BACKCOUNTRY SKI & SNOWBOARD ROUTES

WASHINGTON

BACKCOUNTRY SKI & SNOWBOARD ROUTES

WASHINGTON

MARTIN VOLKEN
& THE GUIDES OF
PRO GUIDING SERVICE

MOUNTAINEERS
BOOKS

MOUNTAINEERS BOOKS

Mountaineers Books is the publishing division of The Mountaineers, an organization founded in 1906 and dedicated to the exploration, preservation, and enjoyment of outdoor and wilderness areas.

1001 SW Klickitat Way, Suite 201, Seattle, WA 98134
800.553.4453, www.mountaineersbooks.org

Printed in the United States of America
Distributed in the United Kingdom by Cordee, www.cordee.co.uk
First edition, 2014

Copy editor: Laura Shauger
Cover design and layout: Jennifer Shontz, www.redshoedesign.com
Cartographer: Pease Press Cartography
Photo overlays: Gray Mouse Graphics
Photograph by Bob and Ira Spring on page 20: University of Washington Libraries, Special Collections, Bob and Ira Spring Photographs, Negative #17324
Front cover photograph: *Forest McBrian during a midwinter descent into Luna Cirque on Day 4 of the Pickets Traverse* (Jason Hummel)
Back cover photograph: *The spirit of the North Cascades* (Scott Schell)
Frontispiece: *Autumn on Mount Baker's Coleman Glacier* (Forest McBrian)

Library of Congress Cataloging-in-Publication Data
Volken, Martin, 1965–
Backcountry ski & snowboard routes / Martin Volken and the Guides of Pro Guiding Service.—First edition.
pages cm
Includes index.
ISBN 978-1-59485-656-3 (trade paper)—ISBN 978-1-59485-657-0 (ebook)
1. Cross-country skiing. 2. Ski mountaineering. I. Title.
GV855.3.V638 2013
796.93'2—dc23

2013031561

ISBN (paperback): 978-1-59485-656-3
ISBN (ebook): 978-1-59485-657-0

CONTENTS

CENTRAL CASCADES

MOUNT RAINIER

AERIAL PHOTO KEY

camp ▲

featured route —··—··—··—

descent - - - - - - - -

alternate ··········

hidden or obscured route -·-·-·-·-

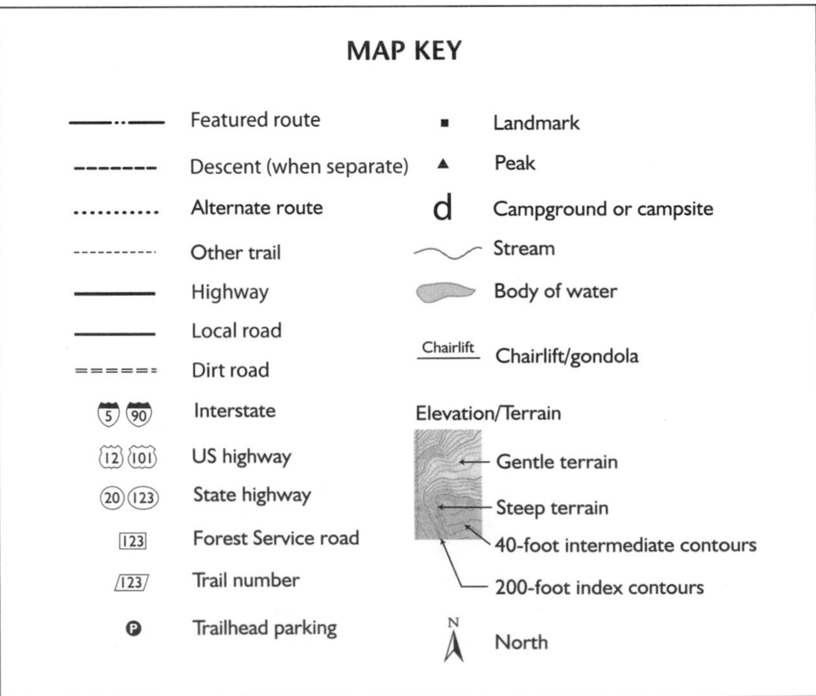

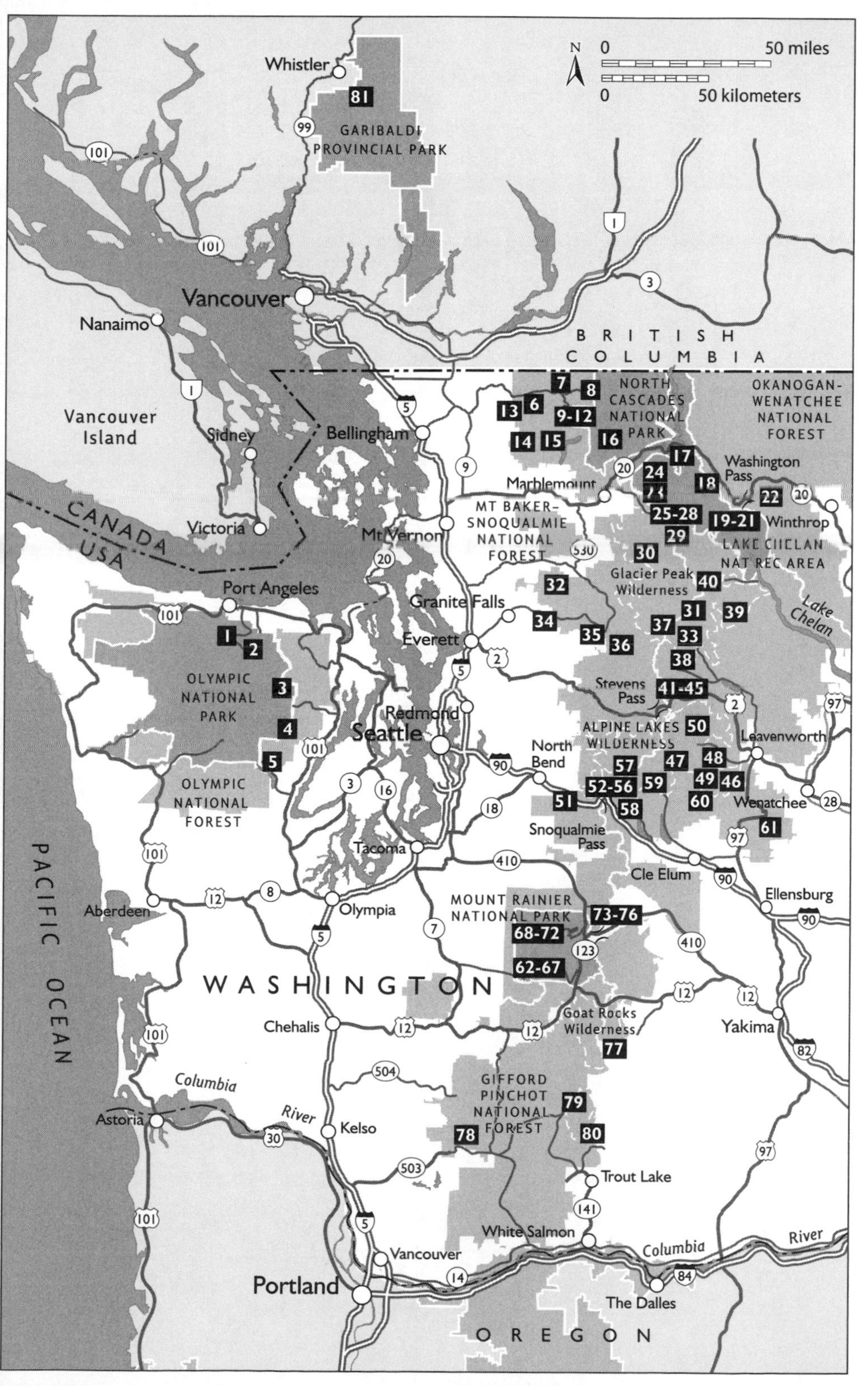

N
0
50 miles
0
50 kilometers
Whistler
81
GARIBALDI PROVINCIAL PARK
Vancouver
Nanaimo
BRITISH COLUMBIA
Vancouver Island
Sidney
Victoria
CANADA
USA
Bellingham
NORTH CASCADES NATIONAL PARK
OKANOGAN-WENATCHEE NATIONAL FOREST
Washington Pass
Marblemount
Winthrop
MT BAKER-SNOQUALMIE NATIONAL FOREST
Mt Vernon
LAKE CHELAN NAT REC AREA
Glacier Peak Wilderness
Port Angeles
Granite Falls
Lake Chelan
Everett
OLYMPIC NATIONAL PARK
Stevens Pass
Redmond
Seattle
ALPINE LAKES WILDERNESS
Leavenworth
North Bend
OLYMPIC NATIONAL FOREST
Wenatchee
Snoqualmie Pass
Tacoma
Cle Elum
Ellensburg
Aberdeen
Olympia
MOUNT RAINIER NATIONAL PARK
PACIFIC OCEAN
WASHINGTON
Goat Rocks Wilderness
Chehalis
Yakima
Columbia River
GIFFORD PINCHOT NATIONAL FOREST
Astoria
Kelso
Trout Lake
White Salmon
Vancouver
Portland
The Dalles
OREGON

TOURS AT A GLANCE

No.	Tour	Tour author	Difficulty	Day trip	Overnight	Multiday	Route pioneers
THE OLYMPICS							
1.	Mount Angeles with Klahhane Ridge	Benjamin Haskell, Peter Leh	Difficult	x			Unknown; probably 1950s
2.	Hurricane Ridge to Deer Park Traverse	Lowell Skoog	Moderate		x		Max Borst and party, 1938, from Deer Park
3.	Mount Deception: Southwest Face and Circumnavigation	Benjamin Haskell	Very difficult		x		Phil Fortier and Sky Sjue via the Northeast Chute, April 2007; Ben Haskell and Matt Schonwald, Southwest Face, May 2012
4.	The Brothers: East Basin	Trevor Kostanich	Difficult	x			Unknown
5.	Mount Ellinor: Ellinor Chute	Chris Simmons	Moderate	x			Unknown
NORTH CASCADES							
6.	Mount Baker: Coleman–Deming Glaciers	Forest McBrian	Moderate		x		Edwin Loners and Robert Sperlin, May 1930
7.	Winchester Mountain and Mount Larrabee	David Jordan	Difficult		x		Winchester Mountain, unknown, probably 1930s; Steve Hindman, Mount Larrabee, c. 1997
8.	Ruth Mountain: Ruth Glacier	David Jordan	Moderate	x			Sigurd Hall, Dwight Watson, and unknown 3rd person, June 1938
9.	Mount Shuksan: White Salmon Glacier	Benjamin Haskell	Very difficult		x		Henry Reasoner and Otto Trott, March 1941
10.	Mount Shuksan: North Face	Forest McBrian	Very difficult		x		Karl Erickson and Greg Wong on center route, June 1979. Jens Kieler and Gordy Skoog on original climbers route, March 1981
11.	Stoneman Couloir	Erin Smart	Moderate	x			Unknown

No.	Tour	Tour author	Difficulty	Day trip	Overnight	Multiday	Route pioneers
12.	Table Mountain Circumnavigation	Kurt Hicks	Moderate	x			Unknown, probably 1930s
13.	Mount Baker: Park Glacier	Martin Volken	Difficult		x		Ben Thompson, Robert Hayes, Milana Jank, and Otto Strizek (ski-climb), June 1931
14.	Colfax Peak: South Couloir	Forest McBrian	Very difficult	x			Martin Volken, Matt Schonwald, and Mason Stafford, May 2006
15.	Mount Baker: Boulder Glacier	Margaret Wheeler	Moderate		x		Unknown, probably 1960s
16.	The Pickets Traverse	Forest McBrian	Extremely difficult			x	Jens Kieler and Carl and Lowell Skoog, May 1985
17.	Ruby Mountain	Benjamin Haskell	Difficult	x			Tony Hovey and Duke Watson, May 1967
18.	Mesahchie Peak: Mesahchie Glacier	Chris Simmons	Difficult	x			Joe Firey and friends, Mesahchie Glacier, 1970s
19.	Black Peak: South Face and Last Chance Pass	Benjamin Haskell	Difficult		x		Rene Crawshaw, Andy Dappen, and Carl Skoog ski descent from summit shoulder of Black Peak, May 1997
20.	Rainy Lake and Lake Ann Loops	Benjamin Haskell	Moderate	x			Unknown, probably 1970s
21.	Washington Pass Birthday Tour	Benjamin Haskell	Moderate	x			Don and Sally Portman, 1970s
22.	Silver Star Mountain	Benjamin Haskell	Difficult	x			Fred Beckey and Mike Borghoff first winter ascent/ski-climb, March 1965
NORTH CENTRAL CASCADES							
23.	Hidden Lake Peaks	Benjamin Haskell	Moderate	x			Dwight Watson and friends, 1930s
24.	The Isolation Traverse	Forest McBrian	Very difficult			x	Gary Brill, Mark Hutson, Lowell Skoog, and Brian Sullivan, March 1983
25.	Sahale Peak	Margaret Wheeler	Moderate		x		Unknown, probably 1950s

No.	Tour	Tour author	Difficulty	Day trip	Overnight	Multiday	Route pioneers
26.	Mount Buckner: North Face	Martin Volken	Extremely difficult		×		Garth Ferber and Lowell Skoog, Southwest Face, July 1999; Martin Volken, Andrew McLean, Fred Marmsater, and Petra Pirc, North Face, June 2002
27.	The Forbidden Tour	Martin Volken	Very difficult			×	Martin Volken, Mike Hattrup, Don Denton, Murray Gailbreth, Greg Lange, Dave Metallo, May 1999
28.	Cascade-Johannesburg Couloir	Forest McBrian	Extremely difficult	×			Jason Hummel and Sky Sjue, first recorded descent, April 2003
29.	Spider Mountain: North Face (Arachnophobia)	Martin Volken	Extremely difficult		×		Martin Volken and Peter Avolio, June 2003
30.	The Ptarmigan Traverse	Forest McBrian	Difficult			×	Dick Easter, Dan Stage, and Brian Sullivan, June 1981
31.	The North Central Cascades Traverse	Trevor Kostanich	Extremely difficult			×	Trevor Kostanich, Peter Avolio, Adam Vognild, and Rob Bolton, May 2011
32.	Whitehorse Mountain	Forest McBrian	Moderate	×			Mountaineers Party led by Walt Little (Lone Tree Pass), May 1947; Jens Kieler (North Face), March 1985
33.	Glacier Peak: Gerdine and Cool Glaciers	Trevor Kostanich	Moderate			×	Sigurd Hall and Dwight Watson (approached from Milk Creek and ascended peak from northeast side), July 1938
34.	Mount Pilchuck: The Gunsight	Benjamin Haskell	Moderate	×			Everett Chapter of The Mountaineers, first recorded ascent of peak, April 1933
35.	Vesper Peak	Erin Smart	Moderate	×			Unknown
36.	Kyes Peak	Martin Volken	Difficult		×		Josh Kaplan, April 2004
37.	Bandit Peak: Black Hole Couloir	Aaron Mainer	Difficult		×		Phil Fortier and Ryan Lurie, March 2008
38.	The Dakobed Traverse	Trevor Kostanich	Difficult			×	Gary Brill, Brian Sullivan, and Joe Catellani, June 1982

No.	Tour	Tour author	Difficulty	Day trip	Overnight	Multiday	Route pioneers
39.	Mount Maude: North Face	Jason Hummel	Difficult		x		Ben Manfredi, July 2002
40.	Bonanza West Peak: Northwest Buttress	Forest McBrian	Difficult			x	Paul Belitz, David Coleman, Phil Fortier, and Sky Sjue, June 2005
CENTRAL CASCADES							
41.	Skyline Ridge to Tye Peak	Erin Smart	Easy	x			Unknown, probably 1930s
42.	Yodelin	Margaret Wheeler	Easy	x			Unknown, probably 1930s
43.	Jim Hill and Arrowhead Mountains	Benjamin Haskell	Moderate	x			Unknown, probably 1930s
44.	Lichtenberg Mountain	Benjamin Haskell	Moderate	x			Unknown, probably 1930s
45.	Rock Mountain to Mount Mastiff Traverse	Chris Simmons	Very difficult	x			Popularized by Andy Dappen, Tom Janisch, and Adam Vognild, February 2010
46.	The Enchantments Traverse	Trevor Kostanich	Moderate		x		Walt Little and George Dennis, earliest recorded skiers, May 1943, but did not traverse
47.	The Central Cascades Traverse	Trevor Kostanich	Very difficult			x	Trevor Kostanich and Peter Avolio, April 2008
48.	Cannon Mountain: Cannon Couloir	Chris Simmons	Very difficult	x			Gordon Briody and Rob Harris, c. 1985
49.	Colchuck Peak: Colchuck Glacier	David Jordan	Moderate		x		Unknown
50.	The Chiwaukum Traverse	Forest McBrian	Difficult			x	John Race and Ben Mitchell, January 2006
51.	McClellan Butte: East Face	Martin Volken	Moderate	x			Martin Volken and Dave Perkins, earliest recorded ski descent, March 2006
52.	Pineapple Pass	Martin Volken	Easy	x			Unknown, probably 1920s–1930s
53.	Chair Peak Circumnavigation	Martin Volken	Difficult	x			A party of four Mountaineers, 1928

No.	Tour	Tour author	Difficulty	Day trip	Overnight	Multiday	Route pioneers
54.	Snoqualmie Mountain: The Slot Couloir via the South Ridge	Martin Volken	Difficult	×			Jan Kordel and Steve Martin, April 1997
55.	Kendall Knob	Margaret Wheeler	Easy	×			Unknown, probably 1930s
56.	Kendall Adventure Zone	Benjamin Haskell	Difficult	×			Ben Haskell, Mason Stafford, Matt Schonwald, Jim Sammet, and friends, mid-2000s
57.	The Snoqualmie Haute Route	Martin Volken	Very difficult			×	Martin Volken, Mike Hattrup, Peter Avolio, Andy Dappen, and Carl Skoog, June 1999
58.	Alaska Mountain Adventure Zone	Margaret Wheeler	Difficult			×	Unknown
59.	Mount Daniel	Trevor Kostanich	Moderate		×		Sigurd Hall and Dwight Watson, 1937
60.	Mount Stuart: Cascadian Couloir	Forest McBrian	Difficult		×		Eric and Kurt Feigl, April 1979
61.	Blewett Pass	Kurt Hicks	Easy	×			Unknown
MOUNT RAINIER							
62.	Camp Muir	Aaron Mainer	Moderate	×			Unknown, 1920s–1930s
63.	Fuhrer Finger	Martin Volken	Very difficult		×		Dan Davis, Tom Janisch, and Jeff Haley, May 1980
64.	Van Trump Park	Trevor Kostanich	Moderate	×			Unknown, probably 1930s
65.	Lane Peak: The Zipper and The Fly	Aaron Mainer	Moderate	×			Unknown
66.	The Tatoosh Traverse	Chris Simmons	Difficult		×		Unknown
67.	Little Tahoma: Paradise Approach	David Jordan	Very difficult	×			Paul Gilbreath and J. Wendell Trosper, April, 1933
68.	Liberty Ridge	Aaron Mainer	Extremely difficult		×		Chris Landry, May 1980

No.	Tour	Tour author	Difficulty	Day trip	Overnight	Multiday	Route pioneers
69.	Emmons Glacier	Aaron Mainer	Very difficult		x		Andew Anderson, E. Lester LaVelle, and William J. Maxwell, first recorded skiing in the area, 1927
70.	Cowlitz Chimneys	Aaron Mainer	Difficult	x			Unknown
71.	Fryingpan Creek Couloir	Aaron Mainer	Very difficult	x			Unknown
72.	Mount Rainier Circumnavigation	Aaron Mainer	Very difficult			x	N.L. Kirkland, Terry Pritchards, Dana Rush, and Dr. Roy Walters, May 1986
73.	Crystal Lakes: G-String and Shoestring	Solveig Waterfall	Difficult	x			Unknown
74.	Crystal Mountain: East Peak	Aaron Mainer	Easy	x			Probably Charles Hessey and friends, 1940s
75.	Sheep Lake Couloir	Aaron Mainer	Difficult	x			Unknown
76.	Crystal Mountain to Chinook Pass	Aaron Mainer	Difficult	x			Unknown, probably 1950s
77.	Goat Rocks: Gilbert Peak	Trevor Kostanich	Moderate		x		Sigurd Hall and Dwight Watson, first recorded ski-trip in area, 1930s
78.	Mount Saint Helens: Worm Flows and Swift Glacier	Solveig Waterfall	Moderate	x			Hans-Otto Giese and Otto Strizek, probably from Spirit Lake, June 1933
79.	Mount Adams: North Face of Northwest Ridge	Trevor Kostanich	Very difficult		x		Charlie Berg and Ben Manfredi, first recorded descent, July 1999; Doug Coombs and Glen Plake, July 1995
80.	Mount Adams: South Ridge and Southwest Chutes	David Jordan and Chris Simmons	Moderate		x		Hans-Otto Giese, Hans Grage, Sandy Lyons, Walter Mosauer, and Otto Strizek (South Ridge), July 1932
BONUS TOUR							
81.	The Spearhead Traverse	Martin Volken	Moderate			x	Karl Ricker group, 1964

Approaching Chair Peak (Brian Hall)

ACKNOWLEDGMENTS

AS WITH ALL BOOKS, there are a lot of people to thank. This book was especially dependent on the benevolent participation of people who simply wanted to help make the project happen. The work that goes into researching and completing a guidebook takes a lot of time away from families, and we would like to thank them for their patience.

We, the guides of Pro Guiding Service would like to thank Kate Rogers from Mountaineers Books for showing the necessary flexibility and vision to let multiple authors bring this project to completion.

We tried hard to provide pictures with documentary value for most of the routes. Doing so would not have been possible without the generous use of an airplane along with the piloting skill of Dan Nordstrom and Greg Zinter. Thanks also to photographers Scott Schell and Alasdair Turner who contributed their time and skill to ensure the quality of many of the images.

Lowell Skoog has been a pioneering figure in the Washington backcountry scene for decades. His contribution provides an invaluable historical context that reminds us that ours is but one of many eras of ski exploration in Washington State. Many thanks to Lowell for adding his perspective to this project.

Jason Hummel's cover shot is a full representation of how we see the adventurous spirit of the North Cascades, and he graciously provided the photo.

Friend and journalist Andy Dappen helped us with tour selections on the east side of the North Central Cascades. Fellow mountain guides Larry Goldie, Peter Leh, John and Olivia Race, and Jeff Ward all shared expert knowledge of and insight about the areas they regularly guide.

Hearty thanks also to Outdoor Research, K2 Skis, and Scarpa whose gear we proudly use. Mike Yost and KC McIvor from Pro Ski and Mountain Service in North Bend, Washington, kept our skis running smoothly in some pretty rough places.

Last but not least we would love to thank the entire Northwest backcountry skiing and snowboarding community. Your love and passion for exploring the mountains of Washington provided the inspiration to write this book. We hope that love and passion have been passed along through our work.

FOREWORD

WHEN MOUNTAINEERS BOOKS asked me to write this book, I initially refused the offer because of the daunting task of completing such a project. Without their flexibility in allowing me to coauthor this book with the guides of Pro Guiding Service, I would have never embarked on this venture. I feel deeply indebted to my guides for bringing this project to completion. It would clearly never have happened without their collaboration. My name happens to be on the cover of the book, but the effort was evenly distributed among all of us.

Selecting the *best* backcountry ski and snowboard routes in Washington State was essentially an impossible task. What we came up with is a *selection* of excellent routes that made sense to us. We are certain that many a backcountry skier or snowboarder could have come up with a different set of routes, but we selected tours that epitomize the spirit of the Olympics and the Cascades and the ambience of adventure that make our mountains a world-class playground.

Coming up with 81 worthy ski tours, descents, and traverses was not that hard a task; the challenge was to create a list that offers something for every ability level in a geographically diverse region. We were trying to produce excellent beginner ski tours, classic moderate routes, long and remote traverses, and also what we proudly call modern American ski mountaineering and extreme skiing challenges. Be assured that the skiable terrain in Washington State is so vast that we could write a second volume, and many of you could argue that your home area deserves its own book. That is probably true. The point of this book was to showcase *one* selection of great routes that make ski touring special here. Along with the described routes you will find mention of sidetrips, adventure zones, and exploratory areas. Let your imagination run wild and have at it.

Thirteen coauthors worked together to make this book happen. Before submitting the manuscript, we spent quite a bit of time reconciling all the different writing styles, but differences remain. People see terrain differently and have different ways of writing and talking about it.

We prioritized the use of aerial photographs to document our routes. This approach sounds great until you realize what covering 20,000 square miles of mountains in a hopefully slow-flying plane entails. We are indebted to the generosity of our pilots, Dan Nordstrom and Greg Zinter, who flew the plane and provided the fuel simply because they liked the project.

All the guides went to great lengths to ski the routes they were writing about (some of them several times) to ensure that their descriptions are as accurate as possible. Different snow years and different times of the year create different impressions of what routes are feasible in an area. Some of these routes pass through extremely remote terrain, and in certain instances we had little information about the routes beyond what we gathered firsthand. Please take the difficulty rating scale and its breakdown into ratings for ski skills, fitness level, and technical skills seriously. We do not call a moderate tour difficult. The difficult tours are—well—difficult.

The Cascades and the Olympics are not the biggest mountain ranges in the world or even in North America. Some ranges are more remote, while others boast a more developed access infrastructure. Some of these coauthors have roamed the mountains of Washington State for more than two decades, and we believe that the sweet spot of size, relief, remoteness, and reasonable access makes ski touring and ski mountaineering in Washington State a pure affair. Many of the described routes are day tours, some are overnight tours, and still others require a multiday effort. All of them are self-sufficient endeavors; no gondolas, no huts, no hotels, no helicopters, no porters—just you and the mountains.

Our intention was to highlight a selection of the best ski tours in Washington State, and while there are certainly good tours to be had in the Kettle Range and the Blue Mountains, they did not make it into the book. Once we decided which areas we would be most eager to share with someone from another state or country, it was very hard to stay away from the Cascade Range, the volcanoes, and the Olympic Mountains.

The young and rugged Cascades are not a gentle mountain range. Many of the range's peaks are heavily glaciated, and their typically enormous snowpack does not come from blue skies. No other mountain range in the Lower 48 can throw such diverse high-alpine challenges at adventurers. Roughly 80 percent of the glaciated terrain in the Lower 48 is located in Washington State. Many of these glaciers are small, but they are relatively fast flowing and therefore surprisingly crevassed. A number of the routes described in this book boast ski descents in excess of 6000 vertical feet—impressive considering that the average crest line in the North Cascades hovers around 8000 feet, and only 14 of its peaks exceed an altitude of 9000 feet.

The range's relatively predictable maritime snowpack allows you a more reasonable chance of completing some of the most challenging routes and descents that are profiled in the book. But please do not let the reputation of the "well-natured" snowpack of the Cascades lead you astray. Our direct action avalanches and especially our climax avalanche cycles in the spring are not to be taken lightly.

Lastly there is the infamous Cascade weather. Dealing with it can be one of the greatest challenges when touring these mountains. The delivery of moisture from the Pacific can be relentless. Remaining safe, healthy, dry, and warm is not always easy in our damp maritime climate. Doing so takes skill, experience, and the appropriate equipment.

All the elements described above create a package that can best be described with two words—adventure skiing! Get out there, experience it, and stay safe.

—Martin Volken and the guides of Pro Guiding Service

Skiers explore the Quien Sabe Glacier in Boston Basin in the 1950s.
(Bob and Ira Spring)

A BACKCOUNTRY RENAISSANCE

IN THE EARLY DAYS, all skiing in Washington was backcountry skiing. There were no chairlifts, ski patrol, gates, or grooming. Miners and fur trappers started it. In the 1890s, skis were sometimes used to run errands in mining towns or to follow trap lines in winter. Skis were used for work rather than pleasure in those days. Skiing for recreation in the Cascades emerged in the first decade of the 1900s. At Scenic Hot Springs near Stevens Pass and Longmire Springs at Mount Rainier, hotels were built to accommodate summer tourists traveling by train. After visitors started to show up in winter, the hotels began stocking snowshoes, toboggans, and skis to attract more guests through the allure of winter sports.

In 1914, The Mountaineers built a lodge near Snoqualmie Pass to make summer and winter outings more accessible to club members. Most skiers at that time were self-taught, and controlled skiing was a novel concept. Lawrence Byington of the club recalled that before European immigrants began sharing the secrets of telemark and christiania turns, "We herring-boned up and ran it straight."

Completion of Rainier's Paradise Inn in 1917 and Mount Baker Lodge in 1927 made it practical to visit these alpine playgrounds in winter. The proprietors, who initially planned for summer use only, gradually responded to the demand for winter lodgings. Within a few years, both Paradise and Mount Baker were full-fledged winter resorts. More club lodges sprang up near Snoqualmie Pass. In 1934, the Seattle Park Board cleared a few acres of forest to create a public ski hill at the site of today's Summit West Ski Area. A couple of years later, the US Forest Service began developing ski grounds at Stevens Pass and at Deer Park on the Olympic Peninsula.

In 1926, William J. Maxwell made one of the earliest recorded ski ascents in the Cascades on Denny Mountain, site of today's Alpental Ski Area. By the mid-1930s, skiers had encircled Chair Peak, climbed Snoqualmie Mountain, and traversed the Cascade Crest from Snoqualmie Pass to Stampede Pass. At Mount Baker, they had explored the backcountry from Shuksan Arm to the volcano itself. At Mount Rainier, Camp Muir, Nisqually Glacier, Indian Henry's Hunting Ground, and the Tatoosh Range were all popular tours. But in all of Washington State, not a single rope tow or chairlift yet existed.

In April 1928, Hans-Otto Giese, Otto Strizek, and Walter Best introduced ski mountaineering to the Cascades; they skied to 12,000 feet on Mount Rainier, stashed their skis, and continued to the summit on crampons. After returning to their skis, they descended in two-and-a-half hours what had taken them two days to climb. Two years later, Edwin Loners and Robert Sperlin skied to the summit of Mount Baker for the first time. By 1933, skiers had summited Mounts Hood, Adams, and St. Helens.

The last of the Washington volcanoes to fall was remote Glacier Peak, which Sigurd Hall and Dwight Watson skied in July 1938.

The 1930s and 1940s brought a surge of ski scouting to the Cascades and Olympics. Skiers explored destinations far from the usual ski centers at Mount Baker, Mount Rainier, and the Cascade passes. Adventurous skiers scouted Mount Pilchuck, Ruth Mountain, Eldorado Peak, North Star Mountain, Whitehorse Mountain, Mount Daniel, Mount Hinman, the Enchantments, the Goat Rocks, and many other isolated peaks. Dwight Watson was the most widely traveled backcountry skier of this period.

Skiers also began exploring high-level traverses. In April 1934, Otto Strizek, Orville Borgersen, and Ben Spellar skied across several of the largest glaciers on Mount Rainier from Paradise to the White River. During the same month, Ralph Calkin and James Mount of the Wy'east Club skied all the way around Mount Hood in less than ten hours. In the 1930s, Ben Thompson and Dwight Watson pioneered separate traverses around and over Mount Baker. In 1938, Max Borst led a party from the Deer Park Ski Area along Hurricane Ridge to the Elwha Road in the Olympic Mountains. Afterward, he recommended building a series of huts along the route.

Like a spring flower killed by a late frost, two events stunted the early growth of backcountry skiing in Washington. First was the introduction of the rope tow. During the 1937–38 ski season, rope tows were installed at Mount Baker, Stevens and Snoqualmie Passes, and Paradise on Mount Rainier. Skiers no longer had to climb to ski, eliminating one of the basic reasons for ski touring. The second event was the outbreak of World War II. Many pioneer skiers were drawn into the war effort, and gas rationing limited the travel of many others. Paradise, the Northwest's premier ski resort, was closed during the war.

Following the war, lift skiing rebounded with vigor, but backcountry skiing did not. In 1946, Fred Beckey proposed to The Mountaineers publication of a climbers' and skiers' guide to Washington, with the skiing section to be written by Dwight Watson. After The Mountaineers turned down the project, Beckey published his guidebook through the American Alpine Club, but Watson's skiing section was left out.

The 1950s and especially the 1960s were boom years for downhill skiing. New ski areas were developed at White Pass, Mount Pilchuck, Hurricane Ridge, Crystal Mountain, Alpental, and Mission Ridge. A few of the old guard lamented that ski mountaineers had become a dying breed. Hans-Otto Giese, one of the earliest pioneers, said in 1969: "People are too lazy now. They'd rather sit on a chair, get hauled up, ski down, and then take the next chair up—just like a yo-yo."

In fact, a small number of skiers kept the backcountry torch aloft during "the dark ages," as one of them called this era. Bob and Ira Spring, renowned outdoor photographers, organized trips to Mount Rainier, Mount Baker, Glacier Peak, and Boston Basin, returning with classic images that were published in newspaper pictorials. Charles and Marion Hessey of Naches spent weeks skiing and making movies at remote cabins in what are now the Glacier Peak and Pasayten Wilderness Areas. Joe Firey and other Mountaineers explored new ski routes on Mount Shuksan, Eldorado Peak, Snowking, Silver Star, Ruby, Blum, and other remote summits.

Yet the backcountry faithful remained few in number. In 1968, The Mountaineers published *Northwest Ski Trails*, a guidebook filled with photographs by Bob and Ira Spring of ski tours from Mount Garibaldi, British Columbia, to Mount Hood, Oregon. To broaden the book's appeal, it included maps and descriptions of all the major ski areas in the region. The publishers hoped the book would offer downhill skiers an alternative to the chairlifts, but the book didn't sell. Most of the growth at that time was in "skinny skiing," Nordic touring on light cross-country skis.

Cross-country skiing grew in the late 1960s and 1970s as a reaction to overcrowding and the steeply rising costs of alpine skiing. The simplicity and light weight of cross-country equipment was a big part of the sport's appeal. As cross-country skiers ventured farther from established trails, they rediscovered the telemark turn as a way to maneuver light Nordic skis. Steve Barnett's 1978 book, *Cross-Country Downhill*, introduced a new generation of skiers to techniques forgotten since the 1930s. Barnett, with Dave Kahn, Bill Nicolai, and others, began using lightweight Nordic gear to repeat classic routes done before World War II and to explore new skiing challenges like Mount Olympus and the Ptarmigan Traverse.

The 1980s and early 1990s were a golden age of ski traverses in the North Cascades, during which skiers established a network of high-level routes from the US–Canadian border to Glacier Peak. The skiers pioneering these routes were using either lightweight telemark equipment or recently developed alpine touring gear such as the Ramer binding. Fred Beckey's new *Cascade Alpine Guide* provided photos and inspiration for many of these ventures. The North Cascades Highway, completed in 1972, was revealed as a treasure trove of spring tours and a launching point for many of the longer traverses. Rainer Burgdorfer's 1986 guidebook, *Backcountry Skiing in Washington's Cascades*, was published during this period.

The 1980s brought a surge of energy to the sport, but the number of enthusiasts remained small by today's standards. Backcountry skiing retained an aura of counterculture, the domain of minimalists who made do with finicky equipment. Skis were narrow. Telemark boots were just beginning to change from leather to plastic. Alpine touring boots were either uncomfortable or heavy or both. Alpine touring bindings were generally considered inadequate for fast, hard skiing.

A few young skiers were attracted to the steep snow climbs pictured in Fred Beckey's guidebooks. In the late 1970s and early 1980s, Karl Erickson and Greg Wong skied the North Face of Mount Shuksan and Ulrichs Couloir on Mount Stuart. A party led by Dan Davis skied Fuhrer Finger on Mount Rainier in 1980. A week later, visiting climber Chris Landry skied Mount Rainier's Liberty Ridge. On Mount Hood in Oregon, Steve Lyford skied many of the classic climbing routes, including Leuthold Couloir, Sandy Glacier Headwall, Cooper Spur, and the North Face. Steep skiers during this period relied on a hodgepodge of equipment. Some used full-on downhill skis and boots, either by fitting crampons over their smooth-soled boots for the ascent or by switching from climbing boots to ski boots for the descent. Others used a combination of downhill gear and early alpine touring gear.

During the late 1990s and 2000s, skis grew wider and more shaped. Manufacturers aimed new gear at resort skiers attracted to the "side-country" by more open boundary policies. Alpine touring bindings became burlier. Telemark bindings added release capability. More and more boot makers offered models compatible with the ultra-light tech bindings popularized by Dynafit. Advances in rescue beacons, survival gear, and avalanche hazard evaluation increased skiers' confidence about venturing into fresh snow and avalanche terrain. Web discussion forums and videos introduced a new generation of skiers to the attractions of backcountry skiing in their local areas. As the number of backcountry skiers grew, it became possible for ski guides to make a living in Washington, which further accelerated the growth of the sport.

Since 2000, skiers and snowboarders have pioneered nearly 200 new ski routes—mostly steep descents, but a few high traverses as well—in the Cascades and Olympic Mountains. A few, but probably not many, of these routes may have been skied earlier. Modern information-sharing not only makes it possible to track these developments, but it also fuels motivation as never before. The increased popularity of the sport can be seen in the growth of annual ski mountaineering races. The first local race was held at Alpental in 2002, with three dozen entrants. Ten years later, the number of participants had grown fourfold.

Backcountry skiing in Washington is in the midst of an unprecedented period of innovation and expansion. New skiers, new routes, and new ideas make this the most exciting time in the history of the sport. Growth brings both new challenges and new opportunities. Next season you may need to get up a bit earlier to find fresh tracks on your favorite run. But you may also find it easier to venture over the ridge to that special place you have been meaning to explore. Backcountry skiing ignites a passion that is constantly being renewed. Every season, every storm opens a blank page and invites us to trace our storylines anew.

—Lowell Skoog

INTRODUCTION

THIS BOOK PRESENTS some of the fantastic ski touring, backcountry snowboarding, and ski mountaineering that Washington has to offer. The information we have compiled will help you plan some incredible adventures, but you must combine it with information from other sources and apply it with the requisite skill. The role of skill and experience in safely attempting any of these tours cannot be overemphasized, and we hope this discussion (and this whole book) will inspire you to pursue mountain education in its many forms.

A quick note about backcountry snowboarding: This book should be as useful for snowboarders as it is for skiers. It is hard to deny, however, that many of the long traverses may not be quite as suited for backcountry snowboarding since tactics like "holding elevation in a traverse" or transition-intensive tours are a bit more cumbersome for snowboarders. We trust that backcountry snowboarders are aware of those limitations and will take them into account as they read our route descriptions.

GET AN EDUCATION

Whether you educate yourself on your own, with a trusted friend or mentor, or under the tutelage of a qualified guide or instructor, make sure you are prepared:

- **Take a ski touring course:** A course in ski touring can teach you how to plan tours, make and follow a schedule, move uphill efficiently and safely, set tracks, transition efficiently, and navigate. It can take a lot of the guesswork and frustration out of trying to figure it all out alone.
- **Sign up for an avalanche course:** Avalanche education has become an accepted prerequisite for new backcountry skiers. A good three-day avalanche course will introduce you to how to assess terrain and the snowpack, read and apply an avalanche forecast, and rescue your companions. You should take a refresher every few years.
- **Study wilderness first aid:** There are lots of ways to get hurt in the mountains, and a good wilderness first-aid course can help you be prepared to deal.
- **Get trained in crevasse rescue:** Do not count on our famously deep snowpack to keep you out of the hole. Learn how to routefind on glaciers, rope up, rescue yourself, and pull your friends out too.
- **Read a book:** We recommend *Backcountry Skiing: Skills for Ski Touring and Ski Mountaineering* by Martin Volken, Scott Schell, and Margaret Wheeler. It covers all of the skills demanded by the tours in this book and will serve you as a reference for years to come.

- **Keep a notebook:** Take notes about your observations, record how your actual tour compares to your time plan, and capture your thoughts about a specific tour and touring in general.
- **Practice with friends:** Use bad weather as an opportunity to hone your skills. Many skills, especially rescue skills, become rusty without continued practice.

EQUIP YOURSELF

When packing for a tour, your goal is to take the smallest pack that carries everything you *need* to have, which can be difficult because so much depends on accurately estimating the conditions with your own skills and comfort zone. The threesomes system that Martin Volken developed for *Backcountry Skiing: Skills for Ski Touring and Ski Mountaineering* will help you remember all the critical items:

The Basics

- Skis, boots, and poles
- Skins, ski crampons, and a pack
- A transceiver, a probe, and a shovel
- Maps, a compass, and an altimeter

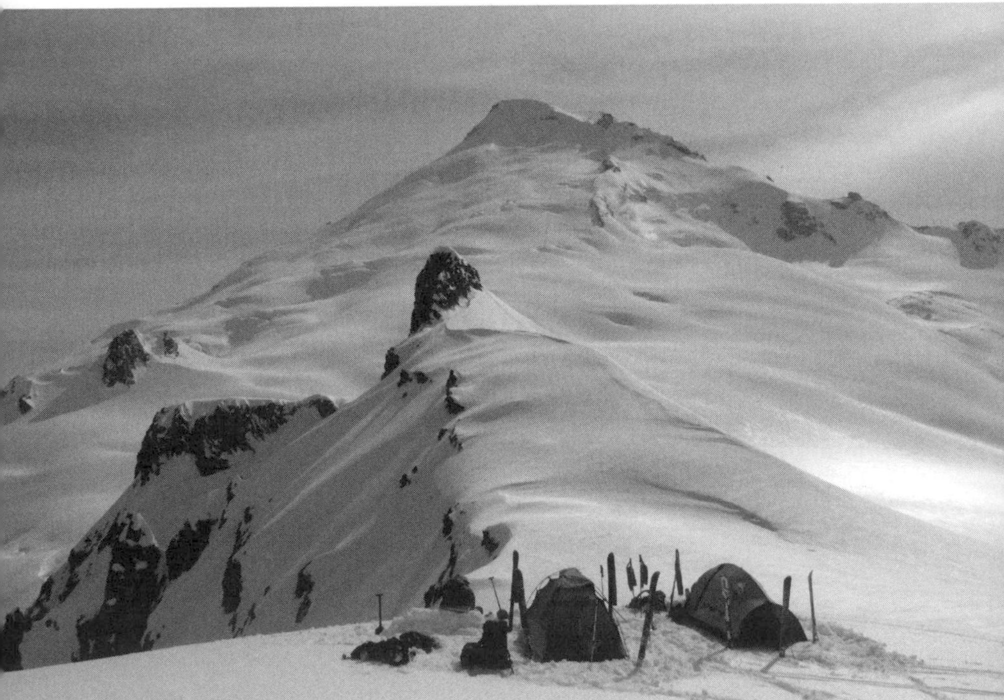

Camping at The Portals on Mount Baker (Jim Bailey)

Ascending the White Salmon Glacier (Ben Haskell)

- A base layer, a midlayer, and outer layers
- A repair kit, a first-aid kit, and emergency shelter
- A cell phone, a GPS receiver, and a rescue sled setup
- Food, water, and an extra layer
- A helmet appropriate for the activity (can be a ski or a climbing helmet)
- A hat, gloves, and goggles
- Sunglasses, sunscreen, and a sun hat
- A headlamp, spare batteries, and a lighter

Ski Mountaineering Equipment

- All the items on the basics list
- An ice ax, crampons, and a rope
- A harness, protection (rock or ice), and a crevasse rescue kit

Overnight Equipment

- All the items on the basics and ski mountaineering lists
- Shelter, a sleeping pad, and a sleeping bag
- A pot, a stove, and fuel
- A bowl, a spoon, and garbage bags

Not all of these are necessary for every trip—the point is not to carry everything on the list, but rather to *address* everything on the list. What you carry for Kendall Peak, which is within sight of Interstate 90, has good cell phone reception, and has a ski descent from the summit to the car, will differ dramatically from what you carry for the committing, remote Picket Traverse.

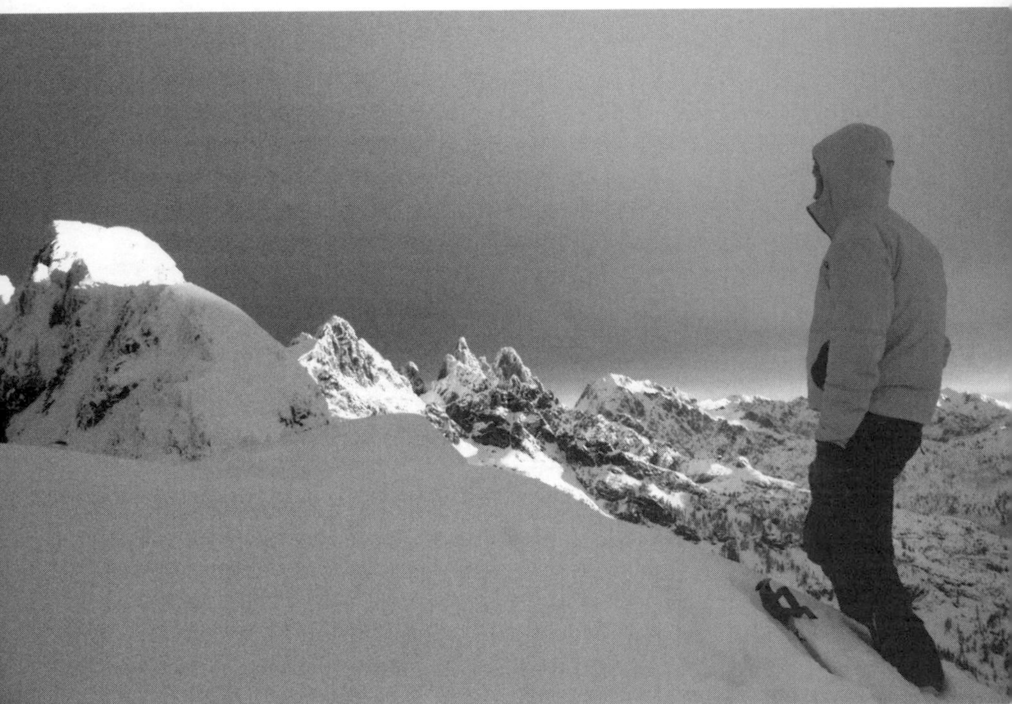

Sunrise on the Four Brothers (Erin Smart)

A Word about Cell Phones, Spot Beacon Locators, and Satellite Phones

Cell phone coverage is very unreliable or nonexistent in many areas of our mountains. However, sometimes we are surprised to find coverage in remote areas. Some form of emergency communication is a very important consideration before you embark on your adventure. Carry a cell phone, and encourage your partners to carry theirs. It can be a valuable tool for calling for help. If you are going on a very remote trip, you might consider an emergency satellite locator device, such as a SPOT locator or a satellite phone. Most of all, you should always be self-sufficient and prepared for whatever conditions and terrain you may encounter.

GATHER WEATHER AND AVALANCHE INFORMATION

The first step in planning a tour is thoroughly investigating weather and avalanche conditions. The Northwest Avalanche Center (www.nwac.us) provides forecasts for mountain weather and avalanche danger throughout the winter and early spring. Real-time weather conditions from remote sensing stations (telemetry) can be found on the Northwest Avalanche Center's website. Additional weather forecasts can be obtained from the National Weather Service (www.weather.gov). Together, these sources provide a good baseline of current conditions in our mountains.

PERMITS AND PARKING

Just a few years ago, it was easy (and free!) to park a vehicle to go ski touring. However, legislation passed in the early 2000s authorized the collection of parking fees for recreational users on our public lands. Although the fees were initially limited to federal lands, the state of Washington soon followed suit. As a result, a confusing matrix of parking permits has evolved. Each tour description defines the permits required for that tour. Be aware, however, that these permits may change, so check with local land managers before you embark on a tour.

Camping

Most of the overnight trips in this book require some type of camping permit. All of the tours in national parks require a backcountry permit that you can acquire at the nearest national park Wilderness Information Center. Tours that lie on US Forest Service (USFS) lands require a free wilderness permit that you can obtain at the trailhead. Some tours access terrain that requires permits only during certain times of year (such as the tour across the Colchuck Glacier, Tour 49); please inquire with the local USFS office for current information.

US Forest Service

Many tours in this book lie on lands managed by the United States Forest Service. These trailheads require either a Northwest Forest Pass or an Interagency Pass. Follow the signage at posted trailheads.

Skinning Jim Hill Mountain (Scott Schell)

On the Upper Nisqually, Mount Rainier (Mike Hattrup)

The cloud sea below Wilson Cleaver camp, Mount Rainier (Mike Hattrup)

National Parks

Parking areas within Mount Rainier National Park and Olympic National Park require either a park entry fee or an Interagency Pass. The Northwest Forest Pass is not valid in national parks. No parking permits or entrance fees are required in North Cascades National Park, including trailheads along the Cascade River road, regardless of jurisdiction.

Washington State Lands

Washington Sno-Parks are plowed winter parking areas that are maintained by the state. These locations require a Washington Sno-Park Permit, which is valid only at these trailheads. The Northwest Forest Pass and Discover Pass are not valid for these locations. Some sno-parks may require an additional permit for groomed trails.

The Discover Pass is required to park in many locations managed by the state of Washington. None of the tours in this book require this permit, but remember that a Discover Pass is not reciprocal with federal passes or sno-park permits.

Parking in Ski Areas and along Highways

Finally, parking vehicles at ski areas and along highways is becoming a concern as our sport grows. It is recommended to check in with ski area management for suitable parking locations for overnight tours. During periods of high snowfall, plowing operations along highways may dramatically reduce or even eliminate parking for some of these tours. Please carpool or consider getting dropped off to avoid leaving vehicles alongside the highway. Lastly, always obey posted signage. The worst way to end a great ski tour is to find your car has been towed!

WILDERNESS ETHICS

The book you hold in your hands was published on the fiftieth anniversary of the Wilderness Act, a law that has defined the evolution of ski touring in Washington State. When faced with the hard work of accessing our wild mountains, you may find yourself fantasizing about a hut beside your favorite glacier or the occasional helicopter ride to a big summit—a fun fantasy, though it ignores the tangible and intangible value we derive from wild places. While you are unlikely to see a helicopter taking skiers to the top of Eldorado, the wilderness *is* changing in serious ways.

Visitors to Boston Basin or the Enchantments, for instance, must deal with a strict permitting system that effectively limits the number of visitors to these extremely popular areas. Showing your permit to a federal officer may not be your idea of a wilderness experience, but remember that these permit systems were a logical step for land managers with a mandate to maintain the wild, untrammeled character of wilderness. Take a moment to imagine a similar system in place at your favorite wilderness ski destination. Ultimately, measurable human impacts will form the basis for future management decisions, and that is where we can have an influence. These strategies will help you control your impact.

Read up on the ecology and natural history of the mountains, as well as the human history, including the Wilderness Act. Understanding the lives of the plants and animals that live in the wilderness can help you situate yourself as a visitor and motivate you to be intentional about your presence there.

Travel in a small group. Three or four is often the optimal group size. Many areas have group size limits, which visitors should always respect. If you prefer being in the mountains with a large group, consider an area that is not part of a wilderness.

Go somewhere new. As more humans visit the backcountry, we can spread out our impact by applying a little creativity. This guidebook leans toward describing many of the most popular and best-loved touring destinations in the state, but each of these outings suggests a dozen others. Look out over the next ridge, find out what that peak is that keeps drawing your eye, and plan a trip to get there.

Travel and camp on durable surfaces. Luckily, snow is a durable surface, but plan ahead for segments of travel that will take you below the snow line. If there is no snow, choose rock or bare ground for hiking and camping. Be careful not to camp on fragile alpine vegetation.

Pack out what you pack in. Repackage foods into larger, zippered bags to avoid the fluttery bits of plastic that result from tearing hungrily into individually packaged snacks, and do a careful check of your campsite for litter before you leave.

Get serious about poop:

- Strategize to maximize use of trailhead facilities and composting toilets, where available.
- Use backcountry toilets appropriately, packing out trash and tampons.
- In forested backcountry areas with deep organic soils, dig a cathole 12 inches deep and 200 feet from water and trails.
- At higher altitudes, there is little microbial action to break down human

waste, and the gold standard is to pack it out. For trips lasting more than one night, try something better than a blue bag. Products like Rest Stop and Wag Bag can make it much easier to carry out waste: powdered agents both solidify and deodorize waste, while the bag is shaped as a backcountry latrine and is durable for packing. It's an inexpensive luxury that will make you feel good.

- Burying waste in snow is never a good idea—it will quickly melt out to become an eyesore and health hazard.
- Pee on rocks or snow away from camp areas; ungulates will chew up vegetation for the minerals left by skiers' urine.

Store food appropriately. Some areas feature food storage requirements to prevent mice, rats, marmots, bears, and other creatures from learning to see humans as a food source. Follow these rules scrupulously, and even where they do not exist, be thoughtful with your food. A rummaging mouse can ruin a night's sleep, or worse. We have few "problem bears" in Washington, and we want to keep it that way.

Respect restrictions on motorized use. For both humans and wildlife, the sound and smell of motors is a disruption, and there are plenty of areas where motorized use is welcome.

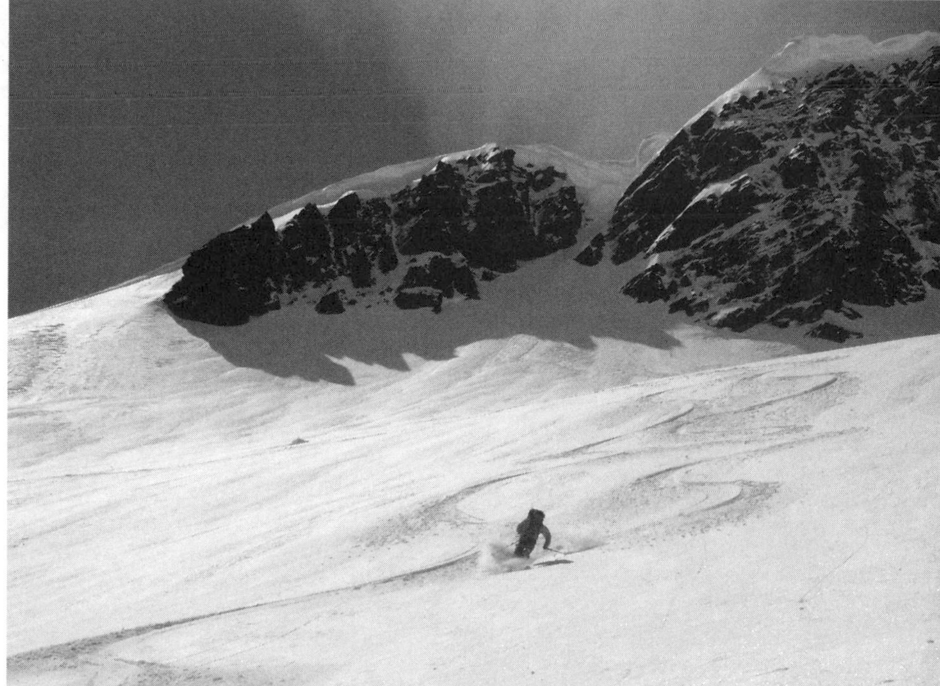

Making turns on the Clark Glacier on the Dakobed Traverse (Trevor Kostanich)

UNDERSTANDING THE ROUTES

The tours in this book are grouped into six regions: the Olympics, North Cascades, North Central Cascades, Central Cascades, Mount Rainier, and South Cascades. Within those regions, they are in order by access. For instance, the Mount Baker tours accessed from Mount Baker Highway (State Route 542) are with the other tours (Winchester, Shuksan, Stoneman, etc.) accessed from there, while other Baker tours are included with tours accessed from the North Cascades Highway (State Route 20) since those are accessed from that side. Tours in the same area (like Snoqualmie Pass on Interstate 90) are in order from day to overnight to multiday. This order revolves around how you access the areas and reflects the effective touring zones. Some tours may be far afield from the other access zones by car even if they are close as the crow flies.

Each tour in this book is made up of several components: the encapsulated summary, an introduction, access directions, a detailed route description, and a map. Some routes include annotated aerial photos that will help you identify major features.

The Encapsulated Summaries

Each tour begins with an encapsulated summary that gives you a quick snapshot of the tour and what it requires in terms of time, skills, fitness, and equipment. Below are notes about how we arrived at these values.

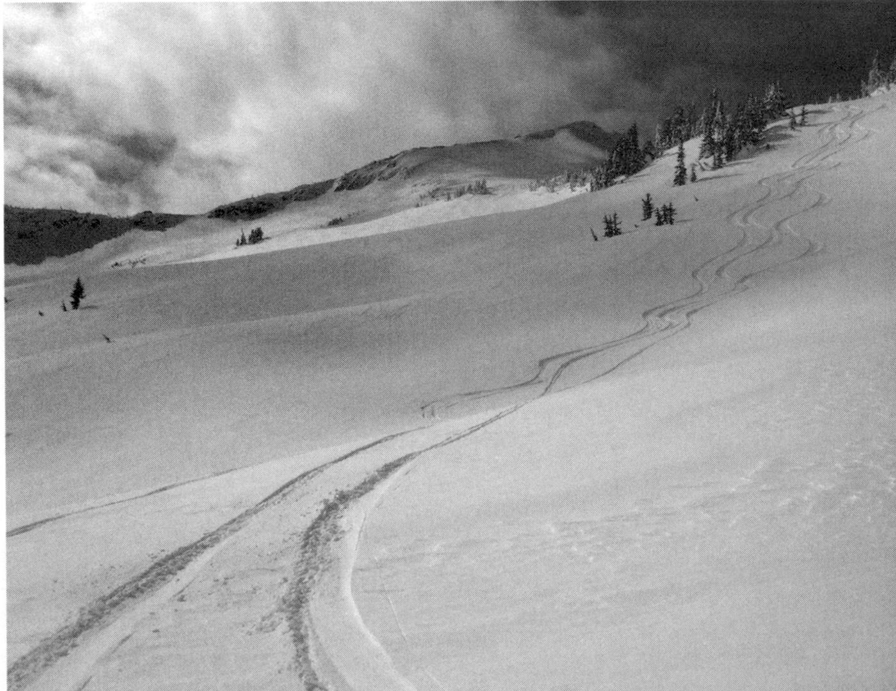

Powder turns on the Rock Mountain to Mount Mastiff Traverse (Chris Simmons)

Starting Elevation/High Point and Vertical Gain/Loss

With the exception of Tour 81, the Spearhead Traverse, all elevations are given in feet since that is how USGS maps are labeled. Each tour lists the elevations of the starting point and high point as well as the total gain and loss to help you quickly assess it in terms of weather, snowcover, and avalanche considerations.

Distance

Distance is given in kilometers first and then miles. This approach facilitates use of the UTM grids present on many topo maps and makes it easier to estimate times on the go using the Munter method.

Estimated Time

On day tours the range of times given is for the entire round-trip tour, starting from and ending at the car (or from one end to the other for traverses). To obtain these times we use the Munter method of time calculation, which breaks a trip down into legs and takes into account horizontal distance and vertical gain, as well as uphill and downhill travel speeds. The low end of the range represents the Munter method time calculation minus 10 percent, while the high end represents the Munter time plus about 20 percent. Note that it includes only travel time, not transitions or breaks. Learn more about time calculations and the Munter method in *Backcountry Skiing*.

Most of the route descriptions include cumulative times to intermediary points, for example: (1 hour to here). These times represent roughly the middle of the range given in the heading. On multiday tours, we use the same convention and start the count over each day. The most complex, involved traverses simply list a number of days.

Difficulty

It is always hard to quantify the difficulty of mountain travel, but the included ratings should make it easier for you to choose a tour. We start with an overall difficulty rating, which, although qualitative, sums up the tour (easy, moderate, difficult, very difficult, and extremely difficult). Day trips are rated relative to other day tours, and overnights relative to other overnights.

To make the overall difficulty ratings more meaningful we include four subcategories: ski skills, fitness level, technical skills, and commitment required. If you consider all these ratings, you should have a good idea of what you are getting into. Please be aware that ratings for a tour are for average conditions in decent weather. Weather and conditions can change rapidly in the high mountains and turn a moderate tour into a serious undertaking. The ratings break down as follows:

Ski Skills:

- *Easy:* 30 degrees or less
- *Moderate:* from 31 to 38 degrees
- *Difficult:* about 40 degrees
- *Very difficult:* about 45 degrees
- *Extremely difficult:* greater than 45 degrees

Fitness Level (effort required per day):

- *Not very strenuous:* up to 2500 feet of vertical gain; 8 kilometers of distance
- *Moderately strenuous:* from 2500 to 3500 feet of vertical gain; 12 kilometers of distance
- *Strenuous:* from 3500 to 4500 feet of vertical gain; 15 kilometers of distance
- *Very strenuous:* from 4500 to 5500 feet of vertical gain; 20 kilometers of distance
- *Extremely strenuous:* more than 5500 feet of vertical gain; 20 kilometers or more of distance

Technical Skills (some or all of the following are required):

- *Low:* requires basic ski touring equipment and skills
- *Moderate:* involves technical skinning or easy booting
- *High:* requires complex transitions and easy glacier travel; involves some third-class sections; requires a formal tour plan and strong navigation skills
- *Very high:* requires the use of an ice ax and crampons; involves some fourth-class sections, rappels, and moderate glacier travel; requires a detailed tour plan and key routefinding
- *Extremely high:* can involve water ice climbing, has some fifth-class sections and difficult glacier travel; requires precise routefinding, and in general the technical nature of the tour has a substantial impact on the overall tour difficulty

Commitment Level:

- *Low:* cell service likely available, fall line to trailhead, and many other people in the area
- *Moderate:* 5 miles into the backcountry, one ridge separated from trailhead, and some other people in the area
- *High:* 10 miles into the backcountry, two ridges separated from trailhead, and few other people in the area
- *Very high:* remote to very remote, no cell coverage, reversal of the route may or may not be possible, and some technical skills are required to ensure a positive outcome
- *Extremely high:* very remote, no cell coverage, reversal of the route might be impossible, rescue may not be possible, and the technical skills required to ensure a positive outcome are very high even in ideal conditions

Gear

This summary section refers to the three included equipment lists: the basics, ski mountaineering, and overnight (see "Equip Yourself" above). Each tour requires the basics and may require items from one or both of the other lists as well. Use these lists as guidelines for packing—checklists that prompt you to at least consider each item. For example, some ski mountaineering outings will require only an ice ax and crampons and not a glacier kit; some skiers will bring a rope while others will leave it at home. What you pack will undoubtedly reflect your skills, experience, and risk tolerance—make sure the gear you bring reflects *all* those things.

Any special items not included in the corresponding list will be noted here. We also include rope-length requirements when an itinerary includes a rappel. For glaciated tours, you should decide what length rope to bring.

Best Season

Every winter is different and so, of course, is each spring. Our recommendation for best season is based in some cases on many, many visits to a given tour, and in others more on an area's general, average evolution of snowpack and its weather.

USGS Maps

In our route descriptions we reference marked features and text labels found on USGS 7.5-minute topographic maps (or in software products based on these maps), and we strongly recommend these as crucial equipment for almost every tour in this book.

Permits

Some trailheads require a Northwest Forest Pass or Sno-Park Permit, which may vary seasonally. Additionally, many tours that take place in wildernesses and national parks require permits and passes administered by the forest or park. Inquire ahead of time about permits because many ranger stations may be closed or have reduced hours outside the summer season, and as backcountry use continues to grow, expect regulations to evolve. Each tour calls out the managing agency and lists the passes and permits you will need, which sometimes vary with the season. Each regional introduction lists specifics for each park, forest, wilderness, and so on.

Introduction

Each tour begins with a brief overview to whet your appetite and give you a sense of why we selected it. It is perhaps the most subjective element of the book—keep that in mind when you read it.

Access

This section describes how to get to the start of the tour beginning at the nearest town with basic services and includes the mileage from that town. For traverses we include directions to both ends and the mileage between them. We also make note of any special parking issues, as some routes may start or end at places other than sanctioned parking lots or trailheads.

Tour Description

Some of these tours are very complex; some take place in terrain with endless options for variation. In describing these tours we have tried to strike a delicate balance between precision and generality. Conditions influence routefinding and track-setting

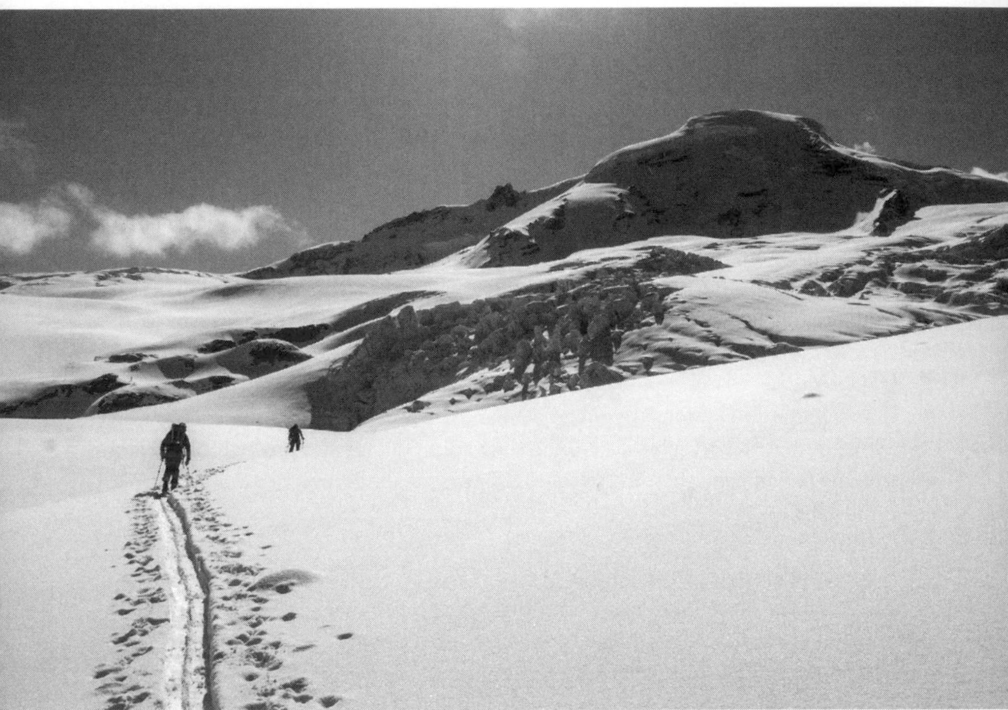

Touring below the Coleman Icefall on Mount Baker (Erin Smart)

so much that a painstaking description would be a disservice to the reader; each party must interpret the general route found here based on the specific conditions and the experience and skill level of its members.

We aim to describe the optimal route through the terrain, with specific mention of key land features and, in some cases, key hazards. We do not point out every avalanche slope or terrain trap, and it is important to realize that the optimal route may be impracticable or dangerous under some conditions; carefully study the map and conditions to decide for yourself. But we do underscore certain hazards that seem likely to catch people off-guard or that have a history of doing so. By the same token, we strongly recommend including a particular GPS waypoint in your navigation plan in places where a navigation gaff could be catastrophic.

In general though, these descriptions do not include GPS coordinates, despite a growing trend toward their inclusion in outdoor guidebooks. The reasons for this are many, but to put it simply: we want the reader to prepare a thorough plan that is appropriate to a tour's demands and conditions. The challenge of ski touring and ski mountaineering lies in decision making in uncertain environments, aided by strong forethought and planning. Any coordinate we could provide can be found through careful consultation of the recommended map; the more time you spend perusing the contour lines of your intended itinerary, the better.

Maps

The maps included in this book are meant to help you understand the text; cross-referencing the route description and optimal route we have drawn will help you have a clear idea of the route in the terrain. These maps are *not* intended as a substitute for high-quality, detailed topographic maps. Some software-mapping products, while providing high-resolution screen images of USGS maps, may yield poor paper maps when paired with your average home printer. Stock up on genuine USGS quads while you still can!

Aerial Photos

Annotated aerial terrain photos complement many of the route descriptions and maps. We collected these photos over the course of many years of touring and during a series of flights around the state and have selected the ones that best describe crucial navigation and safety concerns. We have prioritized illustrative photos over inspiring photos, in an effort to maximize the usable information in this book. Keep in mind that a particular year's snowcover may vary dramatically from what is presented in these photographs.

Tenpeak Mountain and the Dakobed Traverse from the northwest (Trevor Kostanich)

Where Are All the Easy Tours?

You may note a bias toward moderate and difficult tours, but hidden within many of these are shorter, less-committing day tours. We point some of these out, but others will be obvious as you study a route's description and map. Doing the first day or two of any longer traverse can be a great way to learn about overnight touring, as well as a chance to preview terrain for future endeavors. We hope these tours inspire creativity and serve as a jumping-off point for the endless possibilities offered by Washington's mountains.

A NOTE ABOUT SAFETY

Safety is an important concern in all outdoor activities. No guidebook can alert you to every hazard or anticipate the limitations of every reader. Therefore, the descriptions of roads, trails, routes, and natural features in this book are not representations that a particular place or excursion will be safe for your party. When you follow any of the routes described in this book, you assume responsibility for your own safety. Under normal conditions, such excursions require the usual attention to traffic, road and trail conditions, weather, terrain, the capabilities of your party, and other factors. Keeping informed on current conditions and exercising common sense are the keys to a safe, enjoyable outing.

—*Mountaineers Books*

THE OLYMPICS

THE OLYMPIC MOUNTAINS ARE KNOWN for their unique geology, diverse ecosystems, and plentiful precipitation. This is a rugged range with deep valleys, glacier carved ridgelines, dense vegetation, and challenging weather. Nearly all of Olympic National Park is designated wilderness and many of the high peaks of the range are in wilderness areas. Access to these peaks is particularly challenging in winter as the only road maintained for winter access is the Hurricane Ridge Road, which is condition-dependent. Consequently much of the ski touring in the Olympics, and in this book, is focused on the periphery of the range.

The Olympic mountain range is a cluster of peaks often described as a radial formation, with river valleys emanating from the center in all directions. It does not have a distinct north–south crest like the Cascades; the elevation profile is more of a dome with Mount Olympus as the apex. But due to the prevailing weather patterns, the entire range serves as a precipitation barrier that creates a rain shadow on the east and northeast sides of the range. While precipitation on the west side of the range can often be over 200 inches a year, precipitation on the east and northeast can be less than 50. The weather in these leeward areas is correspondingly more reasonable for those who venture there.

Although the summit elevations in the Olympics are modest compared to the Cascades, with many of the alpine summits in the 6500 to 7500 foot range, the terrain is surprisingly steep. And although the elevations are relatively low, the vertical relief is high, with valley bottoms often more than 4000 feet lower than surrounding summits. Mount Olympus itself rises almost 7000 feet from the adjacent Hoh River valley, giving it a much grander appearance than its elevation would suggest.

Of particular interest to skiers is that even though the summit elevations are relatively low, the average elevation of the snow line is also relatively low. In fact, the Olympics have some of the lowest elevation glaciers anywhere in the world for their latitude—a testament to the amount of snow that falls here.

FEES, PERMITS, AND WEATHER INFORMATION

Tours in the Olympics are located within Olympic National Park and Olympic National Forest. Contact information for these two entities, as well as the Hood Canal and Pacific Ranger Stations, is located in Resources.

Parking. An entrance fee or pass is required to park in Olympic National Park. Accepted passes include a single visit pass sold at the park entrances, an Olympic National Park Annual Pass, or an America the Beautiful Pass. Many national forest recreation sites also require a parking fee. Day passes can be purchased at local vendors; an annual Northwest Forest Pass or an America the Beautiful Pass also works.

Camping. Wilderness Camping Permits are required for all overnight stays in Olympic National Park wilderness (backcountry). Permits are limited in some areas. Be sure to check in advance to see if reservations are needed. Call the main Wilderness Information Center in Port Angeles to check on station hours and seasons or

Previous page: Mount Deception through The Needles (Alasdair Turner)

for more information about getting your permit. For camping on Olympic National Forest lands, fill out a free self-issued wilderness permit at the trailhead. Wilderness regulations apply, and Leave No Trace practices are strongly encouraged.

Wilderness Areas. Olympic Wilderness is located in Olympic National Park. Buckhorn Wilderness, Colonel Bob Wilderness, Mount Skokomish Wilderness, The Brothers Wilderness, and Wonder Mountain Wilderness are all located within Olympic National Forest.

Weather. In addition to the Northwest Avalanche Center and the National Weather Service websites, check the Hurricane Ridge site for current local weather and snowpack conditions. See Resources for web addresses.

1 Mount Angeles with Klahhane Ridge

Starting elevation: 4400 feet
High point: 6454 feet
Vertical gain/loss: variable, 4400 feet/4400 feet for Mount Angeles circuit
Distance: 6 km (3.7 miles) for Mount Angeles circuit
Time: 6 hours for Mount Angeles circuit
Overall difficulty: difficult
Ski skills: difficult to very difficult
Fitness level: strenuous
Technical skills: moderate
Commitment: low
Gear: the basics; ski mountaineering equipment can be useful in firm conditions
Best season: December–May
USGS maps: Mount Angeles and Port Angeles
Permits: Olympic National Park entrance fee

Mount Angeles and Klahhane Ridge are the premier ski touring destinations in the Hurricane Ridge area of Olympic National Park. This tour describes chutes, bowls, and glades that you can link in different configurations for a variety of loops around the mountain. Touring on Mount Angeles has a favorable distance-traveled-to-vertical-feet-skied ratio because there is no approach, traversing is minimal, and the incline is consistently steeper than 35 degrees—a modern ski tourer's dream. With its annual average snowfall of over 400 inches and its scenic summit overlooking the Strait of Juan de Fuca to the north and the entire Olympic mountain range to the south, it is clear why Mount Angeles is a popular destination.

ACCESS

As of this writing, the National Park Service currently attempts to plow Hurricane Ridge Road Friday through Sunday during winter months, weather and avalanche

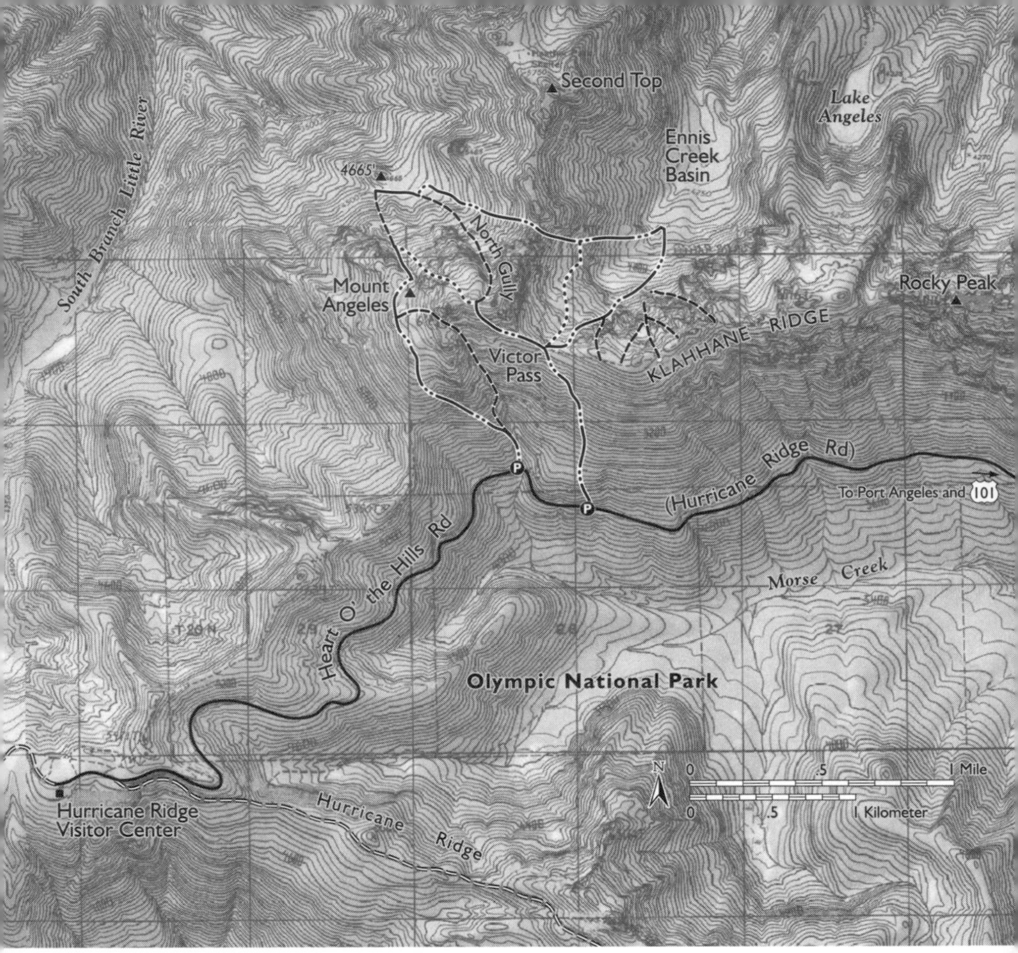

conditions permitting. The road is maintained daily usually starting in April. Be sure to check current conditions through Olympic National Park. From US Highway 101 in Port Angeles, head south on South Race Street and up Heart o' the Hills Road, also called Hurricane Ridge Road, a little less than 16 miles. About 0.3 mile down the road from the summer trailhead for the Switchback Trail up Mount Angeles, look for a small pullout that is normally plowed. Park here.

Observe all parking restrictions, and do not park anywhere that could interfere with plowing operations. When this parking pullout is full, park at the Hurricane Ridge Visitors Center and ski slopes along the route of the Hurricane Ridge Trail toward Mount Angeles's south slope. After avalanche potential has subsided in the spring, you can park at the Switchback Trail summer trailhead.

TOUR

Walk to the summer trailhead, which is at the base of the main south-southeast–facing couloir that descends from the summit area. Head straight up the open drainage or up the treed slopes to the west. Exit climber's left from the drainage at 4800 feet below the first major constriction.

Above 5400 feet trend north through increasingly open terrain to 6000 feet, west of the summit. Head east up the final 400 feet to the summit, wrapping slightly southeast to reach the summit rocks. Resist the temptation to ascend toward any of the false summits before reaching the final ascent slope. Depending on the conditions, the final portion below the summit may require booting (2 hours to the summit).

From the summit, there are many descent options. For a quick return to your starting point down the south-southeast couloir, ski a few hundred feet back down the final summit slope wrapping south around a rocky rib to the slope below the first notch south of the summit. Climb up to the notch to gain the top of the couloir. Ski the couloir down to a rocky constriction near 5000 feet where the summer trail crosses the creek. If the constriction is not filled in enough to ski, bypass it by exiting onto the open slope skier's left, or the treed slope skier's right to regain the drainage below. Ski fall line from there back to the road.

To descend slopes northwest of the summit, follow the northwest ridge down to where the slope angle eases near 5800 feet, and find a broad entrance down to the slopes north of the ridge. Alternatively, cross east around the northwest ridge just below the summit area into the upper north bowl, and find a steeper northwest-facing chute underneath rocks of the northwest ridge at 6200 feet to access the same slopes. At the bottom of these runs, retrace the main descent line back up to the northwest ridge, or continue north or northwest to access the slopes southwest of Point 4665. From there, you can follow glades up to connect to slopes farther east on the mountain.

Mount Angeles and Klahhane Ridge from the north (Alasdair Turner)

East Summit Area and Klahhane Ridge: To access the slopes on the east side of the mountain directly, climb up the south slope from the winter parking pullout, or the summer trailhead for the Switchback Trail, to the broad saddle at 5850 feet on the ridge that connects Mount Angeles to Klahhane Ridge, known as Victor Pass (1.25 hours to Victor Pass).

Options abound here as well. To ski the prominent north-facing bowl below the east summit, climb the southeast ridge until it steepens below rocks. Then continue onto the south face, and work climber's left up through a series of rock bands to reach the ridge crest west of the east summit. From here ski fall line into the north bowl, entering a broad gully via a steep headwall below 6200 feet. Ski down as far as time and conditions merit. You can connect this route with the previous routes described off the northwest ridge when snow levels are low by skiing beyond Point 4665 and touring back up to the southeast.

An alternate option from the bottom of the north bowl is to skin to the col at 5800 feet on Mount Angeles's northeast ridge that leads from the Little River Valley over to the Ennis Creek valley (3.5 hours to the col).

From the col ski skier's left down to Ennis Creek, or descend and traverse right to 5200 feet to reach ascent slopes back to Victor Pass. Scope out the lines off Klahhane Ridge from the Ennis Creek valley.

The views of Klahhane Ridge may inspire you to ski more, especially if the skin track out of Ennis Creek is already in place. To add in a descent off Klahhane Ridge, simply climb up to Victor Pass and traverse along the ridge from the pass to any one of the chutes that looked appealing from below. Of course the lines off Klahhane Ridge are worthwhile tours in their own right and can be accessed directly from the start for shorter tours from your car. To descend from Victor Pass back to your car, ski south or southwest off the pass to link open areas and glades to either parking location.

Tour Author: Benjamin Haskell, with special thanks to Peter Leh

2 Hurricane Ridge to Deer Park Traverse

Starting elevation: 5200 feet
High point: 6700 feet
Vertical gain/loss: 3500 feet/6800 feet
Distance: 35 km (22 miles) from Hurricane Ridge to boundary gate
Time: 2 to 3 days (has been done in a single day)
Overall difficulty: difficult
Ski skills: moderate
Fitness level: moderate
Technical skills: moderate
Commitment: high

Gear: the basics, overnight gear, plus an ice ax, crampons, and ski crampons recommended; plus trail shoes for the last leg along the road
Best season: January through April
USGS maps: Mount Angeles and Maiden Peak
Permits: Backcountry permits are required to camp on the traverse. Check in at the visitors center on the way to Hurricane Ridge.

Hurricane Ridge to Deer Park is the classic ski traverse in the Olympic Mountains. The tour is older than Olympic National Park itself. In 1934, roads were constructed from the Elwha River to Hurricane Ridge from the west and from Danz Ranch (near the current park boundary) to Deer Park from the north. Soon thereafter, the US Forest Service developed Deer Park as the first ski area on the Olympic Peninsula.

In April 1938, Max Borst, caretaker of the Deer Park Ski Lodge, led a party of skiers across Hurricane Ridge to the Elwha Road to survey the terrain for skiing and to plan a proposed series of huts. Other ski expeditions followed during the next few years. In 1957, the Heart o' the Hills Road was completed from Port Angeles to Hurricane Ridge. Deer Park was abandoned as a ski area, and ski operations moved to the ridge.

During the late 1960s, park ranger Jack Hughes reintroduced cross-country skiing to Hurricane Ridge. Hughes skied from the Hurricane Ridge Visitors Center to Elk Mountain and back countless times, often to service a weather station located high on the mountain. Later, park volunteer John Charno skied the full traverse to Deer Park

The Hurricane Ridge to Deer Park Traverse from the east (Alasdair Turner)

To Port Angeles and 101
Lake Angeles
Mount Angeles
Klahhane Ridge
(Hurricane Ridge Rd)
Heart o' the Hills Rd
Morse Creek
Round Mountain
finish
Deer Park Rd
Olympic National Forest
Cox Valley
Maiden Creek
Deer Park Rd
start
Hurricane Ridge Visitor Center
Steeple Rock
Hurricane Ridge
Olympic National Park
Blue Mountain
Deer Park
Green Mountain
Maiden Lake
Alternate camp
Eagle Point
Lillian River
Maiden Peak
Alternate camp
Camp
Obstruction Point
Elk Mountain
Grand Creek
Badger Valley
N
0 .5 1 Mile
0 .5 1 Kilometer

frequently while serving as winter custodian of the Visitor Center. In recent years, the traverse has become increasingly popular and is occasionally guided. Traverse parties that allow a bit of extra time can enjoy delightful skiing on slopes adjacent to the ridge.

ACCESS

Deer Park: The Deer Park Road is normally gated in winter at the park boundary near Danz Ranch, about 7.5 miles from Deer Park. Leave US Highway 101 on the Deer Park Road (about 3.5 miles east of downtown Port Angeles), and drive about 9 miles to the gate. Most parties park a car at the gate for pickup at the end of the traverse.

Hurricane Ridge: As of this writing, the National Park Service attempts to plow the Hurricane Ridge Road Friday through Sunday during the winter months, weather and avalanche conditions permitting. Overnight parking is prohibited at Hurricane Ridge in winter. It is permissible to park about 3 miles down the road from the ridge at a small pullout that is normally plowed. Skiers should contact the main park visitors center (360-565-3100) to inquire about parking. It is important that the rangers know you will be parking there, and you may be able to make arrangements with the rangers to shuttle a car from the parking area to the top of the ridge, where the ski route begins.

From US Highway 101 in Port Angeles, head south on South Race Street and up Heart o' the Hills Road (Hurricane Ridge Road). After about 5 miles, you will come to the park visitors center on the right. After stopping for a backcountry permit, continue driving another 12 miles to Hurricane Ridge.

TOUR

The ski route begins on the Obstruction Point Road, about a quarter mile east of the Hurricane Ridge Visitor Center. The Civilian Conservation Corps (CCC) built this extremely scenic road (snow-covered in winter) in the 1930s. The first 2.5 kilometers (1.5 miles) of the road are flat or slightly downhill. After a short climb to Steeple Rock, the road levels out again. Near the 4-mile point, the road begins a steady climb around Eagle Point. In good snow years, the road may be completely obscured near Eagle Point and beyond. Rolling, gentle terrain continues to Obstruction Point, about 12 kilometers (7.5 miles) from the start (5 hours to here). Many tourers choose to camp in this area near Obstruction Point, with views back toward Hurricane Ridge and Mount Olympus.

In summer, the road ends just south of Obstruction Point, and a trail crosses the east basin toward Elk Mountain. In winter, a shorter, generally safer route leaves the ridge west of Obstruction Point and traverses the northwest flank of the peak to the southwest shoulder of Elk Mountain. Climb the shoulder until it is possible to traverse east near the Elk Mountain summit ridge.

The ridge between Elk Mountain and Maiden Peak is the highest and most exposed section of this traverse. Conditions on this section can vary from bare rock to easy corn snow to boilerplate ice. Hurricane Ridge takes its name from the mighty winds that hammer the ridge from the Pacific Ocean. Prevailing weather will determine the best route along the ridge and whether skins or crampons are the best tools for the crossing. You must pay careful attention to the weather forecast, since navigating in a windy whiteout anywhere between Eagle Point and Green Mountain would be difficult.

As you descend the east shoulder of Elk Mountain, the route threads between wind-scoured slopes on the south and corniced bowls on the north. This section includes the steepest terrain of the traverse. The ridgeline mellows as you climb toward Maiden Peak, 18 kilometers (11 miles) to here, which is normally passed on its south flank. (3 hours to here from Obstruction Point). The ridge bends northward just beyond Maiden, then descends and turns eastward to the Green Mountain divide. Exposed camps with beautiful views out over the Strait of Juan de Fuca can be made at many points along the ridge. As you approach Green Mountain, the route drops below tree line. Follow the ridgeline or slightly to one side or the other to the low point west of Deer Park. About a half mile of skinning uphill will take you to the old Deer Park Road.

Deer Park Road is so steep and narrow that during the days of the ski area, car traffic was restricted to uphill-only in the morning and downhill-only in the afternoon. Stripping off your skins, you will find fast skiing down the road for several miles. The CCC boys knew how to build a road, however, and you may encounter bare ground where the road crosses sun-warmed south-facing slopes. Wearing a pair of trail shoes will make easy work of the final miles to the gate.

Tour Author: Lowell Skoog

Mount Deception: Southwest Face and Circumnavigation

Starting elevation: 2530 feet
High point: 7788 feet
Vertical gain/loss: **Southwest Face:** 7600 feet/7600 feet
Circumnavigation: 8300 feet/8300 feet
Distance: **Southwest Face:** 17 km (10.5 miles)
Circumnavigation: 22 km (13.75 miles)
Time: 2 days
Overall difficulty: very difficult
Ski skills: very difficult
Fitness level: very strenuous
Technical skills: moderate
Commitment: high
Gear: the basics, plus ski mountaineering and overnight equipment
Best season: early season or April–May, depending on snow levels and access on Forest Service Roads 2880 and 2870
USGS map: Mount Deception

Permits: You must display a Northwest Forest Pass or Interagency Pass in your vehicle to park at the trailhead. If you want to camp overnight, get a wilderness permit from Olympic National Park (available through the park's Wilderness Information Center). Reservations for overnight stays in Royal Basin are subject to quota restrictions from May 1 through September 30.

Although Mount Deception is the second highest peak in the Olympic Mountains, it gets relatively little attention as a ski mountain. However, Mount Deception can be much quicker to access for skiing than the highest peak in the range, Mount Olympus. Royal Basin is one of the most popular areas in the Olympics; however, Mount Deception itself has a reputation for loose rock and scree during the summer climbing season,

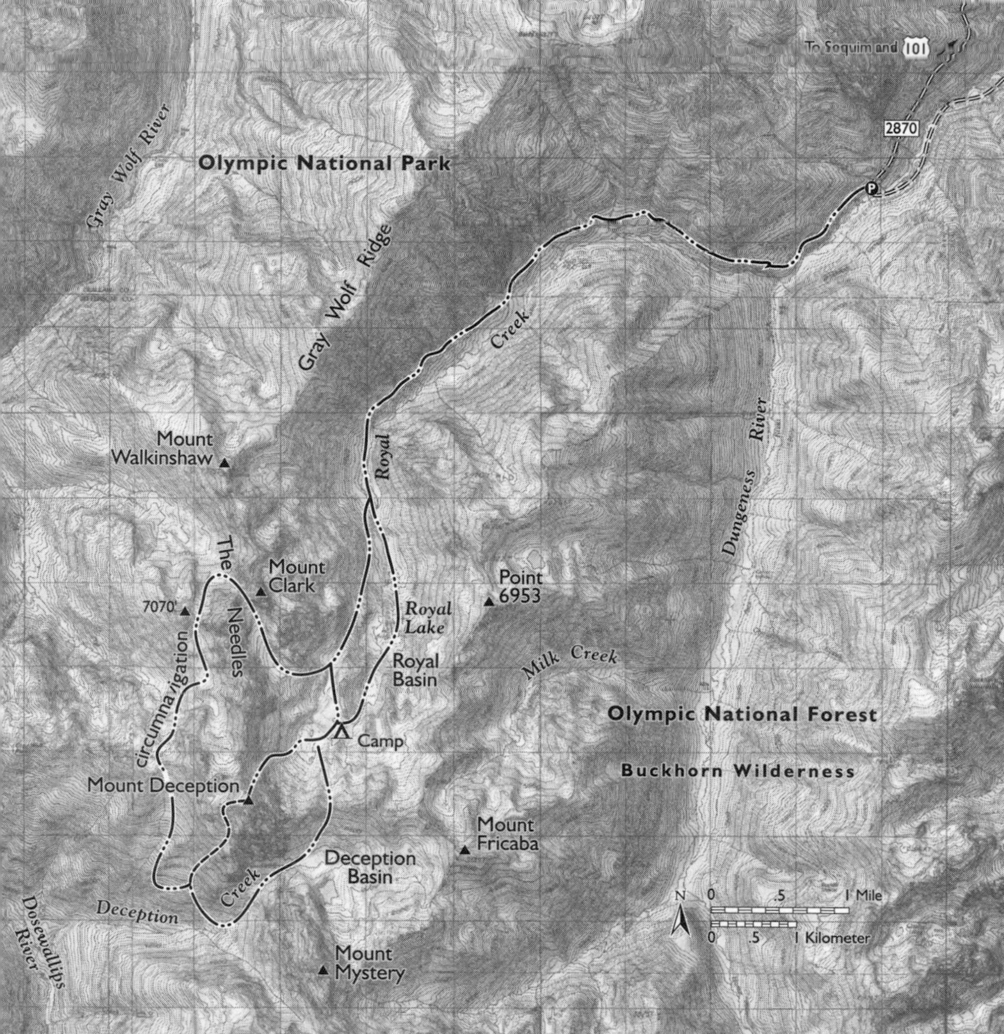

which keeps crowds away from the mountain itself. But given the right conditions, Mount Deception is a great ski mountain with steep ski descents on several aspects, including one of the longer descents in the range: the 3700-foot Southwest Face from the summit to Deception Creek.

For those less interested in steep skiing, more moderate slopes can be linked for an interesting circumnavigation of the Deception massif. A base camp at the headwaters of Royal Creek provides plenty of alternative options for skiers with less ambitious objectives, and the scenery of Royal Basin justifies its name.

ACCESS

Drive US Highway 101 to Palo Alto Road, 3 miles east of Sequim, or 17.5 miles west of the junction of US 101 and State Route 104. Turn south on Palo Alto Road, and follow it a little more than 7 miles to Forest Service Road 2880, which is 0.25 mile beyond where Palo Alto Road turns into FS Road 28. Turn right and follow FS Road 2880 for 1.7 miles to Forest Service Road 2870. Keep left on FS Road 2870, and continue on it, bearing right to continue uphill at 2.6 miles where it intersects FS Road 2860. In another 6.5 miles, park in the lot on the right just after the road crosses the Dungeness River. The Upper Dungeness trailhead is on the north side of the bridge over the river.

TOUR

DAY 1. Begin hiking on the Upper Dungeness Trail, Forest Service Trail 833.2. Continue 1 mile to where Royal Creek flows into the Dungeness River, and turn right onto the Royal Basin Trail. Hike up the Royal Basin Trail to the snow line. Once you are on snow, follow the general line of the summer trail, staying above and to the right of Royal Creek. Be cautious of avalanche paths that sweep into the valley from Gray Wolf Ridge to the northwest.

Where the summer trail meets the creek at 4720 feet, cross the creek and continue past Royal Lake, then head south-southwest through a small valley up to the upper basin below Mount Deception. Alternatively, stay on the right side of the Royal Creek from 4720 feet and begin a slow traversing ascent through a series of small draws and drainages along the base of Mount Clark to reach the same area. Although this route is less obvious than the summer route on the way up, it has the advantage of being almost completely gravity fed for skiers on the way back out and can, therefore, repay your additional routefinding effort during the approach.

Camp in a safe location near tree line at 5700 feet with great views of the mountains surrounding the upper Royal Basin. You have many options from this location, from short low-angle tours on the surrounding ridges, to steep skiing descents on the faces of Mount Deception, to circuits around Mount Fricaba or into Milk Creek on the southeast face of Point 6953.

DAY 2. Start the Southwest Face tour by climbing the northeast couloir to the summit of Mount Deception (7788 feet). Evaluate hazards carefully before committing to the climb. It normally requires an ice ax and crampons, but a rope may also be necessary

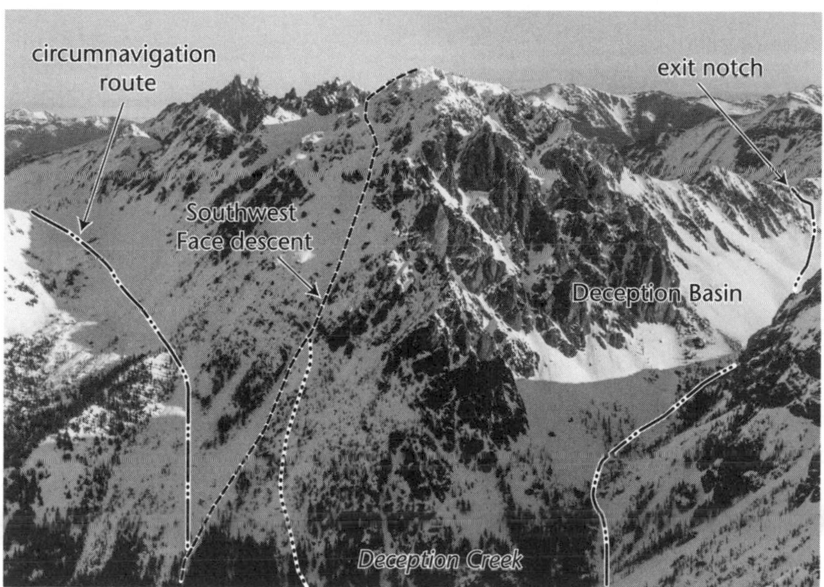

Mount Deception from the southwest (Scott Schell)

to belay in firm conditions. The northeast couloir is a worthwhile steep ski objective in its own right with a 1800-foot continuous fall line, 1000 feet of which is steeper than 40 degrees, with a steeper headwall at the top (2.5 hours to the summit from camp).

Southwest Face Descent. To ski the 3700-foot descent of the Southwest Face, head west off the summit, staying skier's right of the rocks and cliffs that form the upper west shoulder of the mountain. At approximately 7200 feet, turn the corner to skier's left, and begin a short southward traverse on a shelf that leads to the entrance of the couloir bisecting the face at 6800 feet. Enter the couloir, and ski straight down 1800 feet to the forest, or exit skier's left two-thirds of the way down to ski less constricted, lightly treed slopes to the southeast. Enter the forest and find glades trending southeast toward Deception Creek. Ski these to the creek at 4000 feet (3 hours to here).

Ascend the north side of Deception Creek to 4200 feet. If possible, cross to the south side of the creek for an ascent northeast on open slopes below the west face of Mount Mystery. If a lack of snowpack prevents you from crossing the creek, or if avalanches from Mount Mystery are a concern, continue ascending Deception Creek on the north side through a few hundred feet of dense forest, gaining a beautiful open hanging valley above 4800 feet (4 hours to here).

Continue up valley into Deception Basin. After you enter the basin, climb northeast to the notch at the low point on the ridge that divides Deception and Royal Basins. A short, steep step on the north side of the notch leads down onto easy slopes back to camp (5.5 hours back to camp).

Circumnavigation. To avoid the steep terrain on Mount Deception while still enjoying the spectacular setting, circumnavigate the massif through a series of passes that connect with the tour described above. Climb through the pass southeast of Mount Clark (7528 feet), ski down, around left, and up to a small col east of Point 7070. From the col, ski approximately 800 feet or more down and then to skier's right before ascending to the ridge above the unnamed lake that forms the headwaters of the east fork of the Gray Wolf River. From the southeast notch along the ridge, descend 2600 feet and across a treed rib toward Deception Creek to connect with the Southwest Face route up to Deception Basin.

Tour Author: Benjamin Haskell

4 The Brothers: East Basin

Starting elevation: 710 feet
High point: 6650 feet
Vertical gain/loss: 6740 feet/6740 feet
Distance: 22 km (13.5 miles)
Time: 12 hours (1 long day) or 2 days
Overall difficulty: difficult
Ski skills: difficult
Fitness level: strenuous
Technical skills: moderate
Commitment: moderate
Best season: February–May
Gear: the basics, plus an ice ax, crampons, and overnight equipment
USGS map: The Brothers
Permits: You must display a Northwest Forest Pass to park at the Lena Lake trailhead. Fill out a wilderness permit at the trailhead.

A significant landmark looking west from Seattle, The Brothers is a double-summit peak that tempts the adventurous skier to visit its lonely eastern basin. The approach requires many miles of hiking, but for those who are up for it, The Brothers offers up a most fantastic outing. This route describes a ski route off the summit ridge just below the North Summit.

You can do this tour as an overnight or a long day, but we recommend traveling light and doing it as a day trip.

ACCESS

From its junction with Interstate 5 in Olympia, take US Hwy 101 north through Hoodsport, and turn left on Hamma Hamma River Road (Forest Service Road 25). Continue about 9 miles to the Lena Lake trailhead at 710 feet.

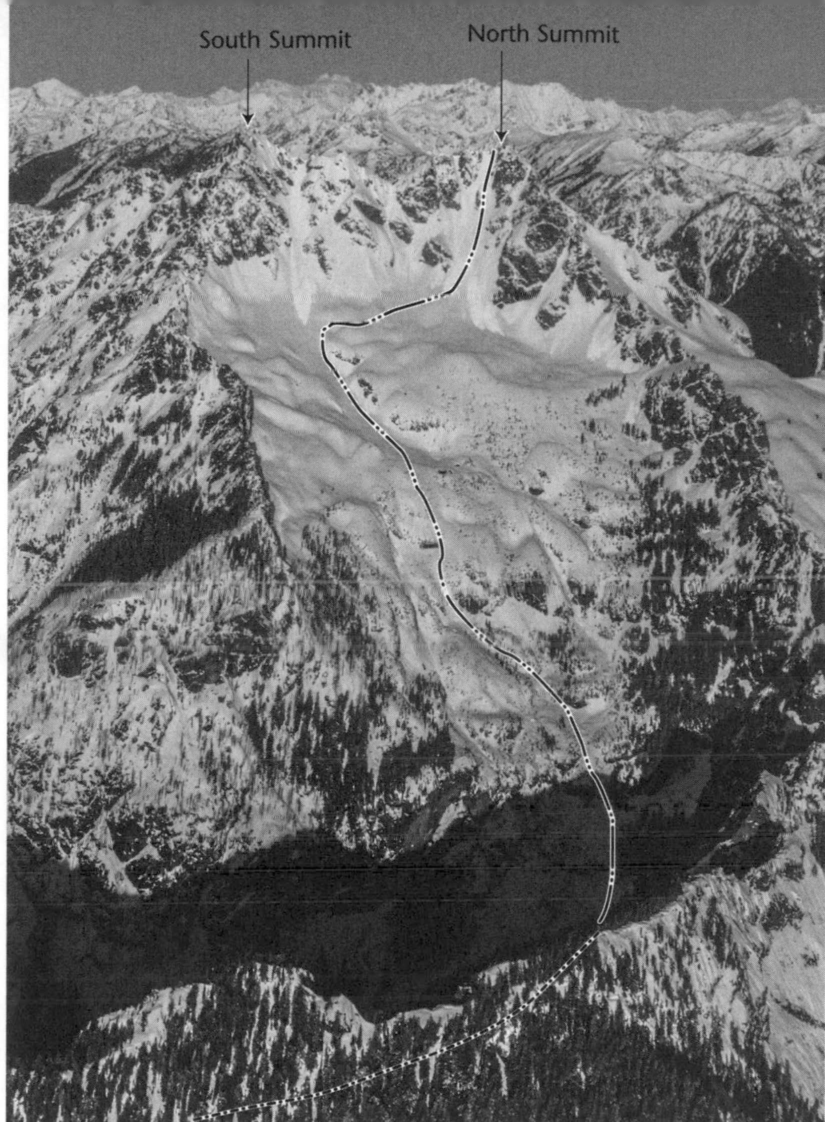

The Brothers from the east (Alasdair Turner)

TOUR

Hike the trail to Lena Lake, passing the final lake campsites and outhouse on the northeast end of the lake (1.5 hours to here). Follow the trail up the East Fork Lena Creek through a healthy forest known as the Valley of the Silent Men. Depending on the time of year and snowpack, you will encounter snow up this drainage and at some point begin skinning. At 3100 feet the valley flattens and the creek forks. Stay right, and continue traveling north-northeast on the east side of the creek drainage. At the fork and shortly beyond are nice camp locations. At 3400 feet and about 8.5 kilometers (5.2 miles) from the trailhead, the terrain begins to steepen (4 hours to here).

The next 2000 feet of climbing requires careful routefinding steeply through trees, rock, and hopefully lots of snow. Skin north up the clearing and stay high while trending west through glades. Traverse left up a steep slope. Continue climbing west up snow gullies to attain the bench at the bottom of the east basin at 5300 feet (5.5 hours to here).

As you tour up the basin, absorb the alpine playground that you worked hard to reach. Traverse right, and climb up past a rock prow. Boot the final climb, and attain the summit ridge at 6640 feet just south of the North Summit (7.5 hours to here).

DESCENT. From the ridge enjoy steep skiing back into the east basin. Execute the first few turns carefully before the slope angle eases and the chute widens down into the basin. Return via the ascent route, and safely navigate the steeper gullies back to the valley floor at 3400 feet (9 hours to here). Relish in the wildness of your descent and current whereabouts before continuing to ski and eventually hike to the trailhead at 710 feet (12 hours to here).

Tour Author: Trevor Kostanich

5 Mount Ellinor: Ellinor Chute

Starting elevation: 2670 feet
High point: 5944 feet
Vertical gain/loss: 3280 feet/3280 feet
Distance: 8 km (5 miles)
Time: 5.5–6.5 hours
Overall difficulty: moderate
Ski skills: moderate
Fitness level: strenuous
Technical skills: moderate
Commitment: low
Gear: the basics
Best season: February–April
USGS maps: Mount Skokomish, Mount Washington, and Hoodsport
Permits: A Northwest Forest Pass or Interagency Pass is required to park at the *upper* Mount Ellinor trailhead. This tour description starts at the *lower* Mount Ellinor trailhead and assumes that you are likely to start even lower than that when the road is snowed in, in which case no permits are required.

Mount Ellinor and its neighbor Mount Washington are the most southerly of the summits in the Olympic Range panorama viewed from the east across Puget Sound. That view, combined with its relatively easy access, makes Mount Ellinor one of the most popular climbs and ski descents in the Olympics. Consistently steep for the final 1300 feet to the summit, Mount Ellinor also provides a fantastic view from the summit westward into wild and woolly Olympic National Park and eastward across the Sound to Seattle, Tacoma, and the Cascades.

ACCESS

From the waterfront town of Hoodsport, head west on Lake Cushman Road (State Route 119) for 8 miles, where the paved road makes a 90-degree bend to the left. Turn right here onto Forest Service Road 24, and drive 1.7 miles. Then turn left onto Forest Service Road 2419 (Big Creek Road), and continue another 5 miles to the Lower Mount Ellinor trailhead or as far as possible before you are stopped by snow.

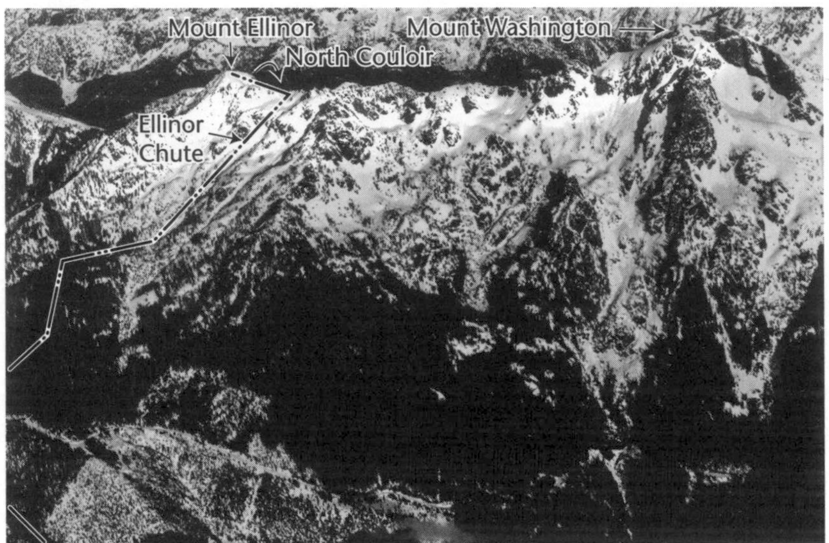

Mount Ellinor from the east (Scott Schell)

Midwinter, if snow has blocked the Forest Service roads lower down, you can park at Big Creek Campground, and follow the trail network up to the Lower Mount Ellinor trailhead. This alternative approach doubles the tour's length and time, with very little to gain except more commitment, remoteness, and a lot of thick tree or trail skiing during the descent. Conversely, if the road is melted out all the way to the trailhead, count on sharing the route with a lot of other climbers and skiers.

TOUR

From the Lower Mount Ellinor trailhead, continue up the road toward the Upper Mount Ellinor trailhead, but turn left (east) to head uphill in the first drainage (3100 feet and 0.25 hour). This drainage has been clear-cut recently. For easier travel, pick a line up and left into the uncut, old-growth forest, then start traversing up and right across the basin, above the clear-cut, around 3400 feet. Continue traversing across and northward to gain the ridge separating this drainage from the North Fork Big Creek, and follow the ridge up to 4400 feet. At this elevation a terrain bench appears, and you may spot the sign for the summer trail to the summit. Head almost due north into a small meadow, called Chute Flats, immediately below the Ellinor Chute (4440 feet and 2 hours to here).

Climb the chute for 1000 feet to a small bowl east and 300 feet below the summit. Avalanches in this couloir have surprised numerous climbers and skiers—be confident about your avalanche hazard assessment before committing to this climb. At the top of the couloir, turn left (west) to cross the bowl and climb the final slopes to the summit at 5944 feet (4 hours to here).

DESCENT.

Ellinor Chute. From the summit area, the obvious line back to the start is to retrace your skin track and descend the Ellinor Chute. This line is super fun, with several logical pull-outs down to Chute Flats. Then simply traverse south into the wooded bowl you climbed up in the beginning, picking a line down and right until you rejoin the road and follow it back to your car.

North Couloir. Between the small bowl at 5600 feet and the summit is the obvious entrance to Mount Ellinor's North Couloir, a steep 2000-foot-plus descent. This is a gem of a line, but since you have not had an opportunity to assess its avalanche hazard *and* you have to climb back up the couloir to get home, be absolutely certain about the avalanche conditions and your time plan. If the conditions are right and you feel confident about your skiing skills and terrain assessment ability, this can be one of the best 5000-foot-plus backcountry ski days in the state! There are numerous additional opportunities for descents and exploration between Mount Ellinor and Mount Washington.

Tour Author: Chris Simmons

NORTH CASCADES

THE NORTH CASCADES ARE SOMETIMES called America's Alps. While it's true that the heavy glaciation and rugged ridgelines are more like the Alps than any other range in the Lower 48, the comparison fails to capture the unique and wild nature of these mountains. Protected in a series of large wilderness areas and the North Cascades National Park, the range gives an idea of what it may have been like before humans arrived in North America. Valleys without roads or trails, sprawling glaciers, and pristine forests and meadows are hallmarks of the North Cascades, and reasons enough to make the trip.

The geology of the North Cascades is a famously difficult story to tell. Mount Baker and Glacier Peak offer the simplest chapters—stratovolcano siblings to Rainier and Shasta. But the rest of the range presents a complex mosaic of unrelated rocks: ocean sediments, basaltic ocean floor, pieces of mantle, and more. These disparate parts have been uplifted, eroded, and in some cases sent to great depth before re-emerging, transformed, at the surface. When the continental ice sheet receded, alpine glaciers remained to carve their U-shaped valleys. The resulting range is modest in height—for the most part the high peaks reach only 7000 to 8000 feet—but world-class in terms of vertical relief: 4000 to 6000 feet from valley floor to mountaintop is not uncommon. There are also 14 peaks that exceed 9000 feet.

Heavy rain and snowfalls define the mood and ecology of the North Cascades. Glaciers and forests change in character as you move from west to east across the range. On the wetter west side, the glaciers and trees are big; look for mammoth Douglas firs, western hemlocks, and western red cedar on your way to tree line, where they often give way to mountain hemlock and subalpine fir—and big, active glaciers. East of the crest—in the rain shadow—you'll encounter ponderosa pine, Engelmann spruce, larch, and grand fir.

The North Cascades are big enough that we have divided them into two sections in this book: this one and the North Central Cascades. These are designations of convenience and don't necessarily correspond to geography. This North Cascades section covers the region accessed by State Route 542, the Mount Baker Highway, and the areas directly accessible from Highway 20.

FEES, PERMITS, AND WEATHER INFORMATION

Many of the tours in the North Cascades are located within North Cascades National Park, Mount Baker–Snoqualmie National Forest, and Okanogan–Wenatchee National Forest. Contact information for these entities, as well as the Sedro Woolley National Park and National Forest Information Centers, and Cle Elum and Wenatchee River Ranger Districts, is located in Resources.

Parking. There is no entrance fee for North Cascades National Park and parking passes are not required to park along Highway 20. Many popular trailheads, however, actually lie on Forest Service lands and require a day pass (available from local vendors), a Northwest Forest Pass, or an America the Beautiful Pass.

Previous page: Crooked Thumb and Mount Blum from Luna Cirque (Scott Schell)

Camping. Wilderness Camping Permits are required for all overnight stays in North Cascades National Park wilderness (backcountry). Permits are limited and are offered on a first-come, first-serve basis. Call the Wilderness Information Center in Marblemount to check station hours and for more information about getting your permit. For camping in both Mount Baker–Snoqualmie and Okanogan–Wenatchee National Forests, fill out a free self-issued wilderness permit at the trailhead. Wilderness regulations apply, and Leave No Trace practices are strongly encouraged.

Wilderness Areas. Stephen Mather Wilderness is located in North Cascades National Park. Mount Baker Wilderness, Noisy-Diosbud Wilderness, and Boulder River Wilderness are found in the Mount Baker–Snoqualmie National Forest. Pasayten Wilderness is located in the Okanogan–Wenatchee National Forest.

Weather. In addition to the Northwest Avalanche Center and the National Weather Service websites, check the Mount Baker and Stevens Pass sites for current local weather and snowpack conditions. See Resources for web addresses.

6 Mount Baker: Coleman–Deming Glaciers

Starting elevation: 3670 feet
High point: 10,781 feet
Vertical gain/loss: 7111 feet / 7111 feet
Distance: 16 km (10 miles)
Time: 10–12 hours (1 long day) or 2 days
Overall difficulty: moderate
Ski skills: difficult
Fitness level: very strenuous
Technical skills: moderate
Commitment: low
Gear: the basics, plus ski mountaineering equipment
Best season: April–July
USGS maps: Mount Baker and Goat Mountain; also recommended: Green Trails Mount Baker Wilderness Climbing map
Permits: A Northwest Forest Pass or Interagency Pass is required to park at the trailhead, which is located in the Mount Baker–Snoqualmie National Forest. Visitors should fill out a self-issued wilderness permit at the trailhead.

A brilliant introduction to skiing on big glaciers, the Coleman and Deming Glaciers provide a moderate, aesthetic route to the top of Mount Baker. The route winds beneath the craggy peaks of the Black Buttes, visits a high col at 9000 feet, and then climbs up the Roman Wall to the summit plateau. Do not be fooled by the weekend crowds and the beaten track up the glacier: this is real glaciated terrain and requires the appropriate skills and equipment.

ACCESS

From the town of Glacier, drive about 1 mile east, and turn right onto Glacier Creek Road (Forest Service Road 39). Follow it 8 miles to the well-signed Heliotrope Ridge trailhead (which has a vault toilet) at 3670 feet.

TOUR

DAY 1. Heliotrope Trail 677 climbs gently through big timber for 2.1 miles to a junction (4980 feet) with the climber's trail to Hogsback Camp. Follow this trail steeply up the moraine crest to Hogsback Camp at 5890 feet. This is a very popular camp with many rock circles for tents (2 hours to here).

If snowcover and stability permit, you can gain upper Heliotrope Ridge more directly from the trailhead by touring south through forest from the trailhead and then traversing slightly southeast to intersect Grouse Creek near 3900 feet. From there, head upstream in steep and complex terrain. Aim to gain the Coleman Glacier just to the east of Point 6058 on the USGS map (Point 6029 on the Green Trails map).

DAY 2. From Hogsback Camp the route climbs steeply to the southeast for 800 vertical feet to reach a very flat area known as the Football Field. Black Buttes Camp, another

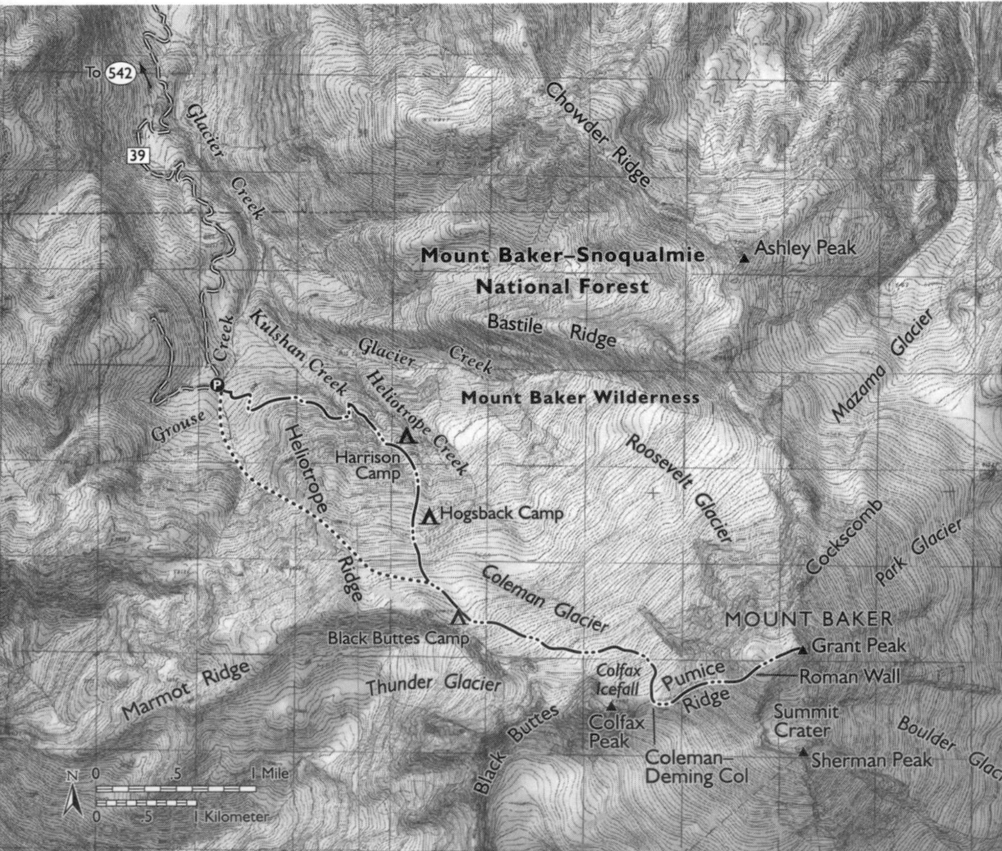

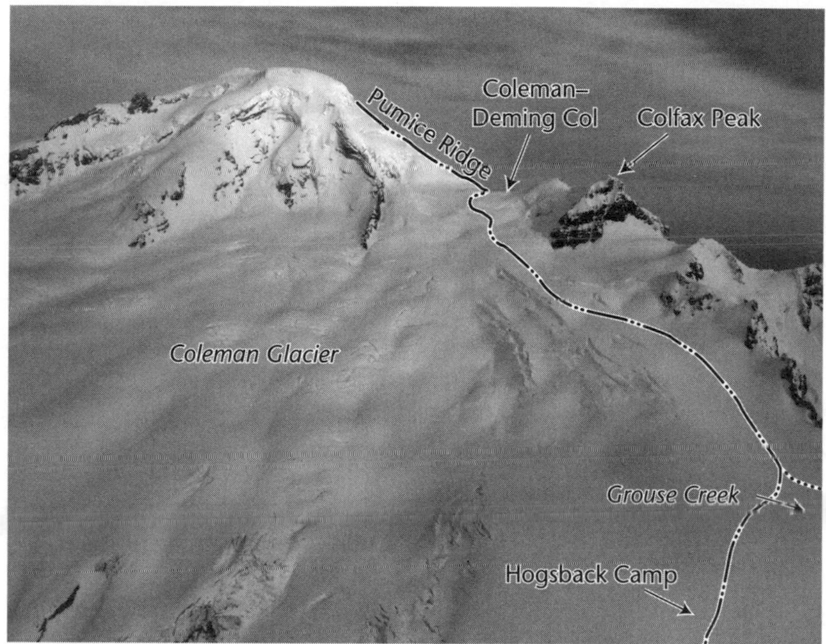

Mount Baker from the north (Martin Volken)

popular staging place for this tour, lies in the wind scoops below the low point in Heliotrope Ridge (7160 feet, 3 hours to here). The route follows a shelf westward on the Coleman Glacier, skirting below the northwest and north faces of Colfax Peak; be sure to steer clear of the icefall zone below seracs on Colfax Peak. Since this area also has large crevasses, evaluate conditions carefully. The route bends south to reach the Coleman–Deming Col at 9000 feet (4.5 hours to here).

From the col, ascend Pumice Ridge (skin, boot, or use crampons as conditions require) to 10,000 feet. From here, choose a line up the Roman Wall, considering snow quality, rockfall hazard, and ease of travel; conditions vary considerably throughout the season and from year to year. Many people will choose to boot this section often with crampons, though in the right conditions, it is possible to skin to the summit plateau.

Once you are atop the summit plateau at 10,680 feet, cross to the northeast to gain the true summit at Grant Peak at 10,781 feet (6 hours to here). Have a look into the crater, enjoy the views of Mount Shuksan and the Pickets, and get ready for the 7000 feet of skiing back to your car. As you descend, beware not only of crevasses, but also of numerous moats and open streams that develop in late winter and during spring at and below tree line. If conditions allow and your party is up to it, skiing the fall line down the Coleman Glacier to exit near Harrison Camp is an incredible way to top off your Baker experience.

Tour Author: Forest McBrian

7 Winchester Mountain and Mount Larrabee

Starting elevation: 2050 feet
High point: 7861 feet
Vertical gain/loss: 7513 feet/7513 feet
Distance: 28 km (17 miles)
Time: 2 days
Overall difficulty: difficult
Ski skills: very difficult
Fitness level: strenuous
Technical skills: moderate
Commitment: high
Gear: the basics
Best season: January–May
USGS map: Mount Larrabee
Permits: A Northwest Forest Pass or Interagency Pass is required to park at the trailhead.

This tour is one of the northernmost ski descents in the state of Washington with the summit of Mount Larrabee being barely 2 kilometers (1.2 miles) from the Canadian border. The roughly 14 kilometers (8.7 miles) of travel to get to the summit reinforces its very remote feeling. Thankfully though, on the summit of Winchester Mountain sits a fire lookout. Built in the 1930s, it served as an observation point for wildfires until the 1960s. It is now open to the public year-round and operates on a first-come, first-served basis. It makes for an outstanding base camp from which you can ski north to Mount Larrabee the next day.

ACCESS

From Glacier, drive the Mount Baker Highway (State Route 542) 12 miles east to a Washington State Department of Transportation highway maintenance shed on the north side of the highway. This is where the tour begins in winter. Parking can be difficult and limited, but there are a few pullouts off the highway that can work. *Do not park in the WSDOT maintenance lot—you will be towed.* Forest Service Road 3065 begins here and is the entry point to the tour. A snow berm normally blocks vehicle access up this road late into the spring.

TOUR

DAY 1. Unless you have a snowmobile, prepare for about a 6-mile skin up to Twin Lakes. From the snow berm, follow Forest Service Road 3065 approximately 4 miles as it winds upslope and into the Swamp Creek drainage to the Yellow Aster Butte trailhead, elevation 3720 feet (3 hours to here). Continue on the road grade to an elevation of approximately 4280 feet at which point you will cross the drainage from

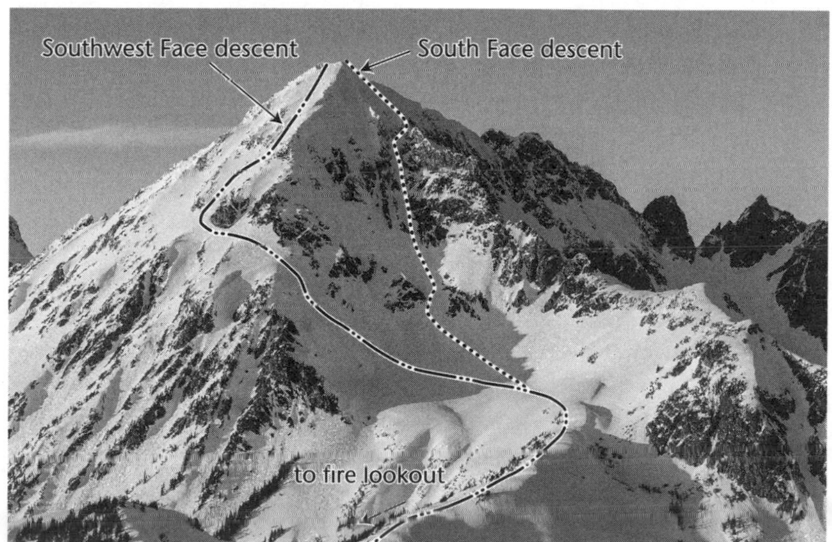

Mount Larrabee from the south (Scott Schell)

Twin Lakes. From here the road grade switchbacks up the southwest-facing slope to the Twin Lakes plateau at a little higher than 5100 feet (4 hours to here).

At this point you leave the road grade and travel cross-country. From the southwest end of the lake, ascend the southeast-facing slope just ahead staying right of the subpeak to gain the summit at 6521 feet (6 hours to here). On the summit you reach the Winchester fire lookout. Camp here.

DAY 2. Mount Larrabee is due north from the summit of Winchester Mountain and the distance between the two summits is about 2.5 kilometers (1.5 miles). From the lookout you descend through pleasant low-angle terrain nearly 1000 feet to an area called Low Pass at 5660 feet. Once you reach the pass, gradually climb to the north to reach an elevation of 6000 feet, an area labeled "High Pass" on the USGS Mount Larrabee quadrangle. Trend slightly east at this point, staying east of the drainage and on the rib that defines High Pass. As you continue north-northeast, the slope angle lessens at around 6200 feet (2 hours to here).

At this point, change your bearing to northwest and work your way from the south face, around the well-defined corner to the southwest face—ideally at around 6600 feet. If you are too low, you will find yourself on the very steep and rocky lower southwest face. Once you round the corner and are on the west face it is a direct shot north-northeast for the final 1200 feet to the summit (7861 feet). This is a fairly steep pitch and booting up the final bit may be necessary (4 hours to here).

DESCENT. Mount Larrabee offers several possible ski lines—some more committing than others. Below are two options: the southwest face and the steeper south face.

Southwest Face. Many areas on the southwest face are steeper than 40 degrees with the potential to take long falls; you must be confident skiing steep slopes. The cleanest line is skier's left near the rib that defines the southwest and south faces. Two areas of concern are constrictions at about 7200 feet and 6800 feet. Your descent is a reversal of your ascent track, so take note of these on your approach. At the 6600-foot contour, follow your skin track around back on to the right-trending southwest slope. Don't get too low here, or you will find yourself on the steep lower face. Trend south at 6300 feet or so on to the rib at High Pass and ultimately down to Low Pass as noted on the quadrangle (5 hours to here).

South Face. If you are an extremely strong skier looking for a little more adventure, the south face may be for you. Its upper reaches are steeper than the west face, and it is comprised of two distinct lines. The far skier's left chute is the widest and the most

attainable. Drop in from the summit, and stay just west of the buttress that divides the south and east faces. Steep skiing aside, the other challenge is a choke point around 7200 feet. Late in the season, it could be an ice bulge, but much of the time it is steep snow. Continue downslope using the rocky buttress as your guide to intersect your skin track around 6200 feet. From there, continue down to Low Pass (5 hours to here).

Both ski descents finish in the same location with a quick skin back up to the summit of Winchester Mountain (6 hours to here).

From the summit of Winchester Mountain a 3500-foot descent awaits. The first pitch is 1500 feet down the southeast face toward Twin Lakes. Just before you reach the lakes, trend to the south, keeping them on your left to stay high enough to avoid the flats and ski the next slope. From an elevation of 5100 feet, head south, keeping right of the drainage. At 4000 feet you are back at the Twin Lakes Road (7 hours to here). Follow the road grade to the west and gradually southwest to intersect your original skin track at 3000 feet. Continue on the road grade back to your car at 2050 feet (8 hours to here).

Tour Author: David Jordan

8 Ruth Mountain: Ruth Glacier

Starting elevation: 3080 feet
High point: 7115 feet
Vertical gain/loss: 4035 feet/4035 feet
Distance: 15 km (9.5 miles)
Time: 7 to 9 hours
Overall difficulty: moderate
Ski skills: moderate
Fitness level: strenuous
Technical skills: low
Commitment: low
Gear: the basics
Best season: January–May
USGS maps: Mount Sefrit and Mount Shuksan
Permits: A Northwest Forest Pass or Interagency Pass is required to park at the trailhead.

Standing at 7115 feet, Ruth Mountain is an attainable day trip for those looking to ski among some of the most iconic mountains of the northern Cascades, most notably Mount Shuksan, Mount Baker, and the Pickets. To the south is the jagged ridge of the Nooksack Cirque. To the southwest is the Nooksack Tower, the intimidating Price Glacier, the summit of Mount Shuksan, and ultimately Mount Baker. Ruth Mountain offers more than 2700 feet of skiing on north and northwest aspects with limited objective hazards.

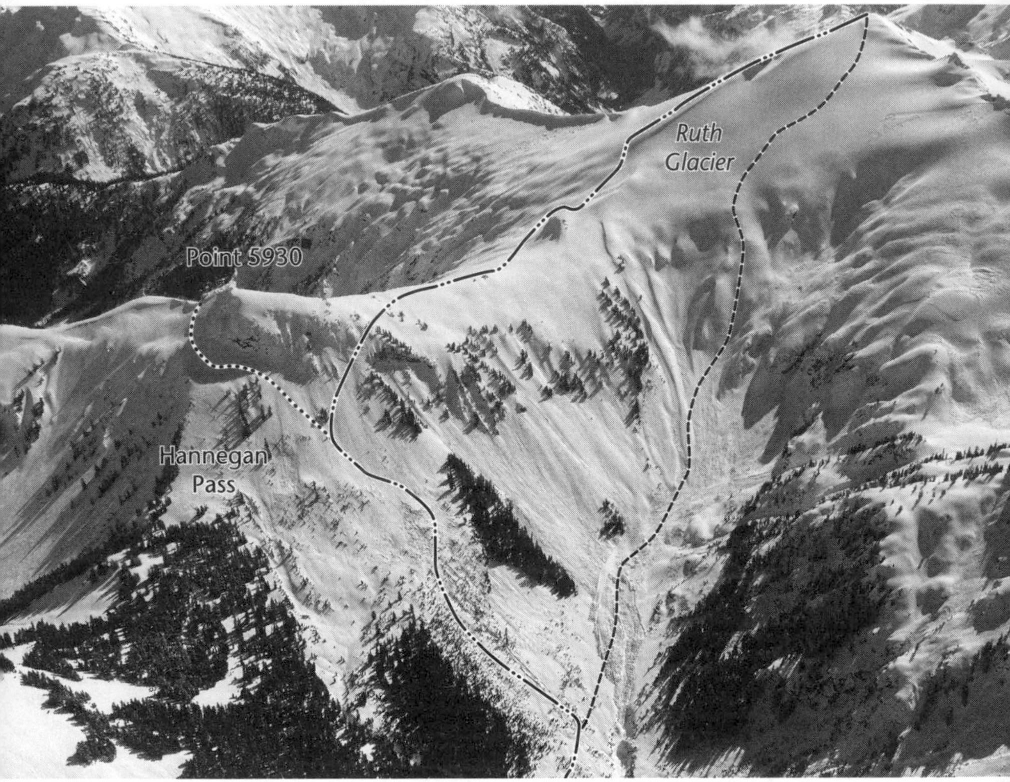

Ruth Mountain from the north (Scott Schell)

ACCESS

From Glacier, take the Mount Baker Highway (State Route 542) eastbound toward the Mount Baker Ski Area. In 13 miles turn left (north) onto Hannegan Pass Road (Forest Service Road 32). In another 1.3 miles, take the left fork, onto Ruth Creek Road, which is a continuation of FS Road 32. Continue on it for 5.4 miles to Hannegan Campground. Depending on the road conditions and snow coverage, the ski tour will start here.

TOUR

You have two options for gaining the ridge at the head of the Ruth Creek drainage. Your choice will depend on the snowpack.

If there is adequate snow coverage at the campground, avoid the trail and stay low in the Ruth Creek valley heading southeast for roughly 5 kilometers (3.1 miles) to an elevation of 4120 feet (2 hours to here). Staying south of the drainage that comes down from Hannegan Pass, travel east up the gentle slope to an elevation of about 5200 feet. At this point you intersect the summer pack trail shown on the USGS map just northwest of Point 5930 (3.5 hours to here).

If the valley floor has melted out or snow coverage is thin, the summer trail is your best option. This long slow traverse of the northwest side of the valley has many creek crossings and some steep terrain. From the campground, head southeast and gain elevation ever so slightly to reach approximately 4600 feet. When you reach the drainage that comes down from Hannegan Pass, the forest opens up a bit. Follow the drainage to the east, and gain the ridge at Hannegan Pass (3–4 hours to here).

Both options take you to the same location just northwest of Point 5930. Depending on conditions, you can stay low and travel west of the bump for a more direct approach, but later in the season this area has dangerous moats. Otherwise, strive for the high point by staying just east of the bump and contour around to the south. Once you have reached this point, due south is the summit of Ruth Mountain. Use caution when on the final 1100 feet on the well-defined ridge to the summit; it runs north–south and can be heavily corniced. Travel south to an elevation of 6400 feet, and then trend ever so slightly south-southwest to the summit (5.5 hours to here).

DESCENT. The longest continuous ski descent is to the north back to the valley floor. From the summit, ski due north just west of your skin track on the ridge. Keep heading north and avoid trending west until you have reached an elevation of about 5700 feet. Skiing north-northwest may feel inviting and easy, considering the fall line, but it will deposit you in steep, complicated terrain. Once you have reached 5700 feet, head more north-northwest, and finish your descent on steeper terrain to the valley floor. Pick up your skin track, and follow it back to the Hannegan Campground.

Tour Author: David Jordan

9 Mount Shuksan: White Salmon Glacier

Starting elevation: 3600 feet
High point: 9131 feet
Vertical gain/loss: 6600 feet/6600 feet, depending on how low you enter the White Salmon Creek valley
Distance: 16 km (10 miles)
Time: 2 days or 1 long day (more than 11 hours) in good conditions
Overall difficulty: very difficult
Ski skills: difficult
Fitness level: very strenuous
Technical skills: very high
Commitment: high
Gear: the basics, plus ski mountaineering equipment and some pieces of rock protection, depending on season
Best season: January–May
USGS maps: Shuksan Arm and Mount Shuksan
Permits: To stay overnight in North Cascades National Park, you must get an overnight backcountry permit which is available at the combined national forest and national park Glacier Public Service Center just east of the town of Glacier. No parking pass is required.

Mount Shuksan is one of the iconic peaks of the North Cascades. As Fred Beckey says in his *Cascade Alpine Guide, Volume 3*, "Shuksan has no equal in the range when one considers the structural beauty of its four major faces and five ridges and variety of routes they provide." Although Beckey was talking about the mountain in terms of climbing, this is also an apt description for its ski mountaineering routes. The mountain combines world-class scenery with a seemingly endless variety of ski routes that run the spectrum from introductory ski mountaineering tours, to extreme descents, and everything in between.

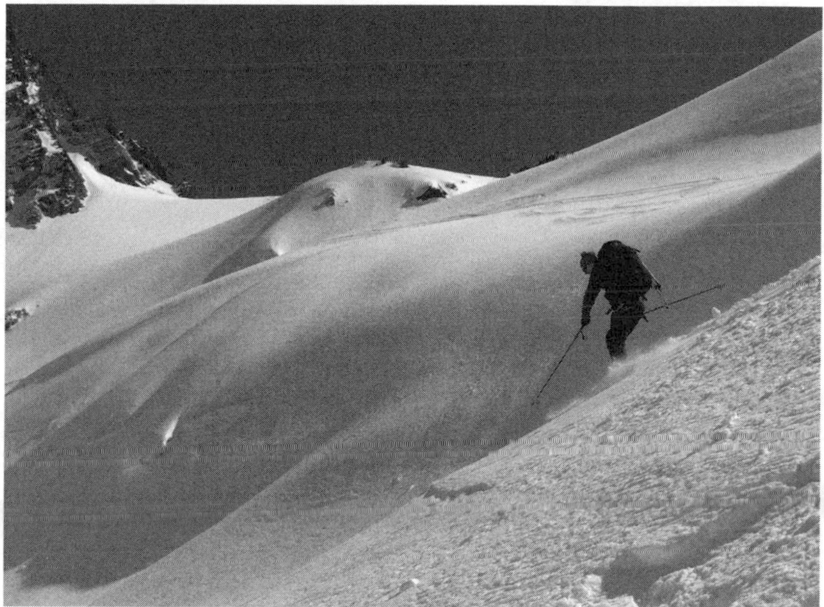

Descending the White Salmon Glacier (Crispin Prahl)

The White Salmon tour combines all the elements that make Mount Shuksan great: a spectacular setting, long descents, and bona fide ski mountaineering challenges. Although the White Salmon Glacier is one of the shortest routes to the summit, do not be fooled: this is a big mountain with enough transitions, routefinding issues, and decision points to captivate new or seasoned ski mountaineers alike.

See the aerial photo for Tour 10 for this route.

ACCESS

This tour begins at the entrance gate to the Mount Baker Ski Area White Salmon Day Lodge. From the town of Glacier, travel 18.8 miles east on the Mount Baker Highway (State Route 542) to the entrance of the ski area's White Salmon Day Lodge parking area. Park in the White Salmon parking area; be aware, however, that the gate to this lot may be closed after hours. Parking outside the lot may be worth the extra walk.

TOUR

Walk through the parking lot to the Mount Baker Ski Area White Salmon Day Lodge. Start skinning from the lodge. Take the snowcat track that starts climber's left just above the lodge and leads to the base of the C-8 chairlift. When the ski area is operating, stay to the side of the track to avoid downhill snowmobile or skier traffic. In a little more than a kilometer (which you should cover in about a quarter hour) from the day lodge, the track turns abruptly uphill to the right to gain the base of the chairlift.

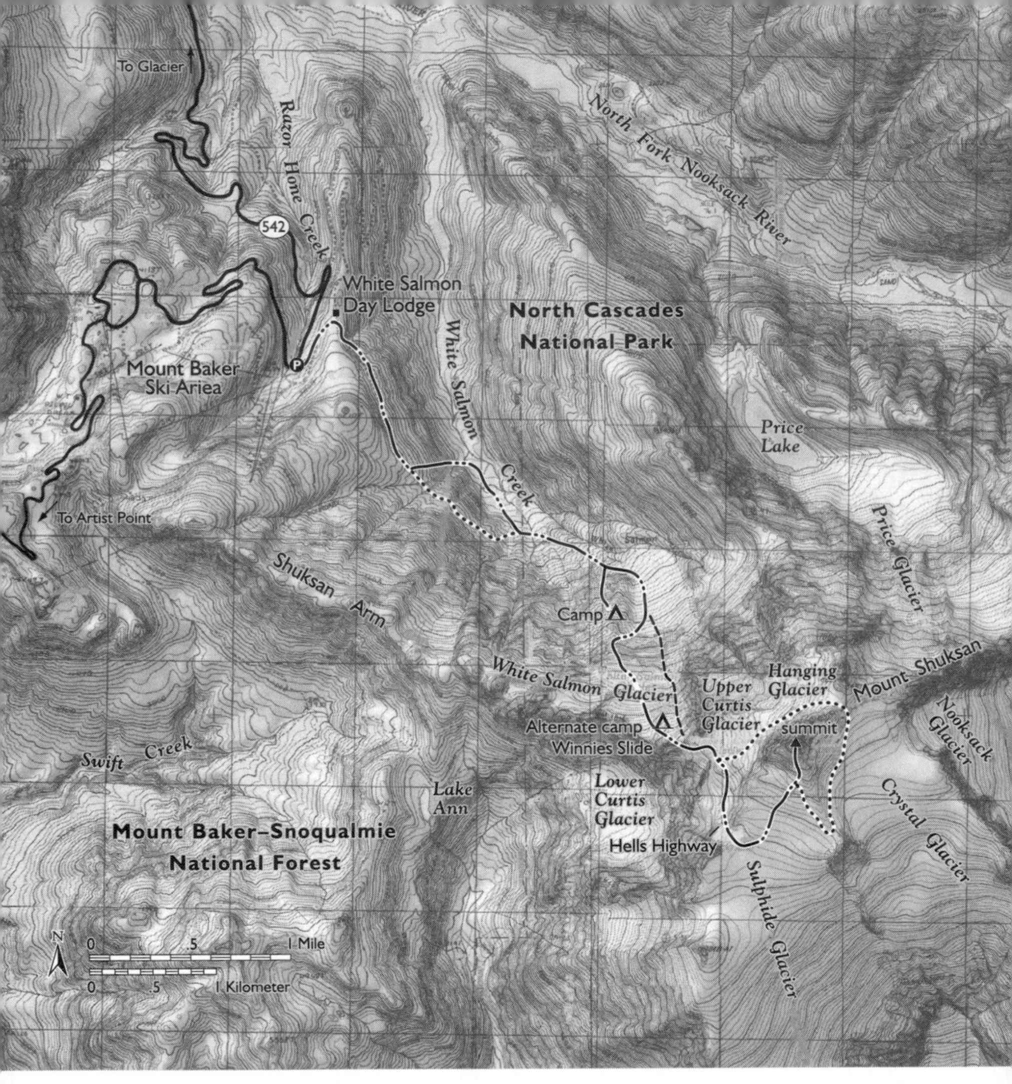

Exit left at this point into an old clear-cut below the ski area; you can strip your skins here. Make a slightly descending traverse to cross to the far side of the clear-cut. Ski the skier's right side of the clear-cut, or link steep steps just inside the forest directly to the valley floor. This direct descent into the valley is generally the most efficient route choice.

Alternatively, if there is snow higher up in the valley but not lower down, you can traverse just below 3600 feet to reach an easy slope and the floor of White Salmon Creek valley at 3300 feet, just west of the "indefinite" boundary line between Mount Baker–Snoqualmie National Forest and North Cascades National Park shown on the USGS map. This traverse requires going in and out of several drainages with steep sidewalls, which often require sidestepping, working through brush, and taking off your skis to climb in and out. Stay as high as possible through the drainages to avoid cliffs and waterfalls below.

If you have any doubt, choose the direct descent option. The east end of the White Salmon Creek valley is usually covered well with snow late into spring due to the many large avalanches that sweep into it during the winter (1 to 2 hours to 3300 feet in the valley, depending on conditions and your route).

Once you are on the valley floor, tour directly up valley toward a lightly treed buttress that bisects the lower White Salmon face. To gain the top of the buttress, either switchback steeply up its west side or more gradually contour around to its east side and then rightward up a draw beneath the glacier. Beware of significant avalanche potential from above through all this terrain (4 hours to tree line on top of the buttress). Look for great campsites near tree line at the top of the buttress if you are spending the night. Marvel at the up close vantage of the Hanging Glacier to the southeast, and enjoy the sensation of being so close to the ski area, yet so far removed as you look back down toward the White Salmon Day Lodge.

From the top of the buttress, climb directly onto the glacier above. Beware of crevasse hazard that starts immediately once you are on the glacier. As you ascend, bypass several headwalls by heading climber's left to reach a bowl high on Shuksan Arm. Continue up and farther climber's left through crevasses and then snow-covered talus to reach the base of a short, steep slope called Winnies Slide, the last slope leading up to the ridge that separates the White Salmon and Upper Curtis Glaciers. Some parties like to camp here to ensure a shorter summit day. The USGS map incorrectly labels Winnies Slide as part of the Hanging Glacier to the northeast. Winnies Slide is steeper than 50 degrees near the top and often merits an ice ax and crampons, even when the lower slopes of the White Salmon are skinnable.

From the top of Winnies Slide at 7000 feet cross through the obvious notch that leads over to the Upper Curtis Glacier. Ascend northeast alongside the rocky ridge for less than 200 feet to reach lower angled terrain. This route may involve a short pitch of low-angle ice late in the season if the snow has melted. If you are unprepared for ice, scramble up the rocky ridge itself to reach the lower angled slopes above. Continue a rising traverse to gain the top of the lower lobe of the Upper Curtis Glacier at 7500 feet.

Transition to downhill mode for a brief descent over to the base of Hells Highway, the segment of the Upper Curtis Glacier that connects to the Sulphide Glacier to the south. The USGS map labels Hells Highway as the "Hourglass," but the latter is actually the hourglass-shaped gully northeast of Hells Highway (6 hours to here). Climb out of a windscoop feature on the northeast flank of Hells Highway, and ascend through the cleft of Shuksan's southwest ridge to access the Sulphide Glacier. Once on the Sulphide, head northeast toward the lower southeast corner of Shuksan's summit pyramid. A longer but scenic alternative to the Hells Highway route to reach the base of the summit pyramid can be made by circling the summit pyramid via the Upper Curtis and Crystal Glaciers.

From the base of the summit pyramid, make a leftward rising traverse up its lower flank toward the central gully that leads to the summit. Many parties depot their skis just before the gully and transition to belayed climbing for the final two to three pitches on either steep snow or loose fourth-class rock in the gully, depending on conditions.

Climb the right side of the gully, then exit left just below the top of the gully to gain the final ridge to the summit.

DESCENT. With good conditions early in the season, those interested in a steep, exposed descent can carry their skis up the summit gully to ski from just below the top. Many parties prefer to downclimb or perform several low-angle 30-meter rappels to protect the gully descent.

Return to your ski depot, and descend the rest of your ascent route, including a short transition to uphill mode to cross the Upper Curtis Glacier. From the top of Winnies Slide, a steeper fall line can be skied directly to the valley bottom if you are not returning to camp on the buttress below the White Salmon face. Exit the valley by retracing your route to the ski area cat track.

Tour Author: Benjamin Haskell

10 Mount Shuksan: North Face

Starting elevation: 3600 feet
High point: 8180 feet (9131 feet with summit)
Vertical gain/loss: 6280 feet/6280 feet (7200 feet with summit)
Distance: 13 km (8 miles), 17 km (10.5 miles) with summit
Time: 7–10 hours (10–14 hours with summit)
Overall difficulty: very difficult
Ski skills: very difficult
Fitness level: very strenuous
Technical skills: very high
Commitment: high
Gear: the basics, plus ski mountaineering equipment and a small alpine rack late in the season
Best season: April–June
USGS maps: Mount Shuksan and Shuksan Arm
Permits: To stay overnight, you must get a free overnight backcountry permit for North Cascades National Park from the Glacier Public Service Center. No parking pass is required.

This tour takes you very quickly into a world of steep, high alpine terrain. It follows the left-hand skyline of Mount Shuksan as viewed from the Mount Baker Ski Area. With or without the optional visit to the summit pyramid, the North Face is a classic steep ski mountaineering outing in a big setting. It may be difficult to find the face in great ski conditions, and a fall here in firm conditions would likely be fatal. Preview the route by climbing it first, and if you do not like the conditions, you can descend via the White Salmon Glacier.

Mount Shuksan from the northwest (Alasdair Turner)

ACCESS

This tour begins at the entrance gate to the Mount Baker Ski Area White Salmon Day Lodge. From the town of Glacier, travel 18.8 miles east on the Mount Baker Highway (State Route 542) to the entrance of the ski area's White Salmon Day Lodge parking area. Enter the parking lot, and park in the southeast corner (be aware that the gate can be closed at any time, even in season, so parking outside the gate may be prudent). When the ski area is closed, park outside the gate, taking care not to block the entrance.

TOUR

Begin with your skins on, going around the east side of the lodge and heading out the level cat track that leads to the C-8 chairlift. Follow this track for about a quarter mile to where it bends sharply uphill to reach the chairlift. Rather than going uphill, continue on a short spur into an old clear-cut, and remov e your skins. From the logging deck you have two options. With very good snow coverage, you may be able to gradually

descend into White Salmon Creek along Shuksan Arm. If snow cover is thin, this route is often plagued by steep creek banks and other obstacles. If you have any doubts, ski the fall line down the right-hand side of the clear-cut, moving rightward into the trees near its bottom. When you reach the valley floor, transition into skin mode (2800 feet, 0.75 hour to here).

Follow White Salmon Creek up valley, remaining aware of the many slide paths descending from Shuksan Arm. The slopes of the White Salmon Glacier also generate large slides, and the resulting debris can inspire creative routefinding. If the area has debris, head for a rib leading from 3400 to 4200 feet between branches of the creek (located just to the southwest of the word "White" on the USGS map). Follow the lowest angle slopes eastward toward the ridge and the toe of the North Face at 5500 feet (4 hours to here).

The lower North Face is a lobe of crevassed glacial ice; parties typically climb up and eastward on it, and then cut back west toward a gully at 7100 feet that gains the upper hanging snowfields. Follow the snow slopes straight uphill through a few rock bands. The slope here averages 40–45 degrees, steepening at the top to 50 degrees. The 8180-foot shoulder above, where the North Face meets the upper Hanging Glacier, is a great place for a break (6.5 hours to here).

Many parties will choose to ski from here. The fall line on the North Face goes over several cliff bands. Follow your tracks back down this steep, exposed face, enjoying the wild views to Price Lake and the border peaks.

If you want to visit the summit pyramid before you ski the North Face, the best way is via the Crystal Glacier. Note that this route features significant crevassed terrain. Skin to the wide col between the Crystal and Hanging Glaciers at 8350 feet (6.75 hours to here). Ski south-southwest to 7920 feet on the Crystal Glacier, and then ascend to the col between the Crystal and Sulphide Glaciers. *Beware: the steep glacier slope guarding access to the Sulphide harbors very large crevasses.* From the col, skin to the northwest, aiming for the base of the summit pyramid at 8100 feet and the head of the Sulphide Glacier (7.5 hours to here).

Ascend the obvious gully in the summit pyramid's southwest face, which reaches 50 degrees and offers excellent but exposed skiing; many prefer to leave their skis at the base. Later in the season, when some rock becomes exposed in the gully, a small alpine rack may prove useful. Take care as you reach the summit (9131 feet), as cornices form on the north side (8.5 hours to here).

DESCENT. After skiing or downclimbing to the base of the gully, reverse your route to Crystal-Hanging Col (9.75 hours to here). From here, traverse northwest across the Hanging Glacier to the top of the North Face. If skiing conditions are poor for the steep descent of the North Face, consider descending the White Salmon Glacier route (Tour 9) instead. From the Crystal-Hanging Col, traverse west then southwest toward a rock ridge at 7800 feet that divides the Hanging and Upper Curtis Glaciers. Follow this ridge on its skier's left side down to the gap that leads to the White Salmon Glacier at 7000 feet. Ski the White Salmon to the valley floor.

Once on the valley floor from either the North Face or the White Salmon descent, follow White Salmon Creek down to 2800 feet. From here, reverse your route up through the trees and into the clear-cut to regain the ski area cat track. Many parties will boot some or all of this final ascent. Glide the cat track back to your car.

Tour Author: Forest McBrian

11 Stoneman Couloir

Starting elevation: 4260 feet
High point: 6030 feet
Vertical gain/loss: 3020 feet/3020 feet
Distance: 7 km (4.2 miles)
Time: 5–6 hours

Overall difficulty: moderate
Ski skills: difficult
Fitness level: moderate
Technical skills: moderate
Commitment: moderate
Gear: the basics, plus a Rutschblock cord or knotted cordelette recommended
Best season: December–May
USGS map: Shuksan Arm
Permits: None during ski area operations. A Northwest Forest Pass or Interagency Pass is required after the resort closes in the spring.

The Stoneman Couloir is the prominent couloir that appears as you make the turn around Picture Lake near the top of Mount Baker Highway (State Route 542). Many Mount Baker locals spend years eyeing this line from Chair 1, just waiting for the right conditions. From afar this couloir may look intimidating, but in fact it maxes out around 38 degrees. However, do not take this objective lightly; avalanches in this couloir have taken lives. Given the right conditions, this excellent outing provides a quieter day away from the Table Mountain and Mount Herman crews, a rewarding objective, and spectacular views. See the aerial photo for Tour 12.

ACCESS

From the town of Glacier, head east on the Mount Baker Highway (State Route 542) for just over 21 miles to where it ends at the Mount Baker Ski Area. Head to the Upper Heather Meadows parking lot, near the start of the Blueberry cat track and the RV parking area. Park in the uppermost lot.

TOUR

From the southwestern corner of the parking lot that points toward Bagley Lakes, head down 50 feet to reach the flat valley below the lot (short enough to transition to uphill mode in the parking lot and then skin downhill). The first part of this tour is often well traveled. Take the climber's left-hand side of the valley to reach Bagley Lakes, and look up at the southeast face above, as this is the last ski descent of the tour (where the USGS map reads "Bagley Lakes").

Once you reach the lakes, Table Mountain is on your left, and Herman Saddle is straight ahead to the west. Head toward Herman Saddle by following more or less the route of the summer trail on the map (while this tour does not visit Herman Saddle, the out-and-back trip is a great, easy ski tour to be aware of). The summer trail climbs up through a boulder field (a wide, open slope on a good snow year), and avoids the gully feature to climber's left. Before you reach Herman Saddle, veer off to the north to gain the col between Mazama Dome and the southwest ridge of Mount Herman at 5400 feet.

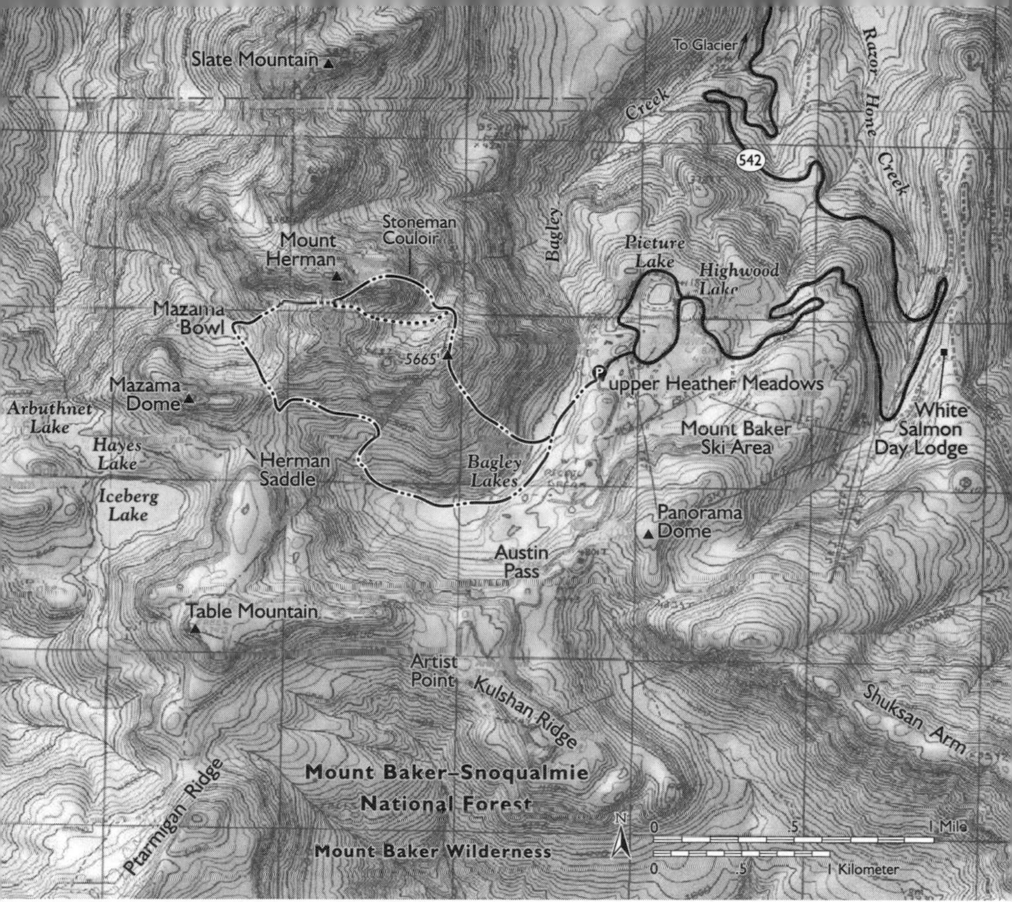

Ski northwest down to the unnamed lake. This run is called Mazama Bowl. Once you reach the lake, climb east toward a col south of Mount Herman's true summit; you cannot see the col until you have reached the low-angle basin above the lake. Steeper skinning leads to a nice low-angle basin where you have a clear view of Mount Herman to the left and the col straight ahead. This col can be difficult to make out on a USGS topo map because the word "Mountain" covers the contour lines, but aim for the area between the "o" and "u."

From the col (5950 feet), it is best to rip skins for the traverse over toward the subsummit of Mount Herman. Be careful here late in the season, as the sun bakes this slope, and it is the perfect angle for loose snow avalanches. If conditions look good, traverse northeast across the steep slope, and then boot to gain the flat eastern spur ridge of Mount Herman. Head due east along the spur ridge to the subpeak on its eastern end, and take a look down at the Stoneman Couloir.

DESCENT. Continue between Mount Herman and the subpeak down a small north-facing chute that heads into the Slate Creek drainage. Be aware that a cornice typically builds here throughout winter. This chute is the steepest part of the tour, but it is short and often filled with powder.

Climbing toward the Stoneman Couloir; Table Mountain and Mount Baker behind (Kurt Hicks)

Make a hard skier's right at the bottom of it, and traverse east until you are below the small pass. Boot up a short way heading due east, until you reach a large platform at 6030 feet—the top of the Stoneman Couloir! Enjoy the views of Mount Shuksan and the surrounding peaks.

In the center of the couloir, the steepest turns are around 38 degrees. Early in the season, it is best to go right of the large rock outcropping at the bottom of the couloir until it fills in more. Late in the season, however, you will likely want to go left because a moat forms on the right side.

Once you exit the couloir, traverse down and skier's right through the trees to reach the basin floor. From here, head south to gain the north-facing ridge of the nameless peak—the eastern flank of the Mount Herman massif. Follow this ridge, mostly skinning with a few bootpacks, to the summit at 5665 feet. Depending on the conditions and time of day, you have many descent options to get back down into the Bagley Lakes drainage. The quickest and most direct option is to head southeast off this nameless peak, and take the fall line down to the flats below the parking area (this is the line you saw at the beginning of the tour). Skate back onto the winter trail, and boot back up to your car.

Tour Author: Erin Smart

12 Table Mountain Circumnavigation

Starting elevation: 4260 feet
High point: 5300 feet
Vertical gain/loss: 1900 feet/1900 feet
Distance: 9 km (4.6 miles)
Time: 4–7 hours
Overall difficulty: moderate
Ski skills: easy
Fitness level: moderate
Technical skills: low
Commitment: low
Gear: the basics
Best season: December–May
USGS map: Shuksan Arm
Permits: none

Table Mountain and Bagley Lakes from the southeast (Alasdair Turner)

The backcountry ski terrain near the Mount Baker Ski Area is one of the few places in the Cascades where you can drive to tree line in the winter months. The area's fantastic access combined with its incredibly deep snowpack make it an ideal touring destination. This loop tour around Table Mountain provides many options for further exploration. Poke around and enjoy some great ski touring.

ACCESS

From Glacier, drive about 21 miles east on the Mount Baker Highway (State Route 542) to its winter end in the uppermost plowed lot at the Mount Baker Ski Area. Park in the southern end of the lot, or obey the ski area employees' parking directions.

TOUR

From the southern end of the parking lot, skin in a southerly direction on the west side of the groomed track. Keep on the far right of the track to avoid downhill traffic. Follow this track as it climbs, passing the ski area boundary, to Austin Pass (4700 feet,

0.75 hour). Continue southwest toward the east ridge of Table Mountain and the large flat area of Artist Point at 5080 feet (1.5 hours to here).

Although there is often a skin track that you can follow on a high traverse along the southeast slope of Table Mountain, it is often safer and more efficient to ski a descending traverse to about 4800 feet and then climb back up to the south shoulder of the mountain at 5200 feet (2.5 hours to here). From this point, you can extend your tour southwest toward Coleman Pinnacle, though this option adds significant time to the day—check your watch and energy levels before committing to it. To continue the circumnavigation, rip your skins and ski northwest down to Iceberg Lake at 4800 feet (3.25 hours to here).

Another short climb up the slopes of Mazama Dome lead to the broad, U-shaped Herman Saddle at 5300 feet (4 hours to here).

DESCENT. You have many descent options from Herman Saddle. The easiest route is to ski fall line from the saddle into the main drainage, and follow it to the valley floor. A steeper option is to take a high traverse to the right (southeast) for a few hundred feet under Table's rocky cliffs until you reach an obvious alcove in the rocks. From here, enjoy steep, gladed skiing to the valley floor. Carry your speed at the bottom of either descent, and glide as far as possible along the left edge of the valley. One final skin leads out of the Bagley Lakes basin along the normally well-packed trail back to the parking lot at 4260 feet (5 hours to here).

Table Mountain, Northeast Face descent. An alternate descent is possible from the midpoint of this tour. From the south shoulder of Table Mountain, climb northwest to the summit plateau. Peel the skins and ski 1300 feet of steep northeast facing terrain into the Bagley Lakes basin. This descent is through big avalanche terrain and must be carefully evaluated.

Tour Author: Kurt Hicks

13 Mount Baker: Park Glacier

Starting elevation: 4260 feet
High point: 10,781 feet
Vertical gain/loss: 9600 feet/9600 feet
Distance: about 30 kilometers (about 18 miles)
Time: 2 to 3 days
Overall difficulty: difficult
Ski skills: difficult
Fitness level: strenuous
Technical skills: moderate to high
Commitment: high
Gear: ski mountaineering and overnight equipment
Best season: March–June

USGS maps: Mount Baker and Shuksan; also recommended: Green Trails Mount Baker Wilderness Climbing map

Permits: A parking permit is not required when the ski area is operating (generally until the second half of April). After that you must display a Northwest Forest Pass or Interagency Pass to park at the trailhead.

The Park Glacier side of Mount Baker is incredibly scenic and arguably the least-visited side of the mountain. Access is quite good thanks to the Mount Baker Ski Area. This ski tour can be divided into two segments: the long, scenic, and moderate tour across the Ptarmigan Ridge to The Portals and the wild, high-alpine, and lonely ascent of the Park Glacier to the summit.

ACCESS

From Glacier, take the Mount Baker Highway (State Route 542) approximately 21 miles to its end at the Mount Baker Ski Area, and look for the Heather Meadows parking lot; it is near the ski area maintenance buildings at around 4260 feet.

TOUR

DAY 1. From the car, tour in a southwesterly direction to Artist Point and beyond to the base of the short but steep east-facing crag of Table Mountain at about 5050 feet.

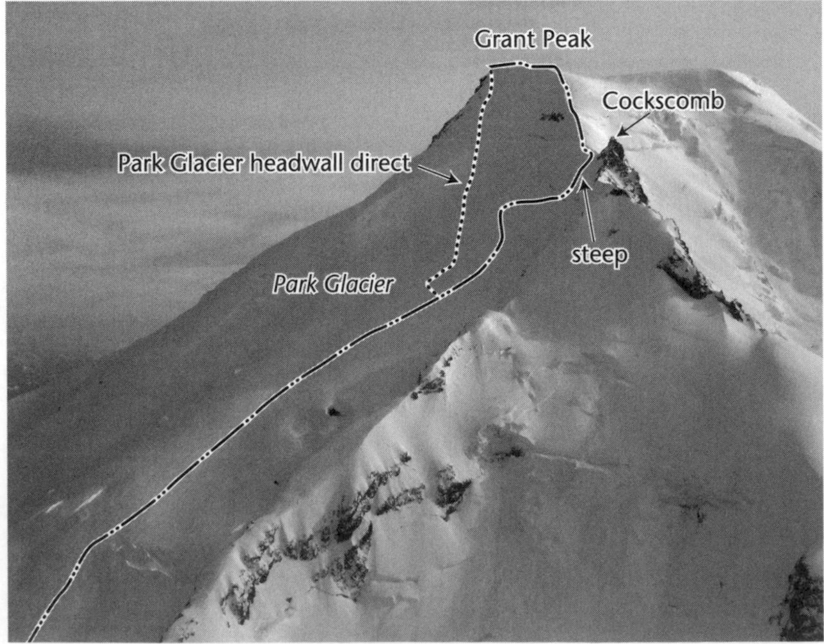

The Upper Park Glacier and Park Headwall from the northeast (Martin Volken)

Ski down the short but steep slope to the south side of Table Mountain. Keep your elevation and traverse this avalanche-prone slope to a gentle pass on the southwest side of Table Mountain at 5100 feet (2 hours to here).

Keep touring in a southwesterly direction on the north side of Ptarmigan Ridge to a little pass just north of Coleman Pinnacle at 6100 feet (3.5 hours to here). From this pass, head across the south-facing cirque, and then carry on to the top of the Sholes Glacier and onward to another pass called The Portals at 6100 feet (4.5–5 hours to here). This area makes for a great campsite.

DAY 2. In good spring conditions, you should be able to stay pretty high while skiing down and across the upper reaches of the Rainbow Glacier. You will most likely have to transition to skins at around 5800 feet, and yes, it is uphill all the way from here.

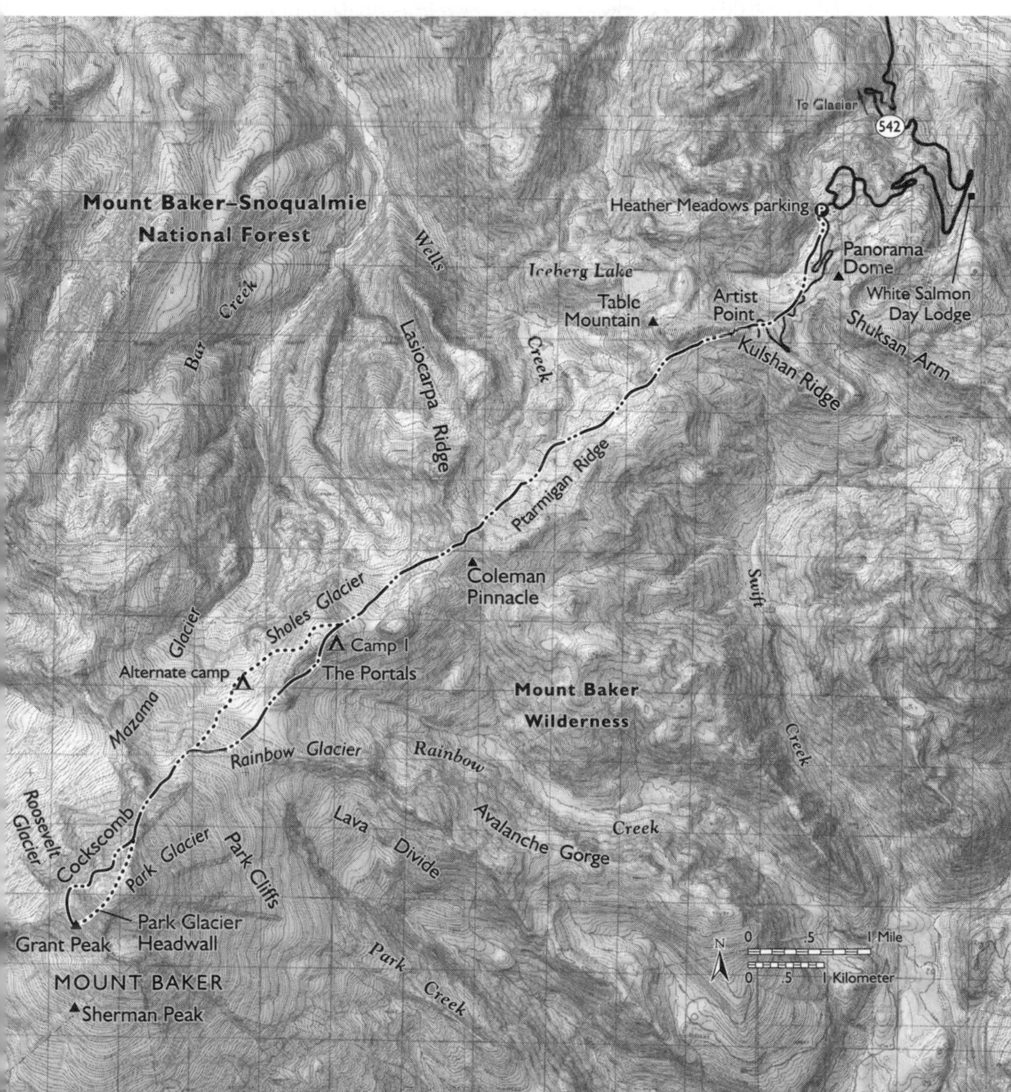

Tour the short distance up to the plateau that divides the Mazama and Rainbow Glaciers at around 6500 feet. From here tour in a southwesterly direction toward the toe of the large cleaver that comes down from the Cockscomb. At around 7800 feet (2.5 hours to here), head toward the center of the Park Glacier.

Keep going in this general direction, and tour through spectacularly glaciated (and crevassed) terrain to about 9600 feet. You are below a steep slope that connects you to the upper end of Cockscomb Ridge at 10,000 feet, just south of the Cockscomb itself (4.5 hours to here). The moat crossing at the base of the slope may be simple or complicated. Either way you want to be here early since this slope receives a lot of sun early in the day. Once on the ridge, follow it to the summit at 10,781 feet (5.5 hours to here).

Variation. If you feel up for it and the conditions are favorable, you can also climb and ski the Park Glacier Headwall. This is an exciting ski descent right off the summit with your first turns after two days of touring exceeding 50 degrees.

DESCENT. The descent down the Park Glacier is what makes spring ski touring in the Cascades excellent. The terrain is huge, and you ski your ascent route for an uninterrupted 5000 feet. Again, be mindful of potential spring avalanche conditions on the steep slope when you are leaving Cockscomb Ridge.

Once you are back at the plateau between the Mazama and Rainbow Glaciers, either carry on to about 5800 feet on the Rainbow Glacier and then skin back to your camp at The Portals, or if you feel like it might be too late and the snow is soft, stay on the north side of the two Portal bumps and access your camp (at 6100 feet) that way (7–7.5 hours to here). As you retrace your route back to the car, do not underestimate the few rises you still have to deal with.

As it is so often in the mountains, the trick is to get started early enough so that you do not run into snags at the end of the day, such as soft conditions on the steep, south-facing slope below Table Mountain at 4800 feet (9–9.5 hours to here).

From Artist Point simply enjoy a few more turns back to your car at 4260 feet (10 hours to here). If it is too late in the day to safely navigate the south slopes of Table Mountain, consider traversing the north side of Table Mountain back to Herman Saddle and the Bagley Lakes basin (Tour 12).

Tour Author: Martin Volken

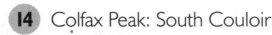

14 Colfax Peak: South Couloir

Starting elevation: 3350 feet
High point: 9440 feet
Vertical gain/loss: 6100 feet/6100 feet
Distance: 19 km (11.8 miles)
Time: 9–11.5 hours
Overall difficulty: very difficult

Ski skills: difficult to very difficult
Fitness level: very strenuous
Technical skills: moderate
Commitment: high
Gear: the basics, plus ski mountaineering equipment
Best season: April–June
USGS maps: Mount Baker and Baker Pass; also recommended: Green Trails Mount Baker Wilderness Climbing map
Permits: A Northwest Forest Pass or Interagency Pass is required to park at the trailhead in the summer. Day-use visitors can fill out a self-issued wilderness permit at the trailhead.

There is definitely more to Mount Baker than skiing the summit, and this tour proves it. With a steep 1500-foot run from the top of a 9000-foot peak amid big, broken glaciers, your efforts are well rewarded. The ambience is big, and while it is not quite extreme, this descent requires the ability to ski steep terrain confidently. The tour crosses serious glaciated terrain and requires careful evaluation of snow conditions

The South Couloir of Colfax Peak and Mount Baker (Forest McBrian)

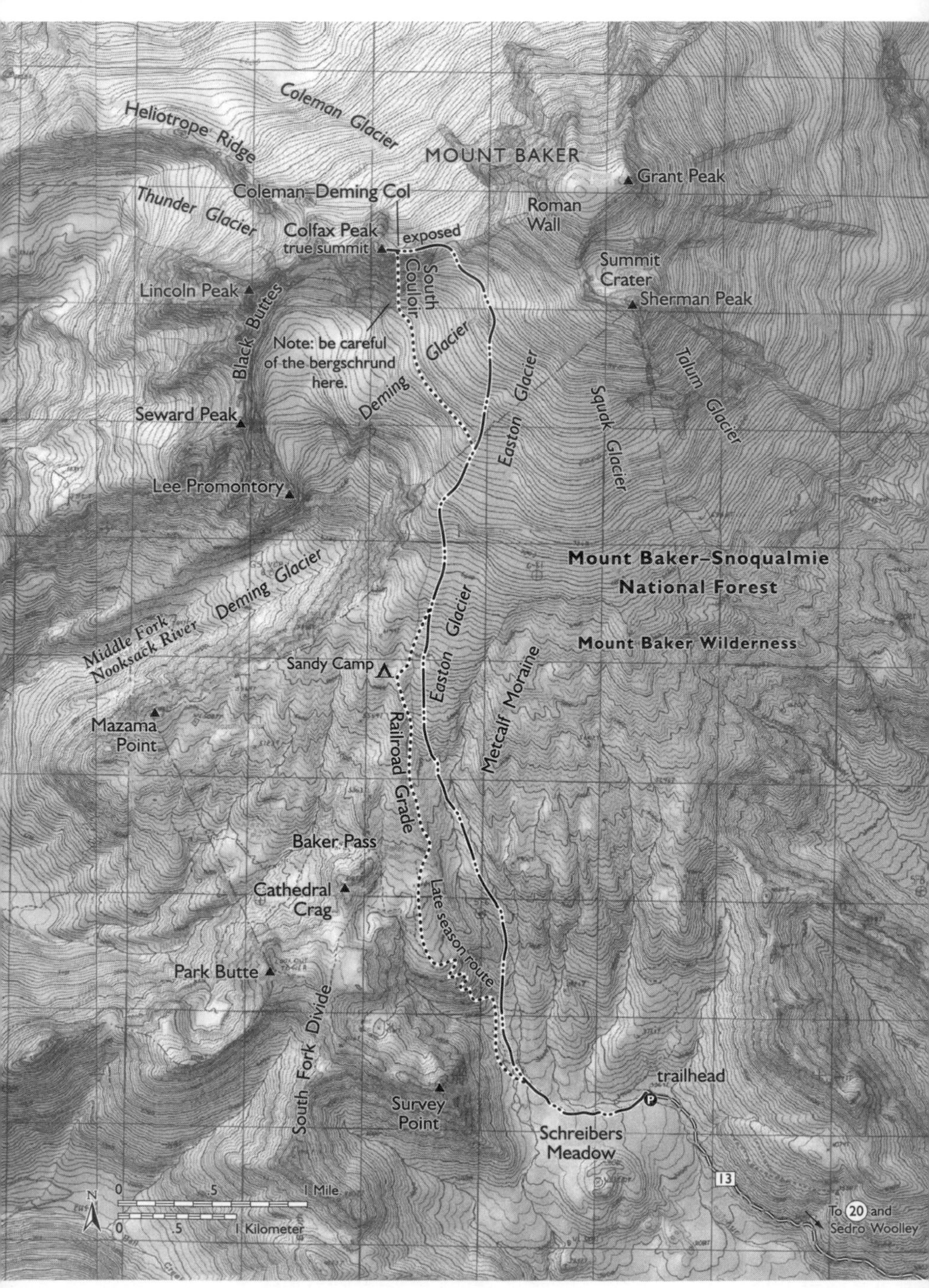
Coleman Glacier
Heliotrope Ridge
MOUNT BAKER
Grant Peak
Thunder Glacier
Coleman–Deming Col
Roman Wall
Colfax Peak
true summit
exposed
South Couloir
Summit Crater
Sherman Peak
Lincoln Peak
Black Buttes
Note: be careful of the bergschrund here.
Deming Glacier
Talum Glacier
Squak Glacier
Easton Glacier
Seward Peak
Lee Promontory
Mount Baker–Snoqualmie National Forest
Deming Glacier
Middle Fork Nooksack River
Mount Baker Wilderness
Sandy Camp
Easton Glacier
Metcalf Moraine
Mazama Point
Railroad Grade
Baker Pass
Cathedral Crag
Late season route
Park Butte
South Fork Divide
trailhead
Survey Point
Schreibers Meadow
13
0 .5 1 Mile
0 .5 1 Kilometer
To 20 and Sedro Woolley

in the couloir. In mid- to late spring the snow on the road melts quickly up to the trailhead, making access a breeze.

ACCESS

From Sedro Woolley, take the North Cascades Highway (State Route 20) east for approximately 17 miles. Turn left at Baker Lake Road, and follow it 12 miles to a left at Forest Service Road 12. Take a right when this dirt road branches again in 3.5 miles, and follow Forest Service Road 13 for 5 miles to the trailhead for Schreibers Meadow at 3350 feet or as high as snow levels allow.

TOUR

When the snowcover allows you to do so, cross the meadows west, and then head north up the drainage of the Easton Glacier (in early season, it is often possible to follow a snowmobile track to nearly 4600 feet on the east side of the creek). Follow the drainage up to gain the glacier at 5200 feet (2.25 hours to here).

Later in the season it is better to hike trails to the glacier's edge. Follow Park Butte Trail 603 for 2.3 miles, then take the right branch for the Railroad Grade Trail 603.2. This narrow lateral moraine leads to the very popular Sandy Camp at 5880 feet.

Head up the Easton Glacier, aiming for the flat area just north of Railroad Grade. Continue north and slightly east up the lowest angle, least-crevassed part of the glacier. At around 8000 feet, start making the ascending traverse toward the Coleman–Deming Col (marked "Coleman Saddle" on some maps). You must have good visibility to safely navigate this crevassed terrain, and you have a chance to assess the condition of the bergschrund at the bottom of the South Couloir (6 hours to here).

From the Coleman–Deming Col, turn to the west and climb up toward the false summit of Colfax (this summit is incorrectly labeled as the true summit of Colfax on the USGS map). At around 9250 feet, turn toward the south side of the false summit, and traverse to the distinct saddle between the false and true summits. This short section is exposed; you may need crampons and an ice ax to gain the saddle. From here, tour or climb up the steep but simple snow slope to the true summit of Colfax Peak at 9440 feet (7 hours to here).

DESCENT. From the summit, ski back down to the saddle. The South Couloir starts here. Your objective line is quite large and wide at the top (you will be skiing through the "x" in "Colfax" on the USGS map). Make sure that you like the conditions in the couloir before you enter it. Be careful of glide cracks and bergschrunds near the bottom; trending skier's left around a distinct solitary rock tower near the bottom may reduce your exposure.

Once you are back on the glacier (8 hours to here), find your way back to your up track by traversing high across the Deming Glacier; be ready to put skins back on and/or rope up if the routefinding proves tricky. Ski your line of ascent back to the trail or to the car if you have snow the whole way (9–9.5 hours round-trip).

Tour Author: Forest McBrian

15 Mount Baker: Boulder Glacier

Starting elevation: 2741 feet
High point: 10,781 feet
Vertical gain/loss: 8040 feet/8040 feet
Distance: 18.4 km (11.4 miles)
Time: 2 days
Overall difficulty: moderate to difficult
Ski skills: difficult
Fitness level: strenuous
Technical skills: moderate
Commitment: moderate
Gear: the basics, plus ski mountaineering equipment
Best season: April–June
USGS map: Mount Baker; also recommended: Green Trails Mount Baker Wilderness Climbing Map
Permits: A Northwest Forest Pass or Interagency Pass is required to park at the trailhead.

The Boulder Glacier is a natural ski line with several options that give you flexibility to choose the best aspect for the conditions. Campsites on Boulder Ridge are many and scenic, with views of Mount Shuksan and the Cascades to the south. If you time your trip when there is no snow at the trailhead (that is, no snowmobile access), you will find that this side of the mountain feels remote and quiet. If the whole route has snow, you can ski the mountain car to car.

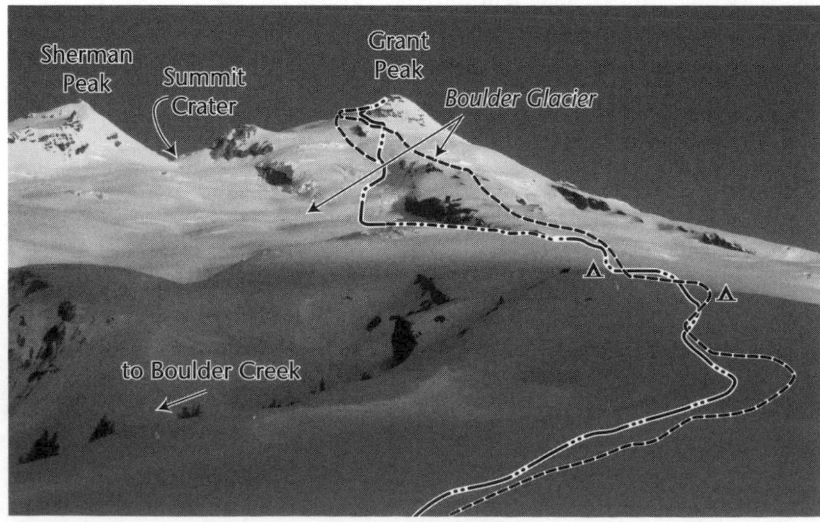

Mount Baker's Boulder Glacier (Margaret Wheeler)

ACCESS

From Sedro Woolley, take the North Cascades Highway (State Route 20) approximately 17 miles to the Baker Lake Road. Turn left, and follow it for 18.2 miles. Then take a left on Forest Service Road 1130, and follow it for 1.5 miles. Turn left on Forest Service Road 1131 (Boulder Ridge Road), and continue for 4.1 miles until it ends in a clearing. The Boulder Ridge trail (Forest Service Trail 605) starts here at an elevation of 2741 feet.

TOUR

DAY 1. Follow the trail as it contours around the ridge for 2.1 kilometers (1.3 miles), passing below the steep treed slopes of the ridge above. The trail gains only 500 feet of elevation before it ends (or becomes "Hard to Follow" on the Wilderness Climbing Map). The snow line will dictate when and where you leave the trail and whether you can skin or if you will need to continue to boot. There are several options; you can gain the toe of Boulder Ridge by ascending the treed slopes south and southeast of point 4328 on the Wilderness Climbing Map, or try to follow the trail to its end and work up along the stream drainage that is northeast of Boulder Creek to gain the ridge at 4500 feet (3 hours to here). Note also that you can work up the terrain east of Boulder Creek and gain the upper ridge via a ramp at 5100 feet.

Once you have gained the end of Boulder Ridge, follow the ridge; if you encounter the steep slope at 4500 feet you can either boot up the steep step right on the ridge

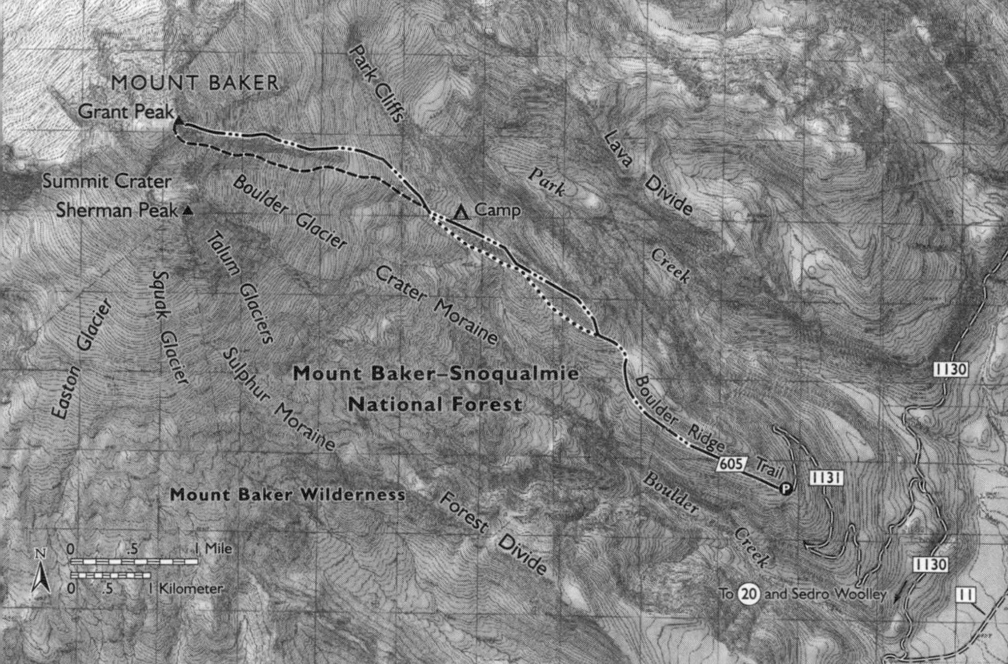

or on the southern (climber's left) side. Above the step, follow the ridge as it merges into the rolling slopes above. There are great spots to camp on the rolling terrain between 5200 and 5400 feet. It is 2.8 kilometers (1.7 miles) from the end of the trail to camp at 5200 feet, and you have gained 1960 feet from the end of the trail to camp (5–6 hours to here). There is also a good spot to camp high on a bench at 6000 feet.

DAY 2. From camp, skin up the broad ramp, leaving the cliffs to climber's left. As you gain the steeper slopes around 9500 feet, you may need ski crampons to proceed. At around 10,100 feet, wrap around to climber's left to pass above a small rock band and below the rocks of the summit cone. Depending on conditions, it can be easier to boot the steep slopes above 10,000 feet to gain the summit plateau. The final slope is steep and serious terrain; watch for crevasses and assess the avalanche hazard carefully. The distance from the camp at 5200 feet to the summit is 4.3 kilometers (2.7 miles), with an elevation gain of 5581 feet (5–6 hours to here).

DESCENT. You have two main descent options. After the first few turns on the initial steep slope off the summit plateau, you can work your way through various rock bands (and possible crevasses) and drop down following the fall line descent on the Boulder Glacier. You may need to work skier's left, along or just below your ascent line, until 9800 feet to avoid steep slopes, and then you can diagonal back right into the scoop of the Boulder Glacier at 9400 feet, leaving the long rock ridge/bench system to your left. This line passes over several areas of crevasses, so evaluate the snowcover and your visibility conditions before you commit to this descent. Traverse back toward your ascent track at 6800 feet and ski the broad rolling terrain back to camp.

Alternatively, to descend from the summit, you can follow your skin track back down via the ramp you ascended. From camp, ski along Boulder Ridge until it ends, then descend the southerly slopes through trees and some fun gully skiing to the elevation of the trail and ski (or hike) back to the trailhead.

Tour Author: Margaret Wheeler

16 The Pickets Traverse

Starting elevation: 900 feet
High point: 8280 feet
Time: 5 to 7 days
Distance: 72 km (45 miles)
Vertical gain/loss: 25,000 feet/24,000 feet
Overall difficulty: extremely difficult
Ski skills: difficult
Fitness level: extremely strenuous
Technical skills: expert

Commitment: extremely high
Best season: March–June
Gear: the basics, plus ski mountaineering and overnight equipment
USGS maps: Diablo Dam, Mount Prophet, Mount Challenger, Mount Blum, Mount Sefrit, and Mount Shuksan; also recommended: National Geographic #233, North Cascades
Permits: To stay overnight in North Cascades National Park, you must get a free backcountry permit from the Wilderness Information Center in Marblemount or the Glacier Public Service Station. You do not need a parking pass on the south end, but a Northwest Forest Pass or Interagency Pass is required at the Hannegan Pass trailhead.

This is as wild as it gets. The climax of the North Cascades, the Pickets offer the most remote and most rugged terrain in the state. A little-known secret is that they are perhaps easier to visit on skis than on foot. However, many stars must align for this tour to be possible; every member of your group must have a high level of fitness and a full array of ski mountaineering skills, the snowcover must be solid, and you need to wait for a spell of agreeable weather. The tour has been done in the summer from north to south and in the winter from south to north; we describe it south to north, but regardless of what variations you choose of the many available or when you do it, this route deserves careful research and planning.

In the event of poor weather or injury, retreat will be difficult at best, with miles of dense thickets in the lowland valleys of McMillan and Luna Creeks and the Baker River. Once you are in the northern Pickets, the ridge extending northeast from the Challenger Glacier is probably the easiest way to exit the alpine zone and reach the trail along Little Beaver Creek, which can take you back to Ross Dam and Highway 20 via Big Beaver. If you plan to fit a water taxi into your itinerary, make sure to make arrangements ahead of time as it runs seasonally and requires reservations.

ACCESS

From Marblemount, drive the North Cascades Highway (State Route 20) east for 20 miles and turn left on Diablo Road. In a little less than 1 mile park on the right side of the road across from the Sourdough Mountain trailhead (at an elevation of 900 feet).

You will need to arrange a car shuttle or pickup at the Hannegan Pass trailhead, which is off the Mount Baker Highway (State Route 542). From the town of Glacier, drive east and in a little more than 13 miles, turn left (north) onto Hannegan Pass Road (Forest Service Road 32). In another 1.3 miles, take the left fork, a continuation of Forest Service Road 32 that is commonly called Ruth Creek Road. After 1.4 miles, take the left or uphill branch, and follow it 4.2 miles to the trailhead.

TOUR

DAY 1. Follow the Sourdough Mountain Trail to about 4000 feet or until you reach continuous snow. From there, follow Stetattle Ridge to the north, cruising over the gentle bumps of its crest. The ridge arcs around to the northwest, and good camping abounds. This day is very straightforward, so it is good to do it when the weather is shifting toward high pressure, leaving the best of the weather for the Pickets themselves. Go as far along the ridge as time allows to set yourself up for success the next day, preferably at least to the col between Points 6245 and 6728 (5000 feet of gain, 7 hours to the col).

DAY 2. This morning you continue toward East McMillan Spire. Climb to the top of Point 6728 and ski into the deep pass just east of Elephant Butte. Climb steeply southwest out of the pass, reading the map and terrain carefully to avoid cliffs. Crest the butte's southeast ridge at 6200 feet, and make a descending traverse to the west, staying as high as possible.

Climb up around the southeast ridge of Point 6914, and continue in a rising traverse toward your objective col; the correct col is just west of Point 6455. At this very committing point, consider whether you still have confidence in the weather, the conditions, and your party to complete the trip.

Drop into McMillan Cirque, and you are now officially in the Pickets. As you make a descending traverse under the north faces of the McMillan Spires, note that you are above cliffs and very severe terrain. Once you are due north of Inspiration Peak, you

Entrance options to McMillan Cirque from the north (Martin Volken)

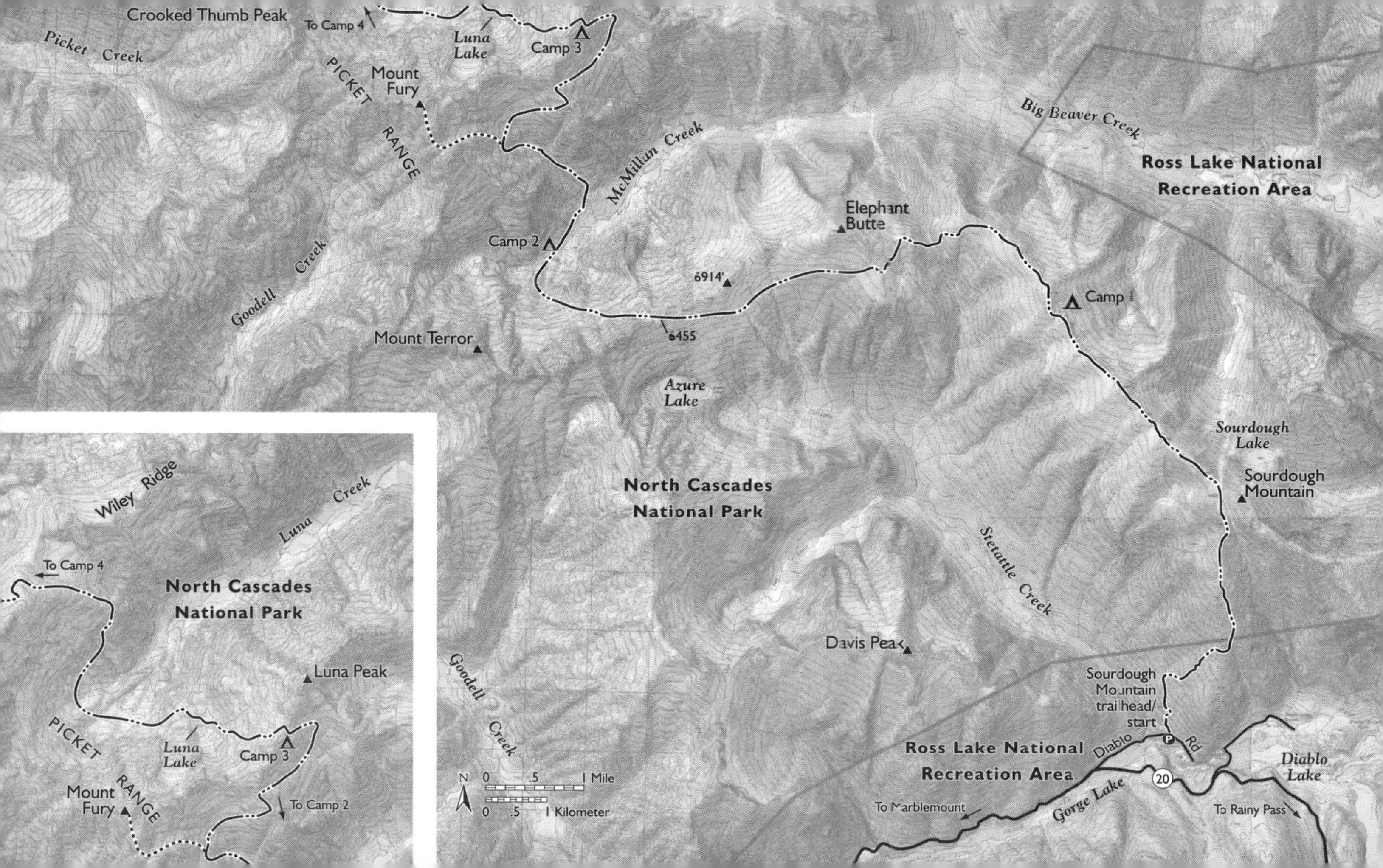
Crooked Thumb Peak
To Camp 4
Luna Lake
Camp 3
Picket Creek
PICKET RANGE
Mount Fury
Big Beaver Creek
Ross Lake National Recreation Area
McMillan Creek
Elephant Butte
Camp 2
Goodell Creek
6914'
Camp 1
Mount Terror
6455
Azure Lake
Sourdough Lake
Sourdough Mountain
North Cascades National Park
Stetattle Creek
Davis Peak
Sourdough Mountain trailhead/ start
Diablo Rd
Ross Lake National Recreation Area
Diablo Lake
20
Gorge Lake
To Marblemount
To Rainy Pass
0 .5 1 Mile
0 .5 1 Kilometer
N
Wiley Ridge
Luna Creek
To Camp 4
North Cascades National Park
Luna Peak
PICKET RANGE
Luna Lake
Camp 3
Mount Fury
To Camp 2

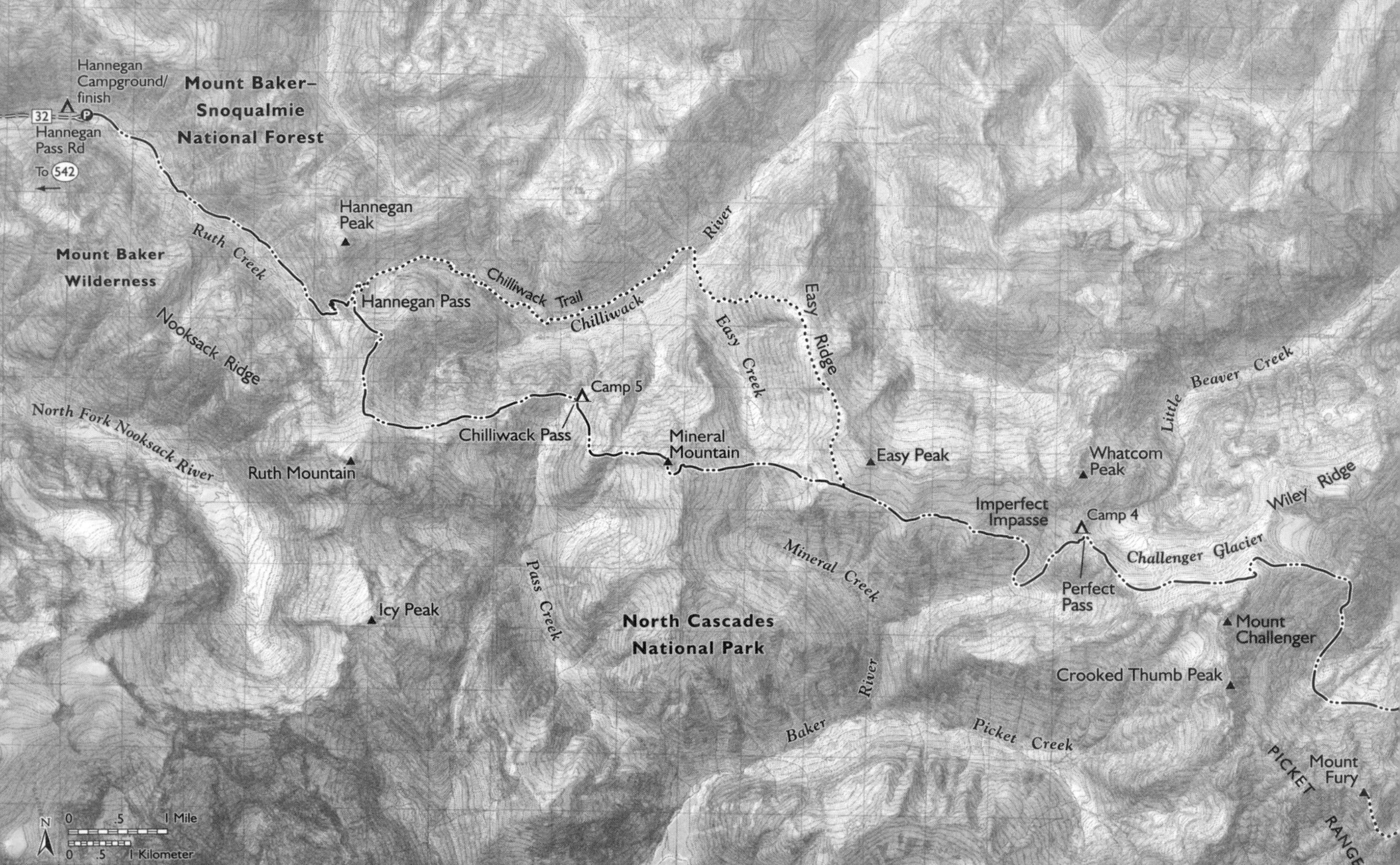
Hannegan Campground/ finish
Mount Baker–Snoqualmie National Forest
32
Hannegan Pass Rd
To 542
Hannegan Peak
Mount Baker Wilderness
Ruth Creek
Hannegan Pass
Chilliwack Trail
Chilliwack
River
Nooksack Ridge
Camp 5
Chilliwack Pass
North Fork Nooksack River
Ruth Mountain
Mineral Mountain
Easy Creek
Easy Ridge
Easy Peak
Little Beaver Creek
Whatcom Peak
Wiley Ridge
Imperfect Impasse
Camp 4
Challenger Glacier
Perfect Pass
Mineral Creek
Pass Creek
Icy Peak
North Cascades National Park
Mount Challenger
Crooked Thumb Peak
Baker River
Picket Creek
PICKET RANGE
Mount Fury
N
0 .5 1 Mile
0 .5 1 Kilometer

should be able to make your way down to the gentle bottom of the cirque; if you try to descend too soon, you will likely run into cliffs. (You may also be able to follow the timbered ridge shown in the aerial photo to drop to the cirque floor directly from the col.) Once you are on gentler terrain, head northeast with McMillan Creek. A good camp can be made where the creek draining Mount Fury's southeast glacier reaches the cirque floor at 2800 feet (3500 feet of gain, 7 hours to here). You will have the option of a ski ascent of Mount Fury on Day 3. In the right conditions this can be incredible skiing, but be aware that it will almost certainly add 3 hours to your day.

DAY 3. Get an early start to climb the drainage to the northwest, as it gets sun early and contains a lot of steep terrain. Follow the creek on its east bank, and check out the amphitheater ahead—the crux of this day and perhaps of the whole traverse (around 4400 feet). A gully or ramp of snow should allow you to surmount the line of cliffs; an ice ax and crampons may be useful.

Once you are above the cliffs, climb to the northeast and crest a spur ridge just above Point 6455. Head northwest up this ridge to a flat spot around 6600 feet. From here, ski down a trough to the northeast, ending at about 5400 feet where the map shows a heart-shaped snowfield. Skin up to Luna Col, just southwest of Luna Peak, booting for some sections. Camping is good at the col or down in the bottom of Luna Cirque, where you will likely have running water (5400 feet of gain and 5.75 hours to Luna Col).

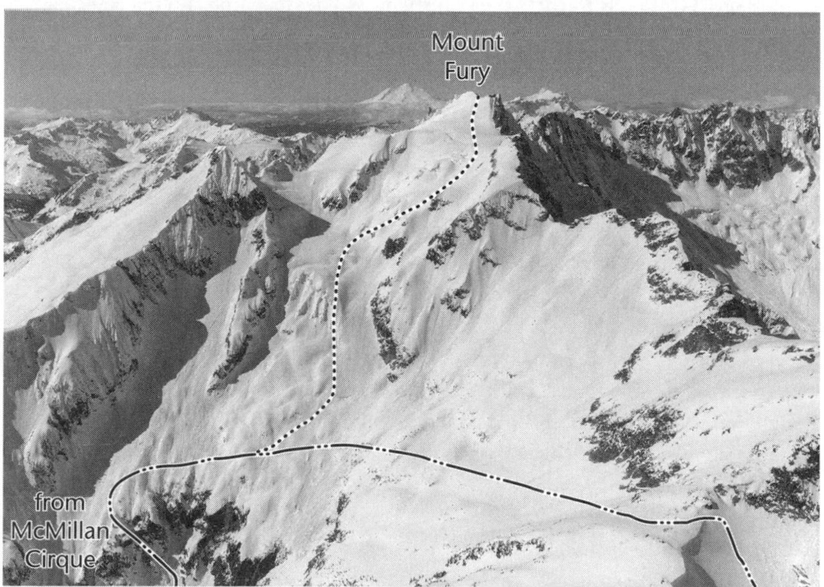

Mount Fury and the exit route from McMillan Cirque from the southwest (Scott Schell)

DAY 4. Ski down through larches to Luna Lake and then west to the cirque floor at 4000 feet, keeping an eye out for your line up out of the cirque. Your goal is the lowest-angle path to gain the broad ridge at 5600 feet that arcs northeast and then east from Mount Challenger. Follow this ridge up onto the Challenger Glacier, and climb southwest to about 7400 feet. Then enjoy a very long and scenic glide across the glacier to Perfect Pass (3600 feet and 6 hours to here).

DAY 5. From Perfect Pass, your next obstacle is the Imperfect Impasse, a deeply eroded dike that appears on the map as a stream (find it on the map just west of Perfect Pass; it runs a little west of due south and is the longer of the two creeks). On a year with a lot of snow, it may be possible to cross it high (about 5400 feet). Otherwise, drop into the bowl below Perfect Pass, and ski due south, crossing the second creek where possible.

Once you are on the south side of both creeks, ski down to 3700 feet where you should be able to cross back north where the map shows a small snowfield obscuring both creeks. Climb back due north, switching back along the west side of the Imperfect Impasse until about 4800 feet. From here you can begin a rising traverse to the west along Easy Ridge.

If spring runoff does not preclude a reasonable crossing of the Chilliwack, you can finish the traverse by taking the Chilliwack River Trail. Head north along the ridge past Easy Peak to the broad col where the word "Easy" appears on the USGS map (5190 feet). From here an unmaintained trail (originally used for the lookout which sat just 1 mile north) descends to the valley on the west side, reaching the river just east of Easy Creek. Enjoy an exciting, cold ford of the river, and find the Chilliwack River Trail a short way uphill on the other side. From here it is a little more than 9 miles to the trailhead over Hannegan Pass (3000 feet of gain and 6.5 hours from Perfect Pass to the Chilliwack River).

Another way to finish the Pickets Traverse is via the Mineral High Route. To do this, head west from Easy Ridge toward the unnamed col between Easy Peak and Mineral Mountain. Climb Mineral Mountain directly, taking the broad drainage leading to the col just south of the summit. Visit the fine summit and enjoy an incredible panorama. Ski down the west ridge of Mineral to a col with a western subpeak.

From here, a direct line to Chilliwack Pass is feasible but quite steep; expect some creative skiing through some sections. You may prefer to ski south into the southwest cirque of Mineral and follow lower-angle terrain west and then north along Pass Creek to reach Chilliwack Pass. Water may be available along the creek immediately south of Chilliwack Pass (4500 feet of gain and 7.5 hours from Perfect Pass to Chilliwack Pass).

DAY 6. From Chilliwack Pass skin west through a gentle col to gain the north slopes of Ruth Mountain's long east ridge. Use benches to work west under Point 6166, and continue on a rising traverse to gain the broad north ridge of Ruth Mountain around 5800 feet, which you can easily follow to the summit (see Tour 8: Ruth Mountain for details). Find the spur trail to Hannegan Pass by skiing north and around the east side of Point 5930. From Hannegan Pass the trailhead is just 4 miles away (1800 feet of gain, 6.5 hours from Chilliwack Pass to the trailhead, excluding the summit of Ruth).

Tour Author: Forest McBrian

17 Ruby Mountain

Starting elevation: 2200 feet
High point: 7408 feet
Vertical gain/loss: 5230 feet/5230 feet
Distance: 12.5 km (7.75 miles)
Time: 8 hours
Overall difficulty: difficult
Ski skills: difficult
Fitness level: very strenuous
Technical skills: moderate
Commitment: low
Gear: the basics, plus ski mountaineering equipment
Best season: January–April
USGS map: Ross Dam
Permits: none

Ruby Mountain entices skiers with a mix of exceptional scenery, friendly fall lines, long descents, and above-average snow quality. Its location in the center of the North Cascades provides a unique vantage on many of the great peaks of the range that are difficult to reach during the winter. These vistas, along with acres of pure north-facing ski terrain, will make you understand why the National Park and National Forest Service once evaluated Ruby Mountain as a potential ski area site during the establishment of North Cascades National Park. Ruby Mountain also boasts significant local relief, giving it the kind of straight up vertical more often associated with skiing on the Cascade volcanoes.

Although the starting elevation for this tour is only 2200 feet, the prevailing weather can provide adequate snowpack to put skis on from the car. Larch trees dotting the mid-elevations indicate this area is drier than other areas normally accessed on the west side of the range, and the drier climate is often reflected in the quality of the snow compared to areas farther west.

ACCESS

From Marblemount, drive the North Cascades Highway (State Route 20) 28 miles west and park at the end of the plowed road near milepost 134 at the Ross Dam trailhead. This trailhead in the Ross Lake National Recreation Area is one of the easternmost points accessible by car in winter outside the cross-state mountain passes. Snowmobilers

Ruby Mountain from the north (Alasdair Turner)

venturing beyond the winter closure gate on the highway, and hikers going to Ross Lake, frequently use this parking area.

Check with the Washington State Department of Transportation for current conditions as the plowing schedule changes based on need and conditions. When the highway east of here is closed for the winter, this area is inaccessible by car from the east.

TOUR

Start the tour by following the highway for less than a kilometer (0.4 mile) east to the Happy Creek trailhead. Enter the summer parking area on the right. Ski on or next to an east-trending boardwalk and trail to the end of the boardwalk loop at the toe of a small ridge on the north side of Happy Creek. Ascend the ridge east-southeast, favoring the north side to avoid fallen timber in the steeper terrain directly above Happy Creek, or follow the climber's trail on the north side if it is visible. Stay to the climber's left side of the creek as, within a few hundred yards, it curves to the south and enters the denser timber of the main drainage.

Just below 3200 feet, start touring up a small, slightly leftward-trending glade just to the east of Happy Creek to gain the valley at the base of the upper mountain at 3400 feet. You have two options from this point. The direct route right of the center of the drainage is short but features dense brush for several hundred feet before breaking into open terrain climber's right above the lower waterfall. A slightly longer but more open route climbs southeast up an avalanche slope and through mature trees climber's right at 3700 feet to reach a higher drainage that can be followed back southwest through a small notch at 4100 feet to regain the main drainage. Be aware of avalanche potential from above on either route.

The angle eases at 4100 feet where you can see the full extent of the potential ski terrain ahead. Large avalanches routinely run into this area from steep terrain directly ahead and climber's right. Be confident of your ability to assess hazards before crossing into the area ahead (2.5 hours to here).

Tour slightly southeast to gain the toe of a broad rib between 4400 feet and 4600 feet. Continue ascending east-southeast and then south up a series of increasingly open benches to gain the divide that separates the Happy Creek drainage from the Lillian Creek drainage at 6300 feet. Views north up Ross Lake and Hozomeen Peak are fjord-like. Straight ahead are the upper alpine bowls that are your reward for the effort of starting at such a low elevation.

Follow the Lillian Creek and Happy Creek divide to the summit ridge, and take the ridge north-northwest to the summit at 7408 feet (6 hours in good conditions). Views into all the great zones of the North Cascades abound in every direction. A

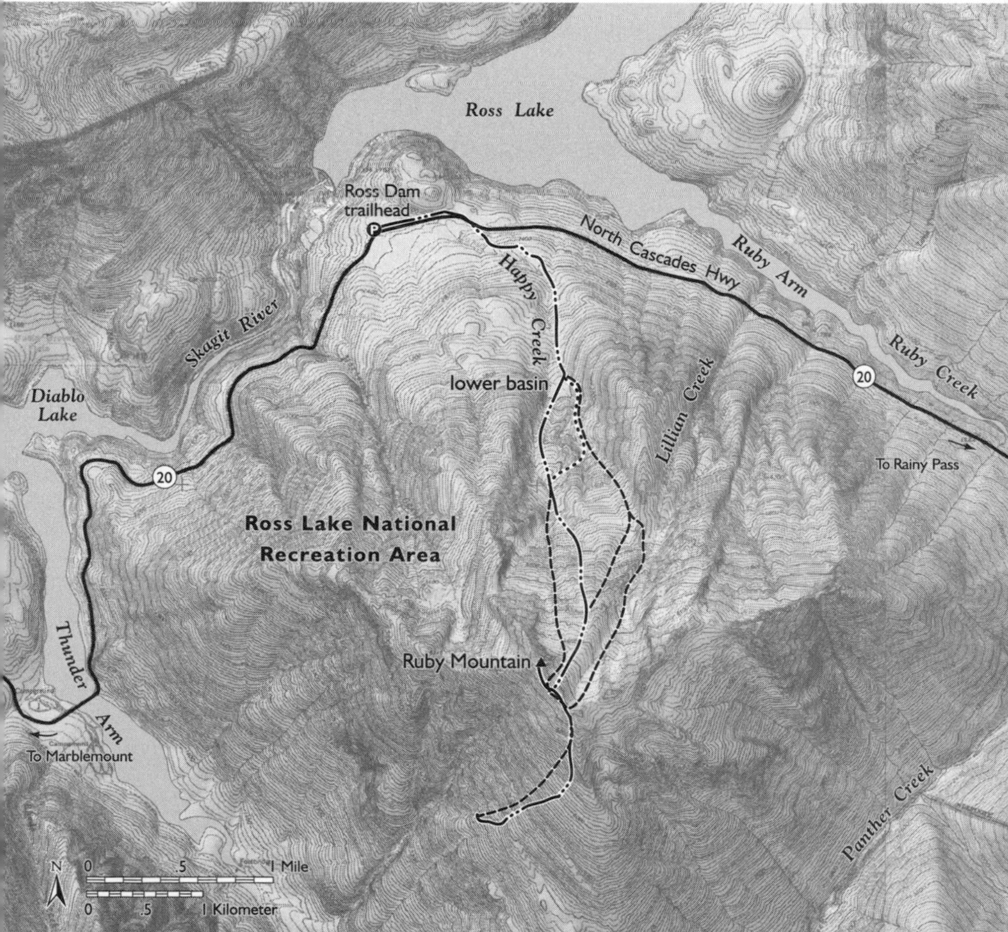

self-contained radio antennae and communications repeater unit on the summit gives a relatively civilized feel to a mountain so deep in such a wild range.

DESCENT. You have a number of attractive ski options from the summit. Follow the summit ridge back to the ascent route, or ski off the ridge earlier into the main bowl just beyond the cliffs of the summit pyramid, to ski slopes northwest back toward Happy Creek. Wrap west under the pyramid to ski a series of short couloirs west of the ascent line that can be linked to the basin at 4100 feet. Reconnect with the ascent route to ski down to the lower basin at 3400 feet.

Alternatively from the summit, traverse farther southeast along the summit ridge to ski into the Lillian Creek drainage. Exit the drainage with a short skin or some sidestepping over a small ridge at 5200 feet to ski slopes northwest. Follow open areas beneath cliffs on the right and above denser forest to the left. Traverse right through the forest at 3800 feet to access the slope leading northwest back down to the lower basin at 3400 feet. For those seeking maximum vertical, ski off the southern end of the summit ridge for several thousand feet on an open, southwest-trending avalanche path before climbing back up tree-covered benches to the east to regain the summit ridge, and following your ascent route back down to the road.

Tour Author: Benjamin Haskell

18 Mesahchie Peak: Mesahchie Glacier

Starting elevation: 3700 feet (finish at 3450 feet)
High point: 7500 feet
Vertical gain/loss: 5200 feet/5500 feet
Distance: 17 km (10.5 miles)
Time: 7 to 8.5 hours
Overall difficulty: difficult
Ski skills: difficult
Fitness level: very strenuous
Technical skills: moderate
Commitment: high
Gear: the basics, plus ski mountaineering gear
Best season: April–May
USGS maps: Mount Arriva and Mount Logan (optional)
Permits: A Northwest Forest Pass or an Interagency Pass is required to park at Easy Pass, which is in Mount Baker–Snoqualmie National Forest.

This tour features two 2000-foot-plus descents, making for a fantastic full day out in North Cascades National Park. It is best to try it immediately after the highway opens,

Climbing the Mesahchie Glacier (Matt Farmer)

but make sure that the road has been plowed widely enough for you to park or that they have cleared the parking at the Easy Pass trailhead.

ACCESS

The North Cascades Highway (State Route 20) is closed during the winter; without a snowmobile, this tour is not possible until the road opens, typically between late March and May. From the town of Marblemount, drive east on the North Cascades Highway for 42 miles. The right turn for the Easy Pass trailhead and parking area is a few miles farther east on the highway (45 miles from Marblemount) between mileposts 151 and 152. You may need to park on the shoulder if the lot has not opened. This tour ends between milepost 148 and 149. If the shoulder is plowed, you can leave a car or bike here. Otherwise be prepared to hike back to the start.

TOUR

From the parking area at 3700 feet, climb up to Easy Pass at 6500 feet. The trail climbs up the climber's right bank of Easy Creek to 4500 feet, crosses the creek, and continues up the climber's left bank to the pass (3.5 hours to here). From the pass, turn right and start heading across the southeast aspects of Ragged Ridge toward Mesahchie Peak. Big cornices form on the opposite side, so stay a healthy distance away from the ridge top. Aim for the 7500-foot notch between Points 8003 and 7985 (5 hours to here). Again, watch out for possible cornice hazards as you approach the north side of the ridge and find an entrance to the slopes on the other side.

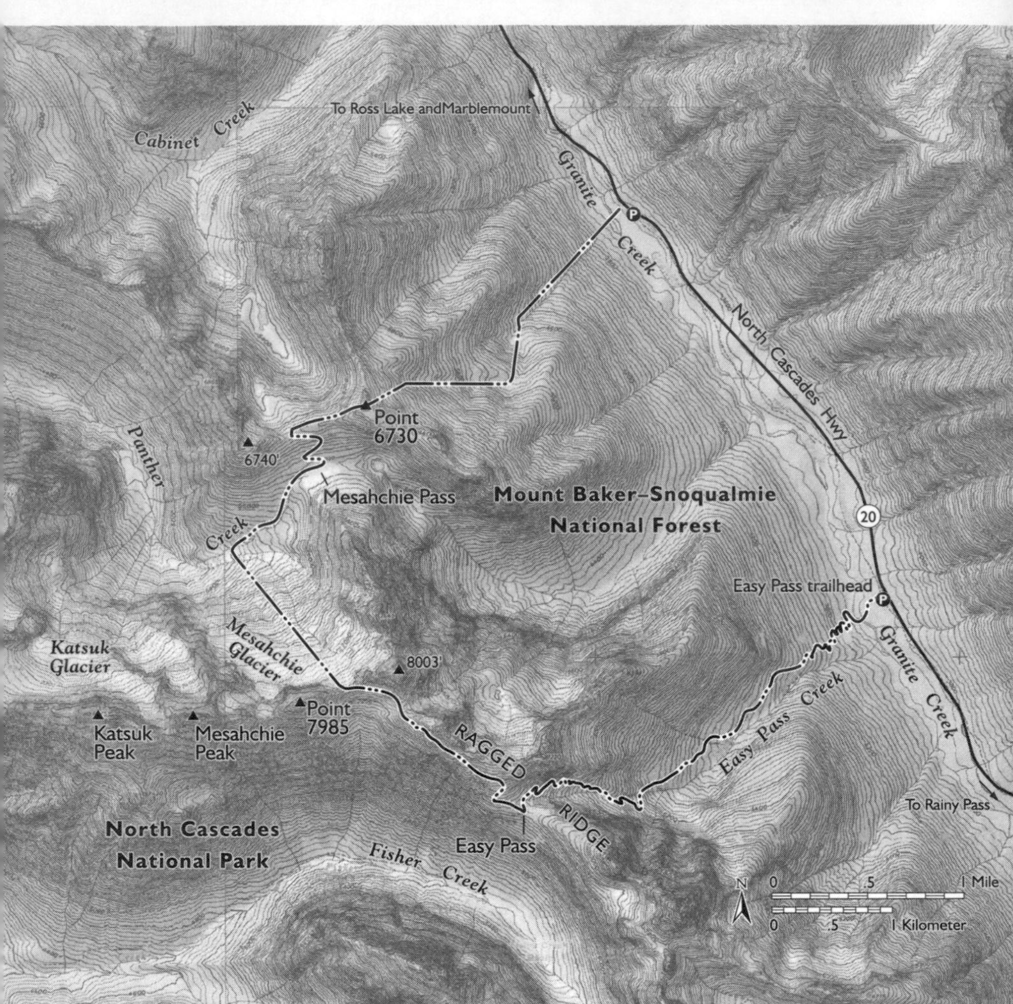

DESCENT. You have earned a 2000-foot run down the immaculate slopes of the Mesahchie Glacier basin and the alpine fields below. The wide, open terrain provides a lot of options, and there are few navigation hazards on this descent. Come to a stop between 5600 and 5400 feet to put your skins back on. Climb northeast, following the drainage marked "Panther Creek" on the USGS map to Mesahchie Pass at 5980 feet. Then turn north and continue climbing to the next saddle between Points 6740 and 6730. Finish the climb by turning right and following the ridge east to the summit of Point 6730 (8 hours to here).

From the summit, choose from among several variations to ski down to the highway. The most moderate is to descend skier's right in the drainage. This is your second 2000-foot-plus descent, and oftentimes that last few hundred feet to the highway turns into a bushwhack. Persevere—the skiing was worth the effort. Return to the start up the road on foot if you have not cached bikes along the highway or shuttled a car.

Tour Author: Chris Simmons, with special thanks to Larry Goldie

19 Black Peak: South Face and Last Chance Pass

Starting elevation: 4840 feet
High point: 8970 feet
Vertical gain/loss: 4630 feet /4630 feet; add 2400 feet with descent into Woody Creek
Distance: 16 km (10 miles), add 4 km for descent into Woody Creek and/or Last Chance Pass exit
Time: 10 hours or 2 days
Overall difficulty: difficult
Ski skills: very difficult
Fitness level: strenuous
Technical skills: high
Commitment: low
Gear: the basics, plus ski mountaineering equipment
Best season: April–June
USGS maps: Mount Arriva, Washington Pass, and McGregor Mountain
Permits: A Northwest Forest Pass or Interagency Pass is required if you park within the Lake Ann trailhead parking area. The North Cascades National Park boundary with Mount Baker–Snoqualmie National Forest coincides with the south ridge of Black Peak. If camping in the national park, you must obtain an overnight backcountry permit.

Black Peak is an impressive pyramid of dark rock with significant vertical relief high above Rainy Pass. It offers classic ski mountaineering requiring careful hazard evaluation, and alpine climbing skills to reach an airy summit. Although often climbed in two days as a moderate alpine climb from the highway in summer, skis can make this a reasonable day tour for a fit party in good conditions. Extend the tour with a long descent into Woody Creek and up through Last Chance Pass to enjoy trail-less areas seldom visited after the snow melts.

ACCESS

This tour begins at Rainy Pass on the North Cascades Highway (State Route 20), 52.3 miles east of Marblemount. This section of the highway is closed to cars in winter starting in November or December, but it is plowed open anytime from late March to May, depending on the snow conditions. Drive to Rainy Pass and park just east of the Rainy Pass sign, at the entrance road to the parking area for the summer trailheads to Lake Ann and Rainy Lake.

TOUR

Ascend southwest from the Lake Ann trailhead at Rainy Pass, roughly following the direction of the summer trail to Lake Ann. After about 0.75 kilometer (0.5 mile),

Black Peak from the northwest (Ben Haskell)

reach a small open basin just above 5200 feet. Gain the small ridge to the south, and traverse into the Lake Ann drainage, using a ramp that coincides with the summer trail at approximately 5400 feet. Continue up the drainage to the lake, and cross to the west end. Ascend moderate slopes northwest and then north to Heather Pass (1.75 hours to here).

Cross Heather Pass, and make a descending traverse toward Lewis Lake. Evaluate avalanche hazards carefully here because you have no protection from large slopes and cornices above and steeper terrain below. Consider also how conditions may change later in the afternoon during the return when you must ascend this quick downward traverse.

West of Lewis Lake, pick up a lightly treed ridge that leads up to Wing Lake. If you are spending the night, look for campsites on the knoll east of Wing Lake. From Wing Lake, ski west up valley to the col at approximately 7900 feet (4.5 hours to here). From the col climb north, trending slightly west off the ridgeline, to the base of a series of steeper gullies that lead up to the false summit. Climb or skin this series of gullies either on the left or right side to just below the false summit at 8900 feet (5.5 hours to here). Depot your skis at the base of the false summit rocks. Many climbers prefer the safety of a rope to continue from here to the summit.

Traverse east around the corner on the south side of the summit ridge, and ascend the first short gully up to the ridge crest. The summit ridge has spectacular fourth-class climbing requiring some "au cheval" moves along the way with several thousand airy feet dropping off in both directions. Although you can access the summit by following ramps and ledges 50 to 100 feet below the ridge on the south side, the ridge itself has less objective hazard in winter and provides a mix of reasonable quality rock and snow features for a particularly aesthetic finish to the climb. Allow 40 minutes for the trip from your ski depot to the summit and back, depending on conditions and your route and belay choices.

DESCENT. Return to where you left your skis. Now you have choices depending on the time you have available and your party's interests. Ski gullies back to the col to retrace the route to Wing Lake, or access a more direct chute to the lake by crossing the south ridge above the col at 8400 feet, just beneath the lower terminus of the cliffs on the south ridge. But if time allows, take full advantage of Black's vertical relief by skiing 3400 feet all the way down the south slopes to Woody Creek. This big descent in open terrain has outstanding views of Mount Logan and the north face of Mount Goode—a classic North Cascade ski run in an incomparable setting. Once you are in Woody Creek, retrace the south slopes back up to the col at 7900 feet to connect with the route back to Wing Lake.

Or to explore farther, continue the Last Chance Pass circuit by following Woody Creek east and climbing southwest up a steep slope starting at approximately 6100 feet to gain an upper bowl that leads to the low point on the Woody and Falls Creek divide at 6920 feet. Traverse across a short slope from the saddle toward Last Chance Pass. Be cautious as you approach the pass—very large east-facing cornices form here. You can often find passage through the cornices above the pass on the north side. To avoid the cornices completely, head south around a small peak at the head of the pass to ski down the northeast trending slope south of the pass.

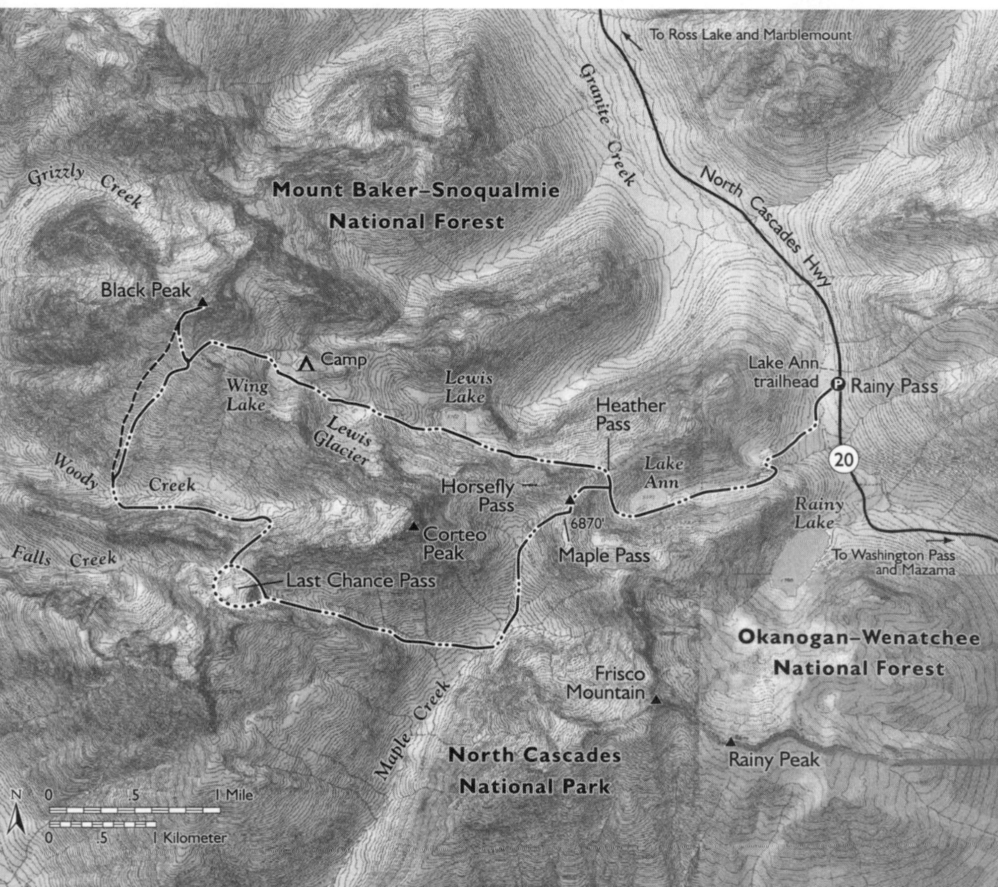

From either entrance, ski down and traverse into the Maple Creek valley. Skin up the valley to the low point on the ridge at the valley's head south of Point 6870, commonly referred to as Maple Pass. Climb up to Point 6870, and ski down to Heather Pass to reconnect with your original ascent route, which you can follow back to Rainy Pass.

Tour Author: Benjamin Haskell

20 Rainy Lake and Lake Ann Loops

Starting elevation: 4840 feet
High point: 7400 feet
Vertical gain/loss: 4200 feet/4200 feet with descent into Maple Creek
Distance: 11 km (6.8 miles) with descent into Maple Creek
Time: 6.5 hours with descent into Maple Creek
Overall difficulty: moderate
Ski skills: moderate
Fitness level: strenuous
Technical skills: moderate
Commitment: low
Gear: the basics
Best season: April–May, depending on when the North Cascades Highway opens
USGS maps: Mount Arriva, Washington Pass, McAllister Mountain, and McGregor Mountain
Permits: A Northwest Forest Pass or Interagency Pass is required if you are parking within the Lake Ann trailhead parking area. The boundary between Mount Baker–Snoqualmie National Forest and North Cascades National Park coincides with the ridge crest of Frisco Mountain. If camping in the national park, you must obtain an overnight backcountry permit.

Who doesn't like a loop tour? This tour offers several options for a quintessential North Cascades day tour loop with fun, mostly moderate ski descents that link the two scenic lakes above Rainy Pass.

ACCESS

This tour begins at Rainy Pass on the North Cascades Highway (State Route 20), 52.3 miles east of Marblemount. This section of the highway is closed to cars in winter starting in November or December, but it is plowed open between late March and May, depending on the snow conditions. Drive to Rainy Pass, and park just east of the Rainy Pass sign at the entrance road to the parking area for the summer trailheads to Lake Ann and Rainy Lake.

Lake Ann and Frisco Peak from the north (Ben Haskell)

TOUR

From Rainy Pass, head south-southeast from the Rainy Lake trailhead, following the route of the summer trail to Rainy Lake. Although technically you are descending slightly, the undulating terrain along the route of the trail is more managcable if you are using skins. Find the bridge that crosses the outlet from Lake Ann just below 4800 feet, about 0.5 kilometer (0.3 mile) from the trailhead. From there continue south-southwest at or just above 4800 feet to enter the Rainy Lake basin. Reach the lake and cross to the far southwest corner.

Ascend slopes leading into the gully at the southwest end of the lake. Alternatively, ascend an aesthetic ramp at the head of the valley that crosses between the upper and lower waterfalls cascading into the lake from the basin above. Neither route is a good choice if there is uncertainty about the stability of the snowpack. Exit the southwest gully climber's left at approximately 5400 feet just below the Y in the gully. You may need to remove your skis for a short bootpack. After you exit the gully, make an ascending traverse through open timber to the flats at the bottom of the Lyall Glacier basin (1.75 hours to here).

You have two options for completing a circuit to Lake Ann and back to Rainy Pass from this location. The short version ascends either a hanging valley west-northwest or slopes just north of the valley to directly gain the divide south of Lake Ann. From the western edge of the divide, ski northwest down and across the undulating ridge that separates the Lake Ann valley from the Maple Creek valley. Cross to the low point on the north end of the ridge, commonly referred to as Maple Pass. If the snow coverage is good, descend steep slopes just east of Point 6870 that lead directly down to Lake Ann. Alternatively, climb up to Point 6870 and descend east-northeast on more moderate slopes to Heather Pass.

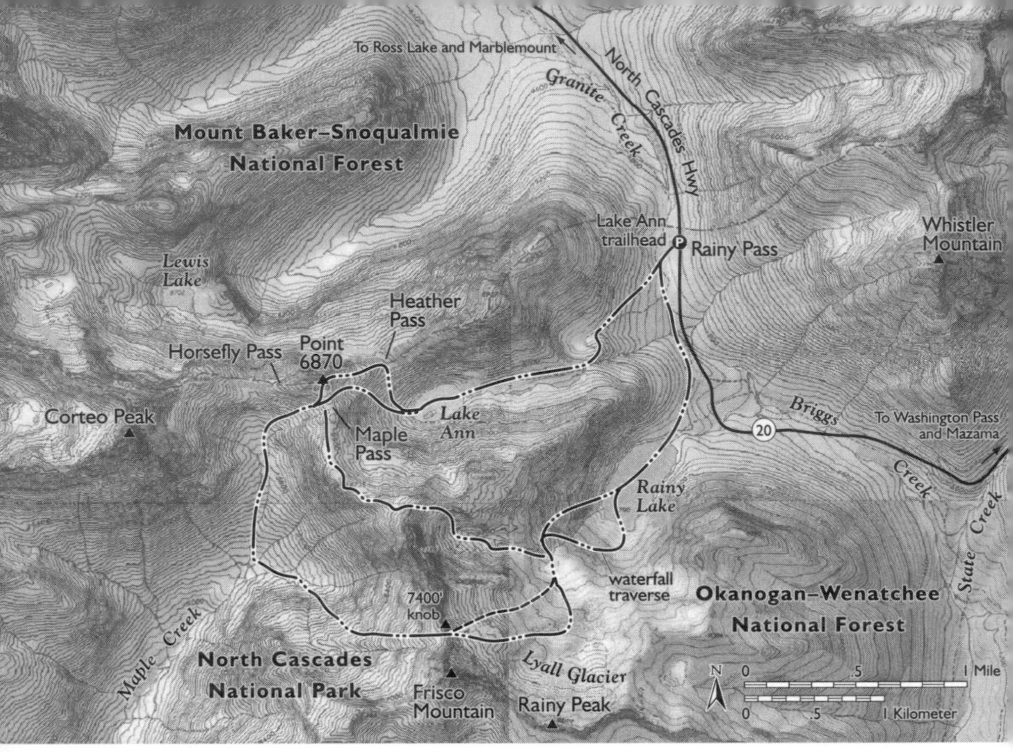

From Heather Pass, descend south or southeast to Lake Ann. Cross Lake Ann and follow the summer route through the Lake Ann drainage, exiting the drainage at 5400 feet onto a small ridge to your left. Ski down the ridge, and cross north into a small open basin. From 5200 feet at the bottom of the basin, descend northeast to Rainy Pass (4 hours for the short loop).

If conditions permit, try a longer circuit with quality skiing from the bottom of the Lyall Glacier basin. Begin by ascending low-angle terrain south toward Rainy Peak to gain the Lyall Glacier. At 6400 feet begin trending west to reach a knob at 7400 feet just north of Frisco Mountain, west of the word "Forest" on the USGS McGregor Mountain map (3 hours to here). If time permits and conditions are good, take the 1500-foot, fall-line ski run back down to the bottom of the basin and retrace your up track to the divide. Heli-ski operators use this run during winter, and it can be a fun objective for a short day tour in its own right when you do not want to complete the loop to Lake Ann.

To continue the loop to Lake Ann from the Frisco divide, drop west from the saddle south of the 7400-foot knob into the Maple Creek drainage. Ski a fun 2100-foot run west and then northwest down to Maple Creek; then climb north up the other side of the drainage toward Horsefly Pass. At approximately 6200 feet, head east to Maple Pass, the low point on the Maple Creek and Lake Ann divide described for the shorter loop option. Ascend to Point 6870 (5.5 hours to here). From Point 6870, descend to Heather Pass to continue the loop back to Rainy Pass as described above (6.5 hours to Rainy Pass).

Tour Author: Benjamin Haskell

21 Washington Pass Birthday Tour

Starting elevation: 5360 feet
High point: 7620 feet (7840 feet with Copper Mountain)
Vertical gain/loss: 3600 feet/3900 feet (4700 feet/5000 feet with Copper Mountain)
Distance: 8 km (5 miles), farther with Copper Mountain
Time: 5 hours (longer with Copper Mountain)
Overall difficulty: moderate
Ski skills: difficult
Fitness level: strenuous
Technical skills: moderate
Commitment: low
Gear: the basics (bring ski mountaineering equipment for Copper Mountain Maple Leaf Couloir)
Best season: April–May
USGS maps: Washington Pass, Silver Star Mountain, McAlester Mountain, and Gilbert
Permits: You must display a Northwest Forest Pass or Interagency Pass to park in the Blue Lake trailhead parking lot.

This is rightfully one of the most popular tours in the Washington Pass area because it offers great skiing on a loop featuring several high cols with outstanding views both far and near. You can choose from among many variations along the way, including summitting Copper Mountain and/or steep skiing objectives. The tour has particular appeal because it uses the highway to finish at a lower elevation than the starting point for some "free" vertical. The tour was originally written up in *Ski Touring Methow Style* by Winthrop local Sally Portman (and published in 1985) after her husband Don pioneered it on his birthday, and the locals and the rest of the Northwest ski community have known it as the "Birthday Tour" ever since.

ACCESS

This tour begins at the Blue Lake trailhead on the North Cascades Highway (State Route 20), 55 miles east of Marblemount or 18.5 miles west of Mazama. This section of the highway is closed to cars in winter starting in November or December, but it is plowed open between late March and May, depending on the snow conditions. You can access it via snowmobile from the east during winter; be aware that heli-ski operations occur in this area during winter.

The tour ends at the highway's hairpin turn, 1.1 miles east of Washington Pass and 2 miles east of the Blue Lake trailhead. Leave a bike or park a car here, or walk back to the Blue Lake trailhead when you are finished.

TOUR

From the Blue Lake trailhead, ascend south for about 200 vertical feet, and then trend east-southeast, breaking into open, gladed terrain near the bottom of an avalanche path at 5800 feet. Continue ascending slopes and benches east-southeast, staying southwest of the lower slopes of Liberty Bell Mountain and Early Winters Spires. Gain the notch in the ridge just south of South Early Winters Spire at 7340 feet (2 hours to here).

For a short tour, cross through the notch and descend straight down to the hairpin turn on the highway, otherwise known as the Spire Gully descent. If you want to tour car to car from the hairpin turn, you can also use Spire Gully to ascend directly to this point.

To continue the Birthday Tour, climb the slope south-southeast directly above the Spire Gully notch; it is usually overhung by an impressive cornice. Stay on the left side, out of the line of fire, and boot up the short, steep final few feet to gain what is commonly referred to as Blue Peak Col, the saddle above the cornice at 7620 feet. Ski down the broad 1600-foot southeast-facing slope into the Copper Creek drainage, commonly called Madison Avenue. From the head of the drainage near 6000 feet, decide if you want to continue the classic tour, or climb to the top of Copper Mountain

Birthday Tour and Copper Mountain from the southeast (Alasdair Turner)

by heading southeast to Copper Pass and ascending the ridge and upper slopes east-northeast to the summit at 7840 feet. The summit of Copper provides a scenic side trip with great views all around.

From the summit, ski back down into the Copper Creek drainage or take advantage of a longer descent off Copper Pass into the North Fork Twisp River drainage. Those interested in steep skiing options can look for a small notch in the ridge southeast of the summit that accesses the Maple Leaf Couloir, which descends steeply 1600 feet directly into the northern spur of the North Fork Twisp River. Depending on the time of year, a cornice may overhang the initial 10–15 feet of the couloir.

If you are bypassing the Copper Mountain summit altogether, skin east up the Copper Creek drainage to the pass north-northwest of Copper Mountain that leads over to the Twisp River valley, often referred to as Copper Col (elevation 7380 feet). You can also drop directly into the Early Winters valley from a higher pass along the ridge west-northwest of Copper Col (4 hours to either pass).

From Copper Col, ski down a few hundred feet and cross the ridge skier's left into the bowl on the north side of the ridge. This location often hides great powder. Ski the bowl east-northeast to below Kangaroo Pass. Kangaroo Pass is the 6671-foot pass at the southeast terminus of Kangaroo Ridge. Once you are north of Kangaroo Pass, traverse down valley, staying high in a northwesterly direction to the finish at the hairpin turn on the highway.

Tour Author: Benjamin Haskell

22 Silver Star Mountain

Starting elevation: 3440 feet
High point: 8876 feet
Vertical gain/loss: 5436 feet/5436 feet (more with side tours)
Distance: 13 km (8 miles), farther with side tours
Time: 8 hours
Overall difficulty: difficult
Ski skills: difficult
Fitness level: very strenuous
Technical skills: moderate
Commitment: moderate
Gear: the basics, plus ski mountaineering gear for summit
Best season: January–May, depending on road access
USGS map: Silver Star
Permits: none

The Silver Star massif makes quite an impression as you crest Washington Pass on the North Cascades Highway (State Route 20). The verticality of the Wine Spires and the Silver Star summit has inspired generations of mountaineers. For ski tourers, Silver Star is no less inspirational, with long descents and multiple tour options surrounded by the impressive granite towers and beautiful larch groves for which the area is famous. The combination of ambience and quality ski terrain make Silver Star a not-to-miss ski touring destination.

ACCESS

The North Cascades Highway may open from the east during winter to the Silver Star Creek gate depending on the snow depth and the Washington State Department of Transportation's (WSDOT) plowing schedule. Otherwise, it is the first part of the road to open beyond Early Winters campground in the spring. Check WSDOT's website for current road conditions. Drive 9 miles west of Mazama, and park in the pullout just east of Silver Star Creek.

Once Washington Pass opens in the spring, this tour is accessible from the west about 8.5 miles from the pass. In winter, you will likely encounter heli-skiers in the areas described in this tour; be aware of their operations and the potential for skiers coming from above you if you are touring here midwinter.

TOUR

Skin up through open forest east of Silver Star Creek, or pick up a faint climber's trail if the snow level starts higher. Stay climber's left and within a few hundred yards of the creek. The angle of the terrain eases briefly near the base of a small clearing on the east side of the drainage above 4400 feet. Start trending back at this point to intersect the creek above 4600 feet. Cross to the west side of the creek, and ascend a short step up

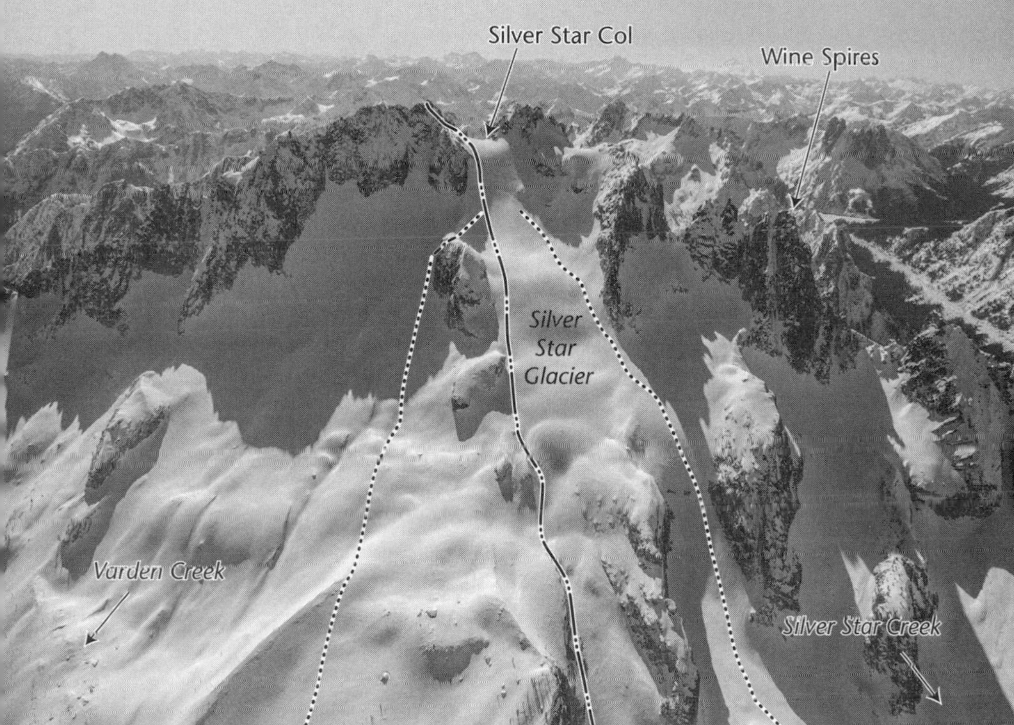

Silver Star Mountain from the north (Alasdair Turner)

through trees to gain low-angle open forest on the west side of the creek. Be careful late in the season to make sure that snowbridges are solid before you cross the creek.

Alternatively, stay on the east side of the creek if solid snowbridges do not exist, or ascend the creek itself if it is well filled in. Continue south to break out into the meadows of the Silver Star basin at 5000 feet. Views of Burgundy Spire are straight ahead, and the summit of Silver Star towers above the left side of the valley. Stay on the west side of the valley floor to the head of the valley (2 hours to here).

Ascend the drainage and avalanche path trending south-southwest toward Vasiliki Ridge. When the path steepens a few hundred vertical feet below the rocky base of the ridge, head southeast (climber's left) out of the drainage. Make a low traverse across rolling, larch-covered terrain. You do not need to get too high in the area below Vasiliki Ridge. Reach the basin directly north of Silver Star Mountain. Continue southeast to the slope running upward alongside the north–south ridge that separates the Silver Star Creek and Varden Creek drainages.

Gain the Silver Star Glacier, and climb directly to what is commonly referred to as Silver Star Col, the prominent saddle west of the summit (5.5 hours to here). From the col, skin or boot east up steeper slopes toward the summit. An easy scramble brings you to the top, with views over the entire northeastern Cascades from 8876 feet.

DESCENT. Options abound from this high promontory. Enjoy skiing directly back down your ascent route for 5400 feet of vertical to the highway. Alternatively, ski the slightly steeper direct face to skier's left of the upper ascent route. Or cross over into the Varden Creek drainage below 8400 feet, and explore the descents there. You can return to the Silver Star drainage by heading over a saddle at 6780 feet on the divide between Silver Star and Varden Creeks. Once you are in the basin below the main face of Silver Star, follow the ascent route back to the start.

For an extended Silver Star circumnavigation, ski *south* from Silver Star Col toward the Cedar Creek drainage. Ski directly down the couloir if it is filled in early season, or trend skier's right partway down the descent to get to slightly lower-angled terrain at the head of the basin. Continue southeast down valley to 6400 feet, and then ascend under a rock buttress and up a short, steep slope to the small pass at the head of Varden Creek.

From there traverse back toward the ridge to cross into Silver Star Creek, or ski terrain down either side of the Varden Creek basin before returning to Silver Star Creek and the route back to the start. The circumnavigation and descent into Varden Creek can add up to 5 kilometers (3 miles) and 3000 feet of climbing to this tour; plan accordingly.

Tour Author: Benjamin Haskell

NORTH CENTRAL CASCADES

THIS CONTINUATION OF THE NORTH CASCADES presents an astounding variety of landscapes. Running south from Highway 20 is a high crest of superb alpine peaks, including Eldorado, Forbidden, and the peaks of the Ptarmigan Traverse. Glacier Peak beckons with massive glaciers pouring out in all directions, while the mysterious and rugged Entiat Mountains farther east hold many seasons' worth of exploration. The Monte Cristo area to the southwest offers similar possibilities only a stone's throw from Puget Sound.

A dedicated band of citizens is responsible for ensuring that these mountains remained a wild refuge for the benefit of society. Congress designated the Glacier Peak Wilderness in 1964 and North Cascades National Park in 1968; more wilderness areas were added through the following decades, making the North Cascades one of the largest continuous wilderness complexes in the Lower 48. When the North Cascades Highway was finally completed, its purpose was overwhelmingly one of recreation.

It's not easy terrain. Travel in the lowland valleys can be slow and laborious without trails, and the high country is fraught with storm, deep snow, and avalanche. But that is the beauty of ski touring in the North Cascades: an opportunity for real challenge, real solitude, and an elemental experience which embodies the spirit of the Wilderness Act. We have the chance to share these mountains with the ones who call it home: mountain goats, wolves, bears, wolverines, marmots, lynx, fox, martens, pikas, bobcats, deer, elk, moose, cougars, and more. There is still much exploration to be done here, and many secrets to learn.

FEES, PERMITS, AND WEATHER INFORMATION

Many of the tours in the North Central Cascades are located within North Cascades National Park, Mount Baker–Snoqualmie National Forest, and Okanogan–Wenatchee National Forest. Contact information for these entities is located in Resources.

Parking. There is no entrance fee for North Cascades National Park and parking passes are not required to park along Highway 20. Many popular trailheads, however, actually lie on Forest Service lands and require a day pass (available from local vendors), a Northwest Forest Pass, or an America the Beautiful Pass.

Camping. Wilderness Camping Permits are required for all overnight stays in North Cascades National Park wilderness (backcountry). Permits are limited and are offered on a first-come, first-serve basis. Call the Wilderness Information Center in Marblemount to check station hours and for more information about getting your permit. For camping in both Mount Baker–Snoqualmie and Okanogan–Wenatchee National Forests, fill out a free, self-issued wilderness permit at the trailhead. Wilderness regulations apply, and Leave No Trace practices are strongly encouraged.

Wilderness Areas. Stephen Mather Wilderness is located in North Cascades National Park. Mount Baker Wilderness, Noisy-Diosbud Wilderness, and Boulder

Previous page: Forbidden Peak from the northwest (Martin Volken)

River Wilderness are found in Mount Baker–Snoqualmie National Forest. Pasayten Wilderness, Glacier Peak Wilderness, and Lake Chelan–Sawtooth Wilderness are located in Okanogan–Wenatchee National Forest.

Weather. In addition to the Northwest Avalanche Center and the National Weather Service websites, check the Mount Baker and Stevens Pass sites for current local weather and snowpack conditions. See Resources for web addresses.

23 Hidden Lake Peaks

Starting elevation: 2400 feet (higher or lower starting points are common)
High point: 7088 feet
Vertical gain/loss: 4688 feet
Distance: 14 km (8.7 miles)
Time: 8 hours
Overall difficulty: moderate
Ski skills: moderate to difficult
Fitness level: strenuous
Technical skills: moderate
Commitment: low
Gear: the basics, plus potentially an ice ax and crampons to gain Sibley High Route; add ski mountaineering gear if you are climbing The Triad
Best season: December–May
USGS map: Eldorado Peak
Permits: No parking pass is required. Although the tour begins in Mount Baker–Snoqualmie National Forest, the North Cascades National Park (NCNP) boundary coincides with the Hidden Lake Peaks ridgeline. You must obtain a North Cascades National Park backcountry permit to stay overnight in the park east of the summit ridge.

When viewed from surrounding vantage points, Hidden Lake Peaks looks every bit the idyllic Cascadian ski alp. Green forested lower slopes rise steeply from the Cascade River valley and give way to acres of open, moderately angled ski terrain, culminating in a beautiful summit pyramid set amidst the craggy peaks of the Cascade Pass area. It cries out to be skied, and it can be much of the year thanks to access provided by the road to the popular Hidden Lake Peaks summer trailhead. Depending on the snow level, you can plan reasonable day trips in this area, or enjoy the expansive ski terrain and scenic ambiance by staying overnight.

ACCESS

From Marblemount, turn right onto Cascade River Road, and continue southeast 10.7 miles to Sibley Creek/Hidden Lake Road (Forest Service Road 1540). Take a left and drive to the snow line or the Hidden Lake Peaks trailhead later in the season.

This road is unmaintained during winter months, so be prepared for possible blowdowns across the road at any point. As with all such unmaintained access roads, consider bringing a saw or an ax to use either on the way in or out. The Mount Baker–Snoqualmie National Forest has information about road conditions on their website, or call the National Park Service and US Forest Service Information Center in Sedro Woolley.

This tour description assumes a starting elevation of 2400 feet (where the road crosses Sibley Creek) since the Sibley Creek Basin often contains snow well into the spring above the outlet from the upper valley. Lower or higher starting elevations are common, so adjust your time plan accordingly.

TOUR

From 2400 feet on Sibley Creek Road, skin the road to the Hidden Lake Peaks summer trailhead. Although you are on a road, do not discount the avalanche potential as you

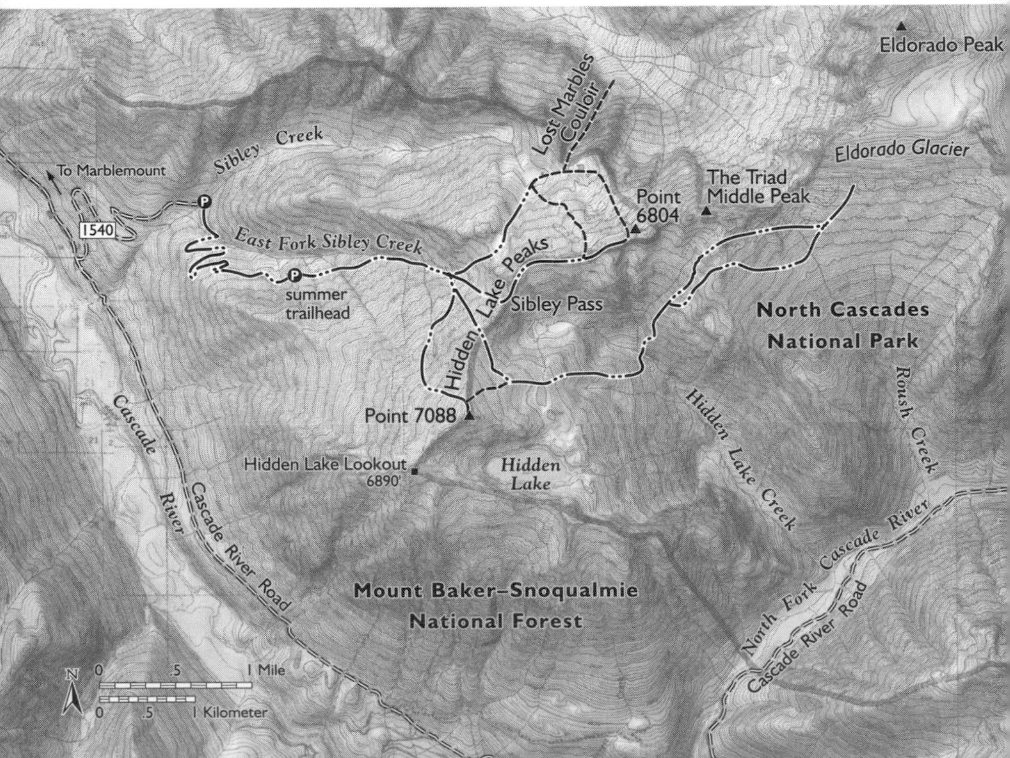

Hidden Lake Peaks from the north (Alasdair Turner)

approach within a half mile of the trailhead. From the summer parking lot, follow the line of the summer trail up through mostly open timber on the east side of the valley, staying within a few hundred yards above the creek. Make an ascending traverse to intersect the creek above 4000 feet (a little more than 2 hours to here).

If conditions are stable, continue up the drainage to open terrain at the head of the valley. Ascend south up the 38-degree lower slopes of Hidden Lake Peaks to gain more moderate slopes above. This open line is subject to avalanche danger from many slide paths. For a safer alternative to reach the upper slopes, leave the route of the summer trail and climb south up through forest prior to reaching the creek or from 4400 feet along the creek itself. Both alternatives involve navigating through a few hundred vertical feet of tight trees that can be a challenge when the snowpack is shallow, but safety and relatively direct improved access to the upper slopes compensate for this challenge.

Once you are in the alpine zone on the primary ascent route, ascend south-southwest toward broad slopes northwest of the summit. At 6200 feet trend east-southeast up to intersect the summit ridge north of the summit, and then climb along the ridge to the top. Stay well back from cornices on the ridge that often overhang to the east. You may have to boot the final few meters of the summit pyramid (5.5 hours to the summit).

DESCENT AND OTHER OPTIONS. Options abound from here. For day trippers starting from 2400 feet, turning around to descend the ascent route makes sense. But the terrain on the mountain's east side is a siren call for any ski tourer interested in moderate skiing in a spectacular setting. For this descent, head north back down the summit ridge to find the first break in the cornices to open slopes below. Ski 1000 feet northeast down to the unnamed lake north of Hidden Lake shown on the USGS map. From there, it is an easy climb up to one of several cols south of what is commonly referred to as Sibley Pass (the main pass along the Sibley Creek and Hidden Lake Creek divide) to make a short loop. Or if time and conditions allow, descend all the way down into the beautiful narrow Hidden Lake Creek valley, and enjoy a uniquely framed view of Johannesburg Mountain before ascending your descent route back up to the divide.

Skiers interested in a more challenging multiday tour can reach the Eldorado Glacier by climbing south out of the Hidden Lake Creek valley via a short, steep slope to the east of the main Triad drainage, which leads to the easier open slopes higher up. Ascend and cross the south shoulder of the Triad at either 7100 feet or the saddle below. Traverse over or under a rock rib to the northeast to reach rolling slopes at the toe of Eldorado Glacier. The Middle Peak (highest) of the Triad also makes a great ski mountaineering objective in its own right, with two 30-meter pitches of fourth-class climbing leading to an airy summit. A small alpine rack is sufficient for the summit ascent.

If you are looking for an aesthetic day-trip alternative to the Hidden Lake Peaks summit tour, ascend the narrow ridge north of Sibley Pass, traverse the Sibley Creek High Route on or just north of the ridge crest, and then ski north-facing terrain toward Sibley Creek. The ridge provides outstanding views into the Marble Creek cirque to the north, Hidden Lake Peaks to the immediate south, and the rest of the Cascade Pass area to the east. An ice ax and crampons can be useful to gain the ridge. After you descend these north slopes, you can make a loop by climbing over the pass above the East Fork Sibley Creek and skiing back to the ascent route. In the other direction, the Lost Marbles Couloir drops northeast 2000 feet straight into Marble Creek after a dogleg entrance, providing exciting access into one of the most impressive cirques of the North Cascades.

Tour Author: Benjamin Haskell

24 The Isolation Traverse

Starting elevation: 2160 feet
High point: 8040 feet
Vertical gain/loss: 13,000 feet/14,000 feet
Distance: 30 km (19 miles)
Time: 3–4 days
Overall difficulty: very difficult
Ski skills: moderate

Fitness level: very strenuous
Technical skills: expert
Commitment: high
Best season: March–June
Gear: the basics, plus ski mountaineering and overnight equipment
USGS maps: Cascade Pass, Eldorado, Forbidden Peak, Diablo Dam, Ross Dam; recommended: National Geographic #223, North Cascades
Permits: A free backcountry permit is required to stay overnight in the North Cascades National Park complex and can be obtained at the Wilderness Information Center in Marblemount. No parking pass is required.

This multiday tour connects the Inspiration and Neve Glaciers, visiting the very wild and isolated country between the Cascade River Road and the North Cascades Highway. It includes some great ski descents, especially when done from south to north as described here. It requires good routefinding and a full range of ski mountaineering skills. The trailheads at either end of the traverse are fairly low (2160 feet and 1150 feet), so many will choose to bring a pair of light shoes to make the walking more comfortable.

ACCESS

This tour requires you to arrange a car shuttle or to get someone to drop you off at the Eldorado parking lot. From Marblemount, cross the Skagit River on the Cascade River Road (Forest Service Road 15), and follow it east 19 miles to the Eldorado Creek trailhead at 2160 feet. To reach your pick-up location at the Pyramid Lake trailhead, follow the North Cascades Highway for 20 miles east of Marblemount to the Gorge Lake Bridge. The trailhead is 0.75 mile farther, with parking at a pullout on the left side of the road, at a sign for Pyramid Lake.

TOUR

DAY 1. Walk a short distance west along the river to cross the North Fork Cascade River on a big log. On the north bank, follow the well-used climber's trail uphill; the grade is gentle at first but becomes very steep. At about 3800 feet the trail breaks out of the trees and enters a boulder field beneath cliffs (1.5 hours to here); ideally this area will be well covered with snow. Skin north, keeping the cliffs on your left. At about 6100 feet gain the divide between the Eldorado and Roush Creek drainages (4 hours to here).

Find an easy place to descend into the Roush Creek side—late in the season you may have to scramble down a gully. Skin northwest to gain the Eldorado Glacier and then north to gain the Inspiration Glacier at 7400 feet where it forms a flat basin below the southeast face of Eldorado Peak (5.5 hours to here). Cross this basin to the northeast to gain the east ridge of Eldorado Peak at 7600 feet (6 hours to here).

North Cascades Hwy
Pyramid Lake trailhead/finish
Pyramid Creek
Diablo Lake
To Ross Lake and Rainy Pass
20
Gorge Lake
Pyramid Lake
Ruby Mountain
Ross Lake National Recreation Area
20
To Newhalem
Pyramid Peak
Paul Bunyans Stump
Colonial Glacier
Colonial Peak
Point 7505
Thunder Creek
Neve Glacier
The Needle
Snowfield Peak
7115'
East Fork
North Cascades National Park
Newhalem Creek
Camp 2
Isolation Peak (Point 7102)
McAllister Creek
Point 6684
Stout Lake
Ice-elation Couloir
Primus Peak
The Coccyx
Austera Towers
North Klawatti Glacier
Backbone Ridge
McAllister Glacier
Klawatti Glacier
Camp 1
8041'
Dorado Needle
Klawatti Peak
Marble Creek
Inspiration Glacier
Eldorado Peak
Moraine Lake
To Marblemount
Sibley Creek
Eldorado Glacier
The Triad
Hidden Lake Peaks
15
Forbidden Peak
Boston Glacier
Rousn Creek
Eldorado Creek
Cascade River
Cascade River Road
Boston Peak
North Fork Cascade River
Eldorado trailhead/start
Mount Baker–Snoqualmie National Forest
15
0 .5 1 Mile
0 .5 1 Kilometer

The Isolation Traverse looking south from the Neve Glacier (Martin Volken)

The Inspiration Glacier presents a big change in character from the gentle Eldorado Glacier—its crevasses can be big and may run parallel to your intended line of travel. Continue north on a gradually ascending traverse, heading for a broad, gentle col among the Tepeh Towers that will gain you access to the McAllister Glacier at 8040 feet (7 hours to here). Wind scoops near the col can provide good camping.

DAY 2. Ski northwest across the head of the McAllister Glacier to about 7560 feet, and transition to uphill mode. Rather than head for the obvious broad col just north of Dorado Needle, aim for a subtle col a little farther north. The col is hard to see on the USGS map, but it is just north of Point 8041, and you must climb a short, steep stretch to reach it. You may be able to find a nontechnical descent onto the northwest-facing glacial slope beyond, but be ready to potentially build a snow anchor and rappel 20 meters (1.5 hours to here). A lower col even farther north, which is easily discernable on the map, requires a short steep climb on the east side and a 15-meter rappel on the west side with good rock horns available for anchors.

Next comes an unforgettable descending traverse. Keep your elevation as you glide northwest under the Backbone Ridge. At about 6000 feet you can climb up and gain the southwest ridge of The Coccyx (3 hours to here). From 6080 feet on this ridge you should be able to ski down into the head of Newhalem Creek without negotiating a cornice or wind lip; ski to 5800 feet. Skin northeast, ascending gently toward a col between the Coccyx and Point 6885 (4 hours to here). Note that neither "Backbone" nor "Coccyx" appears on the USGS map; reference Fred Beckey's *Cascade Alpine Guide 2: Stevens Pass to Rainy Pass* for their location.

Next comes a great ski line. The Ice-elation Couloir leads down 1500 feet at an average angle of 35 degrees. Note that the sidewalls are quite steep and hold snow

The Isolation Traverse exit from the north (Martin Volken)

on a variety of aspects from northwest to east. From the bottom, climb northeast to a treed col, the second col east from Point 6684 (5.5 hours to here).

Ski and then skin to the northeast along the ridge, looking ahead to the south slopes of Isolation Peak, the unofficial name given to Point 7102. (Lowell Skoog and company also thought it a fitting name for the traverse when they first completed it in 1983.) Climb the southeast snow slope to 6600 feet and traverse to the southeast ridge (7.5 hours to here). Ski east and then north, using caution on a few steep slopes. Head for the lake at 5720 feet, where camping provides good views and morning light (8.5 hours to here).

DAY 3. Continue north and gain the flat ridge connecting Isolation and Snowfield Peaks. Cross the ridge at 6640 feet to enter the basin on the southwest side of Snowfield Peak; contour above cliff tops around 6600 feet, dropping a little elevation where necessary to negotiate rock spurs. *This traverse is quite exposed, with steep slopes facing northwest, west, and southwest as you climb counterclockwise toward gentler ground.* Climb to the col between The Horseman and Snowfield Peak at 7680 feet (2.5 hours to here).

A side trip up the west ridge of Snowfield Peak is well worth it if you have the time. Ski the Neve Glacier to the north, staying in the lower angle corridor between icefalls to the east and west. From the intriguing ice plateau, climb north to the col due west of Point 7505 (3.5 hours to here). Colonial Peak makes another worthy side trip with an easy skin to just below the summit and a short bootpack to the top.

Ski due north from the col, heading for the "d" in Pyramid Peak" on the USGS map. *This traverse, from the Colonial Glacier north under the east face of Pyramid Peak, forms one of the cruxes of this tour.* The route crosses a very large avalanche path midslope. Use caution here, and think ahead to this point on the tour before you leave home.

From the ridge that descends off Pyramid to the northeast, you have two options. You can follow this ridge down, making the best of tight trees and dwindling snow, and veer north with the ridge as it becomes broader, heading for Pyramid Lake (look for the summer climber's trail that starts at the lake). Or if snow coverage is good and you feel adventurous, you can follow avalanche swathes under the north side of Pyramid Peak, linking open terrain and avoiding cliff bands until you are able to traverse east to Pyramid Lake at 2640 feet (6.5 hours to here). From here the well-maintained trail leads 3.6 kilometers (2.25 miles) down to the North Cascades Highway at 1150 feet (7.5 hours to here).

Tour Author: Forest McBrian

25 Sahale Peak

Starting elevation: 3240 feet from Boston Basin, 3640 feet from Cascade Pass
High point: 8680 feet
Vertical gain/loss: 5440 feet/5440 feet
Distance: 18.4 km (11.5 miles)
Time: 1–2 days
Overall difficulty: moderate to difficult
Ski skills: very difficult
Fitness level: strenuous
Technical skills: moderate
Commitment: high
Gear: the basics, plus ski mountaineering gear
Best season: April–June
USGS map: Cascade Pass
Permits: A free backcountry permit is required to stay overnight in North Cascades National Park and can be obtained at the Wilderness Information Center in Marblemount. A parking pass is not required anywhere along the Cascade River Road.

Scenic Sahale Peak is known for its central location among the Cascades Peaks. The summit is a technical rock step, and the peak offers ski descents in two directions: either down the Quien Sabe Glacier into Boston Basin or down the Sahale Glacier and the Sahale Arm to Cascade Pass. This tour can be done as an out-and-back from either the Boston Basin side or Cascade Pass; alternatively it can be done as a traverse, up the Quien Sabe and over the summit of Sahale Peak. (Although its official name per the USGS is "Sahale Mountain," it is more often known as "Sahale Peak.")

ACCESS

From Marblemount, take a right onto the Cascade River Road (Forest Service Road 15). Follow this road 22.3 miles to a small parking area and the trailhead to Boston Basin at 3240 feet. The Cascade Pass trailhead is another 0.4 mile up the road at an elevation of 3640 feet. In early season, the Cascade River Road may be gated at the Johnson Cabin gate at the hairpin turn near milepost 21 at 2400 feet, requiring a 1.3-mile walk up the road to the Boston Basin trailhead. Check road conditions on the national park website before you begin your trip.

TOUR

BOSTON BASIN APPROACH. From the hairpin, walk or tour up the Cascade River Road until you reach the Boston Basin trailhead at 3240 feet on the left. Here the old Diamond Mine Road, which is now the Boston Basin Trail, leads off to the north. Follow it up; there is a good chance that the trail will be snow covered. You will ascend several switchbacks until the old Diamond Mine Road ends at 3600 feet (a very steep climbers trail goes up from here). From here, tour up and east through steep terrain for a few hundred feet until the terrain angles back at around 4200 feet. Be careful in this section; it is quite steep and the terrain's openness in this otherwise timbered zone are signs of regular avalanche activity.

From 4200 feet, tour a bit more northeasterly until you are close to Midas Creek. From here, head up the Midas Creek drainage until you are directly south of a very prominent knoll (Point 6482 on the map). Tour up to the south of this knoll, and then gain the top of it by turning north at the 6400-foot level (4–5 hours to here). It is crucial to get to this point early in the day, since avalanches regularly flush the Midas Creek drainage. Point 6482 is a great first camp option, perched atop the moraine with views of Johannesburg Mountain and the Cascade River valley. (Note that you can also climb up on to the glacier and set camp higher if you prefer.)

From your camp on the moraine, skin northeast to gain the Quien Sabe Glacier, and skirt around the rock buttress coming down from Sahale Peak. At 7800 feet, curve to the east to climb the steeper glacial slopes up to the Boston–Sahale Col (watch for crevasses, and evaluate the snow stability thoroughly). If your plan is to descend the Quien Sabe, depot your skis at the col; if you plan to go over Sahale Peak, then bring them with you!

From the col, ascend the ridge, being careful to evaluate any cornices on the ridge and keep clear of them. The rock step to gain the summit is fourth-class climbing

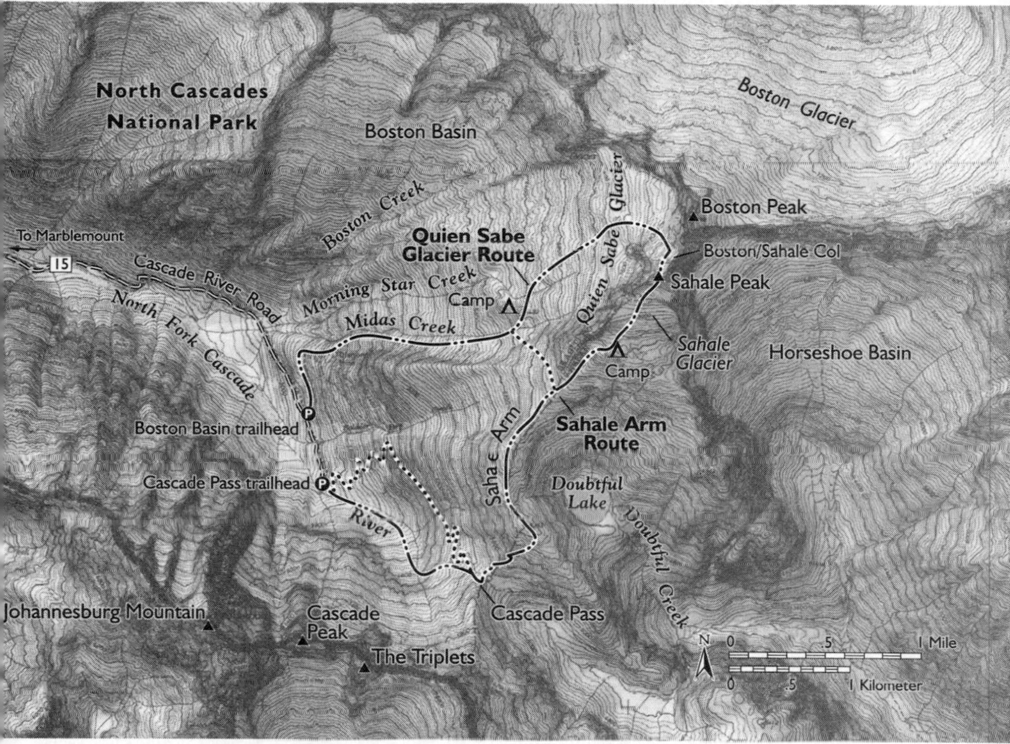

with a good amount of exposure, so a rope and the skills to climb rock are needed to reach the summit proper.

To descend via the Quien Sabe, return to your skis at the Boston–Sahale Col, and enjoy excellent skiing down the same route that you came up.

Another fun option is to make the trip into a traverse and loop back to your camp from Sahale Arm. Do this by descending off the summit to the south. Make a rappel of 25–30 meters depending on the snow levels. This puts you at the top of the Sahale Glacier which you can then ski down to the magnificent Sahale Arm. At about 6800 feet you will have to turn northwest off the Sahale Arm and regain the southern end of Boston Basin and your camp at Point 6482.

CASCADE PASS APPROACH. The snow level will dictate your route to Cascade Pass; the summer trail leads through steep and cliff-ridden terrain, so unless the trail to the pass is clear, your route will go up the gut of the valley until you hit a steep section at around 4600 feet (see aerial photo for Tour 28). Tour or boot straight up until you can trend left at about 4800 feet. The terrain mellows out from there, and you should be able to reach Cascade Pass at 5400 feet easily (3 hours to here).

Be sure to carefully assess the slopes of Cascade Peak and The Triplets above you—when avalanches run here, they can cross your intended route.

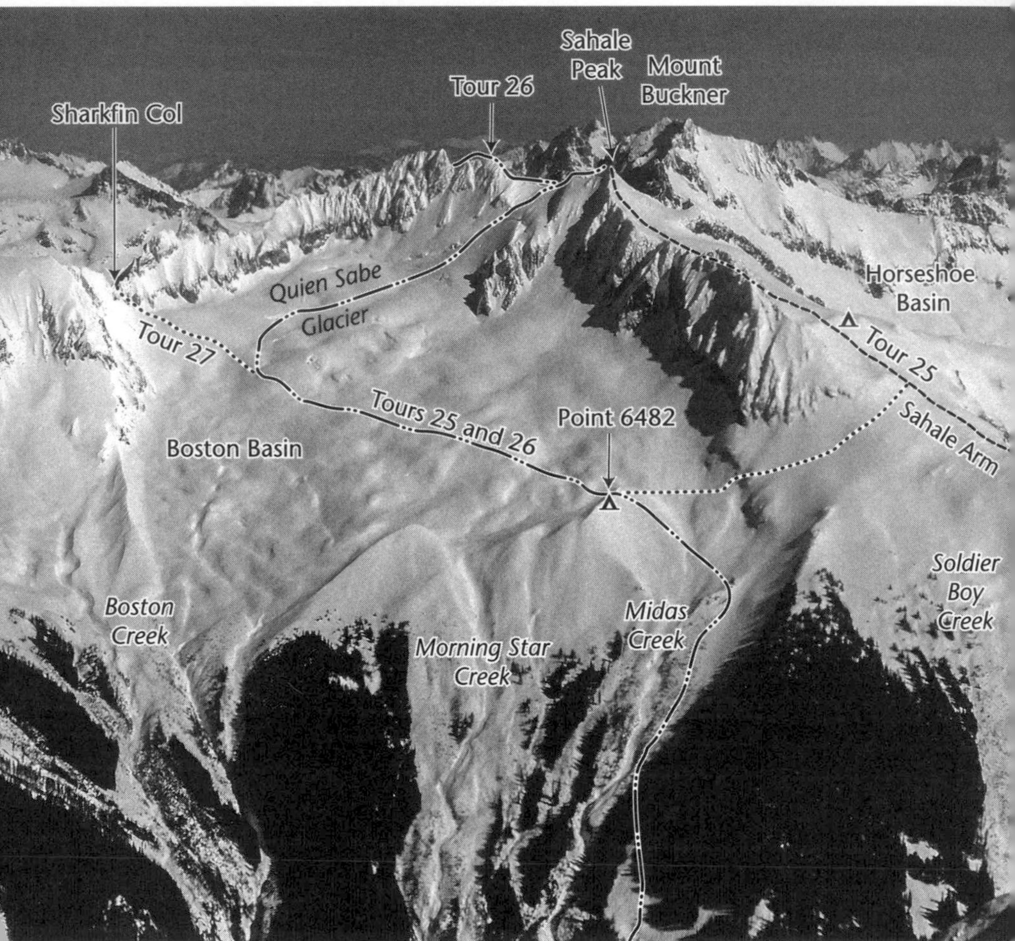

Sahale Peak from the southwest (Scott Schell)

From the pass head northeast on or just climber's right of the ridge to gain lower angle terrain and the beginning of Sahale Arm at 6200 feet. Follow the gentle terrain of the arm up to a broad gully at 7200 feet. Leave the small rock ridge on your right, and ascend a steep slope to flatter ground and excellent camp spots at 7600 feet. The distance from the trailhead to camp is 4.3 kilometers (2.7 miles).

From camp at 7600 feet, ascend the Sahale Glacier to just below the summit pyramid. Summitting from this side requires one pitch of mostly fourth-class rock climbing with a few fifth-class moves.

For the descent, you have your choice of lines down the broad slopes of the Sahale Glacier and Sahale Arm. From Cascade Pass, make sure you follow your up track, as it can be tricky to navigate through the cliffs and benches if you choose a new line.

Tour Author: Margaret Wheeler

26 Mount Buckner: North Face

Starting elevation: 2400 feet
High point: 9112 feet
Vertical gain/loss: 9300 feet/9300 feet
Distance: 23 km (14 miles)
Time: 2–3 days
Overall difficulty: very difficult
Ski skills: extremely difficult
Fitness level: very strenuous
Technical skills: very high
Commitment: very high
Gear: the basics, plus ski mountaineering and overnight equipment
Best season: April–May
USGS maps: Cascade Pass and Goode Mountain
Permits: A free backcountry permit is required to stay overnight in North Cascades National Park and can be obtained at the Wilderness Information Center in Marblemount. A parking pass is not required anywhere along the Cascade River Road.

The Mount Buckner North Face ski descent holds just about every element that makes ski mountaineering in the North Cascades an unforgettable experience. This tour should not be your first foray into the park even if you are fit and a very strong skier; you should have prior ski mountaineering experience. This route involves steep ascents, routefinding challenges, glacier travel, a short but exposed ridge, and an intimidating 50-degree headwall; it also rewards you with unforgettable scenery in the middle of the wild North Cascades. (Although the USGS labels it "Buckner Mountain," it is more commonly known as "Mount Buckner.")

ACCESS

From Marblemount, turn right onto Cascade River Road (Forest Service Road 15), and drive to the Johnson Cabin gate at the hairpin turn near milepost 21 at 2400 feet. Oftentimes the road will be gated here, especially early in the season. If not, continue driving 1.3 miles up the road to the Boston Basin trailhead. Check road conditions on the national park website before you begin your trip.

TOUR

DAY 1. From the Johnson Cabin gate, walk or tour up the Cascade River Road until you reach the Boston Basin trailhead at 3240 feet on the left. Here the old Diamond Mine Road, which is now the Boston Basin Trail, leads off to the north. Follow it up; there is a good chance that the trail will be snow covered. You will ascend several switchbacks until the old Diamond Mine Road ends at 3600 feet (a very steep climbers trail goes up from here). From here, tour up and east through steep terrain for a few hundred feet until the terrain angles back at around 4200 feet. Be careful in this section; it is quite steep and the terrain's openness in this otherwise timbered zone are signs of regular avalanche activity.

From 4200 feet, tour a bit more northeasterly until you are close to Midas Creek. From here head up the Midas Creek drainage until you are directly south of a very prominent knoll (Point 6482 on the map). Tour up to the south of this knoll, and then gain the top of it by turning north at the 6400-foot level (4–5 hours to here). It is crucial to get to this point early in the day, since avalanches regularly flush the Midas Creek drainage. Point 6482 is a great first camp option.

DAY 2. Make sure to consider the length of your tour in relation to the weather and snow conditions. You might have to get up quite early in order to avoid getting trapped by conditions. From camp, tour up northeast to about 7800 feet. Get onto the Quien Sabe Glacier at about 7300 feet; it is hard to tell when you transition onto the glacier. At about 7800 feet, turn more southeasterly and tour up the glacier to the prominent Boston–Sahale Col at 8600 feet (2 hours to here). Choosing to camp at the Boston–Sahale Col makes for a big first day but an easier second day—pick your poison.

From the col, turn toward Boston Peak, and scramble up the shattered but easy ridge. The ridge gets narrow and exposed after a few minutes and can be very tricky if it is

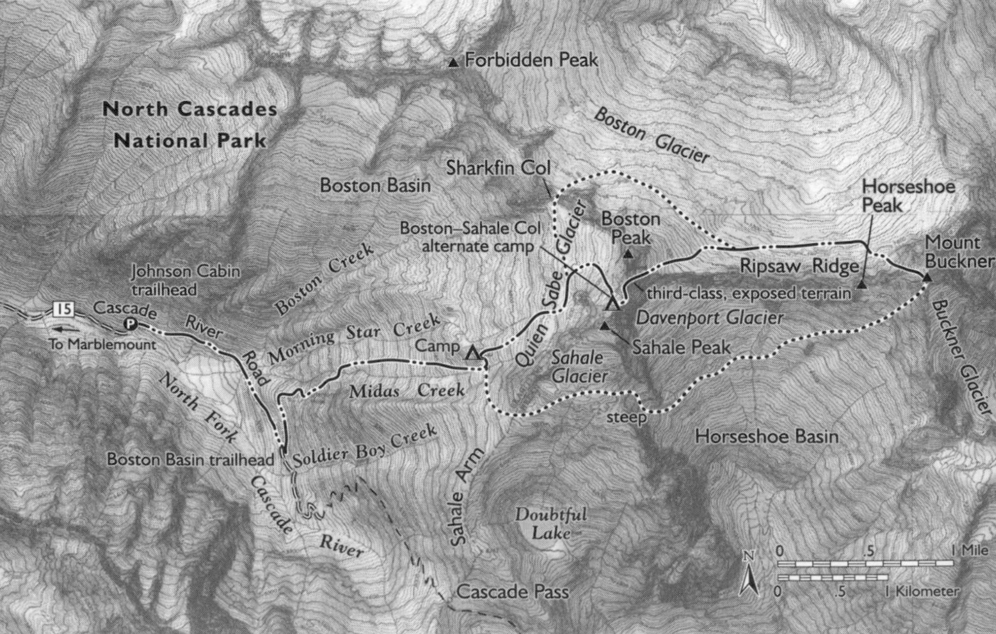

Mount Buckner from the north (Andrew McLean)

corniced. The exposed ridge is short, though, and after a very short downhill section, look for a third-class ledge leading away from a notch across the south face high above the Davenport Glacier. This short, simple, and wild traverse gets you to the top of the triangular apron of the Boston Glacier just south of Boston Peak (3 hours to here).

From here, ski down and across the Boston Glacier straight over to the base of Mount Buckner's North Face. Assess conditions carefully here; you will have to come back up the apron and across the ridge late in the day in potentially much warmer conditions.

The ascent of the North Face is generally straightforward in the spring, and it gives you a good opportunity to assess the conditions before committing to this ski descent. Wiggle through moats if they are present at the bottom of the face, and climb straight up to about 8700 feet. From here, get onto a slightly mellower rib on climber's left that leads to the summit at 9112 feet (5 hours to here).

DESCENT. Ski down the North Face by essentially retracing your ascent tracks. Consider your own condition as well as the weather and snow conditions before you commit to descending this steep face. Once you reach the bottom of the descent, tour back across the Boston Glacier and up the apron to the ridge (7 hours to here). Now climb back across the ridge and enjoy a beautiful descent down the Quien Sabe Glacier back to your camp at 6482 feet (8–9 hours to here). From camp, ski back out to your car via your ascent route from the first day (10–11 hours to here).

Alternate descent. Conditions might be more inviting on the southwest face of Mount Buckner, which is a great descent in its own right. If you choose it, ski down the southwest face off the summit, and keep heading in a west-southwesterly direction down through Horseshoe Basin to about 6200 feet. Now tour around the south ridge of Sahale Peak, and climb up a steep slope to flat benches at about 7200 feet below the Sahale Glacier.

From here, tour across Sahale Arm in a westerly direction. Then get off Sahale Arm at around 6800 feet and ski northwest until you are back in the Boston Basin at around 6400 feet. You are now very close to your camp at Point 6482. Please keep in mind that even this alternate option is a serious descent in big terrain (3 hours from summit to camp).

Tour Author: Martin Volken

27 The Forbidden Tour

Starting elevation: 3100 feet (2400 feet if road is closed)
High point: 8868 feet
Vertical gain/loss: 10,315 feet/11,234 feet
Distance: 36 km (19 miles)
Time: 3–4 days
Overall difficulty: very difficult
Ski skills: difficult
Fitness level: very strenuous
Technical skills: very high
Commitment: very high
Gear: the basics, plus ski mountaineering and overnight equipment
Best season: April–May
USGS maps: Cascade Pass, Forbidden Peak, and Eldorado Peak
Permits: A free backcountry permit is required to stay overnight in North Cascades National Park and can be obtained at the Wilderness Information Center in Marblemount. A parking pass is not required anywhere along the Cascade River Road.

The Forbidden Tour epitomizes what makes the North Cascades a great skiing range. This tour crosses seven glaciers of substantial size and drops deep into Washington wilderness. You will find yourself touring, skiing, and camping in some of the most alpine environs of the Lower 48 on what is essentially a circumnavigation of Forbidden Peak. The tour's commitment level increases substantially once you drop onto the Boston Glacier. All things considered, the Forbidden Tour is a real ski mountaineering adventure that requires skill and commitment.

ACCESS

From Marblemount, turn right onto Cascade River Road (Forest Service Road 15), and drive to the Johnson Cabin gate at the hairpin turn near milepost 21 at 2400 feet. Oftentimes the road will be gated here, especially early in the season. Check road conditions on the national park website before you begin your trip. You can also stage a car or leave a bike at the Eldorado Creek trailhead near mile 19 where the tour ends to avoid the short walk on the road back to where you started.

TOUR

DAY 1. Walk or tour up the Cascade River Road for about 2 miles until you reach the Boston Basin trailhead at 3240 feet. Here the old Diamond Mine Road, which is now the Boston Basin Trail leads off to the north. Follow it up; there is a good chance the trail will be snow covered. Ascend several switchbacks until the trail ends at 3600 feet. From here tour up and east through steep terrain for a few hundred feet until the terrain angles back at around 4200 feet. Be careful in this section; it is quite steep and the terrain's openness in this otherwise timbered zone are signs of regular avalanche activity.

From 4200 feet, tour a bit more northeasterly until you are close to Midas Creek. From here head up the Midas Creek drainage until you are directly south of a very prominent knoll (Point 6482 on the USGS map). Tour up to the south of this knoll, and then gain the top of it by turning north at the 6400-foot level (4–5 hours to here). It is crucial to get to this point early in the day, since avalanches regularly flush the Midas Creek drainage. Point 6482 is a great first camp option.

If you have enough energy, proceed north-northeast to the northernmost tip of the Quien Sabe Glacier, heading climber's right for the Sharkfin Col. There are a few hidden crevasses due to a small icefall about halfway between Point 6482 and Sharkfin Col. The glacier flattens out at around 7500 feet at the bottom of the Sharkfin Col couloir, where you have plenty of room for safe and scenic camping (5–6 hours to here). This spot puts you in a great position for crossing the Sharkfin Col the next day.

DAY 2. From camp, climb up the obvious couloir toward Sharkfin Col. From the bottom of the couloir, another distinct and steep gully leads slightly climber's right. If you go up this way, you will avoid the rock scramble, but the descent on the other side is more difficult and time consuming.

Climb up the obvious couloir, negotiating the bergschrund at the bottom. Keep climbing until you run out of snow. At this point the climber's left side of the gully seems inviting since it is not as steep, but do not go there unless it is snow-covered. The rock quality is highly questionable. Rather, stay on the climber's right edge of the gully and climb up the obvious rocky ledges. Near the top of the gully the terrain angles back, but the rock quality deteriorates again. Move carefully and manage your group to avoid rockfall in this couloir. Climb up to an obvious belay block, equipped with anchor slings of various ages and quality, at 7760 feet at the very top of the gully and to the climber's right of a little tower (1 hour to here).

The anchor block works very well for belays from the Quien Sabe Glacier side and the rappel down to the Boston Glacier side. This point in the tour is an important one, since retreat will likely be difficult once you are on the Boston Glacier.

From the top of Sharkfin Col, make the short, 20-meter rappel down to the Boston Glacier, and ski north to the toe of the prominent rib at 7100 feet. From here, tour up and across the Boston Glacier, still heading north to the northernmost extension of Forbidden Peak's North Ridge at 7600 feet (4 hours to here).

You will see a steep but short slope that leads up to the easternmost edge of the Forbidden Glacier. It is important to get here early in the day because the top of this short slope is very steep and in full eastern exposure. Climb up the slope, and exit its left side by a crumbly rock horn, which puts you onto the Forbidden Glacier at 7700 feet (5 hours to here).

From this col, ski down the scenic Forbidden Glacier on its northern side in a north-northwest direction. At around 6200 feet, you have to decide whether to ski down the snout of the glacier or to move farther north into little trees. From 6200 feet, trend slightly right across a moraine then ski northwest down to the lake. Do not trend too far right as it leads into cliffy terrain. The correct route links snow ramps to the lake. The glacier option is not as steep, but there are big cliffs toward the bottom and you are subjecting yourself to avalanche and icefall danger from the Mount Torment and Forbidden Peak cliffs high above. If you decide on the glacier descent, keep skiing down on the right margin of the glacier all the way to the lake.

The option through the trees is probably safer if the snow conditions are good on the slope leading down to Moraine Lake. Keep in mind that around 3000 feet you will be skiing down 40-degree terrain that is slabby rock in the summer—terrain and condition assessment is of the essence. This fantastic ski descent brings you down to the eastern edge of Moraine Lake. Right by the exit of the lake at 4530 feet are beautiful campsites (6 hours to here).

DAY 3. You have to feel good about the avalanche conditions, weather, and conditions on the lake if you want to reach the plateau of the Inspiration Glacier by crossing Moraine Lake. If you do not feel good about it, you have a couple of choices.

Alternative 1. From your campsite, ski down the short section to the big flat area at 4200 feet. Now traverse north-northwest for about 1 kilometer (0.6 mile), and then turn northwest up the slope toward the eastern border of the massive Inspiration cirque. The slope you are about to tour up is huge and can produce massive slides—be careful. If you do not trust the conditions on the slope, you might be better off sitting tight at Moraine Lake until conditions improve. You reach the ridge that lets you drop onto the Inspiration side at around 7200 feet. From there, you can proceed directly to the Klawatti Col by staying high near the ridge (5 hours from camp).

Alternative 2. Your other choice after camping at Moraine Lake is to battle it out in the West Fork Thunder Creek valley and make it out to Diablo Lake that way. Be aware that a descent down West Fork Thunder Creek bares its own dangers, and

Austera Peak
Klawatti Glacier
McAllister Glacier
Klawatti Peak
Camp 3
Klawatti Lake
Dorado Needle
Towers
Tepeh
West Fork Thunder Creek
Eldorado Peak
Inspiration Glacier
steep above
Inspiration Glacier Plateau
North Cascades National Park
Camp 2
Eldorado Glacier
Moraine Lake
icefall hazard
Forbidden Glacier
North Ridge
Mount Torment
Forbidden Peak
Boston Glacier
Roush Creek
steep climber's trail
Sharkfin Col
Alternate first camp
Boston Basin
Boston Peak
Eldorado Creek trailhead
Johnson Cabin trailhead
Gilbert Creek
Boston Creek
Quien Sabe Glacier
Sahale Peak
Cascade River Road
North Fork Cascade River
Morning Star Creek
Camp 1
Midas Creek
Sahale Glacier
15
To Marblemount
Sahale Arm
Boston Basin trailhead
0 .5 1 Mile
0 .5 1 Kilometer
To Cascade Pass

the ensuing slog through the swampy Thunder Creek lowlands can turn into its own adventure. It is a last resort to say the least.

Standard option. If you are continuing the standard route from your camp at Moraine Lake, ski across the lake then in a northwesterly direction toward the headwall of the cirque. Slightly below the 5000-foot mark on the USGS map, the terrain to the right allows you to climb north up the slope to 5400 feet. At this point, you should be able to put skins back on to again tour in a northwesterly direction toward the Inspiration Glacier. You will find yourself above some sizable cliffs that will remind you that the inventor of the ski crampon is a hero.

Gain the easy entrance to the Inspiration Glacier at around 6000 feet—important but easy to find. If you are too low, ice cliffs will block the passage, and if you are too high, you will run into steep and rocky terrain (2.5–3 hours to here).

Once you are on the lower portion of the Inspiration Glacier, proceed northwest to about 6600 feet. Now, essentially follow a gigantic clockwise turn in order to get up and around a cliff. Refrain from turning northeast until you are on somewhat gentler terrain at around 7600 feet. Tour the remaining distance to your third camp at Klawatti Col at 8000 feet (4.5–5 hours to here).

If time and energy allow, you can make the quick excursion to Austera Peak, which rewards you with views into the spectacular icefalls of the McAllister Glacier. From camp, tour along the west side of Klawatti Peak, and cross from the McAllister Glacier to the Klawatti Glacier right by the toe of Klawatti Peak's north ridge at 7900 feet. Now tour in a northerly direction on the Klawatti Glacier to the first summit tower of Austera Peak.

Just before you get to the top of what might be assumed to be the summit, depot your skis (at around 8300 feet), drop onto the west side of the tower, and follow below an easy but potentially corniced ridge for about 100 feet to the notch of the true summit tower. A short but exposed chimney through rock and snow puts you to the top of Austera Peak (8334 feet and 2 hours from Klawatti Col).

For the descent, downclimb or rappel to the notch, and then retrace the short traverse to your ski depot. From here return to camp via your ascent track (3 hours from Klawatti Col).

Austera Peak is obviously one of many options that you can enjoy as part of your afternoon entertainment, including a circumnavigation of Klawatti Peak or a simple ski down the Klawatti Glacier toward Klawatti Lake. Ascending the tempting South Couloir of Klawatti Peak is not a good option that late in the day, but it would be a fantastic start for the next day.

DAY 4. The summit of Eldorado Peak is the main objective of the day, and this description takes you there via the north side of Tepeh Towers. From camp, ski northwest for a short distance across a shoulder that divides the western and eastern lobes of the McAllister Glacier. Now you can ski safely down to about 7000 feet on the western lobe of the McAllister Glacier, and then regain the Inspiration Glacier via a distinct

Inspiration Glacier from the south (Andy Dappen)

col east of Tepeh Tower 8386. Once you are there, ski south and gain Eldorado's East Ridge at about 7800 feet (2.5 hours to here).

Depot any unnecessary gear, then turn west and tour up the broad East Ridge. Good terrain management and a few kick turns bring you to the base of the short summit ridge at 8750 feet (3.5 hours to here). Depot your skis here, and climb the short but exposed snow ridge to the summit of Eldorado Peak at 8868 feet (4 hours to here).

It is all downhill from here—nearly 6700 feet of it. From the summit, climb back down to your skis, and then ski the very enjoyable East Ridge back to your gear depot at 7800 feet. From here, ski across the East Ridge and the southernmost portion of the Eldorado and Inspiration Glacier plateau south to the Eldorado Glacier at 7400 feet (4.5–5 hours to here).

Now continue skiing southeast and then south along the rib that divides the Roush Creek and Eldorado Creek drainages; you are skiing on its west side. At 6150 feet, find an easy crossing to the other side of the rib—an important spot. You are now in the Eldorado Creek drainage. Ski down this drainage generally staying west of the creek. The terrain steepens at around 4800 feet. You are entering a big talus zone that might not hold all that much snow anymore and could have some treacherous holes. At 4000 feet the terrain gets even steeper. Continue to stay west of the creek, and you should find the climber's trail fairly easily in the trees beyond the talus slope at 3800 feet (6 hours to here).

Follow this climber's trail down into the valley. The trail will lead you to a solid log crossing across the Cascade River about 100 yards west of the Eldorado Creek trailhead parking lot at 2160 feet (7.5–8 hours to here). Your car is a little over a mile east along the Cascade River Road.

Tour Author: Martin Volken

28 Cascade-Johannesburg Couloir

Starting elevation: 3640 feet
High point: 6800 feet
Vertical gain/loss: 3160 feet/3160 feet
Distance: 7 km (3.6 miles)
Time: 6–7 hours from the Cascade Pass trailhead
Overall difficulty: extremely difficult
Ski skills: extremely difficult
Fitness level: strenuous
Technical skills: high
Commitment: high
Gear: the basics, plus ski mountaineering equipment
Best season: May–June
USGS map: Cascade Pass
Permits: none

The Cascade-Johannesburg Couloir from the northwest (Martin Volken)

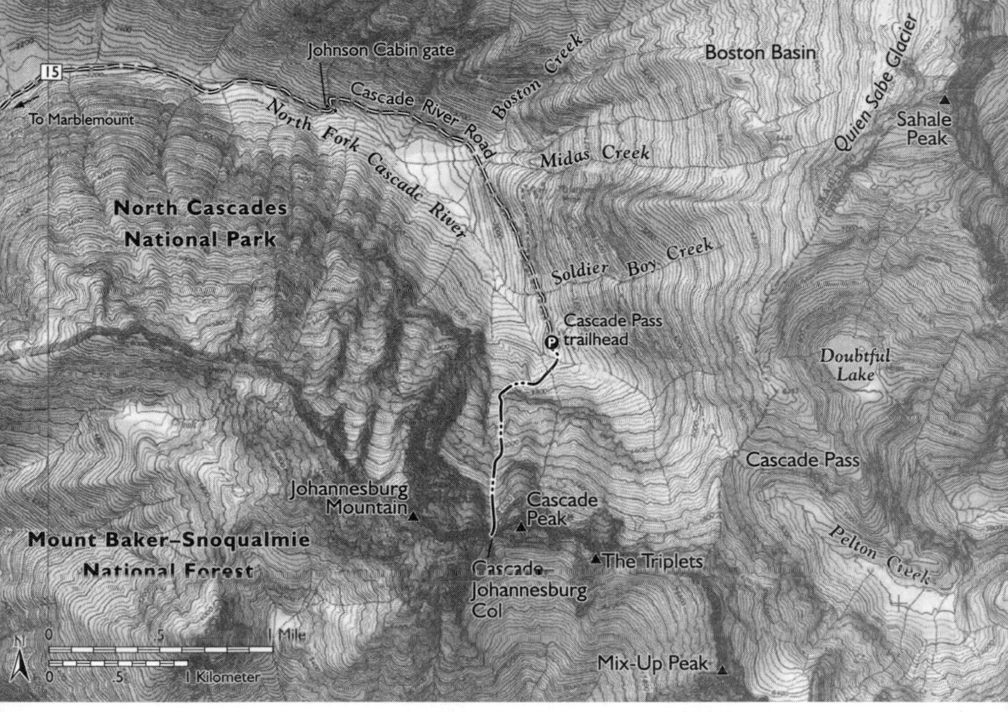

Access to big, steep terrain does not get any more straightforward than this. The iconic Cascade–Johannesburg Couloir catches the eye of any skier who visits the Cascade Pass area, and for good reason—3000 feet of fall line on a huge Cascades north face. Waiting for good conditions is essential here—huge walls overhang the route on either side, and the hazards of rockfall, icefall, and avalanches cannot be overstated. Once you are in the couloir, the exposure is relentless. Insist on excellent conditions, and have a good backup plan in place in case conditions are not as expected. If you climb in the dark, you are more likely to get to the top of the couloir before the mighty Johannesburg Mountain walls receive too much sunlight and start shedding.

ACCESS

From Marblemount, turn right (south) onto Cascade River Road (Forest Service Road 15). Continue 23 miles to its end at the Cascade Pass trailhead. In early season, the Cascade River Road may be gated at the Johnson Cabin gate at the hairpin turn near milepost 21 at 2400 feet. Check road conditions on the national park website before you begin your trip.

TOUR

If starting at the Johnson Cabin gate, ski up the road toward the Cascade Pass trailhead. From the trailhead parking lot head toward the entrance of the couloir by crossing the Cascade River at around 3600 feet and maintaining that elevation. Now head west under the big cliffs of Cascade Peak until you arrive at the exit apron of the Cascade-Johannesburg Couloir. Find a sheltered spot to transition into boot or crampon mode; consider putting on your helmet.

Enter the couloir from the east, climb up a bit, and then exit the couloir quickly to the east around 4200 feet onto a rib. This way you will avoid icefall from the ice shelf that sits at the bottom of Johannesburg Mountain's northeast wall (1 hour to here). You can now follow this rib up to about 5200 feet in relative safety (2.5 hours to here).

Reenter the couloir, and climb the remaining 1600 feet to the top of the couloir. Head up the couloir as directly as possible, noting the snow quality and terrain cruxes for the descent. If things seem to be deteriorating at all, consider turning around. The last few hundred feet of this climb are very steep; keep this in mind before you commit to the descent. If you fall here, you will most likely be unable to self-arrest (4.5 hours to here). In bad conditions, the slopes to the south may look like inviting bail-out options, but routes down to the Middle Fork Cascade River or to Cache Col come with their own set of difficulties and dangers. It is therefore extremely important to recognize the commitment level involved in undertaking this tour.

Breathe deeply at the col as you make your transition, and get ready for a big line! Enjoy the views of Sahale Peak, Forbidden Peak, and the Eldorado and Inspiration plateau, as well as the glimpses to the south of Mount Formidable and the Middle Fork Cascade River. You should be able to ski the couloir all the way back down to 3600 feet (6 hours to here). From here, reverse your ascent route back to the car (6.5 hours to here).

Tour Author: Forest McBrian

29 Spider Mountain: North Face (Arachnophobia)

Starting elevation: 2400 feet
High point: 8286 feet
Vertical gain/loss: 9980 feet/9980 feet
Distance: 24.5 km (15 miles)
Time: 2 days
Overall difficulty: extremely difficult
Ski skills: extremely difficult
Fitness level: very strenuous
Technical skills: very high
Commitment: extremely high
Gear: the basics, plus ski mountaineering equipment and overnight camping gear
Best season: April–June
USGS map: Cascade Pass
Permits: No parking pass is required to park anywhere along the Cascade River Road. A North Cascades National Park backcountry permit is required if you choose to camp on national park lands which are northeast of Cache Col.

The North Face of Spider Mountain from Arts Knoll (Martin Volken)

An extreme ski descent in a remote North Cascadian setting, the physically demanding North Face of Spider Mountain requires expert skiing ability and prior ski mountaineering experience. You will be rewarded with a super scenic camp at Arts Knoll and an unforgettable adventure on the steep flanks of Spider Mountain.

ACCESS

From Marblemount, turn right at a sharp bend in the highway onto the Cascade River Road. Drive up the road as far as possible. Normally you should be able to drive to a little pullout called Johnson Cabin near milepost 21 at 2400 feet, but the road is often gated here until early summer.

TOUR

DAY 1. From Johnson Cabin, tour up the Cascade River Road to its end at 3660 feet (1 hour to here). As you start, keep in mind that this entire tour takes place in extreme avalanche terrain. There will be only a few places where you are not subjected to avalanche hazard from above—careful consideration of snow stability cannot be over-emphasized as you progress.

Proceed toward Cascade Pass by touring up the valley headwall until you hit a steep section at around 4600 feet (see aerial photo for Tour 28). Tour or boot straight up until you can trend left at about 4800 feet. The terrain mellows out from there, and you should be able to reach Cascade Pass at 5400 feet easily (3 hours to here).

Boston Peak
Johnson Cabin trailhead
Cascade River Road
To Marblemount
Sahale Peak
North Fork Cascade River
Cascade Pass trailhead
North Cascades National Park
Doubtful Lake
Cascade Pass
short, steep section
Stehekin River
Johannesburg Mountain
Cascade Peak
Mix-Up Peak
Mount Baker–Snoqualmie National Forest
Yawning Glacier
Cache Col
Magic Mountain
Middle Fork Cascade River
Trapper Lake
S Glacier
Kool-Aid Lake
Glacier Peak Wilderness
Hurry-Up Peak
Arts Knoll Camp
Trapper Mountain
Middle Cascade Glacier
objective hazard above
Mount Formidable
Spider Glacier
true summit
Spider Mountain
N
0 .5 1 Mile
0 .5 1 Kilometer

From Cascade Pass, head south along the ridge to about 6000 feet. Now traverse southeast on the steep terrain of Mix-Up Peak with cliffs looming above and below until you reach the friendlier terrain of the Cache Glacier. Head to its high point and southern tip at 6940 feet (4.5–5 hours to here).

Enjoy spectacular views of Mount Formidable, and ski a long, descending traverse to about 6100 feet, which should get you close to a little pond called Kool-Aid Lake on the USGS map. From Kool-Aid Lake, you have one more gradual ascent to your camp at Arts Knoll. Tour southeast up these last 900 feet of vertical to the incredibly scenic camp right at the knoll at 7000 feet (6–7 hours to here).

DAY 2. From Arts Knoll, ski south, and traverse high enough so that you can make it into the upper basin that holds the Spider Glacier at around 5800 feet. Be mindful that the steep cliffs looming above you on the right get early morning sun. Ideally you want to climb and ski the North Face before the cliffs get too much sun and start shedding their snow. Once you enter the Spider Glacier, tour to the southeast corner of the closer of the two Spider Glacier lobes, which will bring you to the North Face headwall at around 6800 feet (1.5 hours to here).

Navigate the potentially substantial moat, and climb up the northeast-facing 1500-foot face to the summit at 8286 feet (3.5–4 hours to summit). The summit location of Spider Mountain is not indicated correctly on the topographic map; it is farther to the northwest by about 800 feet (250 meters).

From the ridge at 8220 feet, turn northwest and travel over easy but exposed terrain to the proper summit. Move over a gentler middle summit where you leave your skis, then progress on into a little notch, and up to the summit proper. The notch is the entrance to another descent option first skied by Ben Kaufman and Sky Sjue in February 2006, which is equally serious.

DESCENT. From the middle summit, ski back toward your climbing route, and carefully enter the steep face. Keep in mind that you have done a lot of touring and very little skiing before committing to these first, very steep turns—falling is not an option here. Once you are at the bottom (5 hours to here), keep moving quickly back to your camp. You will still have to move through a lot of avalanche-prone terrain as you retrace your route all the way back to your car (9–10 hours to your car).

Tour Author: Martin Volken

30 The Ptarmigan Traverse

Starting elevation: 3500 feet
High point: 8788 feet
Vertical gain/loss: 14,000 feet/16,100 feet
Distance: 66 km (41 miles)
Time: 3–5 days

Overall difficulty: difficult
Ski skills: moderate
Fitness level: strenuous
Technical skills: moderate
Commitment: very high
Gear: the basics, plus ski mountaineering and overnight equipment
Best season: May–July
USGS maps: Cascade Pass, Dome Peak, and Downey Mountain; recommended: National Geographic #223, North Cascades
Permits: Visitors to the Glacier Peak Wilderness must sign the trailhead register at the Downey Creek trailhead (and if you park there, you must display a Northwest Forest Pass or Interagency pass). If you plan to camp between Cache Col and the Cascade River Road, obtain an overnight backcountry permit at the Wilderness Information Center in Marblemount. No parking pass is required along the Cascade River Road.

In 1938 a Seattle climbing club called the Ptarmigans first completed the high route that would later bear their name. Their incredible tour-de-force began at Cascade Pass and headed south to Dome Peak and the Chickamin Glacier. Along the way, they made more than a dozen first ascents, sometimes several in one day. Brothers Lowell and Carl Skoog popularized the high route as a ski tour in the 1980s. With or without any summits, in one day or four, it is a magnificent high-alpine tour through some of the wildest reaches of the North Cascades. The four-day itinerary described here includes the summit of Dome Peak. Especially given the long trail and road walk on the tour's southern end, many will prefer to plan a five-day itinerary.

ACCESS

This tour requires a car shuttle. From Darrington, head north on State Route 530 for 8 miles. Just after you cross the Sauk River on a steel bridge, turn east onto the Suiattle River Road (Forest Service Road 26), and follow it about 12 miles to a barrier and parking pullout where the road was damaged by flooding in 2006. Stop here, or if the road has been repaired, continue on to the Downey Creek trailhead.

To get to your starting trailhead from there, head back out to State Route 530. Turn north on it, and continue on it for 11 miles to the North Cascades Highway (State Route 20). Turn right onto the highway, and drive 8 miles to Marblemount. Stop in at the Wilderness Information Center if you need to. At a sharp bend in the highway in Marblemount, turn right onto the Cascade River Road, and follow it 23 miles to its end at the Cascade Pass trailhead

The Ptarmigan Traverse from the north (Scott Schell)

(the road is often gated at mile 21 in the spring). It takes about an hour to drive from Darrington to the trailhead and an hour and a half to drive from there to the Cascade Pass trailhead.

TOUR

DAY 1. If the snowpack allows, ski directly up the North Fork Cascade River valley following the lowest-angle terrain. You must negotiate one steep section on the way to Cascade Pass just above 4600 feet (see aerial photo for Tour 28). With less snowcover, follow the switchbacking Cascade Pass Trail (2 hours to Cascade Pass). From the pass, turn right and follow Mix-Up Arm south to about 5800 feet. Expect to negotiate a wind lip or cornice here, and evaluate the northeast-facing slope beyond. This steep slope traverses above big cliffs and can be nerve-racking in poor conditions. Consider climbing higher up low-angle terrain on the crest of the arm and then skiing the traverse as a downhill leg. In either case, gain a ridge at 6200 feet, and descend slightly to the edge of the Cache Glacier (unmarked on USGS maps; 3.5 hours to here).

Climb to the 6940-foot Cache Col, the high col on the upper left section of the glacier (4.75 hours to here). Ski a descending traverse to your camping area, the diminutive Kool-Aid Lake, which is often hidden by snowcover (5.25 hours to here).

DAY 2. Skin on a level traverse south, heading for 6320 feet on the west spur of Arts Knoll. This is Red Ledge, the third-class weakness that the Ptarmigan summer route exploits. Earlier in the season, however, it is a steep snow gully requiring a short bootpack (you can also cross the ridge lower and farther west, but you will still need to boot for a stretch). From the crest of the ridge, make a descending traverse to about 6000 feet at the eastern edge of the Middle Cascade Glacier (1 hour from camp).

Skin up the slope immediately above, reaching the glacier where it is gentler, at about 6600 feet. From here make a rising traverse toward Spider-Formidable Col, avoiding the glacier's steeper and more crevassed portions (2.25 hours to here). Head for the easternmost of two notches (the other leads to cliffs on the south side).

Ski down the steep slope on the south side, and start the long descending traverse toward Yang-Yang Lakes (some sidestepping necessary; 3.25 hours to here). From the lakes, locate a steep gully on a ridge to the southwest (the gully is a little southeast of Point 7004). Skin toward and then up this gully to gain the ridge. Follow the ridge south to 7000 feet and a grand view of the Le Conte Glacier (4.75 hours to here).

A long descending traverse to the southeast should bring you to the edge of the Le Conte Glacier at about 6400 feet. Continue to the southeast, climbing the western edge of the glacier to 7300 feet and a big col north of Sentinel Peak (6.25 hours to here).

Ski south-southwest and then south, staying as high as possible on a descent to the head of the South Cascade Glacier. Careful routefinding and a little bit of sidestepping should let you cross the glacier and gain the col west of Lizard Mountain without putting on your skins (6.5 hours to here).

Ski the slope down to White Rock Lakes, watching out for steep rolling terrain and rock islands midway down. Look for great campsites along the southern edge of the middle lake overlooking one of the greatest vistas in all the Cascades (6.75 hours to here).

DAY 3. From White Rock Lakes, begin the traverse toward the Dana Glacier, dropping at first to 5800 feet beneath some cliffs. Ascend toward the toe of the northeast spur of Point 7940, passing just beneath it shortly before leveling off the traverse at 6600 feet. (From this point, an early exit to Cub Lake and Bachelor Creek can be made by climbing the Dana Glacier and passing over the col southeast of Spire Point.) Continue contouring under a steeper, broken portion of the glacier until you are able to climb the gentler eastern slopes of the Dana Glacier. Climb to the easternmost of the two cols (2.5 hours from camp).

If you got an early start, you should be able to drop your overnight gear here, and summit Dome Peak. Skin east-southeast toward a col at the top of the Dome Glacier, northwest of the summit. From the col, climb south via a snow arête that is clearly visible on the USGS map, though it appears as rock, not snow, on the map. Follow it to a false summit; a sharp snow crest leads to the true summit about 50 meters farther on. With some creativity and careful ropework, you can negotiate the exposed traverse. The final step of fourth-class rock makes for an exciting finish (3.75 hours to here).

To Marblemount
North Fork Cascade
River
Cascade River Road
Cascade River
15
Cascade Pass trailhead/start
Horseshoe Basin
North Cascades National Park
Cascade Pass
Johannesburg Mountain
Mix-Up Peak
Cache Col
Magic Mountain
Trapper Lake
South Fork Cascade River
Middle Fork Cascade River
Camp 1
Hurry-Up Peak
Trapper Mountain
Middle Cascade Glacier
Mount Formidable
Spider Mountain
Okanogan–Wenatchee National Forest
Mount Baker–Snoqualmie National Forest
Glacier Peak Wilderness
Le Conte Mountain
South Cascade Lake
South Cascade Glacier
Le Conte Glacier
Sentinel Peak
Old Guard Peak
Lizard Mountain
Mount Buckindy
Downey Creek
Camp 2
White Rock Lakes
Spire Glacier
Spire Point
Dana
Glacier
Chickamin Glacier
Bachelor Creek
Camp 3
Cub Lake
Itswoot Lake
Itswoot Ridge
Dome Glacier
Dome Peak
Downey Creek
Sulphur Creek
Downey Mountain
Downey Creek trailhead/finish
26
Suiattle River Road
To 530 and Darrington
Suiattle River
Sulphur Mountain
N
0 .5 1 Mile
0 .5 1 Kilometer

Ski back to your gear at the col between the Dana and Dome Glaciers (4.25 hours to here). Ski southwest and then west, holding your elevation and taking care around a number of steep rib and gully features in the basin. The ridge east of Itswoot Lake is known as Itswoot Ridge. Cross it at 6200 feet where a short bootpack may be necessary; be wary of cornices here. Several steep rolls guard the way down to Cub Lake (5.5 hours to here).

Skirt Cub Lake on its north side, and climb the 500-foot slope to the northwest, gaining a treed col above Bachelor Creek (6 hours to here). Ski northwest down the gentle basin, following the creek. At 5400 feet make an abrupt turn to the southwest to follow the creek down a slide path. The south side of the creek usually offers fairly open ground for skiing; keep an eye out for the summer climber's trail here. Big trees and boulders provide decent camping at 4600 feet at the edge of the creek (6.25 hours to here).

DAY 4. Follow the climber's path along the south side of Bachelor Creek. The path is faint at times and often overgrown with slide alder. If this area is still snow covered, be sure to plan ahead to where you will join the trail to avoid unnecessary bushwhacking. Cross the creek with the path around 3750 feet—a key transition because the trail becomes much friendlier on the north side (1.5 hours to here). Now follow the rapidly improving trail down to the confluence of Bachelor and Downey Creeks (2.5 hours to here).

Enjoy the deep old-growth forest on the 6-mile trail following Downey Creek down to the Suiattle River. There are many good campsites available along this stretch of trail (5 hours to here).

All that remains is a flat, 8-mile stroll back to your car (8 hours to here).

Tour Author: Forest McBrian

31 The North Central Cascades Traverse

Starting elevation: 3230 feet
High point: 10,541 feet
Vertical gain/loss: 30,290 feet/32,110 feet
Distance: 72 km (45 miles)
Time: 7–8 days
Overall difficulty: extremely difficult
Ski skills: very difficult
Fitness level: extremely strenuous
Technical skills: high
Commitment: very high
Gear: the basics, plus ski mountaineering and overnight equipment
Best season: March–June

USGS maps: Holden, Suiattle Pass, Clark Mountain, Glacier Peak East, Glacier Peak West, and Sloan Peak

Permits: A Northwest Forest Pass or Interagency Pass is required to park a vehicle at the North Fork Sauk River trailhead. Fill out a wilderness permit at the trailhead when you leave Holden.

This traverse follows a high route west across the Glacier Peak Wilderness through continuously phenomenal terrain. The adventurous explorer is rewarded with multiple steep, 3500-foot descents and many transitions above 7000 feet in a remote section of the Cascades. Any one of the suggested campsites could be respected as a multiday destination base camp with the plethora of hard-to-reach ski objectives in its immediate vicinity, and each camp will have you pondering future trips. The opportunity for a summit ski off Glacier Peak makes an excellent bonus.

ACCESS

From Chelan, drive west on State Route 97 for 3.7 miles. Turn right at State Route 971 South (Lakeshore Road), and travel 8.5 miles to Fields Point Landing. You must pay a fee to park overnight either at the dock in Chelan or at Fields Point Landing. Take the *Lady of the Lake* ferry (reserve boat tickets ahead of time) to Lucerne.

From Lucerne, ride the bus up to Holden Village where you can enjoy some time with the friendly people of this camp before beginning the traverse. Contact Holden Village prior to your departure to ensure that there is space for you and your party on the bus up to Holden. Remember to coordinate a vehicle drop-off at the North Fork Sauk River trailhead for your exit.

To get to this trailhead from Darrington, travel south along the Mountain Loop Highway for 16 miles before taking a left on Forest Service Road 49. Follow FS Road 49 for 6.7 miles to the trailhead at 2080 feet.

TOUR

DAY 1. From the bus drop-off area in Holden at 3230 feet, hike the road west a couple hundred feet, and cross Railroad Creek on the first bridge. Hike or skin up the west side of Copper Creek to where the valley flattens out around 4250 feet (1.5 hours to here). You are now in big country that quickly introduces you to the commitment level of this traverse. Cross the valley, and climb through a steep section of trees east of the main drainage. Continue touring south through the flat meadow at 5570 feet, and climb southwest to the col at 7200 feet (4.5 hours to here).

Descend 1500 feet to the Entiat River, and pick a safe camp location where you can relish the ski potential off the north faces of Mount Maude and the Spectacle Buttes.

DAY 2. Leave early for the large climb up and over Mount Fernow's southern shoulder. From camp at 5700 feet, skin west up the valley to about 6500 feet where you turn right and travel north up the glacier on Fernow's southeast slopes. Climb the short, steep

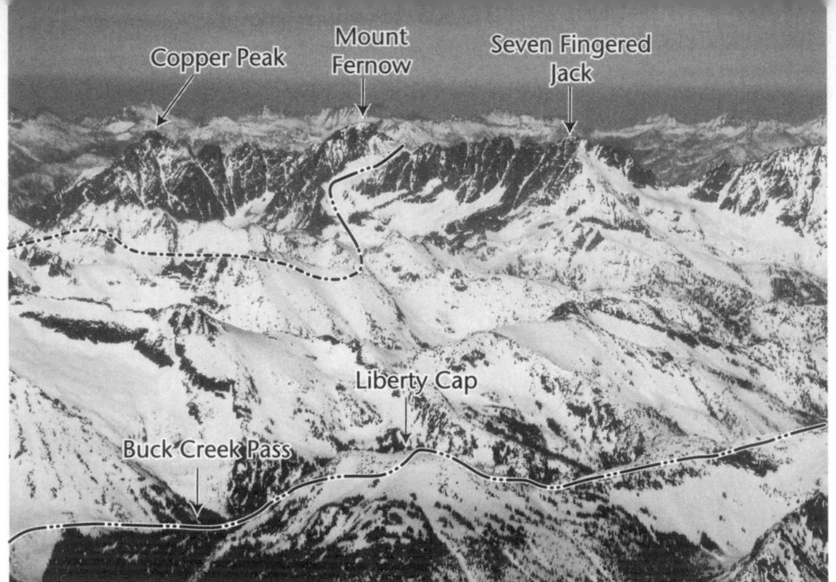

The North Central Cascades Traverse from the southwest (Trevor Kostanich)

gully off the upper right side of this glacier to around 8000 feet to navigate around a cliff band (2.5 hours to here).

Skin or boot west-northwest to the shoulder (8960 feet) south of Mount Fernow's summit. From this high point, you will likely have to downclimb through some rocks to reach more continuous snow.

Ski down to the right enjoying more than 2500 feet of continuously steep turns. From the bench at 7000 feet, ski southwest through a gully and across another flat bench at 6610 feet. Exit this bench west, and enjoy another thousand feet of enjoyable turns among larch trees down the head of Big Creek. Set camp around 5600 feet with access to running water (5 hours to here).

DAY 3. Ski down the drainage staying left of the creek where it steepens near 5400 feet. Traverse left out into open slopes, and transition to skinning. Climb to Dumbell Lake, initially staying left of the drainage and then following the more open slopes to the right. From the lake, climb to the obvious col at 7850 feet north of Dumbell Mountain (3 hours to here). From this col, admire your previous day's descent down Mount Fernow's west side and the endless opportunities stretching from Copper Peak to Fernow to Seven Fingered Jack through unnamed peaks to Dumbell. Then turn around and admire the ruggedness of Bonanza Peak and the friendlier snow-blanketed slopes of North Star Mountain and Cloudy Peak to the northwest.

Ski northwest to 6900 feet. From here, descend more northerly on more moderate terrain, avoiding cliffs on skier's left. Climax slides on rock slabs around 6000 feet sometimes create challenging sections along this generally moderate path. If there is potential for climax slides, you can descend left of the slabs through steep terrain where a 30-meter rappel may be necessary

Variation. From 6900 feet, continue down on the left side through some steep rocks that open up to great fall-line skiing. Ski until the slope flattens around 5200 feet

Holden
start
To Lucerne
Railroad Creek
Copper Creek
Buckskin Mountain
CHELAN MOUNTAINS
Entiat River
Camp 1
Spectacle Buttes
Ice Lakes
Entiat Glacier
ENTIAT MOUNTAINS
Carne Mountain
Mount Maude
Seven Fingered Jack
Mount Fernow
Copper Peak
Big Creek
Camp 2
Phelps Creek
Dumbell Mountain
Red Mountain
Phelps Ridge
Railroad Creek
Lyman Glacier
Chiwawa River
Camp 3
Chiwawa Mountain
Lyman Lake
Okanogan–Wenatchee National Forest
Glacier Peak Wilderness
Buck Mountain
Fortress Mountain
Suiattle Pass
Miners Creek
Buck Creek
High Pass
Continues on inset
Pass No Pass
Helmet Butte
Camp 4
Point 6909
Liberty Cap
Buck Creek Pass
Flower Dome
6247
Small Creek
Middle Ridge
Pacific Crest Trail
Suiattle River
0 .5 1 Mile
0 .5 1 Kilometer
N

(4 hours to here). Take a well-deserved rest here after navigating another sporty descent. You will likely be breaking out the second map for the first time during your trip—yes, you have traveled almost three full days, and all you have needed is the Holden map. This says a couple of things: one, the Holden quad encompasses big terrain, and two, you covered a lot of it.

With reassurance from the Suiattle Pass map, travel south-southwest to the col around 7000 feet that looks down on the Lyman Glacier. From the col, ski left avoiding a cliff band halfway down the slope, and set camp on the bottom of the Lyman Glacier around 6000 feet (6 hours to here).

DAY 4. Your destination today is Buck Creek Pass. An alternate route, that involves ridge climbing over the summits of the Chiwawa and Fortress Mountains, is not described, since poor conditions forced the pioneering party to travel northwest into Miners Creek and then counterclockwise around Fortress Mountain.

Skin southwest up the Lyman Glacier toward Chiwawa Mountain. At about 7600 feet, trend right and attain the subpeak north of Chiwawa's true summit (2 hours to here). From this 8000-foot-plus high point, downclimb to steep snow where a ski belay may be prudent. This descent follows continuous snow, first skiing right to 7400 feet and then traversing left above a cliff band. Now ski the fall line to a bench at 5900 feet and continue down Miners Creek to flatter terrain at 4600 feet (3.5 hours to here).

Travel west along the south side of the creek for a couple kilometers, and then veer south at 4460 feet to climb the unnamed drainage. At 5800 feet traverse west and climb over Middle Ridge just southeast of Point 6247 (6.5 hours to here).

Ski south through trees to Small Creek. Skin up Small Creek until the drainage forks around 4800 feet. Follow the small drainage southeast and then south to a col between Flower Dome and Helmet Butte just above 5800 feet. From this col, maintain your elevation on a clockwise traverse to Buck Creek Pass (8 hours to here). Enjoy some rest and refueling after a demanding day.

DAY 5. Your fifth day follows a high route from Buck Creek Pass toward High Pass that offers fantastic views in all directions, most notably of the bulky massif of Glacier Peak to the west. Skin south up Liberty Cap, favoring its western side. From the south end of the summit, ski south to the col at 6440 feet (1.5 hours to here).

Climb past Point 6909, again favoring the west side, to a saddle at 6800 feet. Ski off the east side of this col and traverse past Point 7276. Climb through a weakness in the corniced saddle between Point 7276 and Mount Cleator (3 hours to here). Ski southwest to 6300 feet, and then climb the ridge south over Triad Lake and finally to the saddle (4 hours to here).

Before descending south from your high point, scan the horizon. If time and energy allow, you have great ski opportunities off Mount Berge to the east and Napeequa Peak to the west. Ski south following the drainage to its confluence with the Napeequa River at 4880 feet (5 hours to here).

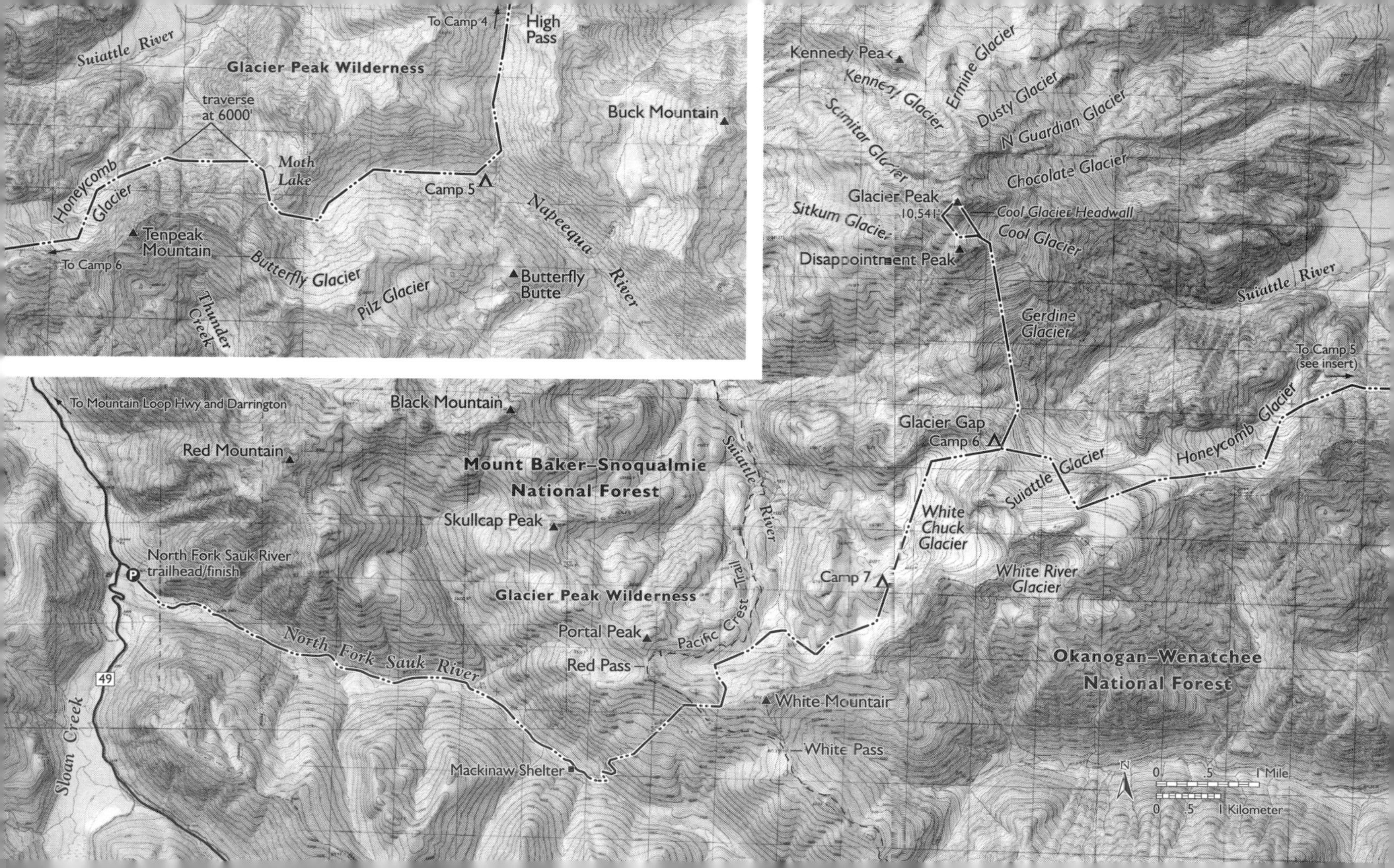

To Camp 4
High Pass
Suiattle River
Glacier Peak Wilderness
traverse at 6000'
Buck Mountain
Moth Lake
Honeycomb Glacier
Camp 5
Napeequa River
Tenpeak Mountain
To Camp 6
Butterfly Glacier
Butterfly Butte
Pilz Glacier
Thunder Creek
Kennedy Peak
Kennedy Glacier
Ermine Glacier
Dusty Glacier
N Guardian Glacier
Scimitar Glacier
Chocolate Glacier
Glacier Peak
10,541'
Cool Glacier Headwall
Sitkum Glacier
Cool Glacier
Disappointment Peak
Suiattle River
Gerdine Glacier
To Camp 5 (see insert)
To Mountain Loop Hwy and Darrington
Black Mountain
Glacier Gap
Camp 6
Honeycomb Glacier
Red Mountain
Mount Baker–Snoqualmie National Forest
Suiattle Glacier
Suiattle River
White Chuck Glacier
Skullcap Peak
North Fork Sauk River trailhead/finish
Camp 7
White River Glacier
Glacier Peak Wilderness
Portal Peak
Pacific Crest Trail
North Fork Sauk River
Red Pass
Okanogan–Wenatchee National Forest
49
White Mountain
Sloan Creek
White Pass
Mackinaw Shelter
N
0 .5 1 Mile
0 .5 1 Kilometer

DAY 6. Skin west up the head of the Napeequa River. Just below the Butterfly Glacier at 6200 feet, climb west to a saddle above Moth Lake (2.5 hours to here). Ski over Moth Lake, continue out its northwest drainage, and then traverse west across Tenpeak Mountain's northern slopes.

Ski west to maintain elevation, and cross through the first of many steep gullies. Transition to skins (and likely ski crampons) to continue traversing at the 6000-foot level, crossing steep slide paths before arriving on a bench at 6020 feet (4 hours to here).

Ski southwest onto the Honeycomb Glacier, and then begin a long, easy climb up this massive flow of ice. Cross onto the Suiattle Glacier at the upper saddle around 7800 feet (6.5 hours to here). Ski down the Suiattle Glacier enjoying smooth glacier turns, and then climb west to Glacier Gap (the saddle connecting the Suiattle Glacier with the White Chuck Basin at 7300 feet). Set camp somewhere on or near Glacier Gap at 7300 feet (7.5 hours to here).

DAY 7. Glacier Peak is the most remote of the five major volcanoes in Washington, and you are now camped on its southern flanks. If conditions are adequate and you have sufficient provisions, make this seldom-skied volcano your day's objective. Leave camp with a day pack, and ski northwest down the Suiattle Glacier gliding left over small ridges to a rocky bench at 7000 feet. Skin north up the Gerdine Glacier contouring around gentle ridges and across friendly faces to the col east of Disappointment Peak at 9150 feet (2.5 hours to here).

Traversing onto the Cool Glacier, you will notice more crevasses and broken terrain than you experienced on the Suiattle and Gerdine Glaciers. While skinning to the saddle north of Disappointment Peak, observe the ski lines on the Cool Glacier Headwall and the bergschrund that is likely starting to open at the bottom. Though steep, these lines can provide better skiing than the bumpy terrain you will climb up on the southwest side. From the saddle on the south ridge, climb out onto the southwest face, and ascend the smoothest gully to the summit ridge. The true summit is on the west end of this ridge at 10,541 feet (4 hours to here).

Descend the Cool Glacier Headwall or south summit gully, and meet back up with your ascent route at the col east of Disappointment Peak at 9150 feet. Enjoy large turns down the moderate Gerdine and Suiattle Glaciers back to the rocky bench at 7000 feet, and then skin back to camp at Glacier Gap (5.5 hours to here). Take a well-deserved rest at camp, and relish in your surroundings before loading up the packs.

The White Chuck Basin is large, and of the several alternate paths through this basin, the described route is the safest and easiest to navigate in case you have limited visibility. Ski west down to 6700 feet, and then transition to skins. Contour south-southwest maintaining the same elevation for 2 kilometers (1.2 miles), and set up camp at the broad saddle at 6700 feet (7.5 hours to here).

DAY 8. Begin the last morning of this traverse by skiing south from camp. At about 6300 feet glide or skate west before enjoying 400 vertical feet of steeper turns. Follow the drainage south, then west, and finally northwest through the flats just under 5600 feet. Traverse left around ridges, and glide down to 5460 feet before putting on your skins for the final time. Skin southwest to 5800 feet, and climb south to the col west of White Mountain at 6620 feet (2 hours to here).

For the last descent, traverse right and then enjoy fantastic fall-line skiing through steeper trees into a flatter portion at 4600 feet that sees many large avalanches from above (3 hours to here). Depending on snow coverage, you may be able to pick up the North Fork Sauk River Trail on skier's right in the forest. If snow persists, ski right into the larger trees, and find the trail to avoid steeper Cascadian bushwhacking at lower elevations. Hike the trail past the Mackinaw Shelter and the final 8 kilometers (5 miles) through healthy forest to the trailhead and your car (6 hours to here).

Tour Author: Trevor Kostanich

32 Whitehorse Mountain

Starting elevation: 915 feet
High point: 6840 feet
Vertical gain/loss: 5925 feet/5925 feet
Distance: 10 km (6.2 miles)
Time: 7–9 hours
Overall difficulty: moderate
Ski skills: difficult
Fitness level: very strenuous
Technical skills: moderate
Commitment: low
Gear: the basics, plus ski mountaineering equipment
Best season: January–May
USGS map: Whitehorse Mountain
Permits: A Northwest Forest Pass or Interagency Pass is required to park at the trailhead, which is in Mount Baker–Snoqualmie National Forest.

Whitehorse Mountain rises dramatically above the town of Darrington, offering a juxtaposition of urban and alpine that is rare in the Cascades. The distraction of Whitehorse and its dramatic relief pose a serious hazard to skiers driving 50 miles per hour on the highway along the Stillaguamish River, and it is hard not to ask yourself what it would be like to ski the line. But catching it in the right condition requires diligence and patience. The lower gullies typically fill with avalanche debris at some point in winter, simplifying travel in the lower elevation section; even then you can expect to become intimate with some sturdy, cliff-dwelling shrubs. This outing is direct, steep, and physical—a one-day extravaganza of Cascadian ski mountaineering.

Whitehorse Mountain from the north (Scott Schell)

ACCESS

From Arlington, follow State Route 530 for 23 miles toward Darrington, and take a right on Mine Road near a gas station and convenience store. Follow Mine Road south past some private residences. At 0.5 mile from the highway, stay left at two forks in the road. The road may be gated here, adding 2 kilometers (1.2 miles) and 400 feet of elevation to your ascent. The road climbs and becomes fairly rough; park 1.8 miles from the highway at the trailhead for the Neiderprum-Whitehorse Mountain Trail (Forest Service Trail 953) at an elevation of 915 feet.

TOUR

Rather than taking the trail, continue along the road 1.3 kilometers (0.8 mile) through some brushy sections to an elevation of 1000 feet where the road ends at Snow Gulch (0.5 hour to here). From here, your line of ascent lies straight up the drainage, staying left at major forks. Diverting left of the gut (terrain crease) in places may get you around some cliffs; shallow snow and scoured bed surfaces may also influence your choice. This is severe avalanche terrain, and you should feel very confident about snow stability. Expect to have your skis on your back for the first few thousand feet.

Eventually the angle eases slightly, and skinning becomes possible. Work south and east toward the ridge that divides Sill Basin from the unlabeled Whitehorse Glacier.

It runs south from Point 5436; you want to reach the flat spot at 5760 feet along this ridge that lies 0.5 kilometer south of Point 5436. Be careful of wind lips or cornices that may form here as you gain the ridge (5 hours to here).

From the ridge, climb onto the So-Bahli-Ahli Glacier, and head southeast up benches toward the summit. Note that on the USGS map "Whitehorse Mountain" is not printed next to the true summit, which lies at the southern tip of the glacier. The final slopes to the summit, which stands at 6840 feet, are steep and will likely require you to carry skis once more (5.75 hours to here).

DESCENT. Now is the time to psych yourself up for the descent—right back down the way you came. Hopefully the ascent will have given you an idea of where to find the best snow. The entire basin abounds in steep rolls, cliffs, and dense bands of vegetation—be careful when leaving your line of ascent for the unknown. Regain the debris-filled gullies of Snow Gulch, and follow the road back to your car (8.5 hours round-trip).

Tour Author: Forest McBrian

33 Glacier Peak: Gerdine and Cool Glaciers

Starting elevation: 2080 feet
High point: 10,541 feet
Vertical gain/loss: 12,960 feet/12,960 feet
Distance: 50 km (31 miles)
Time: 3 days
Overall difficulty: moderate
Ski skills: moderate
Fitness level: strenuous
Technical skills: moderate
Commitment: high
Gear: the basics, plus ski mountaineering and overnight equipment
Best season: April–July
USGS maps: Sloan Peak, Glacier Peak East, and Glacier Peak West
Permits: A Northwest Forest Pass or Interagency Pass is required to park at the North Fork Sauk River trailhead, which is in Mount Baker–Snoqualmie National Forest. Fill out a wilderness permit at this trailhead.

Glacier Peak is the most remote of the five major volcanoes in Washington. Lacking the prominent visibility of Rainier and Baker from west side population hubs, this stratovolcano provides a more isolated experience. For those who would rather tour across wolverine tracks than other human tracks, this is your volcano.

ACCESS

From Darrington, travel south along the Mountain Loop Highway (Forest Service Road 20) for 16 miles. Take a left on North Fork Sauk River Road (Forest Service Road 49), and follow it for 6.7 miles to the North Fork Sauk River Trail at 2080 feet. Vehicle break-ins are common here; leave nothing valuable in your car.

TOUR

DAY 1. Hike the North Fork Sauk River Trail through enormous cedar and fir trees on the north side of the river. After about 8 kilometers (5 miles), pass the Mackinaw Shelter at 2960 feet before the trail begins climbing northeast (2.5 hours to here). Follow the hiking trail until you hit consistent snow and it becomes more efficient to skin—likely around 4600 feet at the bottom of a large slide path. Lighten your backpack by stashing your hiking shoes here. Skin up steep terrain, trending right to the col west of White Mountain at 6620 feet (6.5 hours to here).

All your hard work is rewarded with alpine views north into the White Chuck Basin with Glacier Peak rising beyond. The large White Chuck Basin is primarily

Kennedy Glacier
N Guardian Glacier
Scimitar Glacier
Chocolate Glacier
Lake Byrne
Glacier Peak
10,541'
Cool Glacier Headwall
Sitkum Glacier
Cool Glacier
Disappointment Peak
White Chuck River
Pacific Crest Trail
Mount Baker–Snoqualmie National Forest
Glacier Peak Wilderness
Gerdine Glacier
To Mountain Loop Hwy and Darrington
Black Mountain
Glacier Gap
Red Mountain
Painted Mountain
Suiattle Glacier
49
Skullcap Peak
White Chuck Glacier
North Fork Sauk River trailhead
White River Glacier
White Chuck Cinder Cone
North Fork Sauk River
Portal Peak
Camp 1 and 2
Okanogan–Wenatchee National Forest
Red Pass
Sloan Creek
White Mountain
N
0 .5 1 Mile
0 .5 1 Kilometer
White Pass
Mackinaw Shelter

Glacier Peak from the south; the Gerdine Glacier is on middle-right. (Kurt Hicks)

above tree line, which creates routefinding challenges when visibility is limited. From the col, ski north and then descend the drainage east-northeast to 5460 feet. Skin east over a small rib and then southeast into a flat meadow a little below 5600 feet. Continue climbing east onto a large bench at 6250 feet. Here is a great spot to set up a base camp for the next couple of nights (8 hours to here).

If your team has ample energy and daylight, you can camp closer to Glacier Gap (the col connecting White Chuck Basin and the Suiattle Glacier at 7300 feet) for a shorter summit day.

DAY 2. Leave camp with a day pack destined for Glacier Peak. Climb northeast to a broad saddle at 6700 feet. Contour north-northeast maintaining the same elevation (6700 feet) for about 2 kilometers (1.2 miles) before climbing east-northeast to Glacier Gap at 7300 feet (2 hours to here).

Ski northeast down the Suiattle Glacier gliding left over small ridges to a rocky bench at 7000 feet. Skin north up the Gerdine Glacier contouring around gentle ridges and across friendly faces to the col east of Disappointment Peak at 9150 feet (4.5 hours to here).

Traversing onto the Cool Glacier, you will notice more crevasses and broken terrain than you experienced on the Suiattle and Gerdine Glaciers. While skinning to the saddle north of Disappointment Peak, observe the ski lines on the Cool Glacier Headwall and the bergschrund that is likely starting to open at the bottom. Though steep, these lines can provide better skiing than the bumpy terrain you will climb up on the southwest side. From the saddle on the south ridge, climb out onto the southwest face, and ascend the smoothest gully to the summit ridge. The true summit is the west end of this ridge at 10,541 feet (6 hours to here).

Descend the Cool Glacier Headwall or south summit gully, and meet back up with your ascent route at the col east of Disappointment Peak at 9150 feet. Enjoy large turns down the moderate Gerdine Glacier back to the rocky bench at 7000 feet, and then skin back to Glacier Gap (7.5 hours to here). Retrace your morning ascent route, celebrating fun turns, before having to skin a couple kilometers again at the 6700-foot contour to the saddle above your camp. One final transition here has you sliding into camp content with a clearer understanding why Glacier Peak sees so few visitors (9 hours to here).

DAY 3. Ski west back down to the flat meadow area at 5600 feet. Traverse left around ridges, and glide down to 5460 feet before putting skins on for the final time. Skin southwest to 5800 feet, and then climb south to the col west of White Mountain at 6620 feet (1.5 hours from camp). Begin your descent traversing right and then enjoy fantastic fall-line skiing down to your hiking shoes (2 hours from camp). Hike the trail past the Mackinaw Shelter and the final 8 kilometers (5 miles) through the forest to the trailhead (5.5 hours to here).

Tour Author: Trevor Kostanich

34 Mount Pilchuck: The Gunsight

Starting elevation: 3160 feet (from the summer trailhead)
High point: 5340 feet
Vertical gain/loss: 2650 feet/2650 feet
Distance: 5.5 km (3.4 miles)
Time: 4 hours
Overall difficulty: moderate
Ski skills: very difficult
Fitness level: moderately strenuous
Technical skills: moderate
Commitment: low
Gear: the basics
Best season: April–June, depending on snow levels
USGS map: Verlot
Permits: Although most of this tour is in Mount Pilchuck State Park, the Mount Pilchuck and Heather Lake trailheads are in Mount Baker–Snoqualmie National Forest, which requires a Northwest Forest Pass or Interagency Pass for parking.

Mount Pilchuck is a fun, easily accessible ski tour that includes slopes that were once part of the old Mount Pilchuck Ski Area. The ski area's last season was 1978, but since then Mount Pilchuck has become a popular spring ski touring destination with a unique setting overlooking Puget Sound on one side and the central Cascades on the other. Although Mount Pilchuck's western position in the range means that it receives a healthy mix of both rain and snow during the winter, its north-facing terrain builds and holds snow depth surprisingly late into spring.

Its proximity to lowland population centers allows for quick access once snow melts enough to make the approach up the Mount Pilchuck Road reasonable. Although the trail to the fire lookout on the summit is heavily used by hikers during summer, skiing Pilchuck's less-traveled snow-covered slopes provides fresh perspective on what the mountain is all about beyond the view from the top. Venturing into these areas reveals the variety of open rolling terrain and short, steep descents that attracted skiers here to begin with.

ACCESS

From Granite Falls, drive 12 miles east on the Mountain Loop Highway. Just after you cross the Stillaguamish River, turn right onto Mount Pilchuck Road (Forest Service Road 42). Mount Pilchuck Road is normally only plowed to the Heather Lake trailhead during winter, but once the gate is open, follow the road to the snow line or all the way to the Mount Pilchuck summer trailhead.

TOUR

Start the tour from the summer trailhead at 3160 feet. If the road is blocked by snow lower down, follow the road up to that point. If the snow is deep low on the mountain, clearings can be linked up the east side of Rotary Creek to avoid the last long road switchback before the summer parking area. These clearings coincide with the bottom of the old ski area starting at 2500 feet, but brush is reclaiming the area and makes uphill travel off the road a challenge, depending on the snow depth.

The old ski area slopes continue up from the east end of the summer trailhead parking lot. With good snow coverage found at this elevation, you can skin directly from here. Otherwise, follow the summer trail, or exit left a few hundred yards up the trail to use openings up a moderately timbered slope that leads to an old access road. Follow this road as it wraps around and then ascends southeast to the knoll just north of the tarn at 3800 feet that is unnamed on the USGS map.

Find the draw heading east-northeast that leads to a saddle south of Point 3945. From here climb south up the ridge to 4400 feet and onto open, lower angled north-facing slopes. Trend south-southeast to gain the saddle on the northwest ridge to regain the route of the summer trail as it crosses the ridge (1.75 hours to here from the summer trailhead).

Contour up and around the northwest ridge through small trees, generally on or above the summer route to the summit. At the summit, climb a short ladder to the fire lookout built in 1921 and currently maintained for public use by the Everett Branch of The Mountaineers in conjunction with Washington State Parks. Learn about those who came before and built the lookout through the historical display inside, and enjoy the views that attract the summer masses.

DESCENT. Leave the crowds behind, and ski east from the summit to what has become known as the Gunsight couloir, named for its distinct resemblance to a gunsight when viewed from the west. The Gunsight is a short (500 feet), steep, but wide couloir that

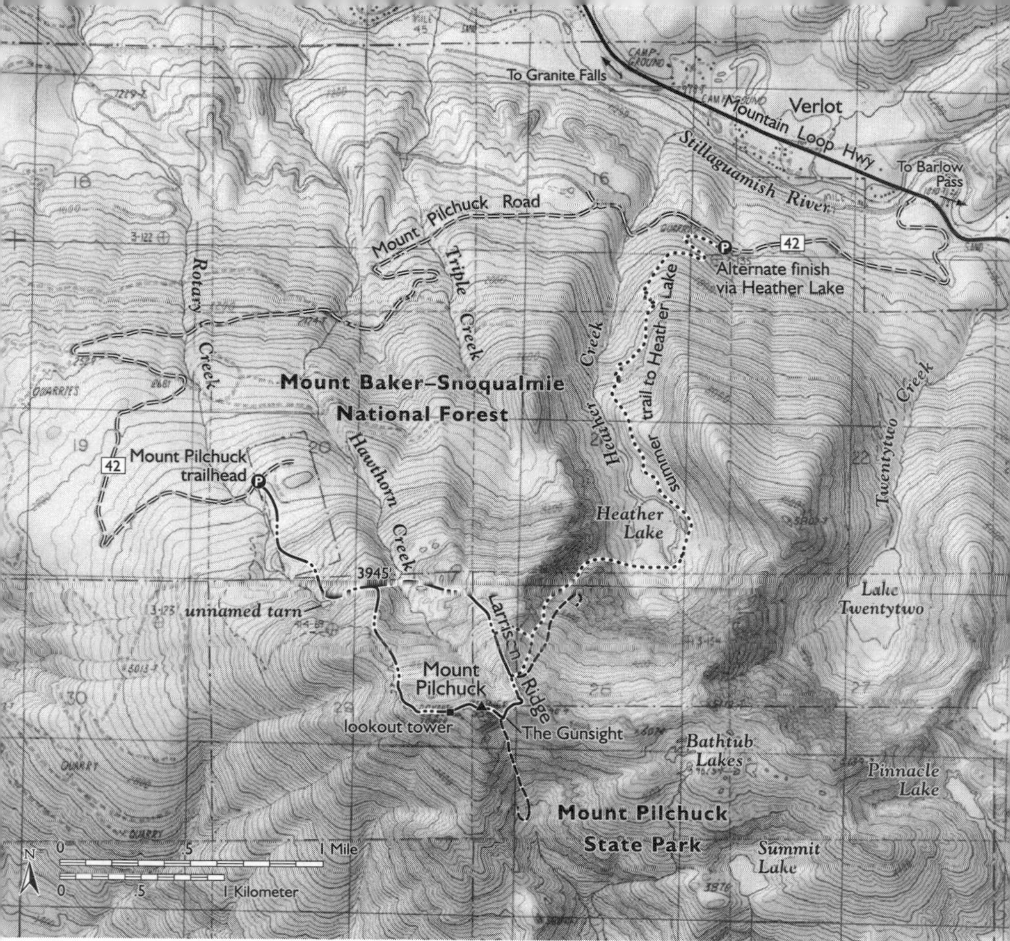

descends east and then southeast into a bowl on the south side of the mountain. The skier's right side has a short section at the top with a slope angle in the upper 40-degree range, while the skier's left is in the mid- to lower 40-degree range. The slope angle eases mid-couloir and then again as it empties into the main bowl.

From the base of the couloir, you can ski an additional 1000 feet down into the lower drainage by trending skier's right near the trees at the bottom of the main bowl to find a straight and narrow line to the valley floor. Climb back up steep trees climber's left of the fall line. If climbing back out of the drainage is not appealing, stop at the bottom of the Gunsight, and skin up or boot to the low point on the east ridge just above to the left. Follow the ridge up the knoll to the east, just west of Point 5198 (3 hours to here with a break at the summit and not descending the south bowl).

From the knoll, ski the rolling benches north-northwest on what is commonly referred to as Larrison Ridge, staying on the ridge crest to avoid cliffs on either side. Continue along Larrison Ridge and over benches to 4000 feet. From 4000 feet, head west into the Hawthorn Creek drainage. Cross the drainage, and skin or boot up 100 feet to the saddle near Point 3945 to regain the ascent route. Follow the ascent route from here back to the trailhead. If there is enough snow coverage, you can also exit

Mount Pilchuck from the northeast (Scott Schell)

by continuing farther down Hawthorn Creek and traversing to the trailhead at 3200 feet (4 hours to here).

Alternate descents can be made from Larrison Ridge into the cirque above Heather Lake. At 4800 feet along the ridge, find a chute to access the cirque, or go another 200 feet down the ridge for an easier entrance off the shoulder. You can make a fun 1400-foot descent on open slopes by staying skier's left onto a rib on the northwest side of the basin.

Climb back up the descent to regain Larrison Ridge and the route back toward the start (1.5 hour for the descent into and climb back out of the cirque).

Descent to Heather Lake. Adventurers seeking more technical terrain can ski a 1300-foot, 40-degree chute all the way down to Heather Lake. This couloir holds snow late into the season and can often be skied to the elevation of the lake even if the overall snow line is higher. This alternative exit requires leaving a second car at the Heather Lake trailhead.

To access the chute down to Heather Lake, stay farther to skier's left on the slopes above Heather Lake into a draw next to the northeast-trending ridge. Stay high to the left out of the draw, and cross into the couloir at the last set of larger mature trees that are northeast of the main buttress above the couloir.

You can choose from several possible entrances, some of which may require 10 feet of downclimbing through brush or small waterfalls if the snow near the top has melted. Bring a rope and crampons if you are uncertain about conditions in the couloir. Ski the snaking, deep-set couloir down to Heather Lake. From the lake, join casual hikers and walk the 2-mile summer trail down to the Heather Lake trailhead.

Tour Author: Benjamin Haskell

35 Vesper Peak

Starting elevation: 2350 feet
High point: 6214 feet
Vertical gain/loss: 4150 feet/4150 feet
Distance: 8.8 km (5.5 miles)
Time: 6–7 hours
Overall difficulty: moderate
Ski skills: difficult
Fitness level: strenuous
Technical skills: moderate
Commitment: low
Gear: the basics, plus a pair of approach shoes
Best season: May–June
USGS maps: Silverton and Bedal
Permits: A Northwest Forest Pass or Interagency Pass is required to park at the trailhead, which is in Mount Baker–Snoqualmie National Forest.

Vesper Peak is a great moderate summit ski destination, but you usually must hike a little to get to the snow if the snow on the roads has melted out enough to access the tour. This ski tour provides a lot of variety in a single day: some classic Cascadian stream crossings, a friendly couloir to boot up and ski down, and a beautiful view from the summit.

ACCESS

From Granite Falls, turn left onto North Alder Avenue, which becomes the Mountain Loop Highway. Drive just over 28 miles, and turn right on the Sunrise Mine Road after passing the parking lot for the Mount Dickerman Trail on your left. Go up the Sunrise Mine Road (Forest Service Road 4065) until it dead-ends at the trailhead.

The Mountain Loop Highway usually closes for the winter near milepost 23 and typically opens in mid- to late spring, depending on the snowfall in a given year. Sunrise Mine Road can be partly blocked by snow a bit longer; typically it is clear by Memorial Day. Be sure to check the Mount Baker–Snoqualmie National Forest website for the road conditions before you head out.

TOUR

Follow the summer trail as it heads southwest into the woods and toward the Stillaguamish River. Crossing the river, which is often swollen with snowmelt, can be challenging at times. If there is no obvious, safe crossing where the trail intersects the river, then bushwhack a bit upstream, where there will likely be a good log crossing on a springtime logjam. Once you are beyond the river, look for the continuation of the summer trail, which switchbacks up a steep meadow and exits through trees to gain the hanging valley to the east of Sperry Peak (1 hour to here).

The hanging valley will likely have continuous snow well into July, and you can usually begin skinning here. Climb toward the head of the valley, threading around avalanche debris as necessary, and look for an obvious couloir on the climber's right-hand side of the valley that climbs up to Headlee Pass (4600 feet). It is best to transition near the bottom of the Headlee Couloir and boot up to the pass.

Note that the Headlee Couloir is next to another, wider couloir to climber's right. The Headlee Couloir (which covers the steep switchbacks of the summer trail up Headlee Pass) is usually the last one to melt out; but in early season, the equally steep but wider couloir just to its right can be another good option for ascending out of the hanging basin and continuing toward Vesper Peak.

Once you have completed the stiff but short climb up either couloir, you will have a great view of Vesper. With luck, you will also have continuous snow so that you can skin all the way to the summit of Vesper Peak. Begin skinning a mellow traverse across a snow-covered rock field toward the small lake basin between Sperry and Vesper (3 hours to the basin). From the basin, take the east-southeast rib to the summit, which offers easy skinning all the way up. Enjoy the spectacular view of Whitehorse Mountain to the northwest and the Monte Cristo Peaks to the southeast from Vesper's summit at 6214 feet (4.5 hours to the summit).

DESCENT. On the descent, enjoy turns down the wide southeast slopes of Vesper. If you ski the fall line, due east from the summit, watch out for potential moats or rock bands. If the snow is continuous, you can coast most of the way back to Headlee Pass.

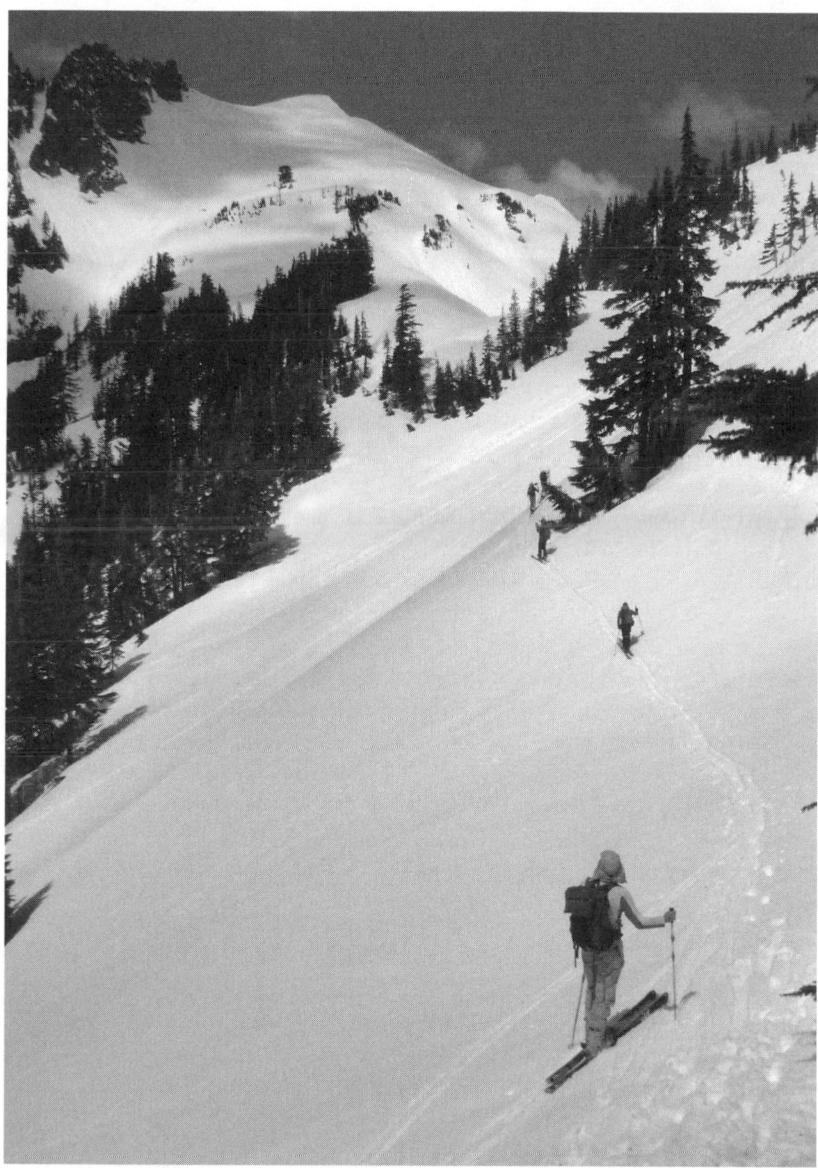

Vesper Peak from Headlee Pass (Douglas Smart)

Once you are back at Headlee Pass, ski down the couloir, but be aware of rocks and boulders at the bottom of the couloir that may have melted out.

Once you are below the couloir, reverse your route across the hanging valley as far as the snow allows, and locate the summer trail leading to the trailhead and your car.

Tour Author: Erin Smart

36 Kyes Peak

Starting elevation: 2361 feet
High point: 7227 feet
Vertical gain/loss: 6160 feet/6160 feet
Distance: 28 km (17 miles)
Time: 2 days
Overall difficulty: difficult
Ski skills: difficult
Fitness level: very strenuous
Technical skills: moderate
Commitment: very high
Gear: the basics, plus ski mountaineering and overnight equipment
Best season: March–end of May
USGS maps: Monte Cristo and Blanca Lake
Permits: You must display a Northwest Forest Pass or Interagency Pass to park at Barlow Pass, which is in Mount Baker–Snoqualmie National Forest.

The mountains around Monte Cristo are a little-visited cluster of very rugged, steep, and even glaciated peaks at moderate elevation. The area was well known and explored in the decades after its intense but short-lived mining boom. What remains now is a lonely area that is relatively easy to reach from the Puget Sound basin. Because these mountains are steep and serious, you will be able to apply your skiing expertise, ability to assess snow stability, and ski mountaineering skills as far as you would like. This great outing embodies the spirit of the Monte Cristo Mountains and introduces you to many other zones in this area that you may want to explore.

ACCESS

From Granite Falls, follow the Mountain Loop Highway just over 30 miles, past the Verlot Ranger Station and hopefully all the way to Barlow Pass. The highway is closed near milepost 23 in winter, so be sure to check current road conditions on the Mount Baker–Snoqualmie National Forest website before setting out. Access beyond Barlow Pass may change in the future due to ongoing mine cleanup operations in Monte Cristo.

TOUR

DAY 1. Walk, ski tour, or ride your mountain bike up the access road that leads to Monte Cristo. Riding a mountain bike can be a great way to reach the end of the road, depending on the conditions. At the time of publication, the newly planned road had not been built yet. Getting to the old town site of Monte Cristo involves crossing the South Fork Sauk River via a massive log after 1 mile where the old bridge got washed out a few years back. From there, simply follow the road to the bridge before the town of Monte Cristo.

At the end of the road at 2750 feet (1.5–2 hours to here on foot or 1 hour on a bike), go left to the little campground, and follow what is now called Glacier Creek. You will be on or near the summer Glacier Basin Trail, which may not be visible if it is snow covered. Cross Glacier Creek at around 2850 feet to its south side, and follow it to about 3200 feet. Now turn southeast and tour up the steep slope to a little pass at 4800 feet (3.5–4 hours to here).

Now tour through the beautiful Glacier Basin with the wild Wilmans Spires looming large over you on the right. Maintain your southeasterly trajectory until about 5200 feet. The terrain steepens here, but you can trend east to about 5400 feet. Then turn southwest to Monte Cristo Pass at 6050 feet. Your campsite should be nothing short of spectacular. (5–5.5 hours to here).

You may wonder why this day is relatively short. The effort of getting to Monte Cristo Pass is pretty substantial, but most importantly, the timing for the second day is crucial.

Kyes Peak from the southwest (Alasdair Turner)

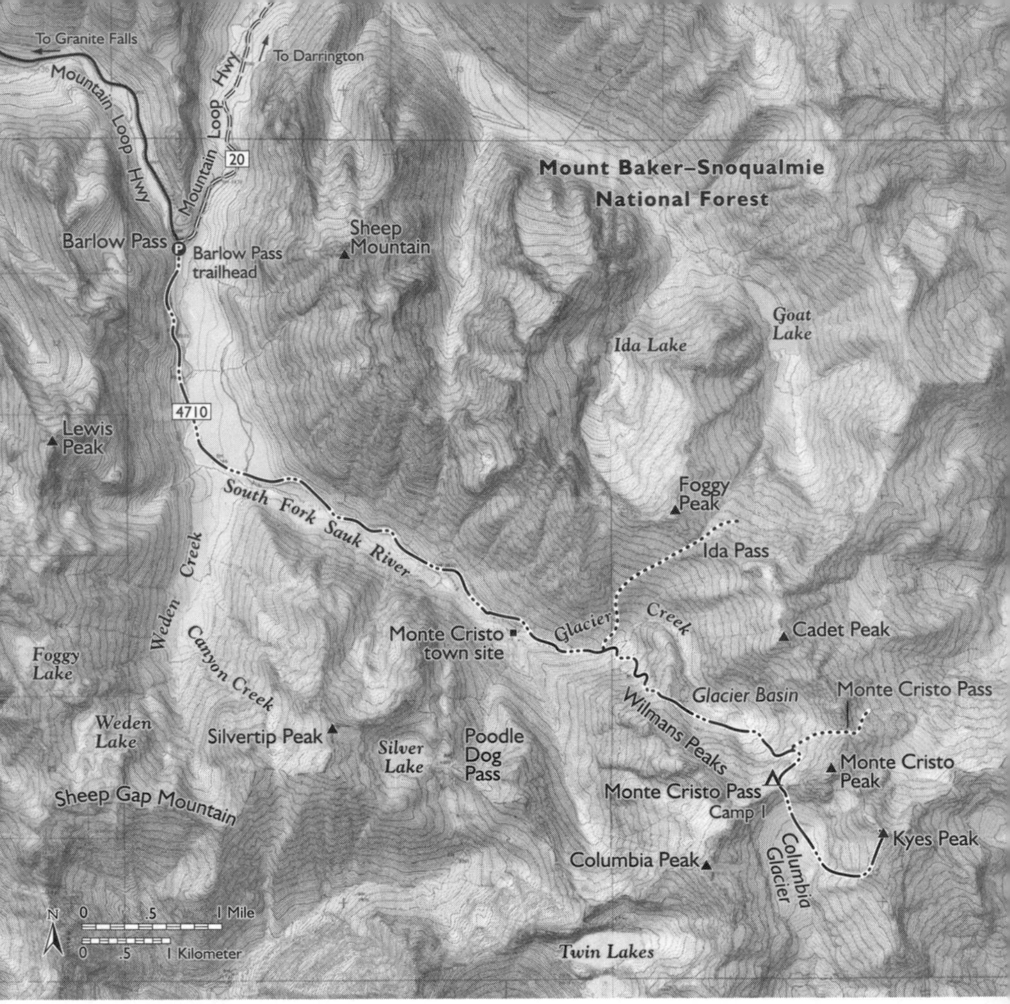

DAY 2. Make sure to get started early for your descent down the steep, south-facing slopes to the Columbia Glacier. Once you are on the glacier, ski down to 5400 feet, and then trend skier's left while maintaining your elevation. You will leave the glacier onto a large west-facing slope that leads up to the subsummit of Kyes Peak, which is falsely named "Monte Cristo 7025" on the USGS map. Gain this summit (2 hours to here), and then turn north along the spectacularly sweeping ridge to the summit of Kyes Peak at 7227 feet (3 hours to here).

From the summit, retrace your ascent route back down to the Columbia Glacier. If the conditions, the weather, and your energy level are good, you can explore this zone further, of course, but keep in mind that you will have to regain Monte Cristo Pass at 6050 feet eventually (4.5 hours back to the pass), and the steep, south-facing slope obviously receives a lot of sun at a high angle. Be careful not to get trapped.

From the pass, enjoy the ski descent back down to Monte Cristo via your ascent route and then out the road back to Barlow Pass (6.5–7 hours back to your car).

Tour Author: Martin Volken

37 Bandit Peak: Black Hole Couloir

Starting elevation: 2000 feet
High point: 7500 feet
Vertical gain/loss: 5900 feet/5900 feet
Distance: 24 km (15 miles)
Time: 14–16 hours in a day or overnight
Overall difficulty: difficult
Ski skills: difficult
Fitness level: very strenuous
Technical skills: moderate
Commitment: low
Gear: the basics, plus boot crampons, depending on the conditions
Best season: December–April
USGS maps: Mount David and Schaefer Lake
Permits: none

The Black Hole Couloir on Bandit Peak is everything that a good couloir should be: deep, dark, narrow, and sustained. The approach is long, but the scenery of the Napeequa River valley keeps things interesting. It is all worth it when you stand at the top and look at a 4500-foot descent to the valley floor.

ACCESS

From Stevens Pass drive 20 miles east to Coles Corner and turn left (north) along State Route 207. Stay on State Route 207 for 10.5 miles as it wraps west around the north side of Lake Wenatchee, then take the right fork on the White River Road (Forest Service Road 167). Continue another 6 miles to the Napeequa Crossing Campground, which is closed in winter. Park here before the end of the road at 2000 feet. This road is privately plowed by Tall Timber Ranch. Please respect this service and park prior to their property. Do not park on ranch property without prior approval.

TOUR

From the campground, cross the road and follow the Twin Lakes Trail up the south side of the Napeequa River valley. The trail ascends 200 to 300 vertical feet before dropping back to the valley floor. From here, continue another 10 to 15 minutes until you reach a large beaver pond. Either link snow-covered beaver dams to get to the other side, or make a number of small creek crossings to skirt it on the climber's left. Once you are on the far side, start turning in a northerly direction to continue up the Napeequa River drainage to 2150 feet (1 hour).

Once you turn north up the drainage, you have another 7 kilometers (4.3 miles) or so to the base of the Black Hole Couloir. To follow the best route, stay on the east side of the Napeequa River and only ascend off the valley floor if steep terrain forces

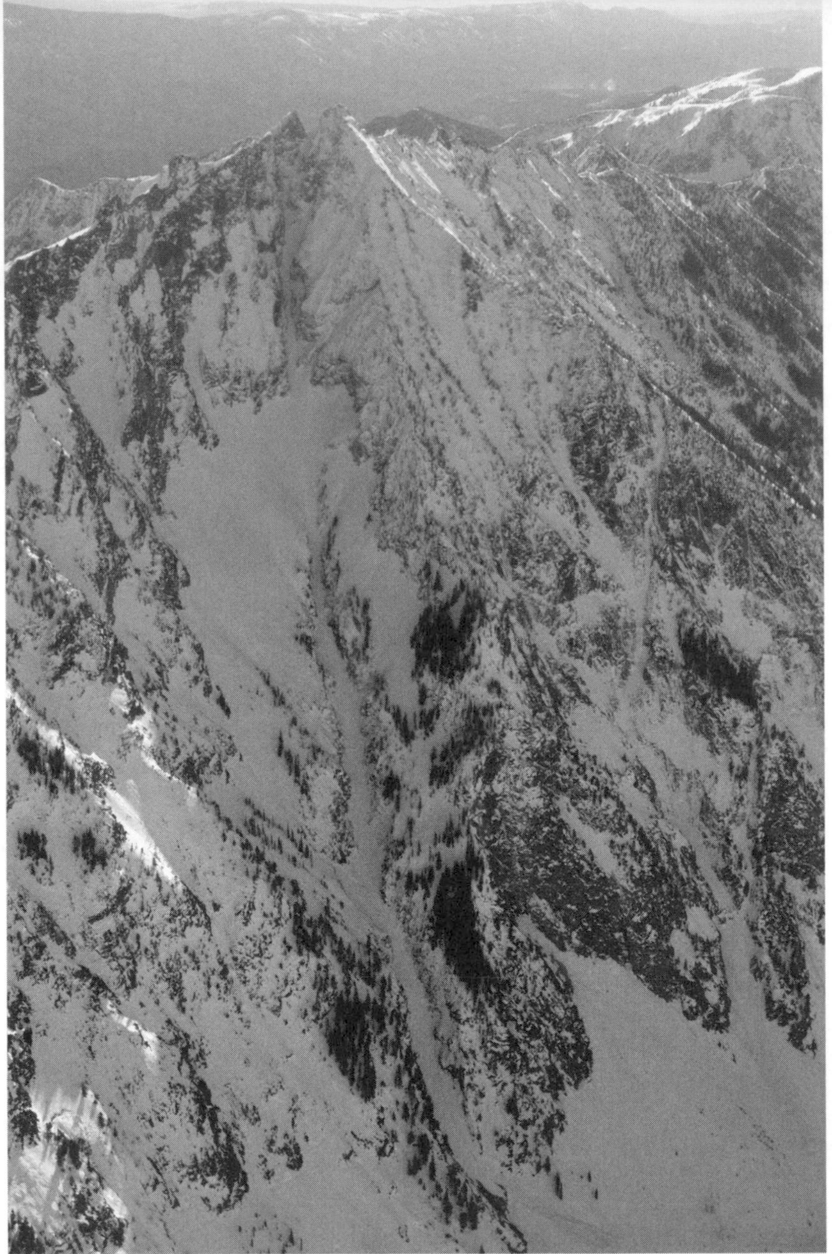

The Black Hole Couloir descends the obvious central line on Bandit Peak's northwest face. (Scott Schell)

you to. Make your way up the valley until you are past Bandit Peak (Point 7625 on the USGS map). There are a number of couloirs low on its western face. Continue past all of these until you reach the base of the Black Hole Couloir on the northwest aspect of the peak at 3200 feet (5 hours to here). Camp can be made near the base of the couloir if you are spending the night.

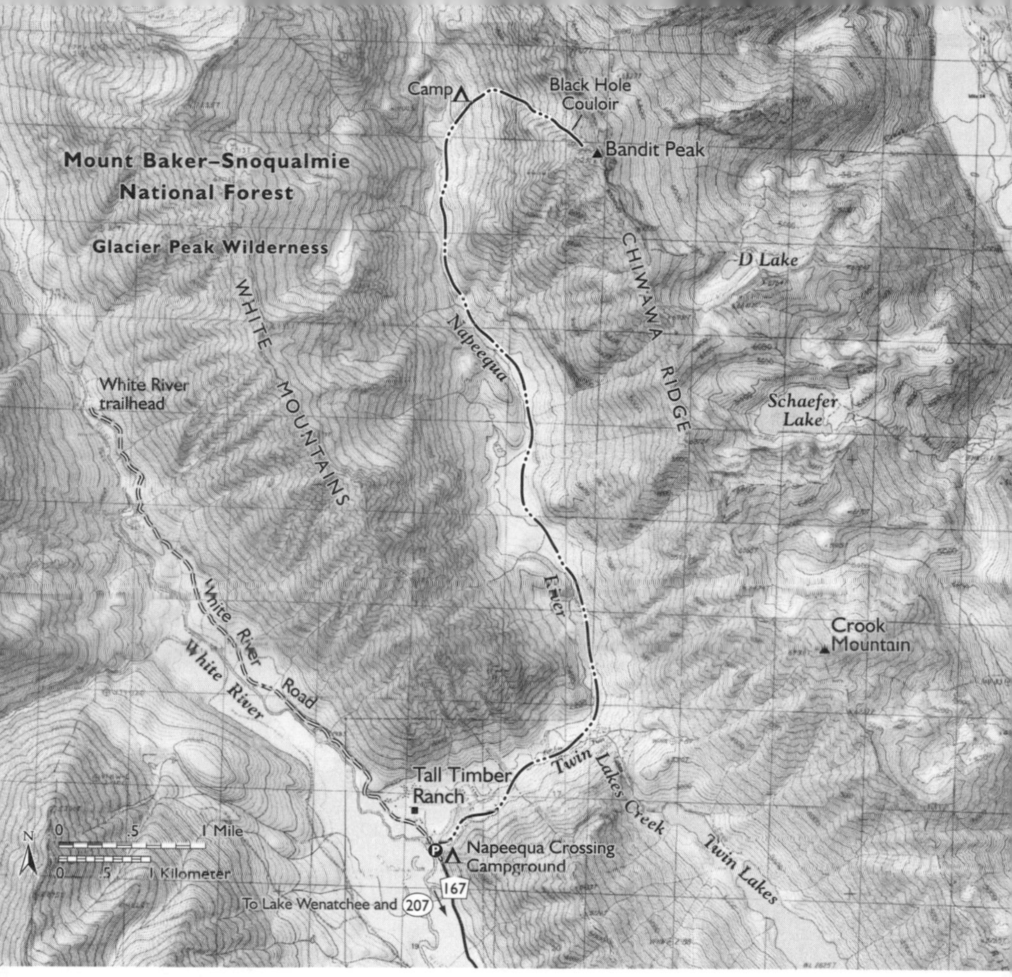

Once you identify the Black Hole Couloir, skin up the apron until you are forced to strap your skis on your back and boot the rest of the way. Like all couloirs that require a bottom-up approach, assess the snow stability carefully before you decide to continue.

About halfway up, the lower couloir gives way to a large open slope at 5600 feet (7 hours to here). Climb through this open section and into the upper couloir. The last 50 feet to gain the ridgeline at 7500 feet approach 50 degrees and is fairly exposed (9 hours to here).

DESCENT. Aside from the top 50 feet, the couloir is not especially steep, but it is quite narrow and has very few "zones of safety." Carefully consider how your group will descend to minimize your exposure to avalanches and sloughing.

Once you are back at the base of the couloir at 3200 feet (10.5 hours to here), reverse your route back down the Napeequa River valley, staying on the east side as previously described before crossing to the route of the Twin Lakes Trail that brings you back to your car at about 2000 feet (14 hours to here).

Tour Author: Aaron Mainer

38 The Dakobed Traverse

Starting elevation: 2000 feet
High point: 10,541 feet
Vertical gain/loss: 17,990 feet/17,990 feet
Distance: 69 km (43 miles)
Time: 4–5 days
Overall difficulty: difficult
Ski skills: difficult
Fitness level: very strenuous
Technical skills: moderate
Commitment: very high
Gear: ski mountaineering equipment and overnight gear
Best season: March–June
USGS maps: Mount David, Clark Mountain, and Glacier Peak East
Permits: A Northwest Forest Pass or Interagency Pass is required to park at the trailhead after the snow has melted. This tour is best when snow blocks the road beyond Tall Timber Ranch. Parking is not allowed at Tall Timber Ranch without pre-approval with its management. You also should fill out a Forest Service wilderness use permit at the White River trailhead about 1.5 hours into the tour.

This traverse follows a high route along the northern slopes of the Dakobed Range. Traveling across many glaciers, this tour ventures across high alpine terrain that holds huge quantities of snow and usually has great skiing late into the season. We recommend that you add Glacier Peak to this route (described here as an extra day). Later in the spring, this traverse requires many miles of hiking on dirt and a longer exit out Indian Creek. We describe this tour as a mid-spring circumnavigation of the Dakobed Range all on snow.

ACCESS

From Stevens Pass, drive 20 miles east to Coles Corner, and turn left (north) along State Route 207. Continue on State Route 207 for 10.5 miles as it wraps west around the north side of Lake Wenatchee, then turn right onto the White River Road, and travel 6 miles to the Napeequa Crossing Campground, which is closed in winter. Park here before the end of the road at 2000 feet. This road is privately plowed by Tall Timber Ranch. Please respect this service and park prior to their property. Do not park on ranch property without prior approval.

TOUR

DAY 1. From the campground, skin up the White River Road to the trailhead at 2310 feet (1.5 hours to here). Skin up the east side of the river, favoring the trail where it

The Dakobed Range from the east (Scott Schell)

is recognizable. Cross Boulder Creek around 2520 feet (3.5 hours to here), and then begin climbing up the north side of this drainage. At 3700 feet, contour east along a bench above Boulder Creek, and cross the creek near where the summer trail crosses at around 4100 feet (5.5 hours to here). Follow the drainage up, eventually climbing through a steeper gully just west of trees at 5600 feet. Continue up to Boulder Pass at 6300 feet and set camp (8.5 hours to here).

DAY 2. Start early for a big day that provides summit ski opportunities if the conditions and your energy levels allow. From camp at Boulder Pass, descend north a short distance before skinning again. Climb northwest up to about 6600 feet, and then begin a counterclockwise contour that wraps you onto the east edge of the Clark Glacier at about 6850 feet (1 hour from camp).

Unless you are quite familiar with the Clark Glacier and its dynamic crevasses, rope up for this next section. Favor the climber's left side of the lower glacier to about 7200 feet, and then traverse right across the main face to 7400 feet. Now travel on more moderate terrain to the col southeast of Clark's summit at 8140 feet (2.5 hours from camp).

If conditions warrant, drop your overnight gear, and travel over to the west side of the col to attain Clark's summit via the southeast face. Skin to the summit, respecting the corniced ridge that overhangs the northeast face, and admire views of your route to the northwest (3 hours from camp). Ski back down to the col, collect your stashed gear, and continue to ski north, enjoying glacier turns. Transition back to skinning above 7700 feet, and climb west to Clark's northwest ridge at 8100 feet (4 hours from camp).

Descend the ridge to a bench at 7830 feet, and then ski west-northwest to a col at 7650 feet that gets you back onto the north side of the ridge. The first couple of turns from this col are steep. Soon transition back to skinning, and traverse west toward Luahna Peak. An alternate route from Clark's northwest ridge at 8100 feet is to ski north-northwest down the Richardson Glacier until you reach 7300 feet.

Mount Baker–Snoqualmie
National Forest
Glacier Peak Wilderness
Vista Glacier
Ermine Glacier
Dusty Glacier
N Guardian Glacier
Chocolate Glacier
Glacier Peak
Cool Glacier Headwall
Cool Glacier
Disappointment Peak
Gerdine Glacier
Suiattle River
traverse at 6000'
Napeequa River
Camp 2
Tenpeak Mountain
Honeycomb Glacier
Suiattle Glacier
Camp 3 and 4
Butterfly Glacier
8022'
Pilz Glacier
Butterfly Butte
Chalangin Peak
Luahna Peak
Richardson Glacier
White River Glacier
Lightning Creek
Thunder Creek
Clark Glacier
Clark Mountain
Boulder Pass
Camp 1
White River
White River
Boulder Creek
Mount Saul
Indian Creek
Mount David
White River trailhead
White River Road
To Tall Timber Ranch parking (see insert)
White River trailhead
White River Road
White River
Tall Timber Ranch
To Lake Wenatchee and 207
0 .5 1 Mile
0 .5 1 Kilometer
N

Skin north to the col east of Luahna Peak at 7950 feet (5 hours from camp). It is a short climb to ski off the summit of Luahna, but you must assess the snowpack carefully as this steep southeast aspect has received sun for many hours. If conditions warrant, drop your overnight gear and enjoy another summit ski. From the col, ski north on the Pilz Glacier to about 7500 feet. Skin west again to the col at 7950 feet between Chalangin Peak and Point 8022 (6.5 hours from camp).

Choices abound from this col about how to end this wonderful day. We recommend that you camp high just east of Neyah Point, but your camp location and route will depend on your group's energy level. From the col, ski onto the Butterfly Glacier, enjoying glacial powder on this northwest aspect. Ski to about 6700 feet, and then climb west-northwest to set camp at the col east of Neyah Point at 8050 feet (8.5 hours from camp).

DAY 3. Ski northeast from camp onto the Moth Glacier trending due north around 7200 feet, and enjoying a couple thousand feet of great skiing. Stop skiing above 6000 feet as this is the elevation you want to maintain while traversing the north slopes of Tenpeak Mountain. If your group camped farther east, you can ski the Butterfly Glacier to 6000 feet, and then climb west to a 6800-foot saddle above Moth Lake. Then ski over Moth Lake, and continue out its northwest drainage before traversing west across Tenpeak's northern slopes.

Ski west, maintaining elevation, and cross through the first of many steep gullies. Transition to skins (and likely ski crampons) to continue traversing at the 6000-foot level, crossing steep slide paths before arriving on a bench at 6020 feet (1.5 hours from camp).

Ski southwest onto the Honeycomb Glacier, and then begin a long, easy climb to the top of this massive flow of ice. Favor its east side throughout the climb, and set camp on the large bench just above 7800 feet (4 hours from camp). For the rest of the day, explore the Kololo Peaks that constitute the upper borders of the Honeycomb, Suiattle, and White River Glaciers. You will not become bored with the plethora of glacier skiing options in this area. A very strong group could ski Glacier Peak during the afternoon of this third day, but it is described here as the fourth day of this five-day traverse.

DAY 4. Leave camp with a day pack destined for the summit of Glacier Peak. Traverse northwest to the high entrance onto the Suiattle Glacier at 7840 feet. Ski northwest down the Suiattle to 6800 feet (1 hour to here). Skin north and contour around gentle ridges and across friendly faces, working your way to the col east of Disappointment Peak at 9150 feet (3.5 hours to here). As you traverse onto the Cool Glacier, you will notice more crevasses and broken terrain than you experienced on the Suiattle and Gerdine Glaciers.

While skinning to the col north of Disappointment Peak, observe the ski lines off the Cool Glacier Headwall and the bergschrund that is likely starting to open at the bottom. Although they are steep, these lines can provide better skiing than the bumpy terrain you will likely climb on the southwest side. From the col on the south ridge, climb out onto the southwest face, and ascend the smoothest gully to the summit ridge. The true summit is the west end of this ridge at 10,541 feet (5 hours to here).

Descend the Cool Glacier Headwall or south summit gully, and meet back up with your ascent route at the col east of Disappointment Peak at 9150 feet (6 hours to here). Enjoy large turns down the moderate Gerdine and Suiattle Glaciers before your final climb up the Suiattle and back to your camp on the Honeycomb (7.5 hours to here).

DAY 5. From camp, make a descending traverse to the right into Lightning Creek basin. Stay on the right side of the upper basin, ski the fall line to the southeast for a couple thousand feet of final alpine turns, and then descend back into the trees. Aim for a gentle bench at 5600 feet on the small ridge between the two main drainages. Follow this ridge down, and trend left below 5000 feet through tighter trees. Cross Lightning Creek around 4760 feet, and ski the open slopes down to 4100 feet (1 hour to here).

Cut left into the trees, and do your best to maintain elevation as you traverse above the White River. Eventually you will be down next to the river and need to use skins for the long slog out. Expect to come up with a creative way to cross Thunder Creek at 2600 feet (2.5 hours to here). The next few drainages will likely be covered in avalanche debris. Continue skinning along the northeast side of the White River to the Boulder Creek crossing at 2550 feet (4.5 hours to here). Follow your route from a few days ago back down to your vehicle at 2000 feet (7.5 hours to here).

Tour Author: Trevor Kostanich

39 Mount Maude: North Face

Starting elevation: 3240 feet
High point: 9040 feet
Vertical gain/loss: 8400 feet/ 8400 feet from Phelps Creek
Distance: 30 km (18 miles)
Time: 1 long (12+ hour) day or overnight, and multiday options
Overall difficulty: difficult
Ski skills: very difficult
Fitness level: strenuous
Technical skills: high
Commitment: high
Gear: the basics, plus ski mountaineering and overnight equipment
Best season: February–June
USGS map: Mount Maude
Permits: You must display a Northwest Forest Pass or Interagency Pass to park at the Phelps Creek trailhead. You must also pay a fee to park at Fields Point Landing if taking the *Lady of the Lake* ferry on Lake Chelan.

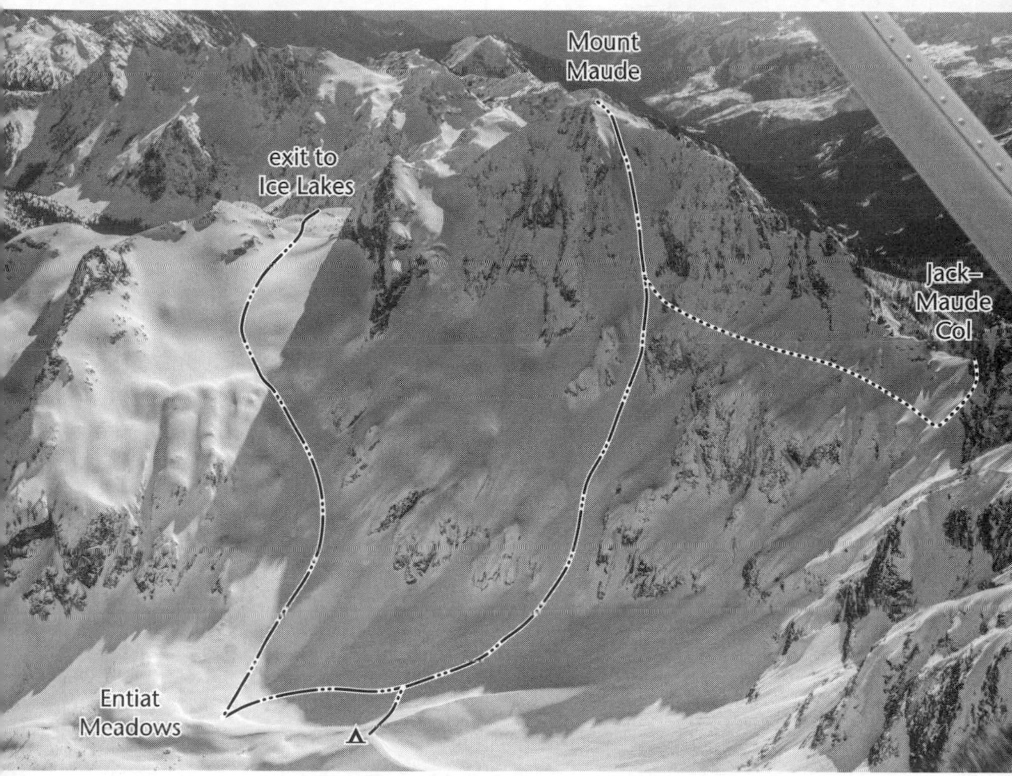

Mount Maude from the north (Alasdair Turner)

On the inside flap of the second edition of Fred Beckey's iconic *Cascade Alpine Guide: Volume 2*, there was a tantalizing image of the North Face of Mount Maude. Although intended to inspire climbers to seek out the challenge of this remote north face, the picture also inspired steep skiing enthusiasts who were attracted to the purity of the line from its 9040-foot summit. But the desire to tackle this remote peak comes with plenty of obstacles. Each of the two very different routes used to access it is challenging, but your reward is a 3000-foot North Cascades jewel.

ACCESS

Phelps Creek access. To reach the Phelps Creek trailhead on the southern end of the tour, drive 20 miles east on US Hwy 2 from Stevens Pass to Coles Corner. Turn left on State Route 207, and continue on it 4.7 miles. Turn right onto Chiwawa Loop Road, and follow it as it curves right for 1.3 miles. Take a left onto Chiwawa River Road (Forest Service Road 62), and follow it around Fish Lake and then north for 22 miles. At Trinity camp, take a final right onto Phelps Creek Road, and park at the end of the road just above 3400 feet. This road is not plowed in winter and requires a snowmobile.

Holden Village access. To reach Holden Village (the northern approach), from Chelan drive west along the south shore of Lake Chelan on State Route 97. After about 3.7 miles, turn right on South Lakeshore Road (State Route 971, Forest Service Road 23). Follow this another 8.5 miles to the turn off for Fields Point Landing on the

Railroad
Creek
Holden
To Lucerne
Copper
Creek
Big Creek
Holden Village
Approach
Okanogan–Wenatchee
National Forest
Buckskin
Mountain
Mount Fernow
CHELAN MOUNTAINS
Camp
Glacier Peak Wilderness
Gloomy
Glacier
Entiat River
Seven Fingered Jack
alternate camp
Jack–Maude Col
Spider Meadow
Entiat
exit route
West Face Couloir
Route
Creek
Mount
Maude
Entiat
Icefall
Glacier
Camp
Ice Lakes
Leroy
Leroy
Basin
south
shoulder
Phelps
Creek
Phelps
Ridge
ENTIAT MOUNTAINS
Chiwawa
River
Phelps Creek
trailhead
Phelps Creek Rd
Trinity
Chiwawa River Rd
62
To Lake Wenatchee
N
0
.5
1 Mile
0
.5
1 Kilometer

west side of Lake Chelan. You will need to take the *Lady of the Lake* ferry up the lake; visit www.ladyofthelake.com for schedules and to make reservations. You must pay a fee to park overnight both at the dock in Chelan or at Fields Point Landing. Take the boat to Lucerne and then the connecting bus to Holden Village. Contact Holden Village to ensure that there is space for you and your party on the bus up to Holden, or if you would like to stay at Holden Village; see www.holdenvillage.org for more information.

TOUR

Phelps Creek Approach. When the snow on the road has melted out, you can ascend and ski Maude's North Face in one long day. Taking two days is not necessarily easier because then you will be carrying heavier packs, but camping can be pleasant, and this allows for a more relaxed itinerary. It should be noted that a day trip is only possible once the road has melted out (or if you have access to a snowmobile).

From the trailhead, follow the Phelps Creek Trail 3.5 miles to where you cross Leroy Creek. A climber's path leads you to Leroy Basin, which has some good campsites near 6000 feet (5 hours to Leroy Basin). From Leroy Basin, you can ascend two routes to the summit of Mount Maude. The direct approach up the west face couloir is sporty. For an easier time, the south shoulder is a walk up. Later in the year, as the snow melts off this route, the boulder fields can be less than enjoyable (3 hours to the summit from Leroy Basin up the south shoulder). A third option is via the Seven Fingered Jack and Mount Maude col with a traverse across steep snow and through rock bands over to the north face.

Holden Village Tour. Since it takes nearly two days to get to and back from Holden Village, it can be difficult to time your trip for reliable weather and conditions. That being said, a direct ascent and descent of the North Face of Maude in winter can be very rewarding.

From Holden Village, ascend Copper Creek to its head near 7200 feet. Descend south from the pass to reach Entiat Meadows (5.5 hours to here from Holden). Good camps can be made at the pass from Copper Creek, or in the Entiat River valley below. Ascend the North Face directly from the valley (3.5 hours to the summit from camp in the Entiat valley). Ski the North Face and reverse your route back to Holden Village (7 hours camp to summit and back to Holden). Extended multiday excursions can be made around Mount Maude, Seven Fingered Jack, and Mount Fernow by linking the Entiat River valley to the Big Creek valley through Leroy Basin and the high col at 8000 feet on the west face of Seven Fingered Jack. This col accesses the appropriately named Gloomy Glacier for routes up Mount Fernow or down Big Creek back to Holden.

DESCENT. You have many choices for descending the north face. From the summit at 9040 feet, you can descend the entire face if the snow pack is continuous. From the base, climb the route back to the summit or exit by traversing below the Entiat Icefall and up the east lobe of Entiat Glacier to Ice Lakes and back to Leroy Basin (6 hours round trip from camp in Leroy Basin).

If the route is not completely filled in, or you are doing a day trip and have limited time, you can traverse horizontally across the North Face to the col between Seven

Fingered Jack and Mount Maude for a shorter circuit back to camp. You can also take this route up if you prefer to check conditions on the North Face prior to skiing it.

Tour Author: Jason Hummel

40 Bonanza West Peak: Northwest Buttress

Starting elevation: 3240 feet
High point: 9400 feet
Vertical gain/loss: 8300 feet/8300 feet
Distance: 31 km (19 miles)
Time: 3–5 days, including travel to Holden
Overall difficulty: difficult
Ski skills: difficult
Fitness level: very strenuous
Technical skills: moderate
Commitment: high
Gear: the basics, plus ski mountaineering equipment and overnight gear
Best season: April–June
USGS maps: Holden and Mount Lyall
Permits: Visitors to the Glacier Peak Wilderness do not need a permit, but they are encouraged to sign the trail register available at many trailheads.

The tallest nonvolcanic peak in the Cascades stands out near the head of Lake Chelan. Bonanza, with its two horns and impressive glaciers, is easy to identify from locations around the range. You can see it clearly from Washington and Cascade Passes, but it sees much less traffic than either of these locations. This is a true adventure in a remote part of the range that you will want to visit more than once. When the Holden copper mine closed in 1957 and the village was leased as a retreat by the Lutheran Church, a unique chapter in the history of Washington mountain culture began. Visiting Holden Village is one of the reasons to do this trip, and if you can afford the time you should consider spending a night or two as a guest.

ACCESS

From Chelan, drive west along the south shore of Lake Chelan on State Route 97. After about 3.7 miles, turn right on South Lakeshore Road (State Route 971, Forest Service Road 23). Follow this another 8.5 miles to the turn off for Fields Point Landing on the west side of Lake Chelan. An overnight parking fee is required both at the dock in Chelan and at Fields Point Landing, a ferry stop that lies to the west along the southern shore. Take the ferry to Lucerne, where you can catch the shuttle to Holden, 10 miles up Railroad Creek at 3240 feet.

Check ferry schedules carefully (www.ladyofthelake.com), as they vary through the seasons, with service only a few days a week in winter. Make sure to let Holden Village know you are coming to ensure that there will be space for you on the shuttle between the lake and the village. You cannot camp in the village itself; plan to head up-valley upon arrival or to pay to stay the night at the village. For reservations and transportation arrangements, visit the village's website (www.holdenvillage.org).

TOUR

DAY 1. Head west out of Holden toward the end of the road, and follow Trail 1256 up valley. At 3440 feet, take a right onto Trail 1251, and follow it (or its approximate route) to Holden Lake at 5278 feet. This route crosses many large avalanche paths, and careful routefinding may be necessary to avoid tedious skinning through debris (3.5 hours to here).

Head around the lake to the northwest, following the lowest-angle slopes, toward the pass between Holden Creek and Sable Creek at 6400 feet. This is a strategic location for a campsite; note that camping is prohibited within 200 feet of Holden Lake (4.75 hours to here).

DAY 2. Ski down into the head of Sable Creek to about 5900 feet, then begin ascending due north. Your goal is a gentle col at around 6200 feet overlooking Company Creek, just south of Point 6354 (0.75 hour from camp). Now ski southwest toward the Company Glacier, using a bench between 5800 and 5700 feet to avoid cliffs. From

Bonanza Peak from the northeast (Scott Schell)

5700 feet, begin a rising traverse onto the Company Glacier, heading southwest and then south to gain a flat area around 8000 feet. This area is just northeast of the low point between Bonanza Peak and Point 8599 (3.5 hours to here).

From here, the west peak of Bonanza is guarded by a steep, intimidating headwall. This big, steep slope has some convexity, and it sits just beneath the ridge; you must be confident about the snow stability in order to continue. Climb the face and trend toward the northwest ridge as soon as you are able. Follow this broad ridge toward Bonanza's summit ridge. Skirt across the top of west-facing slopes to gain the final, steep step (many people will choose to depot their skis here). Climb this via steep snow or, later in the season, easy but exposed scrambling. This is the west peak of Bonanza—a little bit lower than the true summit, but the logical goal of a ski outing to the peak (4.75 hours to here).

DESCENT. The headwall offers exciting skiing, but make sure you like the conditions; the runout is severe. You can reduce your exposure somewhat by skiing the northwest ridge as far as possible, but some exposure on the headwall is unavoidable. Regain the gentle portion of the glacier, and reverse your route to your camp, taking time to savor the wild ambience (7.5 hours round-trip from camp).

As you pack up your camp, check out the Mary Green Glacier and the summit block of Bonanza above. Cruise back to Holden Lake and Holden Village, keeping in mind the shuttle and ferry times necessary to return to your car (2 hours from camp to Holden Village).

Tour Author: Forest McBrian

CENTRAL CASCADES

FOR MOST OF THE POPULATION of Washington State, the Central Cascades are the most accessible ski touring mountains. Roadways over Snoqualmie, Stevens, and Blewett Passes offer year-round access for ski tourers while an interstate (I-90) provides reliably quick transportation between Seattle and Snoqualmie Pass. While I-90 travelers see only the more moderate ski slopes on the south side of the interstate, Snoqualmie Pass offers up a diverse selection of advanced tours north of the highway.

Most of the mountains in the Central Cascades stand between 5000 and 7000 feet tall, but Mount Stuart, the second highest nonvolcanic peak in the state, is 9415 feet. Its huge granite walls jut thousands of feet above the local valleys and help highlight its presence from most vantage points in the Cascades. While the Stuart Range has more overall height, its location east of the crest results in less snowfall and a shorter ski season. With more clear nights, the eastern zones experience freeze/thaw cycles more often and earlier in the year, so you're likely to ski corn down the south side of Mount Stuart in March and April. The corn cycle typically doesn't set up until late April or May, if at all, on the Cascade Crest itself and on the west side.

What the crest may lack in corn season duration, it makes up for in length of powder season. Areas on and west of the crest of the Central Cascades typically receive more than 400 inches of snowfall beginning in November and continuing through April. While skiing powder is common six months of the year, it is also not uncommon to be skiing in very dense snow at any time of the season. Both Stevens and Snoqualmie Passes benefit from "easterly flow": high pressure sitting inland pushes colder air from eastern Washington through the passes toward low pressure off the coast. With this pattern, it is common to see precipitation fall as snow at 3022-foot Snoqualmie Pass when the free air freezing levels are above 5000 feet. The pattern also helps reduce the amount of melt during sunny dry periods.

The terrain in the Central Cascades consists of a great mix of dense forests to craggy alpine basins, all interspersed with many lakes and streams. Similar to most of the range, forests vary with Douglas fir, western hemlock, and red cedar on the west side to thinner stands of subalpine fir, ponderosa pine, and western- and alpine larch on the east side. Approaches via the west side can be challenging due to some mandatory bushwhacking and lack of visibility in "green out" conditions where the forest canopies greatly limit sight distance. While not known to be very glaciated, the central peaks of Mount Hinman and Mount Daniel provide a large quantity of permanent ice. There are also some lingering glaciers in other areas of this region, most notable in the Stuart Range and the Snoqualmie High Peaks of Overcoat Peak, Chimney Rock, and the Lemahs.

FEES, PERMITS, AND WEATHER INFORMATION

Tours in the Central Cascades are located in Okanogan–Wenatchee and Mount Baker–Snoqualmie National Forests. Contact information for these two entities, as well as the Cle Elum, Wenatchee River, Skykomish, and Snoqualmie Ranger Districts, and the Verlot Public Service Center, is located in Resources.

Previous page: Into the Lemahs (Ben Haskell)

Parking. Many national forest recreation sites require a parking fee. Day passes can be purchased at local vendors; or an annual Northwest Forest Pass or an America the Beautiful Pass will also cover your parking.

Camping. Fill out a free self-issue wilderness permit at the trailhead. Wilderness regulations apply, and Leave No Trace practices are strongly encouraged.

Wilderness Areas. Okanogan–Wenatchee National Forest contains Alpine Lakes Wilderness, Glacier Peak Wilderness, and Lake Chelan–Sawtooth Wilderness. Wilderness areas found in Mount Baker–Snoqualmie Nationlal Forest include Henry M. Jackson Wilderness, Wild Sky Wilderness, Mount Baker Wilderness, Noisy-Diosbud Wilderness, and Boulder River Wilderness.

Weather. In addition to the Northwest Avalanche Center and the National Weather Service websites, check the Stevens Pass, Mission Ridge, and Snoqualmie sites for current local weather and snowpack conditions. See Resources for web addresses.

41 Skyline Ridge to Tye Peak

Starting elevation: 4065 feet
High point: 5476 feet
Vertical gain/loss: 2900 feet/2900 feet
Distance: 7.1 km (4.4 miles)
Time: 2–5 hours, depending on variation
Overall difficulty: easy
Ski skills: moderate
Fitness level: moderately strenuous
Technical skills: low
Commitment: low to Skyline Ridge, moderate to Tye Peak
Gear: the basics
Best season: January–mid-April
USGS maps: Labyrinth Mountain and Stevens Pass
Permits: None. Tour takes place in Mount Baker–Snoqualmie National Forest.

Skyline Ridge is a great beginner to intermediate tour with plentiful options, and continuing on to nearby Tye Peak offers variations for advanced skiers, as well as more moderate descents. Many experienced ski mountaineers had their first ski tour on one of these variations. Both the wooded front and backside of Skyline Ridge provide great options when the avalanche hazard is high and powder is plentiful.

ACCESS

From Interstate 5 near Everett, follow US Highway 2 to the Stevens Pass Ski Area, and park on the north side of the highway behind the maintenance building (across from the ski area).

TOUR

From the parking lot, face away from the ski area, and find the groomed or well-traveled trail (a snow-covered maintenance road) that heads north up between cabins and under nearby powerlines. Follow the snow-covered road past the overhead powerlines; pass through woods and switchback up open slopes toward Skyline Lake.

At around 5000 feet, a couple of switchbacks past the first radio tower, the skin track following the road usually diverges. You can keep ascending to the right, up the short remainder of the road to where it ends on the ridge top at the second radio tower; this option offers fall-line descents through the north-facing trees of Skyline Ridge's backside to Nason Creek below. To continue on to Tye Peak, turn left at this fork, about 100 yards before the second radio tower, and traverse northwest to Skyline Lake.

Continue northwest past Skyline Lake toward a col before the rocky pinnacle to the north. From the col, at 5200 feet, transition to downhill travel and head north on the backside of Skyline Ridge down into the Nason Creek drainage and find a nice line through the trees. The farther you go skier's right, the steeper it gets. The skiing is great down to about 4350 feet, but below that the trees get tight. If the snow is good, which it often is on that north aspect, consider taking another lap. Just above Nason Creek, stop to put your skins back on.

Skyline Ridge from the southeast (Alasdair Turner)

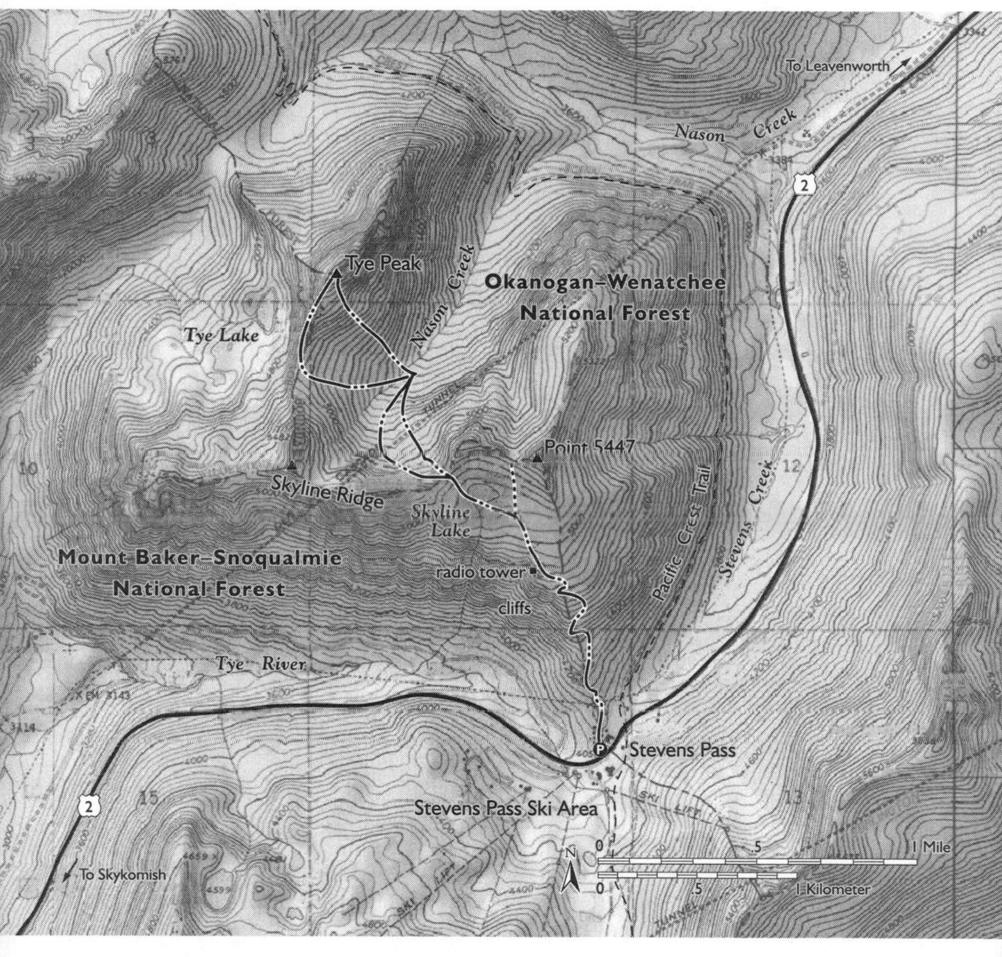

If continuing onto Tye Ridge and the climb up Tye Peak (Point 5476 on the USGS map), head west to gain the col south of Tye Peak. Once at the col, use the ridge to gain the summit. From the drainage, and on the climb up to Tye, there is a good view of the various lines back down into the valley; use this opportunity to note cornices on the ridge and windloading on the easterly slope for your ski back down. Once on the summit, there are a variety of lines to pick from for your descent, the easiest being retracing your up track. Once back in the drainage, don't retrace your down track from Skyline Ridge. It is lower angle to follow the climber's left hand side of the main drainage, and then traverse back over to the col on Skyline Ridge.

Follow your up track back past Skyline Lake and down to the lower radio tower. From there, pick a line on the southeast aspect off the ridge to the parking lot. Be sure to trend left at 5000 feet to avoid the southwest cliffs on the aspect.

Tour Author: Erin Smart

42 Yodelin

Starting elevation: 3600 feet
High point: 5273 feet
Vertical gain/loss: 1400–2500 feet/1400–2500 feet
Distance: 3–9 km (2–6 miles)
Time: 4–6 hours
Overall difficulty: easy to moderate
Ski skills: easy
Fitness level: moderate
Technical skills: low
Commitment: very low
Gear: the basics
Best season: December–March
USGS map: Labyrinth Mountain
Permits: none

Yodelin was once a ski area, and you can see the remnants of old trail cuts and chairlift stations as you explore the area's woods and meadows. It is an excellent area for beginners, but it can also be a great option for more experienced backcountry folks looking to stay out of bigger terrain on a storm day when the visibility is low and the avalanche danger is rising. The area's old road cuts and trails offer easy skinning, and there is enough open skiing that you can make some nice turns without getting into big or steep terrain.

ACCESS

This tour starts along US Highway 2 near the Stevens Pass Ski Area. If you are coming from the west, set your odometer as you drive beneath the pedestrian bridge for the ski area (which is at the pass); the parking area for Yodelin is on the right 1.7 miles from the pedestrian overpass.

If you are coming from the east, follow US Highway 2 from Leavenworth until you reach the section of road where it divides (31 miles from Icicle Junction). The turnoff to park for Yodelin is 2.2 miles west of where the divided highway ends.

TOUR

From the parking lot, skin around the building to the south, and set a line up through the small slope above. Pick up the road grade at the top of the meadow, and follow it up through two switchbacks. The road curves gradually to the right and then straightens in a flat spot at 4240 feet. From here you have two options to ascend.

Your first option is to continue up the road grade as it curves to the south and winds up the broad southwest rib above. From the top of the open ground near 4700 feet, you can work your way left onto open slopes to the high point, or you can stay right and wiggle through the trees to reach the top at 5023 feet.

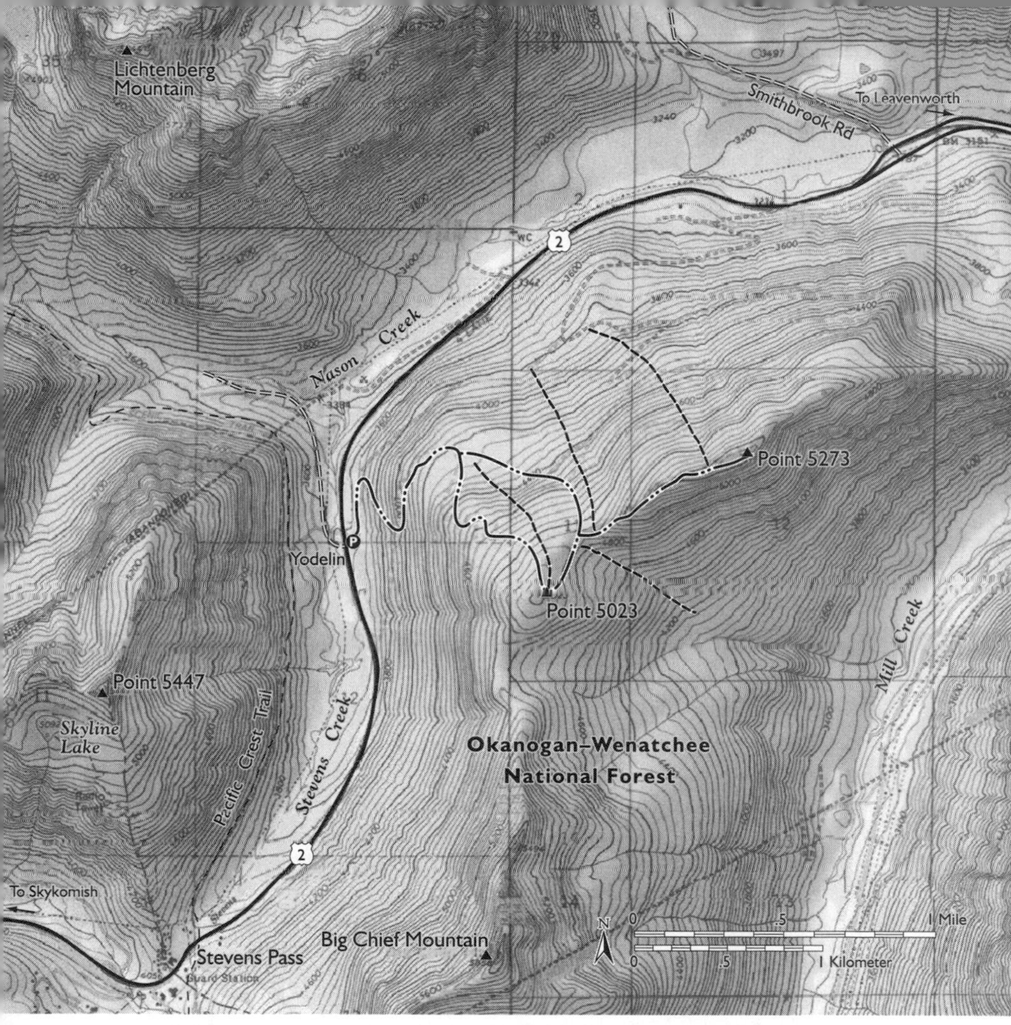

From the flat spot at 4240 feet, you can also traverse to the east across the meadows; you will see an old chairlift station off to your left. Begin an upward traverse at 4400 feet, and cross a steep slope with second-growth trees, emerging in open terrain as the angle eases at 4600 feet. From here, you can skin southwest to gain the gentle knob of Point 5023, or you can continue southeast to gain the col and then skin up the ridge to the northeast above it.

You are now well situated to choose from a variety of aspects, and Yodelin can be a great spot for laps or circuits—especially on a storm day. You can lap the open slopes (the old ski trails), or you can find your own line through the trees as you link clearings.

From the col at 4840 feet, ski the fall line down the northwest slopes until the trees get thick. For a steeper start and a longer shot, skin up the ridge to the northeast, and drop in from there.

You have yet another descent option. From the top of Point 5023, you can ski the fall line back to the meadow at 4240 feet, or you can stay slightly skier's left and keep dropping down to catch the road you skinned up on.

Skiing the trees at Yodelin (Alasdair Turner)

Finally, it is also possible to drop off the back of the col or the knob, where there are lines down the east and southeast slopes. Choose terrain carefully here, as these slopes feature big slide paths. If you plan ahead for a car shuttle, you can head out Mill Creek to the Stevens Pass Nordic Center.

Tour Author: Margaret Wheeler

43 Jim Hill and Arrowhead Mountains

Starting elevation: 3020 feet (Jim Hill) / 2900 feet (Arrowhead)
High point: 6765 feet (Jim Hill) / 6030 feet (Arrowhead)
Vertical gain/loss: 3900 feet/3900 feet for Jim Hill via Lanham Lake; 3130 feet/3130 feet for Arrowhead starting at Henry Creek
Distance: 11 km (6.8 miles) for Jim Hill via Lanham Lake; 7 km (4.3 miles) to Arrowhead and back starting from Henry Creek
Time: 7.5 hours for Jim Hill via Lanham Lake; 4.5 hours for Arrowhead and back starting from Henry Creek
Overall difficulty: moderate
Ski skills: difficult
Fitness level: strenuous
Technical skills: moderate
Commitment: low
Gear: the basics
Best season: December–April
USGS maps: Labyrinth Mountain, Mount Howard, Stevens Pass, and Chiwaukum Mountains
Permits: none

Jim Hill and Arrowhead Mountains are popular destinations just east of Stevens Pass. Their popularity is undoubtedly due to their relatively easy access to the big, moderately angled, north-facing alpine bowl on Jim Hill and the variety of open glade and tree skiing options on Arrowhead. Lower down, logging activity has opened up small slopes suitable for novice backcountry skiers. The obvious ski lines are worthwhile objectives, but these mountains also reward exploration. The fit and adventurous can combine the two for extended loops to sample both together.

ACCESS

Parking is limited close to this tour. From Stevens Pass, drive east on US Highway 2 a little less than 7 miles to the Cascade Railroad Tunnel East Portal buildings, which you can see on the north side of the highway just after the divided highway ends. From the east, you can see these buildings 0.5 mile west of where US Highway 2 crosses under the main railroad line at 2800 feet.

Henry Creek approach. Plowed shoulder pullout spaces may be available just west of the East Portal access road entrance or farther west along the highway at an access road immediately east of the end of the divided portion of the highway. These are not designated winter access public parking areas. Observe all "no parking" signs, and do not park in any way that interferes with plowing operations, traffic, or railroad and Washington State Department of Transportation access.

Lanham Lake approach. There is ample designated public parking at the Stevens Pass Nordic Center and Lanham Lake trailhead, 5.8 miles east of Stevens Pass. Park in the outer lot designated for public access and kindly plowed by the Stevens Pass Ski Area.

TOUR

JIM HILL MOUNTAIN: LANHAM LAKE APPROACH. Jim Hill Mountain can be accessed via Lanham Lake. This approach makes the most sense if you park at the Lanham Lake trailhead at the Stevens Pass Nordic Center, and it has the advantage of a slightly higher elevation start and slightly shorter distance to the summit compared to the Henry Creek approach.

For the Lanham Lake approach, find the marked backcountry corridor access trail at the east end of the Stevens Pass Nordic Center inner parking lot, just inside the gate that separates the outer lot from the inner lot. Follow this trail as it ascends along the west side of Lanham Creek, crossing under powerlines to reenter the forest above 3400 feet. Continue on the west side of the creek along the route of the summer trail to Lanham Lake.

Reach a clearing at 3900 feet, and start a rising traverse southeast linking open areas on steep, tree-covered slopes. Work up through small cliff bands to gain lower-angled terrain higher up. Be aware of the potential for avalanches on small features that can run through these timbered areas. Continue working up and southeast to a low point on Jim Hill's north ridge at 5520 feet. Be careful not to trend too far south into steeper terrain on the way up to the ridge (2.75 hours to here). From 5520 feet,

Jim Hill Mountain from the north (Scott Schell)

climb south along the ridge to find easy ramps traversing into the north bowl of Jim Hill—your playground for the day.

The false summit of Jim Hill presides over the north bowl, and you will be able to find good ski lines from either shoulder of the false summit pyramid. To reach the true summit, ski up parallel to or on the north ridgeline to 6200 feet where you can cross back over the ridge into the small hanging valley west of the false summit. Ski up the hanging valley to the small col that separates the true summit pyramid from the false summit pyramid.

Depot your skis here, and boot up the final 150 feet along the northeast ridge to the summit, which may include a short third-class section, depending on the conditions. Alternatively, ski up the northwest face of the false summit to maximize your ski descent (4 hours to the top).

After taking in the great views of the Chiwaukum Range to the south and the peaks of Nason Ridge to the north, return to your skis for the fun part: 2200 feet of north-facing, moderately angled powder heaven when conditions are right. Ski whatever looks good into the Henry Creek valley to 4400 feet, above the lower basin waterfalls.

From 4400 feet, climb back up the bowl to the low point on Jim Hill's north ridge at 5520 feet to ski the trees back down the Lanham Lake ascent route.

ARROWHEAD MOUNTAIN AND JIM HILL MOUNTAIN: HENRY CREEK APPROACH. When parking is available near Henry Creek, you can access Arrowhead Mountain and Jim Hill Mountain from a logging road that heads south from US Highway 2 just west of the creek; this is called the Henry Creek approach. Older USGS maps show this logging road as a short spur ending at Henry Creek. More recent maps show the full length of Forest Service Road 687, which extends above 4200 feet on Arrowhead Mountain. Reach the road to Henry Creek by walking east along the highway if the shoulder is wide enough and plows are not operating. Alternatively, skin on the south side of the road to avoid plows and the hazards of vehicles traveling at freeway speeds.

To access Arrowhead Mountain, tour up FS Road 687 to the clear-cut east of Henry Creek. Make a rising traverse east to regain the logging road near 3600 feet. Follow the road east as it crosses the creek that flows from the Arrowhead Basin at 3800 feet. Stay on the road or tour through forest to bypass switchbacks up the east side of the creek to an upper clear-cut above 4100 feet (1.5 hours to here).

Climb the east side of the upper clear-cut, and reenter forest above 4500 feet below a rock outcropping on Arrowhead's upper west slope. Climb east-southeast, linking

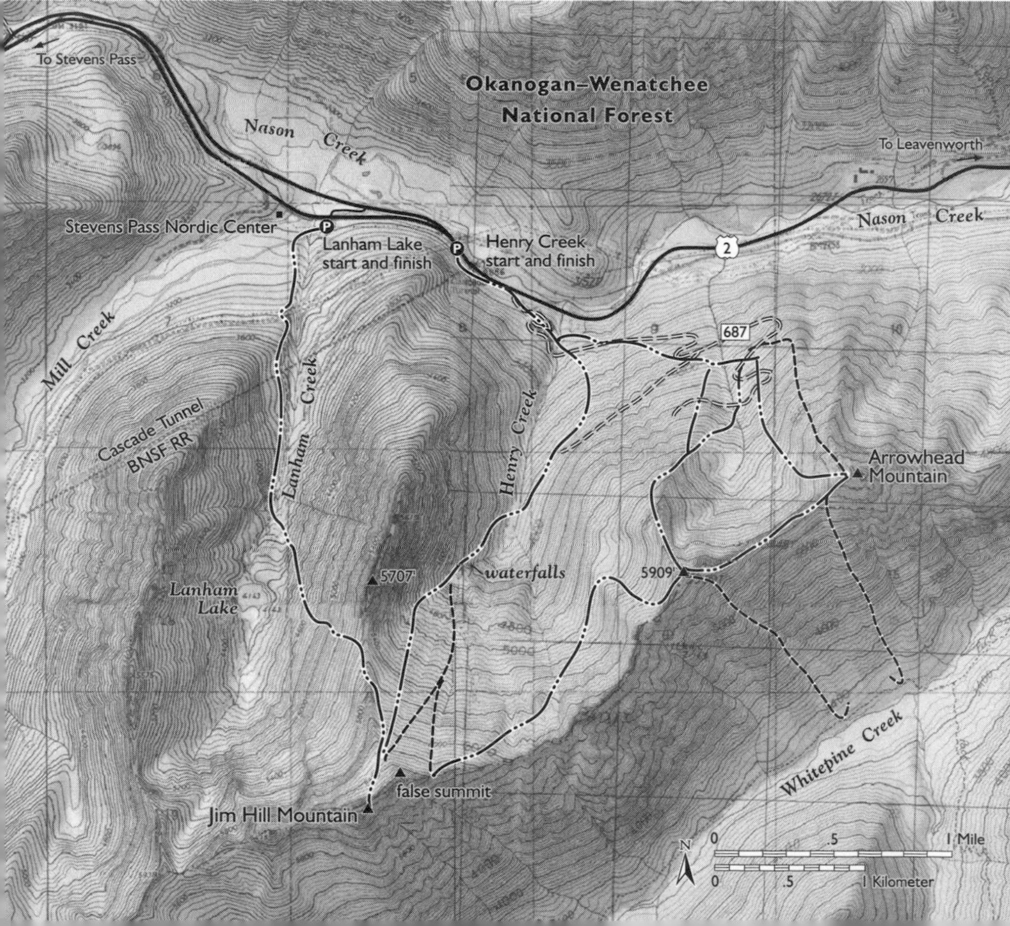

open glades on Arrowhead's west face, or, for a safer alternative, tour more directly south through denser trees to reach the southwest ridge at 5440 feet. Climb the ridge to the summit, bypassing a small rock rib on the north (3.5 hours to here).

From the summit, ski the glades of the west face, or descend and traverse north to ski the broad northwest ridge, traversing back to the logging road below 4000 feet. Alternate glades in tight trees can be found off Point 5909, which forms the west portion of the Arrowhead cirque.

For a steeper descent, you can ski south-facing glades and avalanche paths from the ridge crest down to Whitepine Creek. You must have excellent snow stability to safely ski this area and then climb 2400 feet out of the valley to meet back up with your ascent route. You can also link the Arrowhead area to Jim Hill by descending the short treed bowl southwest of Point 5909, rounding a rib, and making a climbing traverse up through steep terrain, tight trees, and several small gullies on the north side of the ridge crest.

To access Jim Hill Mountain from Henry Creek, enter the clear-cut east of Henry Creek, and start climbing south to gain the spur road at the top of the clear-cut that contours southwest. Follow the road to its end, take off your skins, and make a moderately descending traverse through a short section of trees to a slope that leads down to the open lower basin of Henry Creek near 3800 feet (1.5 hours to here).

Continue by crossing the creek and touring up the west side of the valley to get above the lower waterfalls of Henry Creek. Above 4400 feet, stay on the west side of the valley, or make a short traverse east to gain the most open path in the main Henry Creek drainage to the upper north bowl. Tour up the bowl to connect with the ascent route described in the Lanham Lake approach.

Tour Author: Benjamin Haskell, with special thanks to Olivia Race

44 Lichtenberg Mountain

Starting elevation: 3160 feet
High point: 5844 feet
Vertical gain/loss: 2700 feet/2700 feet
Distance: 12 km (7 miles)
Time: 4–7 hours, depending on your route
Overall difficulty: moderate
Ski skills: moderate to difficult
Fitness level: moderately strenuous
Technical skills: moderate
Commitment: very low
Gear: the basics
Best season: December–April
USGS map: Labyrinth Mountain
Permits: none

With a variety of slopes suitable for introductory, intermediate, and more advanced ski tours, Lichtenberg Mountain offers a little something for everyone. Its mix of alpine bowls and treed slopes ensures good skiing in many different conditions. Prominent ski lines visible from US Highway 2 and easy travel for other winter recreationalists along Smithbrook Road, make it a popular destination. But skiing can be found on every aspect of the mountain, so Lichtenberg Mountain rewards those who are willing to explore. Views into the Union and Jove Peak areas to the north provide enticing possibilities for additional exploration in this area.

ACCESS

Drive US Highway 2 to the Smithbrook Road pullout near mile 69, 4.7 miles east of Stevens Pass off the westbound lanes of the divided highway. If you are driving

Lichtenberg Mountain from the north (Scott Schell)

eastbound, drive a little less than 6 miles from the pass to the U-turn at the Stevens Pass Nordic Center (Mill Creek) exit to turn westbound and backtrack about 1.2 miles to the pullout.

From the east, the pullout is approximately 2 miles west of the start of the divided section of US Highway 2. The pullout is usually (but not always) plowed wide for winter access by the Washington State Department of Transportation crews. Heed all posted closure or no parking signs. Cars parked outside the pullout will likely be towed. Park and walk a short way west to the Smithbrook Road (Forest Service Road 6700) to start the tour.

Alternatively, you can access Lichtenberg from the Yodelin area, 2.5 miles to the west. (See Access for Tour 42.) Do not park in the plowed entrance road on the north side of the highway, which is maintained and reserved for parking by Yodelin residents only. The Stevens Pass Ski Area maintains the parking lot on the south side of the highway for employee and overflow skier parking. Respect ski area operations, and do not park here on predictably busy ski weekends.

TOUR

Skin up the mostly flat Smithbrook Road. At the first switchback, head west through the woods to access the northeast slopes of the mountain. Skin up through steep, mature trees climber's right of the main drainage from Lichtenwasser Lake. Gain the lake (2 hours to here). Some people prefer to continue farther up Smithbrook Road to gain the bottom of the north ridge at 4000 feet and then follow terrain across benches to the lake.

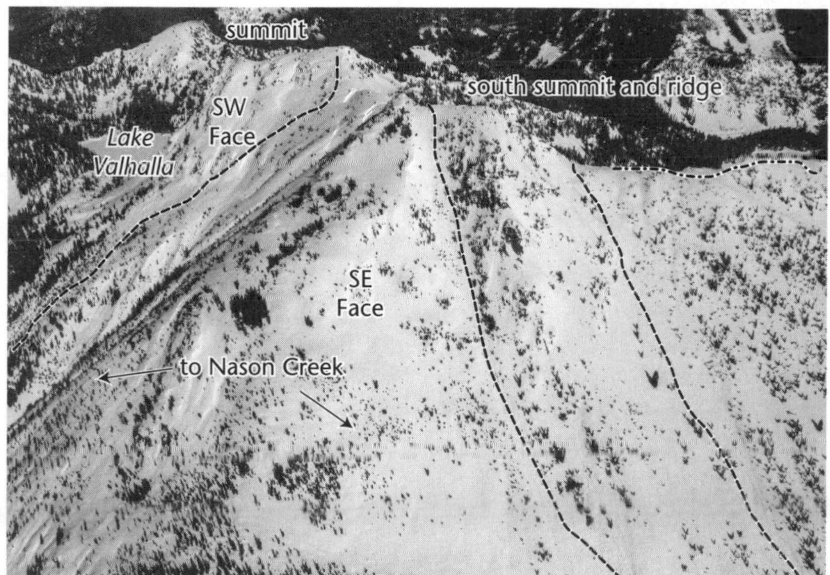

Lichtenberg Mountain from the south (Scott Schell)

Options abound from the lake. If cornices allow, climb directly up valley to the saddle between the main summit and south summit. Or gain the moderate northeast ridge, and follow its direct, undulating line to the top (3 hours to the summit). If you want to ski from the south summit, ascend the climber's left side of the valley through a draw that gains the ridge northeast of the south summit.

If avalanche conditions preclude you from skiing from the summit area, take advantage of well-spaced tree skiing on the ascent slopes below the lake. To extend your lower elevation or tree skiing options, climb the ridge east of the lake, and ski east of the main drainage or ski the left side of a small bowl coinciding with the word "Lichtenwasser" on the USGS map.

From the summit, you can ski more than 2800 feet southwest and then south directly into the upper Nason Creek drainage. Or enjoy shaded, lower-angled slopes northeast back toward the Smithbrook drainage. The northeast slopes also provide access to several steeper, fun, north-facing slots that lead to the valley floor north of the mountain.

From just east of the south summit, you can access the prominent 2300-foot, southeast-facing, shallow couloir visible from US Highway 2. Or ski southeast from either of the low points along the ridge down to the meadows below the southeast face. You can link the meadows to tour flat terrain for 2.5 kilometers (1.6 miles) back to the start by staying skier's left of Nason Creek. If you choose this return, be sure to stay well away from the base of the mountain to avoid the avalanche runouts that roll into this valley.

Tour Author: Benjamin Haskell

45 Rock Mountain to Mount Mastiff Traverse

Starting elevation: 2900 feet (finish at 2670 feet)
High point: 7063 feet
Vertical gain/loss: 7740 feet/7970 feet
Distance: 21 km (13 miles)
Time: 10.5–12.5 hours
Overall difficulty: very difficult
Ski skills: difficult
Fitness level: very strenuous
Technical skills: moderate
Commitment: moderate
Gear: the basics
Best season: January–early March
USGS map: Mount Howard
Permits: none

Nason Ridge follows US Highway 2 for miles just east of Stevens Pass, and this tour follows the ridge for three summits (Rock Mountain, Mount Howard, and Mount Mastiff) and 12 kilometers (7 miles) of alpine terrain. Even with four quality descents, you still pass numerous bowls and chutes in order to make it back to your car in a day. This a great tour to extend into an overnight to have more time to ski, but that adds some car shenanigans. This tour description is for a one-day itinerary.

ACCESS

The tour starts at the unnamed road at the Rock Mountain trailhead, at milepost 73.1 on US Highway 2, 8.5 miles east of Stevens Pass. You will want to either stage a car or bicycle 3 miles farther east, at the Merritt Lake trailhead (milepost 76.1), or be prepared to walk back up the road to your starting point. Your exit point is several hundred feet lower than the starting point, so be ready for some hiking if you do this tour later than mid-March. The shoulders are plowed at both points, but your car will be towed if plow operations occur while it is parked there. This is why most people do this tour in one day.

TOUR

Follow the road for the Rock Mountain trailhead under buzzing electrical wires, and start climbing. Hug the same ridge that the summer trail follows, climbing up almost 4000 feet into the alpine zone, leaving the trees at 5800 feet, and finally spotting the summit of Rock Mountain. The route logically gains the southern subsummit at 6680 feet (4 hours to here), and then traverses the ridge north to the true summit at 6860 feet (4.5 hours to here). Drop off and skier's left down the north face of Rock Mountain for a 1200-foot run to 5600 feet. Then turn east and climb up to the visible low point and notch in the ridge at 6380 feet, between two unnamed summits that separate Rock Mountain and Mount Howard (6 hours to here).

Ski your second descent—almost 1000 feet—to Crescent Lake at 5460 feet (6.5 hours to here). This is the only bail-out point on this tour; it is possible to follow the summer trail east to rejoin the Merritt Lake Trail and the tour's final descent.

From Crescent Lake, climb up the south slopes of Mount Howard, the high point of the tour at 7063 feet (8 hours to here). The actual summit is at the very top of the north ridge; the northeast ridge, where the next descent starts, is a couple of hundred feet downhill to the east and is not very pronounced where it joins the summit ridge. Look for a rock thumb that marks the junction and provides a great entrance. Ski down the northeast ridge for 400 to 500 feet, and then turn right and ski almost due east for another 700 feet to Canaan Lake at 5920 feet (8.5 hours to here).

Another straightforward climb up the southwest slopes of Mount Mastiff leads to its summit at 6741 feet (9.5 hours to the summit) and the final alpine descent. The east face of Mastiff is big and steep. While a continuous, direct line to the Lost Lake may be possible, most skiers will want to veer north at 6200 feet in order to gain a gully leading to open slopes north of the lake. Follow those slopes down to the lake at 4930 feet, and cross to its southern shore. Then climb one last time through big trees to the bench and notch over Merritt Lake at 5580 feet (10.5 hours to here).

Rock Mountain from the northeast (Chris Simmons)

Ski down and left to stay in open glades to Merritt Lake at 5003 feet, and skate or shuffle across it. Then follow Merritt Creek, and ski a rightward traverse that roughly follows the trail. Aim to reach the ridge before 4200 feet, and at that elevation, drop down the south side and ski the fall line for 1200 feet. Start looking for the trailhead road at 3000 feet, and follow it right back to the highway at 2670 feet (11.5 hours to here).

Tour Author: Chris Simmons

46 The Enchantments Traverse

Starting elevation: 1320 feet
High point: 7800 feet
Vertical gain/loss: 7250 feet/6510 feet
Distance: 31 km (19 miles)
Time: 2 days
Overall difficulty: moderate
Ski skills: moderate
Fitness level: strenuous
Technical skills: moderate
Commitment: moderate

Gear: the basics, an ice ax, crampons, and overnight gear
Best season: January–March
USGS maps: Leavenworth, Blewett, Enchantment Lakes, and Cashmere Mountain
Permits: You do not have to display a parking pass during winter, but we recommend that you get and display a Northwest Forest Pass. Fill out the Wenatchee National Forest self-service wilderness permit at the trailhead. This tour is best done in midwinter, and you'll want to be aware that overnight camping is subject to permit limitations after June 15. Check the Okanogan–Wenatchee National Forest website for current details on obtaining a permit if planning a trip into this area in late spring.

The Enchantments are a high lakes basin in the Stuart Range full of larch trees and polished granite. It is one of the most desirable summer hiking destinations in the state, resulting in responsible regulation of overnight use. In winter there is no cap on permits, since only a hardy few will visit the frozen landscape of this beautiful high country. This traverse goes in through Snow Lakes and out via Aasgard Pass over Colchuck Lake. Because it takes great effort to get into the Enchantments, we recommend that you add a day to your trip to ski off nearby peaks such as Little Annapurna, Cannon Mountain, or Dragontail Peak.

ACCESS

From Leavenworth, drive south on Icicle Road (Forest Service Road 76) for 4 miles to the Snow Lake trailhead on your left. If you can, shuttle another vehicle about 4.5 miles farther where Eightmile Road (Forest Service Road 7601) starts on your left. Icicle Road is usually plowed only to this point in the winter.

TOUR

DAY 1. Start up the hiking trail, either booting or skinning depending on snow levels. Follow the trail up switchbacks and finally into the creek basin around 2800 feet. The trail ascends left from the creek and becomes tough to follow above 3600 feet. If the trail is not obvious, climb the fall line to about 3920 feet, and make an ascending traverse right above rock bands and eventually back to Snow Creek. Continue skinning along the trail or climber's right of the creek beyond Nada Lake to where you climb a more exposed slope southwest. Travel through the forested saddle northeast of Snow Lake, and proceed down to the lake at 5420 feet (6 hours to here).

Cross Snow Lake (staying on the south banks if you cannot find a stable crossing), and then ascend west along the right side of the creek. The tight trees in this section make for tougher travel until the terrain opens up around 6100 feet. Climb right away from the drainage up steep slopes before traversing left at 6800 feet to the outflow of Lake Viviane.

Tour the path of least resistance (mostly tracing the route of the summer trail) west to Perfection Lake, being cautious of the windloaded slopes that are often prevalent on these northeast aspects. Find a protected camp spot among the larch trees north of the lake (8.5 hours to here).

DAY 2. Tour west onto Inspiration Lake, and again follow the general route of the summer trail to Aasgard Pass (labeled as Colchuck Pass on the USGS map) at 7800 feet. You will likely have to remove your skis early on the descent to walk over short rocky sections. Ski northwest, being cautious where the snow thins and you must sidestep through rocks, until the terrain finally opens up to fantastic fall-line skiing. Enjoy more than 2000 vertical feet of great turns alongside Dragontail Peak down onto Colchuck Lake (2 hours to here).

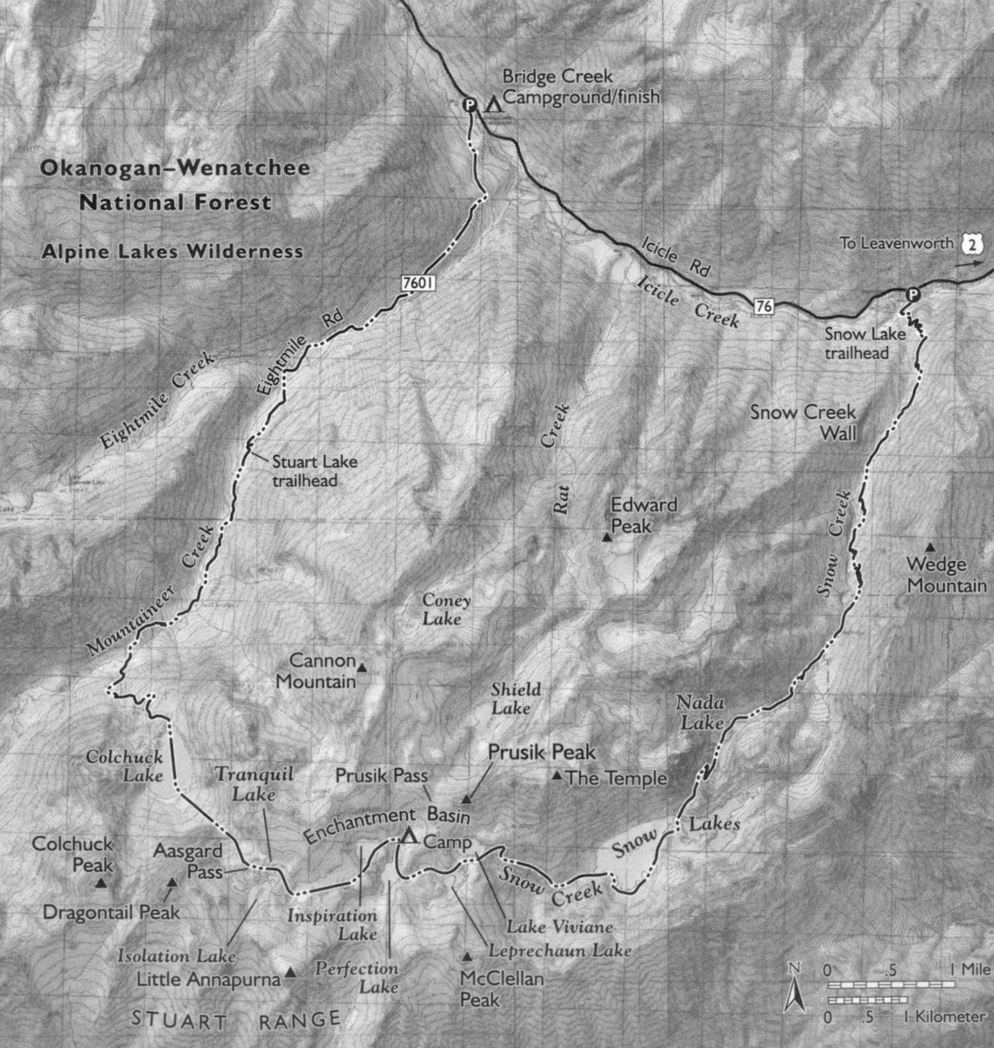

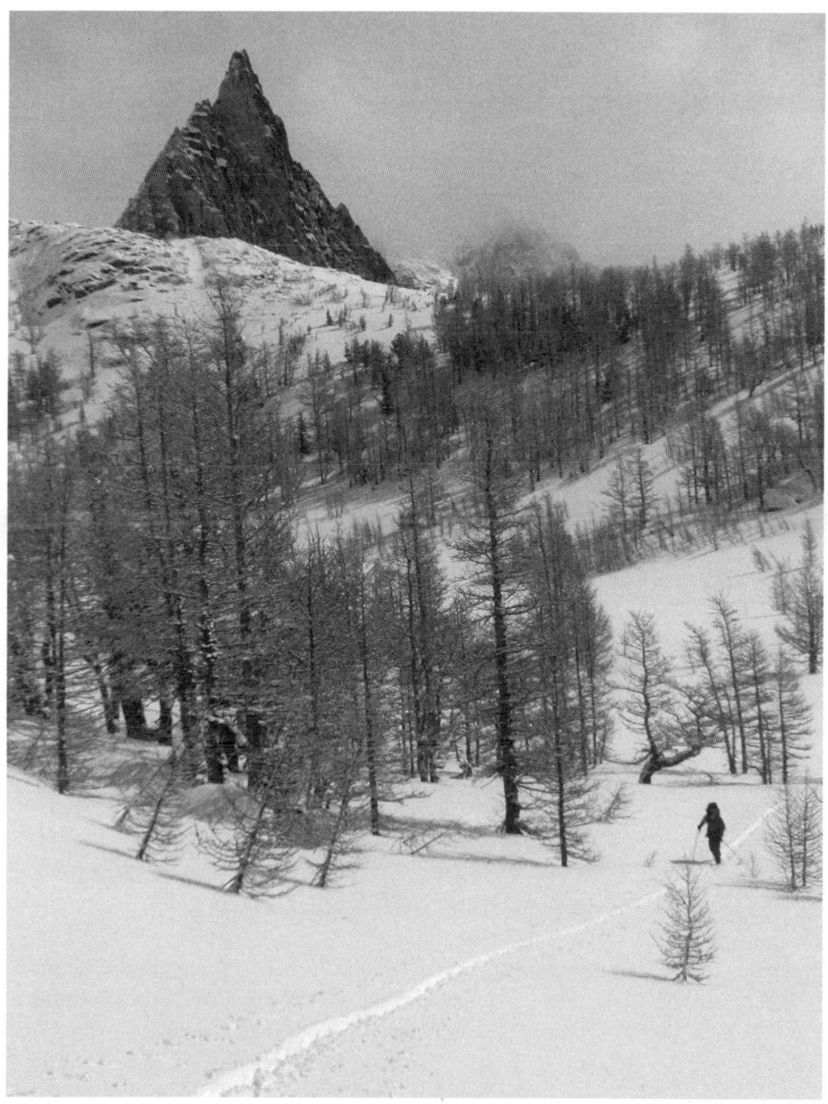

Touring across the Enchantment Plateau underneath Prusik Peak from the west (Trevor Kostanich)

Cross Colchuck Lake, and pick up the hiking trail about 100 meters (300 feet) west of the lake outflow. Follow the trail northwest down to Mountaineer Creek and finally out to the Stuart Lake trailhead. This trail's tight trees and quick turns make it challenging. You end this traverse with an easy 6-kilometer (3.75 mile) glide down Eightmile Road to Icicle Road at 2640 feet (5 hours to here).

Tour Author: Trevor Kostanich

47 The Central Cascades Traverse

Starting elevation: 1320 feet
High point: 7960 feet
Vertical gain/loss: 31,200 feet/30,320 feet
Distance: 90 km (56 miles)
Time: 7 days
Overall difficulty: very difficult
Ski skills: very difficult
Fitness level: extremely strenuous
Technical skills: high
Commitment: very high
Gear: the basics, plus ski mountaineering and overnight equipment
Best season: March–May
USGS maps: Leavenworth, Blewett, Enchantment Lakes, Mount Stuart, Jack Ridge, The Cradle, Mount Daniel, Big Snow Mountain, Chikamin Peak, and Snoqualmie Pass
Permits: Display a Northwest Forest Pass or Interagency Pass to park your vehicle at the Snow Lake trailhead starting in the spring, and display a Sno-Park Permit in a vehicle left at Gold Creek. Fill out a self-issued permit for the Alpine Lakes Wilderness at the trailhead. This tour is best done in early spring, but be aware that overnight camping is subject to permit limitations in The Enchantments after June 15. Check the Okanogan–Wenatchee National Forest website for current details on obtaining a permit if planning a trip into this area in late spring.

This wild crossing links traverses through The Enchantments, Wenatchee Mountains, and Snoqualmie High Peaks and is intended to inspire creativity in Cascadian exploration. These three spines form an obvious link-up when you view them from the North Cascades, and the diverse terrain they offer will not disappoint you.

As with any big traverse, the weather, snowpack conditions, and your team's energy level can mandate alternate routes. Equally challenging is the decision to skirt remote summits in order to cover the necessary mileage to stay on plan. Since this route bypasses a desired high leg through some of the Wenatchee Mountains, consider it a general guide for this large crossing; perhaps some future skiers will build on it.

Opposite page:
(Left) Western portion of The Central Cascades Traverse from the southeast; (Right) Central portion of The Central Cascades Traverse from the southeast (both photos by Scott Schell)

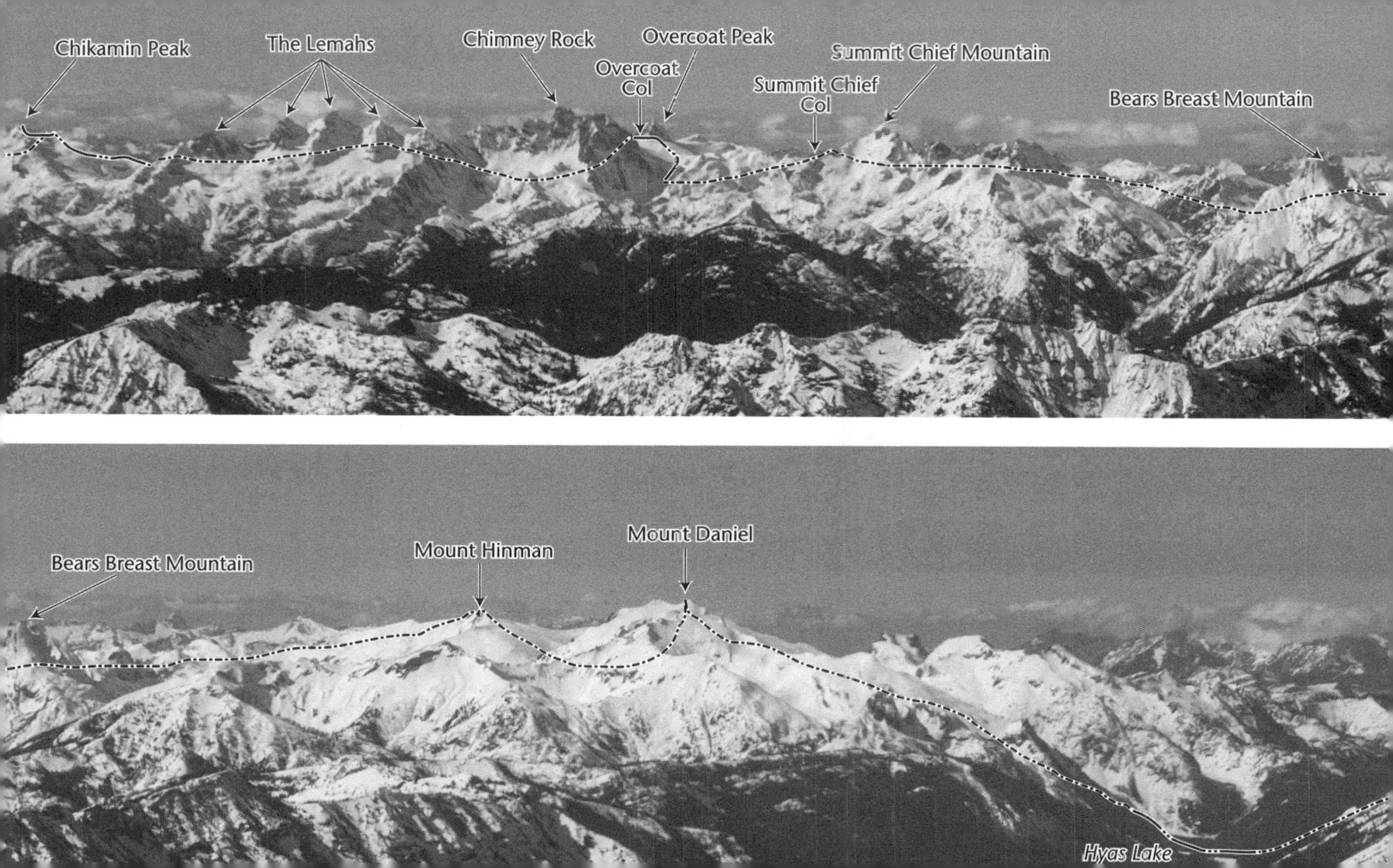
Chikamin Peak
The Lemahs
Chimney Rock
Overcoat Peak
Overcoat Col
Summit Chief Mountain
Summit Chief Col
Bears Breast Mountain
Bears Breast Mountain
Mount Hinman
Mount Daniel
Hyas Lake

ACCESS

From Leavenworth, drive south on Icicle Road (Forest Service Road 76) for 4 miles to the Snow Lake trailhead on your left. You will want to coordinate a vehicle drop-off at the Gold Creek trailhead near Snoqualmie Pass for your exit. Gold Creek is located 2.3 miles east of Snoqualmie Pass on Interstate 90. Take exit 54 and travel east a few hundred yards to park at the Washington State Gold Creek Sno-Park on the southwest end of the Gold Creek valley.

TOUR

DAY 1. Start up the hiking trail, skinning once there is ample snow. Follow the trail up switchbacks and finally into the creek basin around 2800 feet. The trail ascends left from the creek and becomes tough to follow above 3600 feet. If the trail is not obvious, climb the fall line to about 3920 feet, and make an ascending traverse right above rock bands and eventually back to Snow Creek. Continue skinning along the trail or climber's right of the creek beyond Nada Lake to where you climb a more exposed southwest slope before reaching Snow Lake (6 hours to here).

Cross Snow Lake (staying on the south banks if you cannot find a stable crossing) and then ascend west along the right side of the creek. The tight trees in this section make for tougher travel until the terrain opens up around 6100 feet. Climb right away from the drainage up steep slopes before traversing left at 6800 feet to the outflow of Lake Viviane.

Tour the path of least resistance (mostly tracing the route of the summer trail) west to Perfection Lake, being cautious of the windloaded slopes that are often prevalent on these northeast aspects. Find a protected camp spot among the larch trees north of the lake (8.5 hours to here).

DAY 2. This short travel day provides great opportunities to explore nearby peaks. Tour west onto Inspiration Lake, and again follow the general route of the summer trail to Aasgard Pass (labeled as Colchuck Pass on the USGS map) at 7800 feet. Enjoy more than 2000 vertical feet of great turns alongside Dragontail Peak down onto Colchuck Lake. You may have to remove your skis early on the descent to walk over short rocky sections. Cross Colchuck Lake, and then ski northwest down to Mountaineer Creek. Transition back to skinning, and ascend west to make camp near Lake Stuart (3.5 hours to here).

DAY 3. Follow the drainage west up to Jack Lake, and climb northwest over Jack Ridge at 7350 feet (2.5 hours to here). A great ski west into Jack Creek commits you to an area that can otherwise be hard to reach in the snowy months; bad weather forced the pioneering group to follow Jack Creek north. This section has tight trees, and you will need your skins for small rises along the downhill slog to Meadow Creek (5.5 hours to here). Turn west up Meadow Creek, and set camp around 4020 feet (6.5 hours to here).

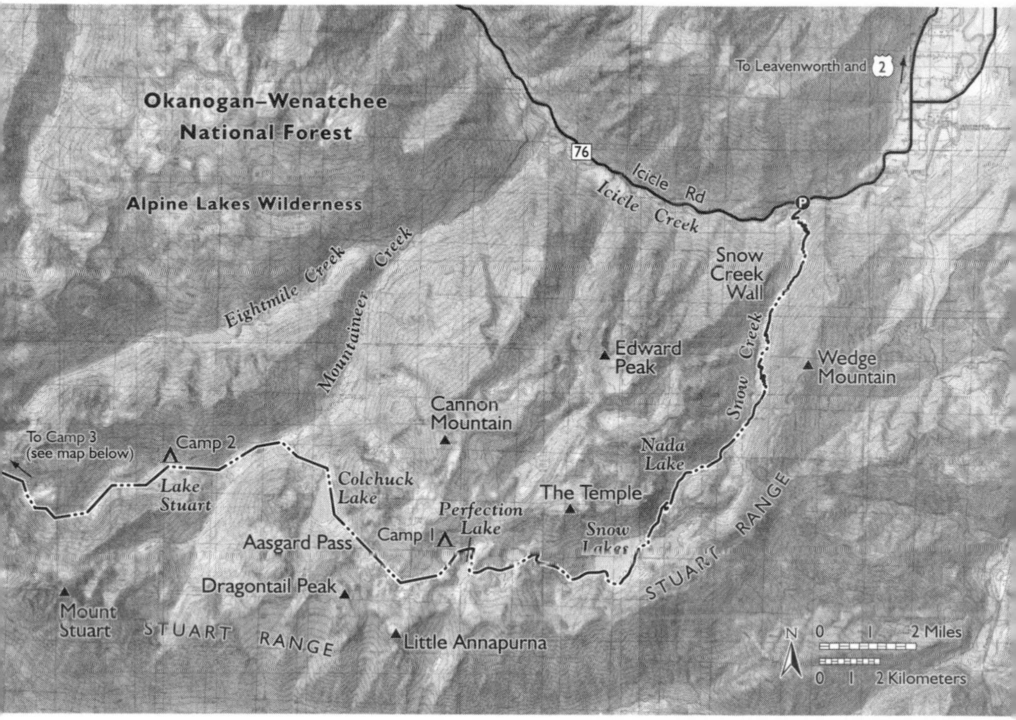

Okanogan–Wenatchee National Forest

Alpine Lakes Wilderness

To Leavenworth and 2

76

Icicle Rd

Icicle Creek

Eightmile Creek

Mountaineer Creek

Snow Creek Wall

Snow Creek

Edward Peak

Wedge Mountain

Cannon Mountain

To Camp 3 (see map below)

Camp 2

Lake Stuart

Colchuck Lake

Nada Lake

The Temple

Perfection Lake

Camp 1

Aasgard Pass

Snow Lakes

Stuart Range

Dragontail Peak

Mount Stuart

Little Annapurna

0 1 2 Miles

0 1 2 Kilometers

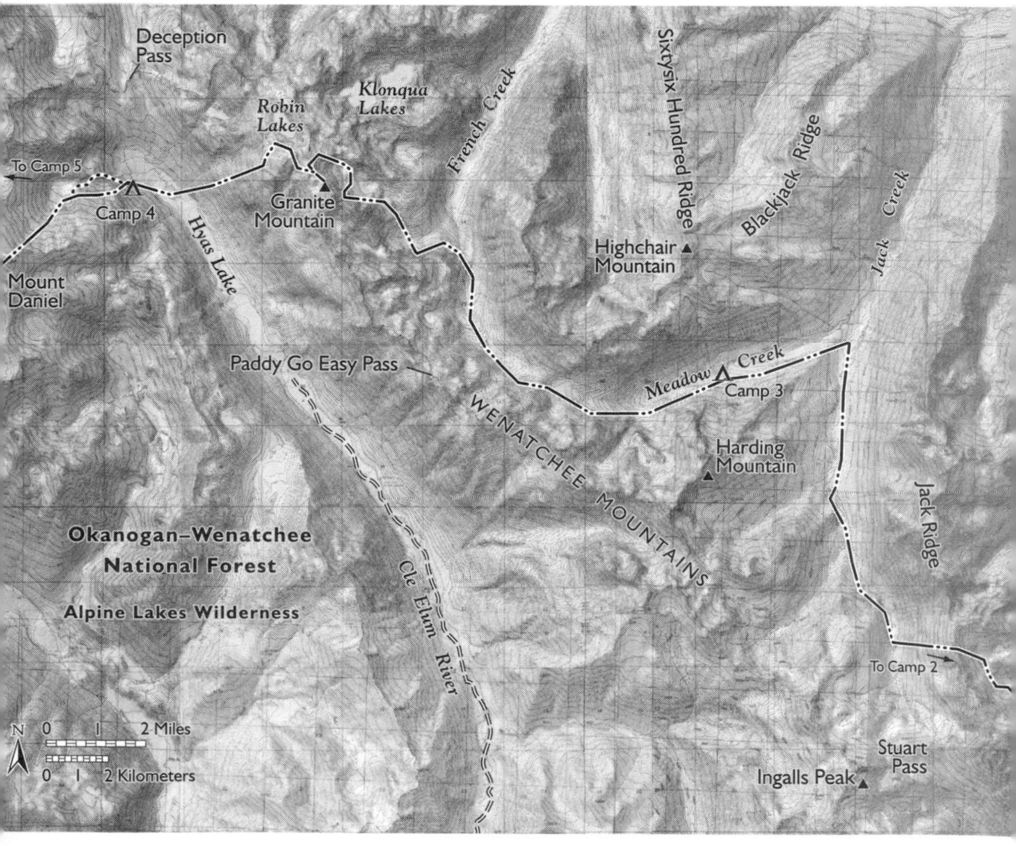

Deception Pass

Robin Lakes

Klonqua Lakes

French Creek

Sixtysix Hundred Ridge

Blackjack Ridge

Jack Creek

To Camp 5

Camp 4

Granite Mountain

Hyas Lake

Highchair Mountain

Mount Daniel

Paddy Go Easy Pass

Meadow Creek

Camp 3

Wenatchee Mountains

Harding Mountain

Jack Ridge

Okanogan–Wenatchee National Forest

Alpine Lakes Wilderness

Cle Elum River

To Camp 2

0 1 2 Miles

0 1 2 Kilometers

Stuart Pass

Ingalls Peak

DAY 4. Travel west to the saddle at 5350 feet (2 hours to here). Ski northwest and then north down the valley to about 4200 feet where you traverse left. Transition to your skins, ascend a drainage west to 4400 feet, and then climb north up the right side of a creek. At 5250 feet, the bottom of Granite Mountain's southeast basin welcomes you back into the high country (4 hours from camp).

Tour up the basin onto a bench on climber's right at 5750 feet. Climb north up the ridge onto a saddle at 6250 feet. From this saddle, continue northwest over flatter terrain before climbing counterclockwise up this basin to the summit of Granite Mountain (6 hours to here).

From this perch, observe the great distance you have traveled from the Stuart Range before turning around and admiring the snowy massif of Mount Daniel you will explore tomorrow. Bring your focus back to closer ground, and prepare for a most pleasant descent.

Ski northwest through a saddle at 6750 feet before enjoying a fun line directly to the largest of the Robin Lakes. This protected north-facing shot holds good powder snow late into the season. Traverse west over the lakes, and then enjoy almost 3000 feet of fall-line turns down to Upper Hyas Lake (7.5 hours to here). Stay left on the upper half of the descent, and then trend right lower in the trees. Camp near open water above Upper Hyas Lake.

DAY 5. You spend most of this big day in alpine terrain. With an early start and confidence in the snow's stability, your most direct route is to climb the obvious cleft west into the bottom of Mount Daniel's northeast basin. An alternate route travels north of this terrain trap using the forested ridge on climber's left. From the flat spot at 5200 feet, descend a short, steep pitch south into the base of the northeast cirque at 4900 feet (2 hours to here).

Climb southwest up the Daniel Glacier using terrain features to set a safe and efficient skin track. Gain the saddle between the East and Middle Summits, and continue northwest to the Middle Summit at 7960 feet (4.5 hours to here). Look down onto the Lynch Glacier, and soak in massive acreage of treeless terrain rare in the Central Cascades.

Descend the vast Lynch Glacier, and continue northwest to a low point around 5100 feet. Transition back to skins, and tour southwest over large, moderate slopes to the top of Mount Hinman at 7490 feet (8 hours to here). Ski west off the summit, traveling over a ridge and maintaining a westward traverse. At 6650 feet drop west off the glaciated slope, skiing some steeper turns down to the col between La Bohn Lakes and Chain Lakes. Cruise south over the Chain Lakes, following the drainage down to Williams Lake (9 hours to here).

DAY 6. Ski down to about 4250 feet, and then tour south into the beautiful Summit Chief basin. With mean rocky veins of Summit Chief's north face on your left, follow the easier terrain right up to the col at 6140 feet (2.5 hours to here). Ski steep slopes

Mount Baker–Snoqualmie
National Forest
Alpine Lakes Wilderness
La Bohn
Lakes
Mount
Hinman
Mount
Daniel
Iron Cap
Mountain
La Bohn
Gap
Camp 5
Bears Breast Mountain
Big Snow
Mountain
Dutch Miller Gap
Summit Chief Mountain
Overcoat Peak
Chimney Rock
Waptus Lake
Mount
Price
Snoqualmie River
110
Middle Fork
Lemah Mountain
Camp 6
Huckleberry Mountain
Chikamin Peak
Mount Thomson
Joe Lake
Snoqualmie
Mountain
Alaska Mountain
Chikamin Ridge
Red Mountain
Kendall
Katwalk
Gold Creek
Kendall Peak
Snoqualmie Pass
Gold Creek
Hyak
Gold Creek Sno-Park
90
Keechelus
Lake
Little Kachess Lake
N
0 1 2 Miles
0 1 2 Kilometers

south trending left until the terrain eases below 4700 feet. Tour southwest toward the large east face of Chimney Rock, and then turn northwest following the least steep terrain onto the upper reaches of the Overcoat Glacier. An alternate route stays high from Summit Chief Col and traverses steeper terrain where you may need to rappel a short distance to reach a southeast traverse to the Overcoat Glacier. Tour west to Overcoat Col south of Overcoat Peak, a picturesque spot for a quick lunch break (5 hours to here).

The descent from Overcoat Col to Iceberg Lake is steep and south-facing. Assess the slide hazard carefully, and be comfortable camping in this gorgeous location if need be. From Overcoat Col, descend cautiously before traversing right above a small cliff band. Finally, enjoy relatively low-consequence skiing down to Iceberg Lake. From the lake, tour south to an aesthetic notch at 6020 feet. Remove your skins to expedite the time you are exposed under The Lemahs, and make a quick traverse of this slope. Transition back to your skins, and tour through the saddle just north of Chikamin Lake. Climb a short, steep slope west into a ramp that allows for easier touring up the north side of Chikamin Peak. A pleasant perch at 6700 feet makes for a great campsite with fantastic views of the peaks you just traveled through (8.5 hours to here).

DAY 7. Climb a few hundred feet to the expansive summit ridge of Chikamin. The true summit is the high point to the southeast; to reach it, climb its north chute or contour around the rockier south side to its southeast slope. In stable conditions, you can ski from the summit following the chute southwest and finally traversing into the main gully down low. The top half of this descent can be fantastic, steep corn snow, while the bottom half is usually full of large avalanche debris.

The standard descent from the summit ridge travels skier's right through some rocky sections. The terrain opens up a bit below 6200 feet where you traverse right to the ridge located northeast of Huckleberry Mountain. Continue traversing past Point 5524, and finally descend to the outlet of Joe Lake (2 hours to here).

A longer but more interesting finish to Snoqualmie Pass is via Alaska Mountain, Kendall Katwalk, and Commonwealth Basin. This route describes the exit out Gold Creek. From Joe Lake, follow the outlet down to Gold Creek, maintaining a gliding traverse as long as you can. The exit out Gold Creek becomes a tour. Succumb to skins, and enjoy the long march out knowing you just crossed an extensive section of the Cascades (5 hours to here).

Tour Author: Trevor Kostanich

48 Cannon Mountain: Cannon Couloir

Starting elevation: 2080 feet
High point: 7800 feet
Vertical gain/loss: 5620 feet/ 5620 feet
Distance: 15 km (9.5 miles)

Time: 8–9 hours
Overall difficulty: very difficult
Ski skills: very difficult
Fitness level: very strenuous
Technical skills: moderate
Commitment: high
Gear: the basics, plus an ice ax and boot crampons for icy conditions
Best season: January–early March
USGS map: Cashmere Mountain
Permits: You do not need a permit for day use in the nonwilderness portion of the Okanogan–Wenatchee National Forest. If Eightmile Road is open, you must display a Northwest Forest Pass or Interagency Pass to park at the trailhead.

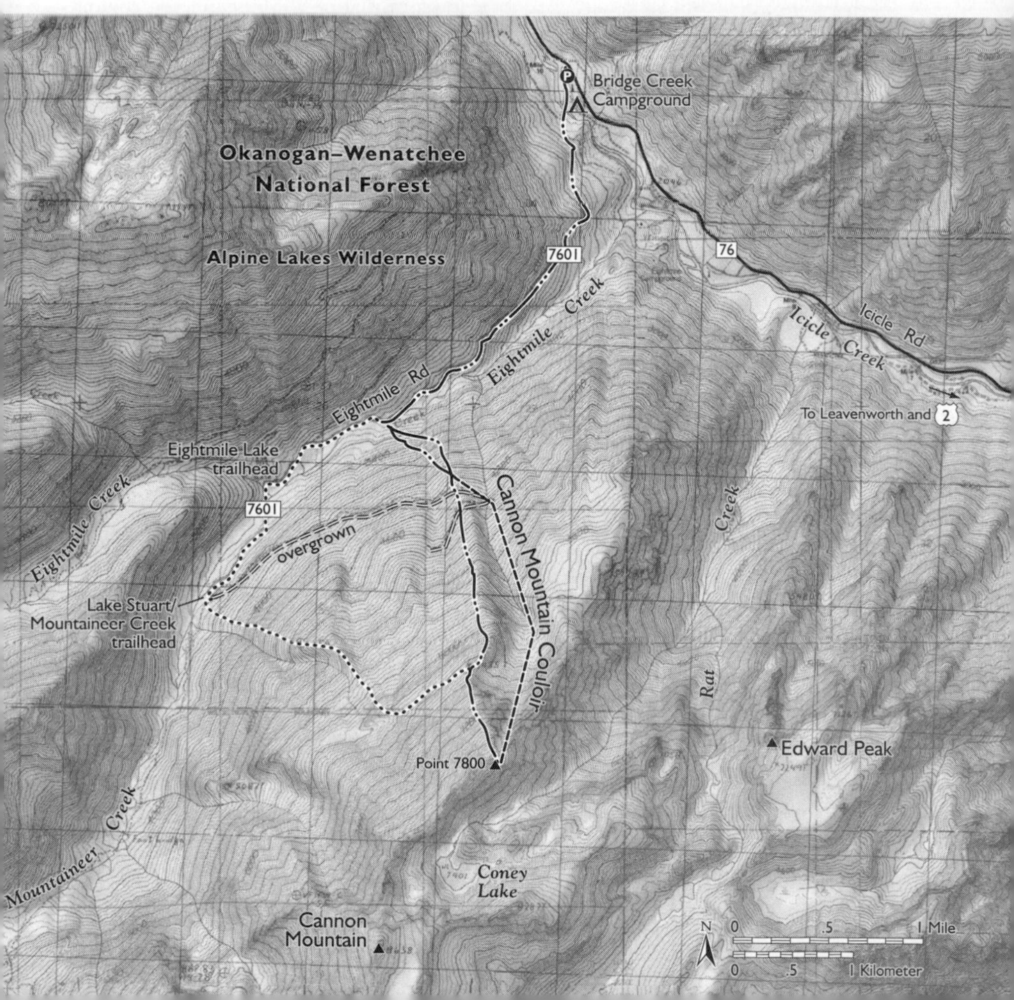

Just like a number of tours in this book, skiing the Cannon Couloir shows you another half-dozen objectives to add to your tick list. From the approach route, the couloir is so obvious and in-your-face that you cannot help but want to ski it. It is a must-do day trip for every local skier. Like many tours in this book, icy conditions earlier in the day may require ski mountaineering equipment, such as an ice ax and boot crampons.

ACCESS

From Leavenworth, drive about 8 miles up Icicle Road (Forest Service Road 76) until the end of where it is plowed near Bridge Creek Campground. The tour starts here.

TOUR

Follow Eightmile Road (Forest Service Road 7601) 2.5 miles to 3000 feet (1.5–2 hours to here). You will have ample opportunity to look straight up the Cannon Couloir, as well as the upper approach to the top of the couloir. Find a way across Eightmile Creek, and then climb upward and left to gain the slope and ridge immediately west of the couloir, reaching a bench at 6500 feet. Continue up the ridge to the couloir entrance just above 7800 feet (6–6.5 hours to here).

Alternatively, if the creek crossing at 3000 feet looks too treacherous, continue up the road another mile to its end at the trailhead for Lake Stuart Mountaineer Creek Trail. Follow the trail for about 300 feet before turning left and uphill. Aim to climb just north of a tributary creek to a bench at 6200 feet. Turn left and follow this bench in a rising climb southeast until you are able to rejoin the first approach near 6500 feet. This alternative adds an hour to the tour.

The Cannon Couloir descends the obvious slanting gash on Cannon Mountain's northeast face. (Alasdair Turner)

The old logging road that appears on the topo maps leading from the trailhead to 4700 feet is a sucker's trap. Alder and maple have fully overgrown it, and the surrounding terrain has deadfall-strewn slopes from multiple forest fires—it's best to stay away!

DESCENT. Sometimes the 40-degree entrance to the couloir is very firm or has a lot of exposed rocks, so it is possible instead to descend 100 feet on the ridge and traverse into the couloir. The approach should have provided you with ample observations to determine the avalanche hazard. Enjoy the excitement of a steep entrance and the aesthetic of a long, continuous descent down the couloir. As the couloir starts to fan out, favor the left side until you reach 4400 feet.

Leave the drainage and start descending leftward to rejoin your up track. Recross the creek, and follow Eightmile Road back to your car. If you do not want to commit to the couloir, you have numerous other descent options along the ridge between the couloir and the true summit of Cannon Mountain—just be aware that multiple forest fires over the years have filled the lower elevations with deadfall and new growth.

Tour Author: Chris Simmons

49 Colchuck Peak: Colchuck Glacier

Starting elevation: 2000 feet
High point: 8705 feet
Vertical gain/loss: 6705 feet/6705 feet
Distance: 19–24 km (11–14 miles), depending on road conditions
Time: 1–2 days
Overall difficulty: moderate
Ski skills: difficult
Fitness level: strenuous
Technical skills: moderate
Commitment: moderate
Gear: the basics, boot crampons, an ice ax, and overnight equipment
Best season: January–April
USGS maps: Enchantment Lakes and Cashmere Mountain
Permits: You must display a Northwest Forest Pass or Interagency Pass to park along Eightmile Road. You do not need to display a permit to park along Icicle Road during winter. You must fill out a free wilderness use permit at the trailhead. To stay overnight at Colchuck Lake after June 15, the Forest Service also requires a camping permit. These permits are limited. Check the Okanogan–Wenatchee National Forest website for current details on obtaining a permit if planning a trip in the late spring.

The Colchuck Glacier is a 2500-foot, north-facing ski descent nestled in the scenic terrain of the Stuart Range. From a col above 8000 feet down to Colchuck Lake, the craggy granite northwest face of Dragontail Peak makes for an incredible backdrop to this sustained fall-line ski descent.

ACCESS

From US Highway 2 just west of the town of Leavenworth, turn south on Icicle Road (Forest Service Road 76). At approximately mile 10, look for Eightmile Road (Forest Service Road 7601) on the left-hand side. This tour begins at the end of the maintained road during winter. As the season progresses, Road 7601 quickly melts out but may remain gated for many weeks; a pair of shoes can be a great help with the road walk.

TOUR

DAY 1. If your tour starts from the access point described above, you can expect a 6-kilometer (3.75-mile) skin up Eightmile Road during which you will slowly gain about 1400 feet to the trailhead for Stuart Lake Trail at 3400 feet (1.5 hours to here). From here, travel and navigation along Mountaineer Creek south-southwest is straightforward. Do your best to follow the summer trail. You will be traveling in heavily forested terrain on the valley floor, which can be disorienting at times—follow a solid compass bearing. At around 3900 feet, look for a footbridge for the creek crossing. Depending on the snow conditions, it can be difficult to cross the creek without it (2.5 hours to here).

The Colchuck Lake cirque from the north (Scott Schell)

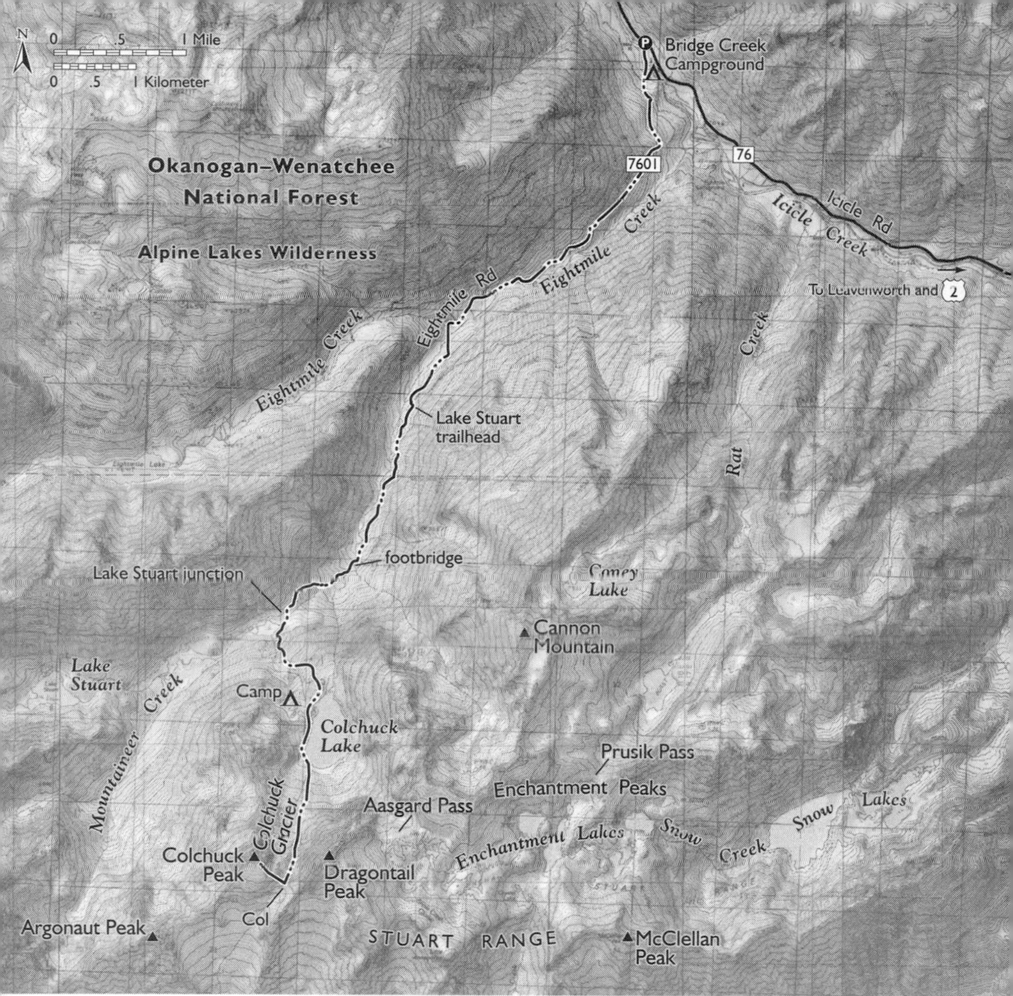

Continue up valley in a southwest direction to approximately 4480 feet, and reach a trail junction and clearing where you should start following a southeast bearing. It is important that you keep heading southeast; if you end up on the south side of the falls, reaching the lake will become much more complicated. This stretch will be your steepest yet on this tour, gaining about 1100 feet in less than 1 kilometer (less than 0.6 mile). The slope levels off, and you will soon see Colchuck Lake at an elevation of 5570 feet and the Colchuck Glacier farther south (5 hours to here). The northern edge of the lake makes for a very good campsite, well away from avalanche terrain. Running water is often available here.

DAY 2. The ski up toward the Colchuck Glacier is very direct and does not pose many navigation difficulties. At 5500 feet, you are at the upper reaches of tree line, and the col is quite obvious to the south between Dragontail Peak and Colchuck Peak. From camp at approximately 5500 feet, you gradually climb to nearly 6400 feet to reach the toe of the Colchuck Glacier.

The Colchuck Glacier is fairly benign and does not present the typical glacial hazards; nevertheless, it is a glacier—proper awareness is important. Keep in mind that you are traveling up a steep northeast aspect and that snow stability is critical. If you have any doubts, do not proceed. Once you are on the glacier, it is a direct 1600 feet to the col keeping just east of the rib that divides the north face of Colchuck Peak from the Colchuck Glacier (2.5 hours from camp to the col). Taking time to make the final climb to the summit (8705 feet) is well worth it (3.25 hours to summit).

DESCENT. For the descent, simply reverse your approach route. Enjoy a sustained, 2500-foot fall-line ski descent back to the lake (4.5 hours to this point). The distance required to get back to the car can make this a strenuous day, but getting an early start may allow you to take an extra lap. From camp, follow your skin track back to the trailhead and ultimately down Eightmile Road to your car (7 hours to here).

Tour Author: David Jordan

50 The Chiwaukum Traverse

Starting elevation: 2700 feet
High point: 8081 feet
Vertical gain/loss: 9800 feet/9400 feet
Distance: 27 km (17 miles)
Time: 2–4 days
Overall difficulty: difficult
Ski skills: moderate
Fitness level: strenuous
Technical skills: moderate
Commitment: high
Gear: the basics, plus ski mountaineering and overnight equipment
Best season: December–May
USGS maps: Mount Howard, Chiwaukum Mountains, and Jack Ridge
Permits: The Chiwaukums are part of the Okanogan–Wenatchee National Forest. Fill out a self-issued permit for the Alpine Lakes Wilderness at the trailhead.

A winter visit to the Chiwaukum Range west of Leavenworth will reignite your love of wilderness. Visible from Stevens Pass Ski Area, the Chiwaukums are the quiet cousins of The Enchantments. Characterized by broad cirques and long, attractive ski lines, this range is rugged and yet free of glaciers. This is a ski mountaineering tour, but you may choose to forego the rope.

Described as a three-day outing beginning with a snowmobile tow up Icicle Creek, this route includes the summits of Snowgrass Mountain and Big Chiwaukum and even

The Chiwaukum Mountains from the north (Scott Schell)

leaves time for some side trips. Without a snowmobile, you can still do the traverse comfortably in three days. It is not unreasonable to complete it in two bigger days, but you will wish you had taken four—there is just too much good skiing here.

ACCESS

This tour requires a car shuttle. Where US Highway 2 exits Tumwater Canyon into Leavenworth, turn south onto Icicle Road, and follow it to its winter closure point at about 10 miles. Park as far off the roadway as possible as a courtesy to the maintenance crew. For the shuttle or pick-up point, drive 14 miles east of Stevens Pass on US 12, and turn south onto Whitepine Road. Follow this about 2 miles to where the plowing ends.

Park here only if the spaces have been plowed out; do not park on wide spots along Whitepine Road. Consider making a donation to Cascade Meadows Camp (a Baptist retreat) to help with the plowing costs. Take note of the big slide path, The Swath, on the triangular face immediately south, where the tour descends to Whitepine Creek.

TOUR

DAY 1. It is 7 miles up snow-covered Icicle Road to the Chatter Creek trailhead. If you can wrangle a snowmobile ride, it is well worth it; allow an additional 3.5 hours if you elect to skin the road. Follow the Chatter Creek Trail as it switchbacks north, climbing into a high basin at 5000 feet (3 hours to here). Do not miss the opportunity to make useful observations of the flanks of Grindstone Mountain as you continue climbing northwest to a col between Points 7112 and 6801 (4.5 hours to here).

If you do not feel confident about the north-facing slope beyond, it is a good time to turn around; the tour ahead involves numerous descents on similar aspects. If

2
Nason Creek
To Stevens Pass
Cascade Meadows
Camp/finish
To Leavenworth
Gill Creek
Whitepine Creek
Point 6602
Lake Ethel
CHIWAUKUM MOUNTAINS
Point 7132
Loch Eileen
Point 6935
Lake Donald
Point 7423
Chiwaukum Lake
McCue Ridge
Wildhorse Creek
Point 7534
Larch Lake
Jason Lakes
Camp 2
Deadhorse Pass
Cup Lake
Chiwaukum Creek
Glacier Creek
Big Chiwaukum
Okanogan–Wenatchee
National Forest
Point 7804
Knox Lake
Lake Grace
Alpine Lakes Wilderness
Upper Grace Lake
Lake Charles
Snowgrass Mountain
Point 7955
South Fork Chiwaukum Creek
Lake Brigham
Lake Margaret
Lake Flora
Lake Mary
Index Creek
Ladies Pass
Lake Edna
Upper Florence Lake
Cape Horn
Camp 1
Lower Florence Lake
Lake Alice
Icicle Creek
Grindstone Mountain
Chatter Creek
Icicle Ridge
Larch Lake
Chatter Creek
trailhead/start
Icicle Rd
76
Icicle Creek
To Leavenworth and 2
N
0
.5
1 Mile
0
.5
1 Kilometer

conditions are satisfactory, glide and then skin north along benches to a camp among larches at Lake Edna (5.5 hours to here).

DAY 2. Skin north to the col immediately northeast of Cape Horn (0.25 hour to here). Make a long descending traverse to the north, maintaining your elevation. From about 6400 feet, you can begin climbing north to the summit of Snowgrass Mountain (2.25 hours to here). Note the cliffs immediately north of Lake Brigham; the route traverses above these. If conditions make this route a poor idea, consider skiing down between Lakes Brigham and Flora to 5200 feet on the South Fork Chiwaukum Creek and ascending south-facing slopes to reach Snowgrass Mountain.

Ski the north-facing bowl off the summit of Snowgrass. From flat terrain among the moraines, climb east up a gully to gain the ridge (3.25 hours to here). (From the summit of Snowgrass, you can also skirt eastward on the south side of Point 7955 and then cross north to the slopes above Lake Charles as soon as the ridge permits.) Ski north, holding your elevation. Once you are past the east spur of Point 7804, begin climbing northwest to the summit (unlabeled on the USGS map) of Big Chiwaukum at 8081 feet (4.25 hours to here).

Ski northeast to cross the ridge at 7400 feet, and descend north-facing slopes down to Cup Lake. Camp near Cup or Larch Lakes; you will have a better chance of finding flowing water at the outlet of Larch (5 hours to here).

The last day from this camp is a short one, leaving time for an early morning adventure without overnight gear. Point 7534 is close by and offers good lines on a variety of aspects. You can reach the base of the northeast couloir on Big Chiwaukum via Deadhorse Pass, which in appropriate conditions can provide an unforgettable descent. This big, steep feature deserves plenty of respect—save it for the right day.

DAY 3. From camp, follow the outlet stream of Cup Lake on its west side. At about 5840 feet, begin to contour north, leaving the stream as it veers east. Aim for the col between Points 7423 and 6935; this long downhill leg should end at 5600 feet on the south-facing slope below this col (0.5 hour to here). Skin and boot up to reach the col at 6650 feet (1.25 hours to here).

Skin north to reach 7000 feet on the east side of Point 7132 (1.5 hours to here). Enjoy the views north to Mount Howard and Glacier Peak, and get ready for your very long, final descent. Ski northeast along the flat crest of the ridge to Point 6602—the top of The Swath, the big slide path visible from US Highway 2. In the right conditions, it is great skiing; for a more conservative option, ski down the northwest-trending ridge from Point 6602 until you can gain the trees on skier's left of The Swath. Note that the logging road along the west side of The Swath switchbacks up to 4200 feet, much higher than the USGS map shows.

Wherever the skiing begins to deteriorate in quality, cut left (west) onto this logging road, and follow it back to your shuttle or pickup, at or just beyond Cascade Meadows Camp (3.5 hours to here).

Tour Author: Forest McBrian

51 McClellan Butte: East Face

Starting elevation: 1450 feet
High point: 5162 feet
Vertical gain/loss: 3714 feet/3714 feet
Distance: 8–9 km (5 miles)
Time: 5–6 hours
Overall difficulty: moderate to difficult
Ski skills: very difficult
Fitness level: strenuous
Technical skills: moderate
Commitment: low
Gear: the basics, light crampons, and an ice ax or a whippet
Best season: January–May
USGS map: Bandera
Permits: You must display a Northwest Forest Pass or Interagency Pass to park at the trailhead. This tour takes place in the Mount Baker–Snoqualmie National Forest.

McClellan Butte is located on the south side of Interstate 90 just beyond milepost 40. The very horn-shaped summit is striking and skiing off its summit is exciting. The described line is unusual. It features an uninterrupted fall-line descent of nearly 3000 vertical feet off a very narrow summit. Good snow stability assessment skills along with expert-level skiing ability are highly recommended due to the avalanche-prone and exposed nature of the descent.

McClellan Butte from the east (Martin Volken)

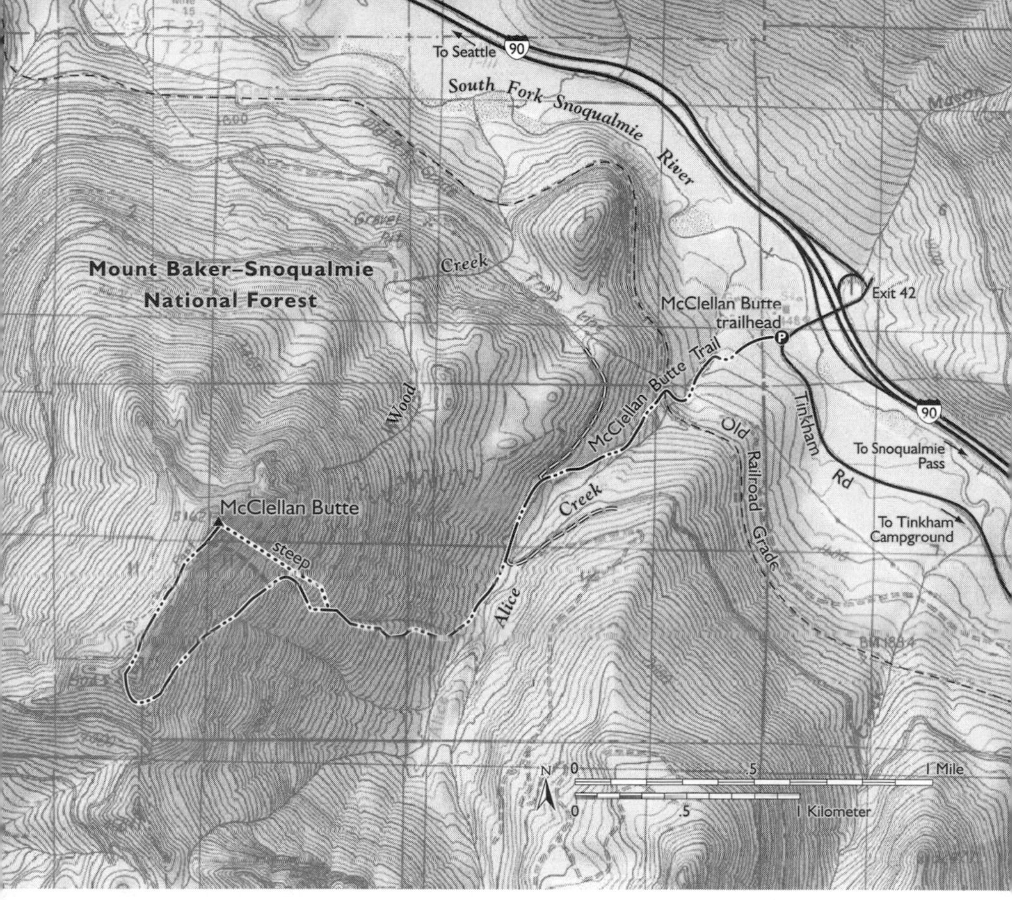

ACCESS

Drive Interstate 90 to the Tinkham Road exit (exit 42). Turn southwest onto Tinkham Road, and park your car at the McClellan Butte trailhead at 1450 feet.

TOUR

Start out your tour (most likely) by walking up the McClellan Butte Trail. Head southwest on the trail across the Old Railroad Grade. The trail crosses a logging road at 2000 feet. Leave the trail here, and follow the logging road almost due south until the road hairpins across Alice Creek (1 hour to here). Leave the road and keep heading south on the west side of Alice Creek for about 400 meters (0.25 mile) to the bottom of a large slide path that comes straight down from the summit (1.5 hours to here). This important spot allows a clear view of your objective. The slope above is very big; proper timing and stability assessment are imperative for you to continue.

Tour up the slope to the 4000-foot level (2.5–3 hours to here). The terrain above you is quite steep. If conditions are appropriate, you can keep climbing straight up the slope to the summit saddle located southwest of the proper summit (5000 feet). You might need light crampons and an ice ax for this. Please note that you would be fully committed to very steep avalanche terrain (4 hours to here).

The less direct but more cautious option is to effectively follow the summer hiking trail (it will be buried, of course) to the southern tip of the mountain at around 4650 feet. Now turn west for a bit, and then start heading north near the ridge (3.5 hours to here). You will follow near or slightly below the ridge northeast until you are below the previously described summit saddle (4 hours to here). Skinning around the mountain can be challenging and even a bit exposed.

Climb up to the summit saddle. From the summit saddle, proceed with caution along the exposed ridge to the proper summit (4.5 hours to here).

DESCENT. Be cautious here; your first turns must be solid since there are cliffs right below you. Trend slightly skier's right until you are below the summit saddle. From here, ski straight down the obvious slide path that you came up to about 2400 feet (5.5–6 hours to here). Now turn north to regain the logging road and then the trail at 2000 feet. Return to the trailhead via the trail (6.5–7 hours to here).

Tour Author: Martin Volken

52 Pineapple Pass

Starting elevation:	3240 feet
High point:	5240 feet
Vertical gain/loss:	2000 feet/2000 feet
Distance:	6 km (4 miles)
Time:	4 hours
Overall difficulty:	easy
Ski skills:	moderate
Fitness level:	moderately strenuous
Technical skills:	low
Commitment:	low
Gear:	the basics
Best season:	December–May
USGS map:	Snoqualmie Pass
Permits:	none

This excellent introduction to the Alpental backcountry takes you to the pretty Pineapple Basin and past the east face of The Tooth, which is many a Seattle mountaineer's first summit. Even though this tour is short and near the Alpental Ski Area, you still must consider its avalanche potential.

ACCESS

Reach Snoqualmie Pass from the west via Interstate 90, and take the West Summit exit. Turn left and follow Alpental Road past the ski area to the uppermost parking lot at an elevation of 3240 feet.

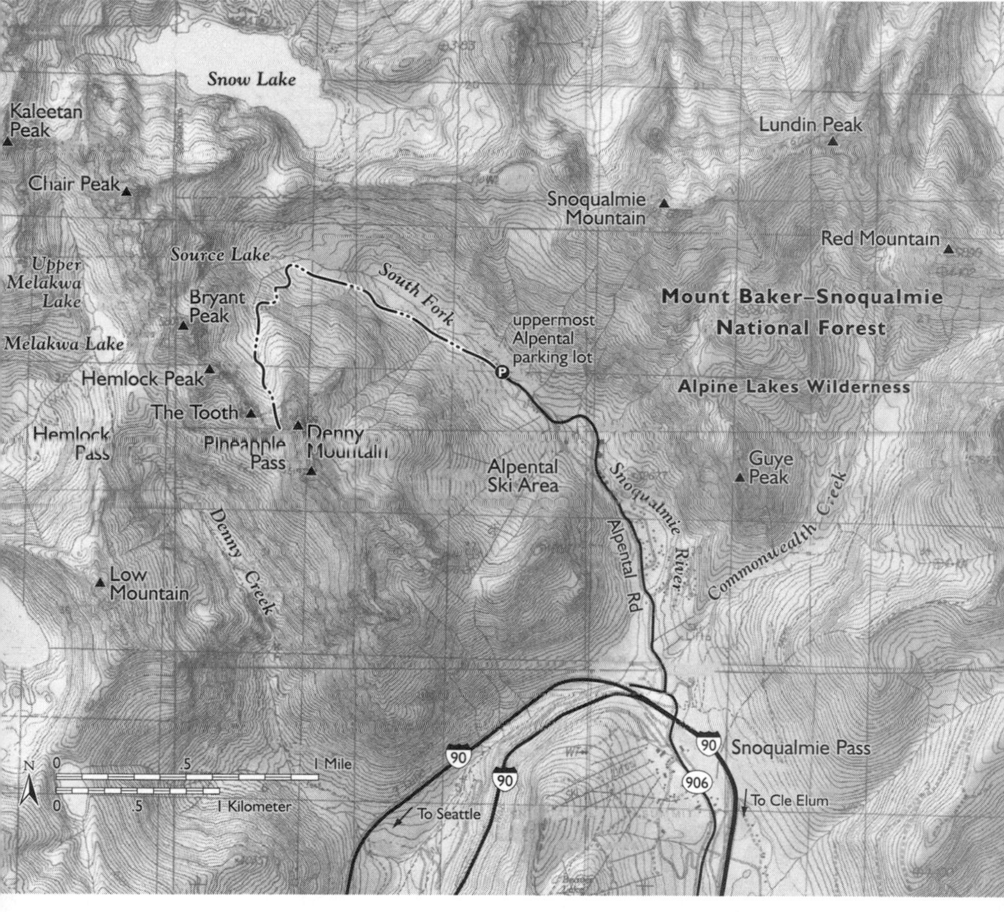

TOUR

From the parking lot you will most likely see a groomed path leading deeper into the Alpental Valley. Follow the path to its end. From here continue up the valley, staying well above and south of the Snoqualmie River. Be aware that the north slopes of the valley are steep and avalanche prone in parts. Tour to Source Lake at 3760 feet (0.75 hour to here). Beware of downhill skier traffic on this trail.

Continue south through old-growth timber, staying on the east side of the creek that comes down from the Pineapple Basin. This is the objectively safest way to reach the gentle upper valley at 4400 feet (2 hours to here). You are now entering the Pineapple Basin proper, which is rimmed by the steep northeast faces of Bryant Peak, Hemlock Peak, and The Tooth on its west side.

From here keep touring south up the basin. The terrain remains gentle up to about 4800 feet. Use care on the last 400 feet of climbing because you are now touring up increasingly steep terrain that is subject to frequent wind loading. Reach Pineapple

Pineapple Basin, The Tooth (middle), and Bryant Peak (right) from the north (Martin Volken)

Pass at 5200 feet (3 hours to here). For the descent, simply ski back down your ascent track to the car (4 hours to here).

Tour Author: Martin Volken

53 Chair Peak Circumnavigation

Starting elevation: 3240 feet
High point: 5460 feet
Vertical gain/loss: 4510 feet/4510 feet
Distance: 12 km (8 miles)
Time: 6–8 hours
Overall difficulty: moderate to difficult
Ski skills: difficult
Fitness level: strenuous
Technical skills: moderate
Commitment: low
Gear: the basics
Best season: December–May
USGS map: Snoqualmie Pass
Permits: none

This tour around the dominating peak of the Alpental Valley has become a classic in the area with beautiful ski descents, somewhat committing terrain, considerable vertical gain, beautiful surroundings, and a natural line of travel. The tour is described via the Chair Peak North Slope descent, but you can and should do it in reverse in spring conditions to avoid sun-affected slopes in the afternoon. The described way offers nicer ski descents, but the other way is less committing in questionable weather and lets you "stay ahead of the sun" later in the season.

ACCESS

Reach Snoqualmie Pass from the west via Interstate 90, and take the West Summit exit. Turn left and follow the Alpental Road past the ski area to the uppermost parking lot at an elevation of 3240 feet. (From the east, take exit 53. Turn left to cross under the freeway and then turn right at the T toward the Summit at Snoqualmie: Summit West ski area. Pass the ski area and continue back under the freeway onto the Alpental Road.)

Chair Peak from the north (Martin Volken)

TOUR

From the parking lot, you will most likely see a groomed path leading deeper into the Alpental Valley. Follow the path to its end. From here continue up the valley, staying well above and south of the Snoqualmie River. Be aware that the north slopes of the valley are steep and very avalanche prone—abandon this tour if you are not confident about the snow stability. Once you reach Source Lake at 3760 feet (0.75 hour to here), tour up the open slope that comes down from the Chair Peak basin.

At around 4300 feet, start trending north toward a flat spot, the Snowlake Divide at 4450 feet. From here ascend the steep slopes west up into the Chair Peak basin. Upon entering the basin, you should see a very distinct rocky feature called The Thumb Tack in the middle of it. From it, turn north and gain the ridge above you via an easy couloir. Once you are on the ridge, turn left again, boot up a short but steep step, and then tour a couple hundred meters to near the base of the Northeast Buttress of Chair Peak at 5460 feet (2.5 hours to here).

You have another option for ascending from The Thumb Tack. Keep touring west for about 200 meters (0.1 mile), and then climb straight up into a distinct notch above

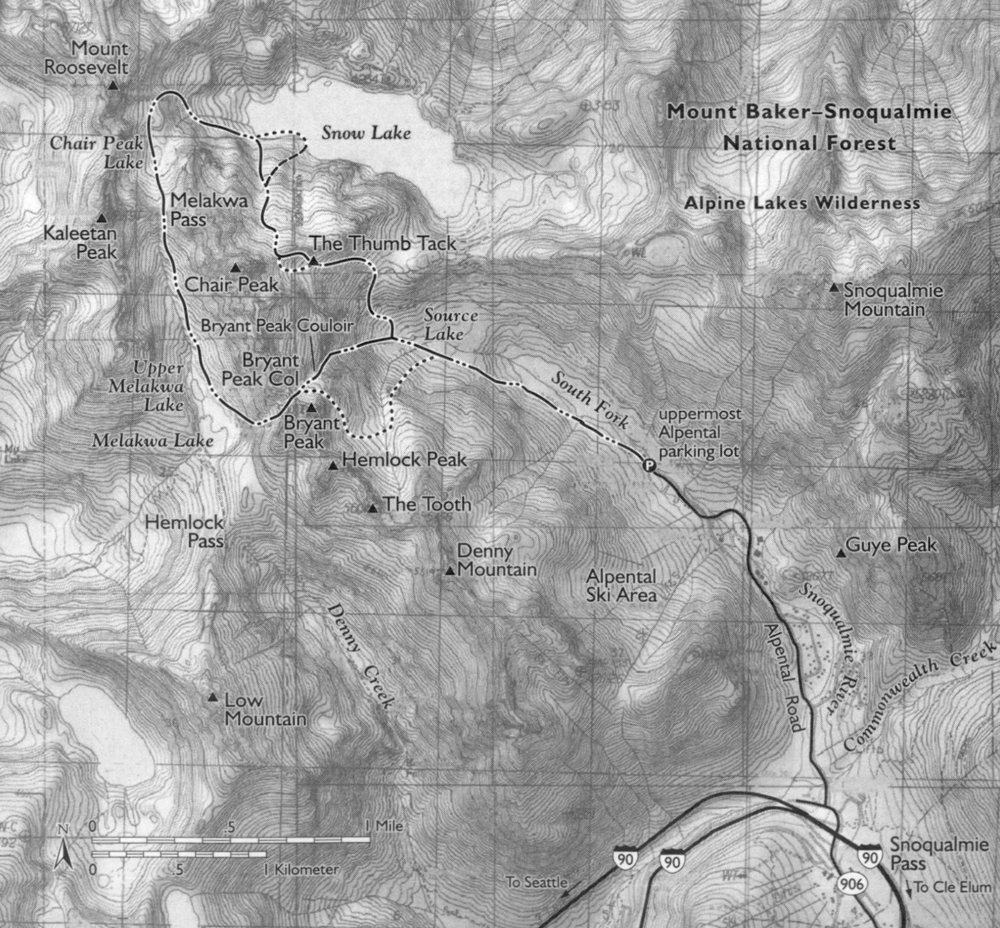

you. Be careful—this route is very steep and not advisable in any conditions other than very good snow stability.

After you have ascended from The Thumb Tack, you are at the first of the three 5400-foot cols you will pass. Now start your ski descent to Snow Lake by skiing north-northwest until you come to the cliffs that form the western border of the north slopes. The following section is a funnel for avalanches—assess it carefully. Ski down to the lake, staying close to the cliffs (3–3.5 hours to here).

From the lake, tour west to about 4350 feet. The terrain steepens here, and you swing north and then west again before heading south to the bench located above Chair Peak Lake. Traverse down to the lake, and tour across it and up to Melakwa Pass (5 hours to here). This ascent is very scenic but quite committing in terms of avalanche potential.

From the pass, ski down the beautiful little valley below the spectacular southwest flanks of Chair Peak to Upper Melakwa Lake (5.5 hours to here). Then tour southeast to about 4700 feet until you reach a steep access slope that leads to the final slopes below Bryant Peak Col. Gain this col by touring northeast up the slope (6.5 hours to here).

You will be looking down into the Bryant Peak Couloir. This inviting 1700-foot descent down to Source Lake can be either a spectacular run or a very bad idea, since the couloir is a catch basin for the avalanches that occur higher up on the east slopes of the South Shoulder. Enjoy the descent down the couloir. Depending on the snow-pack height, you might consider exiting the couloir at the very bottom on skier's left.

Now ski along your ascent track out to the parking lot (7.5 hours to here).

Descent variation. If you do not like the conditions in the Bryant Peak Couloir, you can opt to ski out via the Pineapple Basin. To follow this route, ski down the couloir only a few turns, and then trend east. Within 200 to 300 meters (0.2 mile) you arrive at a distinct shoulder below the north side of Bryant Peak's summit headwall.

At about 5100 feet, turn south and ski down the steep but short slope into the Pineapple Basin. From here ski to the east side of the basin and then down through old-growth hemlocks to the Source Lake area (7 hours to here). And then follow your ascent track out to the parking lot.

Tour Author: Martin Volken

54 Snoqualmie Mountain: The Slot Couloir via South Ridge

Starting elevation: 2980 feet
High point: 6278 feet
Vertical gain/loss: 4000 feet/4000 feet
Distance: 8 km (5 miles)
Time: 6 hours
Overall difficulty: difficult
Ski skills: difficult

Fitness level: strenuous
Technical skills: moderate
Commitment: moderate
Gear: the basics, plus a sling, locking carabiner, and short rope, depending on conditions
Best season: January–May
USGS map: Snoqualmie Pass
Permits: none

You can approach the now classic Slot Couloir descent several different ways. The described ascent to the summit of Snoqualmie Mountain can be the safest, but it is not the most direct or easiest in terms of routefinding. This tour offers a lot of diversity by traveling to the summit via the open south ridge and then descending north into the narrow, deeply inset couloir.

Snoqualmie Mountain from the southwest (Trevor Kostanich)

ACCESS

Reach Snoqualmie Pass from the west via Interstate 90, and take the West Summit exit. Take a left and drive up Alpental Road. (From the east, take exit 53. Turn left to cross under the freeway and then turn right at the T toward the Summit at Snoqualmie: Summit West ski area. Pass the ski area and continue back under the freeway onto Alpental Road.) Park in the maintenance parking lot, the next lot up the road from the main Alpental parking that accesses the Alpental bridge. Park here.

TOUR

From the maintenance parking lot, tour north up the distinct Phantom Slide path, which is the open slide path down the middle of the southwest face of Snoqualmie Mountain. Tour to the base of the obvious waterfall, and then turn west at about 3400 feet to make your way around the waterfall up through the forest. The terrain from 3400 to about 3800 feet is quite steep and strenuous, and you may not make very efficient progress up it. Once you reach about 3800 feet, you can head back toward the Phantom Slide path; travel will be easier from here on out. Now tour up the large slide path to about 4400 feet (1.5 hours to here).

Turn east through a narrow band of trees along flatter terrain, and head for a distinct shoulder located at around 4700 feet that lets you access the scenic south ridge of Snoqualmie Mountain west of where the little creek exits the Cave Ridge drainage. This gentle ridge leads to the summit, which stands at 6278 feet. Touring is beautiful and sweeping here, but be aware that this ridge does not provide much protection from avalanches when hazard conditions are high (3 hours to here).

DESCENT. From the summit, ski south trending skier's right until you hit the right margin of the slope at around 6150 feet. You cannot see the Slot Couloir until you are at its entrance, a slight notch in the west ridge of the mountain. Another couloir entrance looks similar, but it demands a rappel. If it is not clearly apparent that you can ski from the top, you might have gone a bit too low. The descent is fun, but committing. You can safely assess the couloir's snow stability near the entrance thanks to a tree anchor. Note that the top portion receives quite a bit of windloading. While the first few turns can approach 40 degrees, most of the descent averages between 35 and 40 degrees.

You can ski the exit apron of the couloir all the way to the bottom at about 4600 feet, or turn south once you are out of the couloir (4 hours to here).

Either way you have to tour out of the Thunder Creek drainage back up to the exit notch of Snoqualmie Mountain at 5240 feet (5 hours to here). Remember that the final slope leading up to the exit notch is very steep and frequently windloaded.

From the west notch, start skiing southeast to about 5100 feet. You should then be able to ski straight down the Phantom to rejoin your ascent route. At around 3800 feet, you arrive near the top of the waterfall, which some skiers head down in good conditions, but since it is steep (about 50 degrees) and slabby, be careful if you head that way. If you are not sure about this sporty option, navigate west through the forest around the falls. Once you are below the falls, regain the slide path, and ski down to maintenance buildings on Alpental Road.

If you feel that the exit out of Thunder Creek via the exit notch is too hazardous, tour west over a col at 4850 feet. Descend the other side to the Snow Lake area, and then head back into the upper Alpental Valley via the Snowlake Divide and Source Lake, but take into account that this escape route will add at least two hours to your day.

Tour Author: Martin Volken

55 Kendall Knob

Starting elevation: 3000 feet
High point: 5000 feet
Vertical gain/loss: 1680–2000 feet/1680–2000 feet
Distance: 3–6 km (2–4 miles)
Estimated time: 4–6 hours
Overall difficulty: easy to moderate
Ski skills: easy
Fitness level: not very strenuous
Technical skills: low
Commitment: very low
Gear: the basics
Best season: December–March
USGS map: Snoqualmie Pass
Permits: none

The Kendall Knob provides multiple options for shorter tours and offers skiing on a variety of aspects. If you are learning to backcountry ski, this area is a great place to practice, but it also provides direct access if you are a more experienced skier looking for a short tour. Even though it ascends through the clear-cut that you can see from the Summit West Ski Area, this tour has a lot of tree skiing. As such, it offers the full spectrum of northwest backcountry travel: open slopes, beautiful second-growth tree skiing, and wiggling among tight trees. In addition to the Kendall Knob, the trees immediately to the north offer great storm skiing, and together both areas provide an excellent playground with less exposure to avalanche hazard and steep, open terrain.

ACCESS

The parking lot for this tour is at the Summit West Ski Area, off Interstate 90. If you are driving east on Interstate 90, take exit 52 and go right at the end of the ramp. Then turn immediately into the parking lot for the ski area.

If you are traveling westbound on Interstate 90, take exit 53, and go left at the end of the ramp to cross under the freeway. Then take the first right onto State Route 906. Follow this to the northernmost parking lot for Summit West, which will be on your left.

To reach the trailhead, cross SR 906 (carefully, if it is a weekend) and walk north along the side of the road, passing under the interstate. The trailhead for the Pacific Crest Trail (PCT, which is also the turnoff for the Commonwealth Campground) is 500 feet past the bridge on your right. It is not plowed in the winter, but there is often a track or steps cut through the snowbank.

TOUR

From the trailhead, follow the summer access road as it curves right, and take the right fork, which leads you across the snow-covered parking lot to the PCT trailhead (marked with a sign, but more easily located in winter by the pit toilets, which are still visible when buried in snow). Follow the general direction of the PCT, heading southeast. Resist the urge to start climbing uphill as you wind through the trees; if you start climbing too soon, you can end up in tight trees and tougher going.

Finding the easiest way through the trees and up into the old clear-cut can be tricky since you are in thick timber. Begin climbing when you are 0.6 kilometer (0.4 mile) from the PCT trailhead (where the pit toilets were) and before you reach the first switchback of the PCT at an elevation of 3200 feet. Remember that the PCT is sometimes well traveled in the winter, but it can be tough to follow when it is buried in snow; this tour is a great chance to practice with your map and compass or to test the new GPS app on your smartphone.

From this point, work upward through second-growth trees until you cross into the old clear-cut. Several gullies through the lower part of the clear-cut offer steep going but more open travel; find and follow one of these until you break out into more open terrain. The slopes above you are steeper on climber's right and lower angle on climber's left.

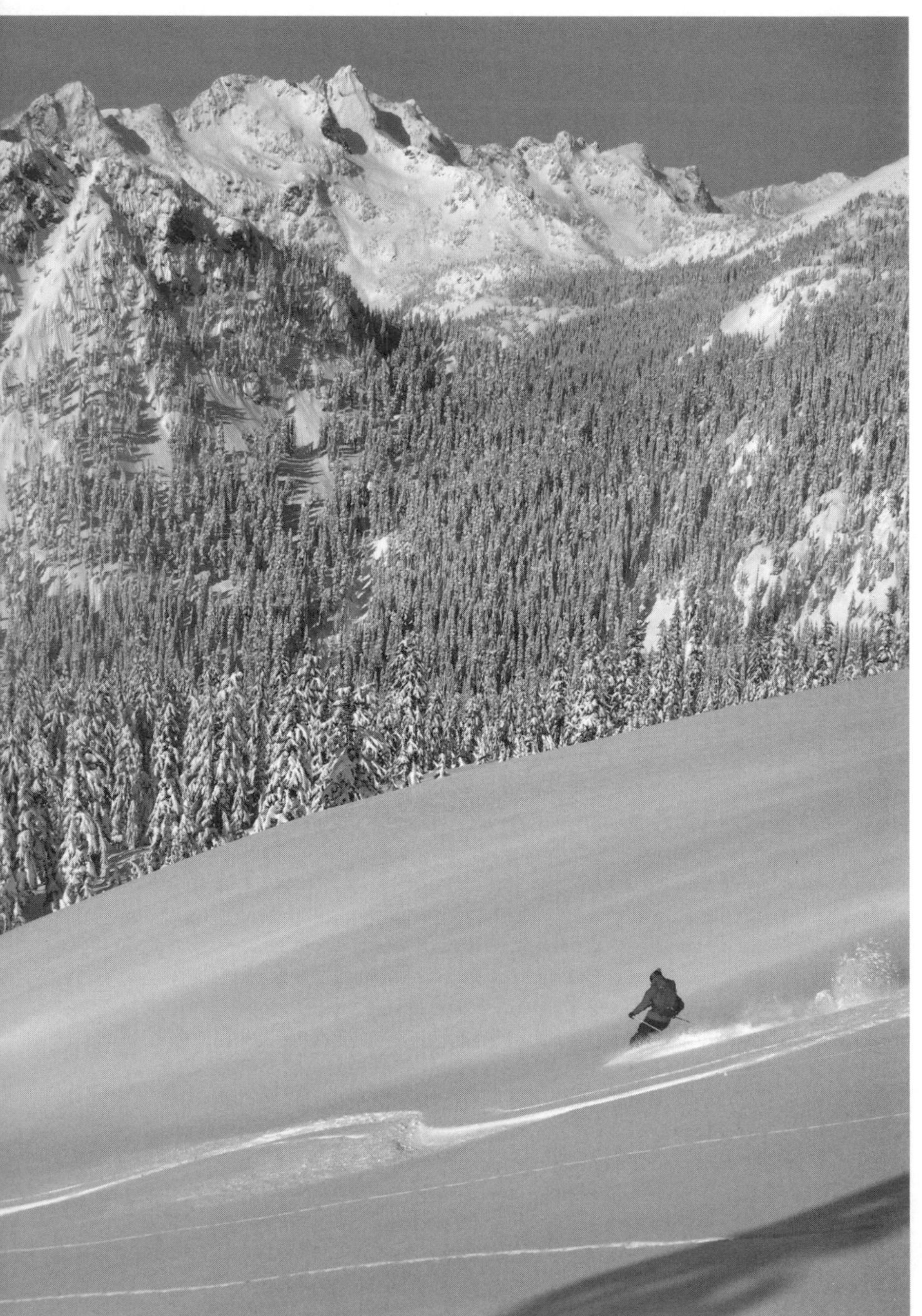

Skiing the Kendall slide path; Chair Peak in the background (Kurt Hicks)

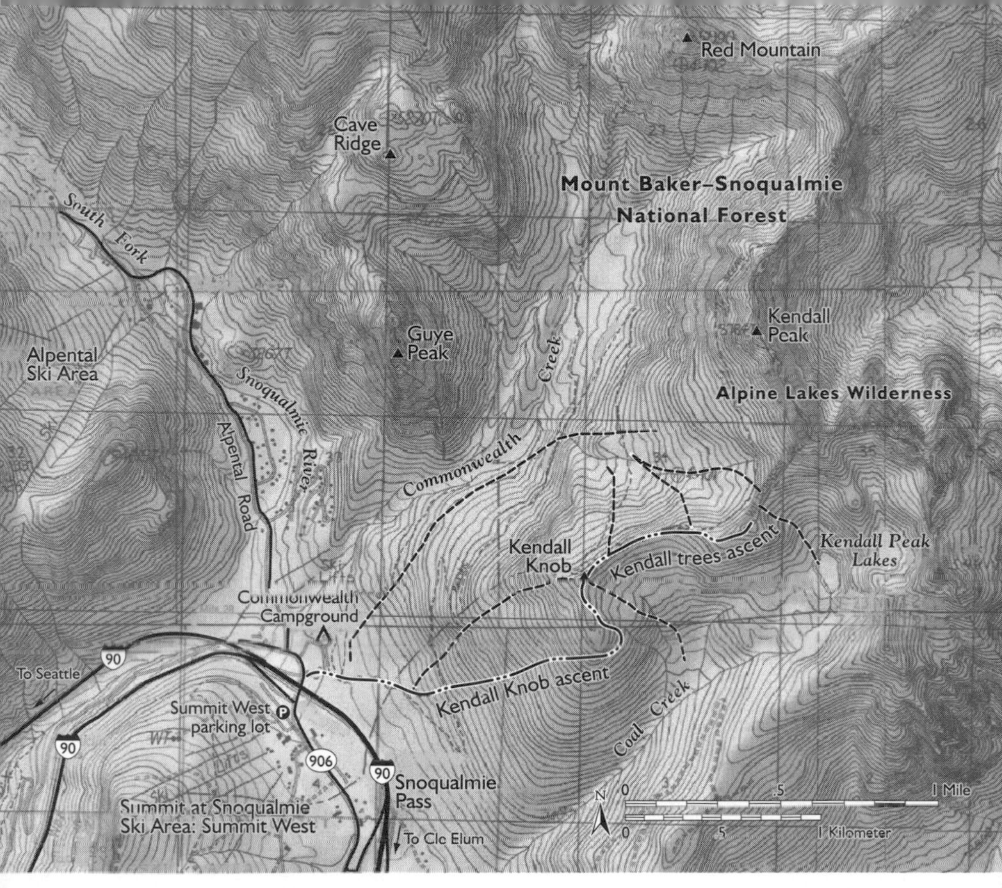

Climb through the increasingly open terrain to gain the top of Kendall Knob at 4680 feet. You can also follow the old road cut around the southeast side of the knob and ascend the final several hundred feet to the top. From here, you have a myriad of options for your ski descent!

KENDALL KNOB. From the top of Kendall Knob, you can choose from a variety of aspects. For a quick lap, you can ski the open gentle slopes that face north and east, and then skin back to the knob for another run. The trees start to get tight at about 4200 feet, but if you are willing to wiggle, you can ski down to the flats at 4000 feet. If you ski this line, it is best to ascend back up to the knob for your descent; Coal Creek is a steep, tree-filled gully—steer clear of it as a descent.

If you are comfortable skiing the trees, a nice line follows the edge of the second-growth trees and then finishes with some nice pitches and a few wiggles through tight trees. From the knob, descend to the southwest, staying in the bigger trees and following a line skier's right of the clear-cut line. The pitch steepens at 4100 feet, and you can work your way from clearing to clearing, keeping generally on the fall line while working slightly to the right. You will cross the PCT on your way by, and you will need to sniff out a way through a few tight spots, but this line leads you back to your up track and eventually the PCT trailhead.

From the top of the knob, the most straightforward line is to descend the same way you came up, and ski the open rolling terrain on the southwest-facing slope of the clear-cut. You can choose from several gully lines, all of which lead you to the low-angle and open treed terrain where you began. Begin traversing skier's right around 3300 feet so that you can glide and shuffle back to the trailhead without putting on your skins.

KENDALL TREES. If you are looking for a longer run and you are comfortable skiing through trees, follow the treed ridge that leads northeast and then east. Skin over several small bumps, and then reach a high point on the ridge in a little more than 1 kilometer (0.6 mile) at an elevation of 5000 feet.

From this high point, you can descend to the southeast through big tree trunks and enjoy great powder skiing down to the middle Kendall Peak Lake. If you are concerned about avalanche hazard, be wary of the open slopes facing east and southeast, and stick to the big trees. Skin back up to the col north of the high point, repeat, and then descend the knob the same way you came up it.

Alternatively, from the 5000-foot high point, you can descend to the northwest through steep and open trees. Make it a short lap and turn around near 4600 feet, or keep descending and work right into the open slopes of the slide path below Kendall Peak. If you choose to ski out this way, you will drop into the Commonwealth Creek Basin by skiing in or near the slide path, descending to the west. Make sure you cut skier's right to cross that slide path above 4300 feet; you can work in one more pitch if you keep going to the bottom of the path, but then you will need to sidestep out of the flats.

To descend into the Commonwealth, find the bench at 4200 feet and move skier's right of it. Just below the bench is a cliff and a waterfall, but to the right there are treed slopes that can offer great powder skiing with a few gullies to choose from. You can ski to the basin floor and sidestep out the snowshoe trails, or you can cut left at 3840 feet (where you cross the PCT) to traverse under the waterfall and slide most of the way out.

Follow the well-packed trail past Commonwealth Creek, making sure you are skier's left of the creek, and wiggle down the steep trail to the trailhead. This track turns into a heavily used luge trail that can be full of people traveling uphill and down. Go slow and watch for uphill traffic.

Tour Author: Margaret Wheeler

56 Kendall Adventure Zone

Starting elevation: 3000 feet
High point: 5640 feet
Vertical gain/loss: variable, minimum 4000 feet
Distance: variable, minimum 9 km (5.5 miles)
Time: variable, minimum 6 hours
Overall difficulty: difficult

Ski skills: very difficult
Fitness level: strenuous
Technical skills: moderate to high
Commitment: moderate
Gear: the basics, plus ski mountaineering equipment
Best season: January–early May
USGS maps: Snoqualmie Pass and Chikamin Peak
Permits: You must display a Washington State Sno-Park Permit if you park at Gold Creek Sno-Park. This tour takes place in the Mount Baker–Snoqualmie and Okanogan–Wenatchee National Forests.

Yin and yang. Hot or cold. Heads or tails. No matter how you look at it, Kendall Peak has two distinct personalities. Its mellow south and west sides welcome backcountry skiers with easily accessible, relatively moderate ski tours with a variety of safe options in a variety of conditions. But venture to the north and east sides, and you quickly realize that it's steeper, wilder, and a lot more committing. While Kendall's south side is suited for introductory tours, the north side requires strong fitness, and advanced ski, routefinding, and hazard evaluation skills. It is not an area for the backcountry novice.

A common reaction among skiers when they first see the many steep chutes and couloirs that drop into Silver Creek is to think, "I need to ski those some day." But "some day" gets further and further away due to the temptations of easier objectives close by or bigger objectives farther away. However, if part of the appeal of ski touring for you is waiting until conditions are right for aesthetic, difficult-to-reach ski lines, then this is the place for you. This somewhat unusually detailed description is also intended to convey what could be extracted out of other zones in the book. Let your imagination run wild.

ACCESS

The most common starting point for skiing Kendall is up the east side of the Commonwealth Creek Basin after parking at the Summit at Snoqualmie Ski Area: Summit West lower parking lot. From eastbound Interstate 90 at Snoqualmie Pass, take exit 52 for the West Summit. From the east, take exit 53. Take a left to cross under the freeway and then turn right at the T toward the Summit at Snoqualmie: Summit West ski area. Park in the lot on the right that the ski area plows; obey any closures and choose other destinations on predictably busy ski area days.

Alternatively, continue another 2.3 miles on Interstate 90 to exit 54 for Hyak. Head north a few hundred yards from the exit and park at the Washington State Gold Creek Sno-Park on the southwest end of the Gold Creek valley. This lower starting point provides easy and relatively safe, if not particularly interesting, access up to Kendall Peak Lakes and allows you the possibility of exiting out Gold Creek if necessary.

TOUR

Kendall Peak is a series of points along an L-shaped massif surrounding the headwaters of Silver Creek northeast of Snoqualmie Pass. You can access the Adventure Zone from many different points along the ridge, depending on your objective. All of these lines can be climbed from the Silver Creek side, but part of the fun is the challenge and sense of discovery you will feel locating their sometimes improbable entrances from the south and west sides.

Choosing to ski into the Adventure Zone is a significant commitment since returning back over Kendall Peak is subject to avalanche hazard from multiple start zones regardless of your route. The alternative Gold Creek exit can be a challenge, too, depending on the snow levels and your tolerance for rolling terrain in forest and brush. Cell coverage is poor in the Silver Creek valley.

The Kendall Adventure Zone can be broken into three general areas based on access. The ***Central Zone*** is most easily accessed from Upper Kendall Peak Lake. The ***East Zone*** can be accessed several ways, but these tours assume an approach up and over the east section of the Central Zone from Upper Kendall Peak Lakes. The ***West Zone*** is approached up Commonwealth Creek. This tour describes some of the descents in each zone, with more specific guidance regarding approaches. The exit options are described in a separate section at the end. Benjamin Haskell and Jim Sammet named these descents after explorations started in 2004.

CENTRAL KENDALL ADVENTURE ZONE. The central part of the Kendall Peak massif offers the zone's largest concentration and variety of ski lines. These descriptions assume that you start from Upper Kendall Peak Lake, which you can reach in several ways. To rely on the relative safety of a ridgeline, start by touring up to Kendall Knob as described in Tour 55, Kendall Knob, and then ascend the ridge northeast that coincides with the wilderness boundary on the USGS map. Contour east off the ridge just below the ridge top, traverse into trees, and then ski down to Upper Kendall Peak Lake.

The most prominent lines in this zone from west to east are: Mainline Chutes and the Silver Twins, Not So Super Steep, The Kingpin,The C. T. Chutes, and The Silver Lining.

Mainline Chutes and the Silver Twins. Mainline Chutes and the Silver Twins provide the easiest access into the Silver Creek valley. They feature short, moderately steep starts that exit onto much mellower slopes below. If you are using the approach up the ridge as described above, traverse directly to these lines rather than descending down to Upper Kendall Peak Lake.

If you are approaching from Upper Kendall Peak Lake, tour up to the low point on the ridge northwest of the lake. A small knob separates the Silver Twins on climber's right from the Mainline Chutes on climber's left. Depending on the conditions, some people may want an ice ax self-belay for the entrances to the left-hand Mainline Chutes. The most straightforward descent entrance is from the skier's right entrance of Mainline Chutes, just before the knob that separates the Mainlines and Silver Twins; however, the Silver Twins feature the longest consistent fall lines from this part of the ridge.

Red Mountain
Cave Ridge
(see map below)
West Zone
Silver Creek
East Zone
Guye Peak
Kendall Peak
Silver Lining
Commonwealth Creek
Trail
Alpental Rd
Crest
Silver Twins
Central Zone
Kendall Knob
Kendall Peak Lakes
Pacific Crest Trail Snoqualmie North trailhead
Pacific
Summit West parking lot
90
Snoqualmie Pass
Coal Creek
Gold Creek
Alpine Lakes Wilderness
Summit at Snoqualmie Ski Area: Summit West
Gold Creek Valley
906
Mount Baker–Snoqualmie National Forest
Summit at Snoqualmie Ski Area: Summit East
90
Gold Creek Sno-Park
Mardee Lake
Hyak
To Cle Elum
0 .5 1 Mile
0 .5 1 Kilometer
0 .5 1 Mile
0 .5 1 Kilometer
Sterling Direct
West Zone
Silver Creek
Spoonman
East Zone
Commonwealth Creek
Crest
Kendall Peak 5784'
Not So Super Steep
Kingpin
C.T. Chutes
Silver Lining
Old Man
Pipeline
Gold Creek
Silver Twins
Kendall Gold
Pacific
Trail
Icy Gash
Silver Lining
Central Zone
To Snoqualmie Pass
To Gold Creek Sno-Park

Not So Super Steep. This 1000-foot, 40-plus-degree, straight chute is not quite as steep as it looks when you view it head-on from north of Silver Creek. From Upper Kendall Peak Lake, climb the first small gully east of the large, westernmost rampart north of the lake. You may have to climb fourth- or low fifth-class rock or an ice step, or it may simply be steep snow when it is completely filled in. Climb straight up to the entrance, which is the saddle between the western rampart mentioned above and the next peak to the east. Be aware of the potential for avalanches to feed into this chute from the large slopes above on the skier's left side.

The Kingpin. The zone's biggest prize (and highest elevation) and a true steep skiing and ski mountaineering objective, The Kingpin features exposed climbing, a rappel entrance, and a straight 500-foot, 45-degree chute set in a cleft next to a vertical rock wall before exiting onto a large open slope below. Climb to the entrance of Not So Super Steep as described above. From there, ascend an exposed snow ramp on climber's right to the top of the peak east of Not So Super Steep. Climb over the peak to the couloir's entrance at the low point along the peak's summit ridge. As of this writing, a snag provides a solid anchor point for a 20-meter rappel into the couloir.

The C. T. Chutes. You can ski down either of these two short chutes or a steep rib to get to one of the zone's larger open slopes. Approach from above Upper Kendall Peak Lake, up the slope just east of the peak that forms The Kingpin. Head for either the left or right notch along the low point of the ridge, or gain either notch and climb over the small knob to the other.

The Silver Lining. For pure ski enjoyment, the zone's longest ski line is hard to beat. Its upper third drops east down a moderate draw to reach a notch that accesses the lower, north-facing two-thirds. Be sure to exit the upper draw on the left side as soon as it opens up so that you do not end up below the notch that accesses the north side. You can ski straight down the lower north-facing slopes, or for added interest, ski the secondary slot just to skier's right of a mid-slope gendarme.

Approach The Silver Lining from Upper Kendall Peak Lake; go up the same slope that accesses The C. T. Chutes. Just below The C. T. Chutes entrance, traverse climber's right and up a short 50-plus degree slope that tops out on a broad, flat portion of Kendall Ridge that marks the top of the run.

EAST KENDALL ADVENTURE ZONE. Kendall's east portion has the massif's lowest elevation starting points and is also the most difficult zone to reach. But do not be deterred—it harbors some of Kendall's most aesthetic lines. And although the start is low, the bottom is lower, so there is plenty of vertical to be had. Some of the lines from west to east are: The Icy Gash, Old Man, Pipeline (Number Four), and Kendall Gold.

The Icy Gash. This moderately steep line hard up against a cliff has a beautiful ice flow that forms seasonally on the cliff face partway down it. From the notch that accesses the lower two-thirds of The Silver Lining, climb east up the ridge and over a wild corniced hump to the entrance. Alternatively, bypass the corniced hump by dropping farther down the upper Silver Lining draw below the north slope notch and ascend the first slope on skier's left up the south flank of the east ridge directly to the entrance.

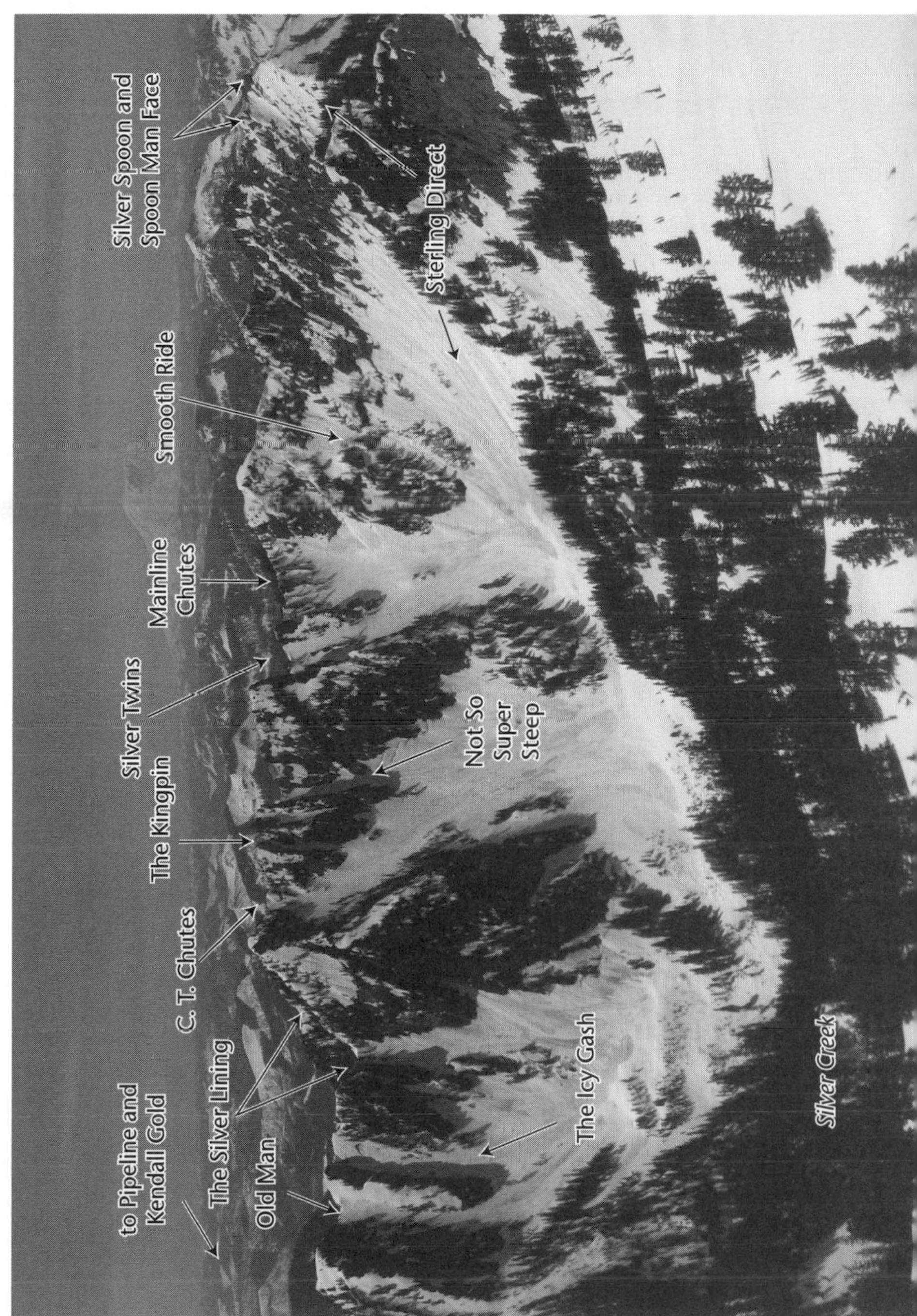

The Kendall Adventure Zone from the north (Martin Volken)

Old Man. This run is named for the proud, solitary old-growth tree in the middle of the run that has survived years of avalanches in this wild cirque. The long, moderate fall line doglegs left into the Silver Creek valley after exiting the couloir itself. From below the entrance to The Icy Gash on the south side of the east ridge, contour farther east and up a small draw to reach the entrance at the top of the ridge.

Pipeline and Number Four. Pipeline is a pure and natural 1000-foot halfpipe. To access it, traverse north-northeast from the top of The Old Man to the left side of the tower that forms the unlabeled northeast summit of the east spur of Kendall. Find a small notch immediately to the west of the tower. You may have to boot to gain the notch after traversing from The Old Man. To avoid a waterfall at the bottom of the Pipeline, exit skier's right into the trees, and either ski the trees themselves or traverse over into Number Four chute, which is the next chute farther east. You can also climb the Number Four chute to reach the entrance of Chute 4703, which drops into Gold Creek from a notch southeast of Point 4703.

Kendall Gold. Despite its lower elevation start, Kendall Gold is one of the mountain's biggest lines because it drops into Gold Creek and, therefore, has a much lower finishing elevation than the lines that drop toward Silver Creek. This long, S-shaped couloir snakes down the east side of the mountain for more than 2000 feet before opening out into the valley below. The start of this line is north-northeast from the entrance to The Old Man. Approach it as if you are going to Pipeline, but drop skier's right down a broad, lightly treed slope that funnels into the couloir itself.

WEST KENDALL ADVENTURE ZONE. The West Kendall Adventure Zone includes the summit of Kendall Peak, and provides long, sustained fall lines on both east and west aspects. Cornices often guard the east-facing lines into Silver Creek. The east-facing lines described here from north to south are: Sterling Direct, Spoon Man Face, Silver Spoon, and Smooth Ride.

Sterling Direct. Skiers often use this open, moderately angled slope as an exit route from Silver Creek after they ski other chutes in the area. Approach it by touring up Commonwealth Creek into the valley between Kendall Peak and Red Mountain. At the head of the valley, tour several hundred feet up a rightward-trending (climber's right) drainage. Exit climber's right as early as possible, and link benches and forest to traverse climber's right up to the ridge crest, ideally topping out at the entrance to the Sterling Direct or just to the north and traversing over.

Spoon Man Face. The upper portion of this line is reminiscent of a small Alaskan-style face. Descend the skier's right side of the face into a small chute that empties to the valley below, or work through trees and small cliff bands near the bottom if you are skiing the middle of the face. To get to this run from the entrance to Sterling Direct, continue southeast along the ridgeline toward the top of the next peak southeast along the ridge. You can follow the ridge to the top, bypassing a small corniced notch by dropping onto the southeast face. Alternatively, drop off the north side of the ridge just after it steepens, and contour across two small bowls to reach a broad northwest-facing rib that leads to the top.

You can also access this northwest rib directly from the small unnamed lake below the Sterling Direct ridgeline entrance. This route also connects to the notch on the far side of the Spoon Man Face that is the entrance to Silver Spoon.

Silver Spoon. This long, straight fall line runs through an initial chute opening to the wide slope below. Its entrance is just south of Spoon Man Face. The easiest access route is to climb the northwest rib to the top of Spoon Man Face and traverse southwest to the top of the line.

Smooth Ride. With an often intimidatingly wind-scoured entrance, the Smooth Ride can transition to better snow below in an interestingly sinewy line that ends up dropping through a slot directly to the middle of the Silver Creek valley. From the Kendall slide path above Commonwealth Creek, locate the summit of Kendall Peak. Head to the second notch right of the summit and gain it via steep skinning or booting. From the notch, ski into the Silver Creek drainage, trending right to access a narrow slot leading to the valley below.

EXIT OPTIONS. You can exit the zone one of three ways: over the ridge to Kendall Peak Lakes, over the ridge into Commonwealth Creek Basin, or out Gold Creek. You can boot back up Mainline Chutes to the ridgeline above Kendall Peak Lakes for a direct exit back down the approach. This option makes the most sense if skiers have already cleared the snow in the chute. Another option is to skin Sterling Direct to the top, and then exit out upper Commonwealth Creek.

Exits out Gold Creek are notoriously painful, but with good snow coverage down low, you can minimize your pain by staying near an elevation of 2800 feet after you exit the constricted portion of the valley to intersect the logging road that will take you back down to the Gold Creek Sno-Park. In addition to the exits described above that lead back to civilization, you can also exit Silver Creek to the north to tour beyond Ridge and Gravel Lakes and into the Alaska Mountain Adventure Zone (Tour 58).

Tour Author: Benjamin Haskell

57 The Snoqualmie Haute Route

Starting elevation: 2980 feet
High point: 7492 feet
Vertical gain/loss: 19,000–20,000 feet, depending on variations and how much you explore the Mount Hinman and Mount Daniel zone
Distance: 60 km (38 miles)
Time: 6 days
Overall difficulty: very difficult
Ski skills: difficult
Fitness level: very strenuous
Technical skills: moderate to high

Commitment: very high
Gear: the basics, plus ski mountaineering and overnight equipment
Best season: March–end of May
USGS maps: Big Snow Mountain, Mount Daniel, Chikamin Peak, and Snoqualmie Pass
Permits: You must display a Northwest Forest Pass or Interagency Pass to park at Dingford Creek trailhead, and a self-issued wilderness permit is required for trips to the Alpine Lakes Wilderness. This tour visits the Mount Baker–Snoqualmie and Okanogan–Wenatchee National Forests.

The multiday Snoqualmie Haute Route was intended to draw the most out of Snoqualmie Pass's "Hinterland." The area has an amazingly rugged character, and this tour is, therefore, very committing. Even though it does not cross many glaciers, this is a more difficult tour than many a high-alpine tour in the Cascade range. The terrain is wildly scenic, the skiing is challenging, it involves demanding navigation, and the total vertical gain is taxing. You will smile when you are back there and remember that you are never farther than 15 miles from Snoqualmie Pass.

In *Backcountry Skiing: Snoqualmie Pass*, this classic was described north to south, so this description approaches it from south to north. The main advantages of the latter are that you will ski mostly north-facing aspects and tackle many of the big south-facing ascents early in the day. Either way, it should be an unforgettable adventure.

ACCESS

Reach Snoqualmie Pass via Interstate 90 and take the West Summit exit. Try to get dropped off, since The Summit at Snoqualmie Ski Area will not want you to park your vehicle in their parking lot for a week. We recommend that you park a vehicle at your exit point at Dingford Creek before you begin unless you can organize a pick-up via satellite phone while you are out there. To reach Dingford Creek, take exit 34 off Interstate 90 in North Bend. Travel 0.5 mile north on 468 Ave SE. Turn right on the Forest Service Road 5600 (SE Middle Fork Road) and follow it about 1.5 miles to where the paved road turns to dirt, then another 9.6 miles to cross the Taylor River bridge where the road becomes Forest Service Road 110. Take a right to continue another 5.4 miles to road's end at the Dingford Creek trailhead.

TOUR

DAY 1. From the West Summit exit, go up Alpental Road for about 100 meters (300 feet) to the turnoff for the Commonwealth Basin parking lot. Turn north here, and head up the valley well east of Commonwealth Creek. You come close to the creek at the flat spot at around 3560 feet. Stay east of the creek and keep touring up the valley for about 1.5 kilometers (0.8 mile) past the west flanks of Kendall Peak.

At about 3850 feet, you run into the tributary stream that drains into Commonwealth Creek from the basin between Red Mountain and Kendall Peak. Tour up this drainage, staying right (south) of the tributary stream up to about 4600 feet. Where the terrain steepens, tour to the left out of the trees and then right to the col at 5400 feet (3 hours to here).

At this pass you should see the famous Kendall Katwalk traversing the steep southeast flank above Silver Creek in a northeasterly direction. If you cannot see the obvious catwalk that has been blasted out of the rock, it is either snow covered or you are off-route. Do not attempt to tour across the slope unless you are absolutely sure of the snow's stability. You may be better off climbing up the short, rocky, and exposed ridge to the north for about 60 meters (200 feet).

After you cross the catwalk, the slope angle eases back quite a bit, and you can tour again in a northeasterly direction, staying at about 5500 feet. Before you see Ridge Lake, follow the almost flat ridge that trends southward to its end. Then turn east and ski down a gentle shoulder to the exit of Alaska Lake at 4200 feet (4.5 hours to here).

From the lake, climb the steep but wooded slopes of Alaska Mountain northeast to its summit at 5745 feet (6–6.5 hours to here). From here enjoy a simple ski descent through virgin trees to Joe Lake, your camping area, at 4600 feet (7 hours to here). You should be able to find running water at the lake exit.

DAY 2. It is crucial to get an early start since the slope to Chikamin Ridge is steep, long, and south-facing. From your camp at the east end of Joe Lake, tour north on the eastern edge of Huckleberry Mountain's south face. At around 5100 feet, you can wrap around to the eastern side of the mountain, and keep touring north onto a bench that becomes very distinct and wide at about 5350 feet. Pass Point 5524 to the west, and continue for another 300 meters (1000 feet) until you come to the gentle saddle that connects Huckleberry Mountain and Chikamin Ridge (1 hour to here).

Turn northeast and follow the ridge to where it meets a steep buttress coming off Chikamin Ridge. At about 5700 feet, turn east and start making a rising traverse up the steep flank of Chikamin Ridge. Gain Chikamin Ridge by touring up (or climbing up) the northwestern part of Chikamin Ridges' southwest flank. You will reach the ridge about 200 meters southeast of Point 6926 on the map. Make sure not to get drawn too far to the southeast while climbing the flank (2.5–3 hours to here).

From the ridge, ski southeast until you are just north and below the summit gully of Chikamin Peak at 6700 feet. Depot your skis here. Ascend the gully to the summit col. This saddle may be corniced, making the final ascent from the col up the summit blocks to the climber's right more difficult. If conditions allow, Chikamin Peak is a worthwhile summit and a fantastic viewpoint in the middle of this traverse. Even though the ascent is short and nontechnical, you must remain cautious, and consider the time of day. You may want to forego the summit in order to get to your next camp on Overcoat Col before the steep final slopes leading up to Overcoat Col get too much sun.

Once you are back at the ski depot at the bottom of the gully (4 hours to here), start skiing straight north past the southwest end of Chikamin Lake at 5600 feet, which will situate you just west of the southernmost Lemah Tower. From here you have to ascend the short distance to the col at 5920 feet, east of Point 6022 on the map (5.5 hours to here).

The following ski descent from the col to Iceberg Lake is easy, and spectacular. The steep looming walls of the Lemah Towers hold a surprising amount of snow in classic Cascade fashion. Be aware that avalanche conditions can make the upper Burnboot Creek Valley a very dangerous spot to be.

Skirt Iceberg Lake on its east side, and start touring northeast up the valley. You will tour right up toward the southwest face of Overcoat Peak. At around 6200 feet, turn east and then northeast again to climb the steep slope leading up to Overcoat Col. Conditions vary on this slope from year to year, but you may find easy snow climbing on the northern edge of the slope (climber's left). Camp on Overcoat Col at 6800 feet (7–8 hours to here).

The final slope up to the Overcoat Col is steep, and you will have been touring for about seven hours already. If you do not feel good about the conditions on this slope, you can start touring north from 5600 feet up the southern slopes of the Burnboot Creek Valley. This will put you on the ridge due west of Overcoat Peak, which is a good campsite as well. The views into the towers are outrageous. From here you can circumnavigate Overcoat Peak clockwise the next day, staying at about the same elevation. You will eventually reach the Overcoat Glacier north of Overcoat Peak and hook back up with the route (2–3 hours from the Burnboot Creek Valley to Overcoat Col).

DAY 3. You have options today. The first option described here is the most committing, but it also leads you into the seldom-seen east side of Chimney Rock's north summit. This descent essentially consists of a double S–turn down an old glacier bed that used to connect the Overcoat and Chimney Rock Glaciers. You end up descending nearly 3000 feet below the southwest slopes of Summit Chief Mountain.

East Chimney Rock Glacier Descent. If you have more time and energy, start your descent by first climbing into the saddle between a small tower called the Finger of Fate and the North Summit of Chimney Rock. From there, ski north to about 6600 feet, turn east, and then ski down below the massive east face of Chimney Rock's north summit. Keep skiing down the naturally curving terrain to about 4600 feet (1 hour to here).

Now climb up the steep southwest-facing slopes of Summit Chief Mountain to about 5800 feet. Here the terrain angle eases enough so that you can start heading due north for the Summit Chief Col at 6140 feet (2.5 hours to here).

Enjoy the easy ski descent down the spectacular Summit Chief Valley with the impressive wall of Little Big Chief looming overhead. Keep skiing northeast all the way to the valley floor of the Middle Fork Snoqualmie River at around 4300 feet. Your goal for the day is a knob at 5700 feet near the western edge of the Chain Lakes zone. To get there, tour around Williams Lake on its east side, and follow the gentle terrain right to the Chain Lakes and up to your camp at 5700 feet (4 to 5 hours to here). What a spot. If you prefer it, camping down at Williams Lake is also great.

Mount Baker–Snoqualmie National Forest
Alpine Lakes Wilderness
To North Bend
110
trailhead/finish
Middle Fork Snoqualmie River
Dingford Creek
Myrtle Lake
Snowflake Lake
Big Snow Lake
Gold Lake
Camp 5
Big Snow Mountain
Hardscrabble Lakes
Hardscrabble Creek
Hester Lake
Crawford Creek
Middle Fork Snoqualmie River
Chetwood Lake
Crawford Lake
Iron Cap Mountain
Williams Lake
Chain Lakes
Camps 3 and 4
La Bohn Lakes
Hinman Glacier
Lynch Glacier
Mount Hinman
7492'
Mount Daniel
Lake Rowena
La Bohn Gap
Venus Lake
Lake Rebecca
Bears Breast Mountain
Shovel Lake
Spade Lake
Dutch Miller Gap
Okanogan–Wenatchee National Forest
Summit Chief Mountain
Summit Chief Col
Waptus River
Overcoat Peak
Overcoat Lake
a ternate Camp 2
Overcoat Col
Camp 2
Chimney Rock
Iceberg Lake
Lemah Towers
Avalanche Lake
Lemah Mountain
Burnboot Creek
Chikamin Lake
Huckleberry Mountain
Chikamin Peak
Mount Thomson
Joe Lake
Camp 1
Snow Lake
Snoqualmie Mountain
Alaska Lake
Alaska Mountain
Chikamin Ridge
Red Mountain
To Snoqualmie Pass (see inset)
N
0 .5 1 Mile
0 .5 1 Kilometer
To Camp 1 (see main map)
South Fork Snoqualmie River
Red Mountain
Kendall Katwalk
Guye Peak
Commonwealth Creek
Alpental Ski Area
Kendall Peak
Denny Mountain
Kendall Peak Lakes
Snoqualmie Pass parking lot/start
90
906
To Seattle

This day is a little shorter, but an easier day might be welcome in light of the overall physical effort you will expend on the rest of the tour. Of course you could also explore some more around camp.

Alternate Descent: Overcoat Glacier to Summit Chief Col. If you do not like the deep descent described above, but you would still like to experience the Summit Chief Valley, you can also ski north from the Finger of Fate Col (or straight from camp) as described. At 6600 feet, start traversing on initially gentle terrain above the steep east-facing terrain high above Chimney Rock Creek. Keep heading northeast, and stay at an elevation of around 6400 feet. The terrain becomes steeper, and there are cliffs below you. Maintain your elevation, and find a potentially snowed-in ledge system that lets you boot around a steep rocky rib that seems to block the way—it gets easier after that. Depending on the snow conditions, you may have to use crampons, an ice ax, and maybe even a rope to safely traverse this section.

Once you are around the ledge, follow easy and beautiful benches to get to Summit Chief Col (1.5 hours to here).

Alternate Descent: Overcoat Glacier. If the weather and or snow conditions do not favor either of the previously mentioned options, you can also ski down the relatively mellow Overcoat Glacier. Once you exit the glacier at around 5700 feet, you have to navigate a steeper zone that gets you down to about 4800 feet. From there keep skiing northeast until you hit the valley floor of the Middle Fork Snoqualmie River at around 4000 feet. Now tour up valley until you regain the other route (2.5 hours to here).

This option makes for a truly short day, and if conditions are good, you might want to check out a short but stout ski mountaineering adventure up Overcoat Peak. To ascend Overcoat Peak before continuing the tour, break down your camp near Overcoat Col and ski counterclockwise around Overcoat Peak until you come to the bottom of the north-facing snow finger. Drop any unnecessary gear here, and prepare for the ski mountaineering portion of the tour. Climb up the snow finger, carrying your skis, and deposit them at the top of the finger. From here, climb left up some most likely snow-covered ledges. After a couple of rope lengths, you will come to a short but steep chimney. Climb up the chimney, and proceed up to the summit ridge. Cross the slabby ridge and follow its southwest side to the summit (2 hours to here).

Reverse your ascent route to descend. There is a good rappel block just when you cross back onto the north side of the ridge. One rappel will take you back down to the mentioned ledges. From here, reverse your ascent route back to your ski depot.

DAY 4. This is a great day because you are only carrying a day pack. You will return to the same camp after the ascent of Mount Hinman or your exploits in the Mount Daniel or the Hinman Glacier zone. The character of the landscape you will visit today is quite different from that of the landscape you traveled through yesterday. You will enjoy a lot of wide open skiing.

From your camp near the Chain Lakes, turn east and gain the distinct La Bohn Gap at 6100 feet. Traverse the steep cirque above the cliffs high above Lake Rowena toward

Overcoat Col from the north (Martin Volken)

an obvious plateau at 6400 feet. Please be aware of the exposure on this slope—a fall here might have dire consequences.

Keep traversing east for about another kilometer until you see the easy slopes that let you gain the gentle west ridge of Mount Hinman at 7280 feet. From here follow the ridge and just left of the ridge east to the summit at 7492 feet (2.5–3 hours to here). The exploratory possibilities on the north-facing flanks of Mount Hinman and Mount Daniel are endless, and the skiing is amazing. Enjoy!

DESCENT: MOUNT HINMAN. You can follow your ascent route to descend, but be careful. The conditions of the cirque above Lake Rowena change very quickly since it gets a lot of sun exposure. Even a little sluff or a simple slip could carry you over the cliffs. You can also ski the gentle west ridge down high above the Hinman Glacier. This easy, very safe, and scenic descent is probably the preferable option.

You will reach a little col between La Bohn Lakes and Chain Lakes. Turn south here, regain your ascent route, and return to camp that way. The described descent route is obviously a very good ascent route as well, if the conditions or your comfort level preclude you from trying the La Bohn Gap option.

DAY 5. You are covering quite a bit of distance to your final camp near the summit of Big Snow Mountain. If the weather is good, you will have great views of much of the terrain you have covered so far. Start out by skiing down from your camp past Williams Lake. Stay on the north side of the Middle Fork Valley until you are right under the steep south face of Iron Cap Mountain. Now tour up those steep slopes to access the beautiful basin that contains Crawford Lake at 5200 feet (2 hours to here).

Tour across the lake to its northwestern edge, and access a col at about 5800 feet, about 300 meters (1000 feet) north of Point 5915 on the USGS map. Ski down steep terrain to Crawford Creek at about 4200 feet (3.5 hours to here). Continue southwest, and tour up on the south side of a little creek to a high cirque. To get out of this cirque, tour over a col that is located about 200 meters (650 feet) north of Point 6080 (5 hours to here).

You are now entering the characteristic bench-covered zone on the north side of Big Snow Mountain. The quickest way to get to your camp area is to traverse west for about 400 meters (1300 feet), ski north to about 5200 feet, and then tour southwest to your camp, which is at about 5860 feet, a bit northwest of Point 6131 on the map (6 hours to here).

You are rewarded with outstanding views in the rarely seen Big Snow Cirque and the Lemah Towers across the valley.

DAY 6. Your final day of this tour with its last ascent. The short ascent up the gentle but spectacular summit ridge of Big Snow Mountain at 6680 feet should be memorable (0.75 hour to here).

From the summit, ski down northwest just west of Big Snow Lake and Snowflake Lake until you reach the Dingford Creek drainage at around 3200 feet. If the valley still has snow, you will be able to ski all the way to about 2400 feet. You definitely want to be on the north side of the creek to find the trail before you head down the last stretch into the Middle Fork Valley at 1400 feet (3–6 hours, depending on conditions).

Alternate exit. If you do not think that the conditions warrant a Dingford Creek exit, you can also regain Middle Fork Snoqualmie River Road by skiing down to the Upper and Lower Hardscrabble Lakes and then out just east of Hardscrabble Creek to Middle Fork Road. The 10-kilometer (6.25-mile) trek down Middle Fork Road might be a bit painful, but it is a safe alternate.

Tour Author: Martin Volken

58 Alaska Mountain Adventure Zone

Starting elevation: 3000 feet
High point: 5745 feet
Vertical gain/loss: 7600–8600 feet/7600–8600 feet (depending on the route)
Distance: 18–21 km (11–13 miles), depending on the route
Time: 2–3 days
Overall difficulty: difficult
Ski skills: very difficult
Fitness level: strenuous
Technical skills: moderate
Commitment: high

Gear: the basics, plus ski mountaineering and overnight equipment
Best season: January–April
USGS maps: Snoqualmie Pass and Chickamin Peak
Permits: You do not need a permit for this tour, either to park or travel in the backcountry. This tour takes place in the Alpine Lakes Wilderness within the Mount Baker–Snoqualmie National Forest.

The terrain immediately north of Snoqualmie Pass is both rewarding and deceiving. As the crow flies, the distances are small, but the compact nature of the ridges and valleys create high value for the backcountry traveler looking for new lines. Consider the route described here as a starting point for exploring the diverse terrain that flanks both sides of the Pacific Crest Trail as it winds north from the pass. Pack light and bring extra food; if you plan to explore this zone in only three days, you may find yourself wishing you could stay longer to explore the many couloirs tucked away in this terrain. The terrain here is steep and committing, and as such, you must have solid avalanche hazard assessment skills. There are few ways around this tour's avalanche terrain.

ACCESS

The parking lot for this tour is at the Summit at Snoqualmie Ski Area: Summit West, accessible from Interstate 90. If you are headed east on Interstate 90, take exit 52 and go right at the end of the ramp, then turn immediately into the parking lot for Summit West Ski Area.

If you are traveling westbound on Interstate 90, take exit 53 and go left at the end of the ramp to cross under the freeway. Then take your first right onto State Route 906. Follow this to the northernmost parking lot for Summit West, which will be on your left. Park on the northern side of the lot if you plan to leave your car for a few days.

To reach the trailhead, cross SR 906 (Alpental Road)—carefully, if it is a weekend—and walk north along the side of the road, passing under the interstate. The trailhead for the Pacific Crest Trail (PCT, which is also the summer turnoff for the Commonwealth Campground) is 500 feet past the bridge on your right. It is not plowed in the winter, but there is often a track or steps cut through the snowbank.

TOUR

DAY 1. The first portion of this tour shares the same access as the Kendall Adventure Zone (Tour 56), so you can choose to start with any of the lines from that zone to reach the Silver Creek Valley. The most direct line ascends the Kendall Knob and drops into one of the Silver Twins couloirs. You either boot up along the ridge that coincides with the wilderness boundary on the USGS map above the knob or ascend via the Kendall Peak Lakes. From the high point of both routes you can pick your line of descent. From an elevation of 4400 feet in Silver Creek Valley ascend to the bench at 4700 feet, and traverse it to reach the steep slopes beyond. Maintain your elevation and cross the slope, keeping an eye on the avalanche hazard and cornices above.

Cross under the Kendall Katwalk of the PCT, and begin climbing as soon as you reach the trees. Ascend the slight gully feature to gain the bench, and then traverse north (you are on the PCT now) at 5400 feet. As an alternative to crossing under the catwalk to avoid traversing some of the steep slopes, drop to 4000 feet into the Silver Creek basin and then ascend through the trees to the north. Either way you can follow the bench at 5400 feet and round the corner at the col above Ridge Lake. Or for a satisfying extra line, ascend to 5500 feet as you round the north side of the ridge above Gravel Lake. Ski down to camp above Gravel or Ridge Lakes; there is no water in winter or early spring (6–8 hours to here).

DAY 2. Today you get to explore the area northeast of your camp with a day pack. To gain the ridge between Gravel Lake and the Thomson basin, skin up the west-facing slope above the lake, and work your way climber's right into the gentle scoop below the ridge. The climb from 5600 feet to the ridge is steep—you may need to remove your skis to go up. From the ridge top, there are multiple descent lines; pick the one that looks the best to you, and enjoy the scenic ski into the Mount Thomson basin. Enjoy the view of Mount Thomson, which is an excellent ski mountaineering or steep skiing objective up the east ridge.

Continuing down valley toward Edds Lake, stay skier's right through the flats around 4900 feet, and you are rewarded with open skiing all the way down to the lake. Make sure you pause on your way through to look up at the descent couloirs above you to your right; you get a good look from below, so you can evaluate the cornice hazard and scope out potential lines of descent. Once you reach the lake, move across it until you are on the northernmost third of the lake to get a clear view of the ramp that leads back southeast and up to the gentle treed col. Skin up the ramp to the col at 5100 feet.

From here, you can either keep working up the north ridge of Alaska Mountain, or you can ski down to and across Joe Lake. The outlet at the east end of Joe Lake is usually accessible as a water source, and there are great campsites all around. For an extended tour, a camp at Joe Lake gives you access to ski lines in all directions. There are lines to be had from the east shoulder of Huckleberry or on its south slopes, or you can push north past the east shoulder and ski down Huckleberry's north side. The bowl on its west side can be a great place to explore as well, either from camp or on your way by from Edds Lake.

To continue a circuit up Alaska Mountain and back to Gravel or Ridge Lakes, skin up Alaska's gentle east ridge. Be sure to take the bench at 5500 feet on the northeast slopes of Alaska; traversing the summit ridge puts you in steep, and rocky terrain. The summit of Alaska (at 5745 feet) provides views in all directions and is a great vantage point from which to plan future tours!

To descend, ski the ridge to the north, and then follow it west until you reach the notch that marks the entrance to the couloir you scoped out earlier from Edds Lake. If the cornices allow you to, ski the couloir down toward Edds Lake, and then put your skins back on and work up the Thomson basin. Skin or boot up to the ridge, and then take your pick of the steep lines back to your camp at Gravel Lake (6–8 hours to here).

To descend from Alaska's summit, you can also ski a few steep pitches on its southwest slopes, while staying high enough so that you can traverse hard skier's right starting at 5400 feet. Maintain as much elevation as you can as you traverse. You can extend this traverse by climbing back up across steep terrain directly to Ridge Lake, or you can ski all the way down to Alaska Lake via the main gully that goes through to it. The gully drops down from the third notch, commonly called Bumblebee Pass, that you can see on the map as you move east to west.

Once you are in the gully, you should be able to see down to the lake; if you cannot see the lake, you are probably not in the right gully—and the other ones all end in cliffs. Ski the gully to the lake at 4219 feet, and then skin up the gentle ridge until you reach the bench and the PCT at 5400 feet.

DAY 3. Skin up to the col above Ridge Lake, and traverse south along the bench at 5400 feet, following the PCT. Drop down into the Silver Creek Valley (the Kendall Katwalk is above you), and ski down into the flats at 4000 feet. Skin around the clusters of trees in the middle of the basin, and ascend the open slopes of the basin.

From here you can return to the trailhead by ascending the Mainline Chute and exiting via Kendall Lakes, or you can skin up the southeast slopes of the basin and

Thomson basin from the northeast; Mount Thomson on the right (Margaret Wheeler)

boot up the Sterling Direct couloir to gain the ridge at 5400 feet. From the ridge, descend into the Commonwealth Creek basin by working skier's right through trees and benches, and then following the main track skier's left out of the Commonwealth to your car (6 hours to here).

Tour Author: Margaret Wheeler

59 Mount Daniel

Starting elevation: 3380 feet
High point: 7960 feet
Vertical gain/loss: 5380 feet/5380 feet
Distance: 18 km (11 miles)
Time: 2 days
Overall difficulty: moderate
Ski skills: moderate
Fitness level: strenuous
Technical skills: moderate
Commitment: moderate
Gear: the basics, an ice ax and crampons in the spring, and overnight equipment
Best season: February–May

USGS maps: Mount Daniel and The Cradle

Permits: You must display a Sno-Park Permit to park at Salmon La Sac. A Northwest Forest Pass or an Interagency Pass is required at Hyas Lake trailhead later in the season. Fill out a wilderness permit at the Hyas Lake trailhead for the Alpine Lakes Wilderness; this tour takes place in the Okanogan–Wenatchee National Forest.

Mount Daniel is a huge massif that anchors the Central Cascades. The Snoqualmie High Peaks stretch to its west and to the east the Wenatchee Mountains run into the Stuart Range. Its north-facing glaciers and snowfields are enormous and often surprise one looking south from the North Cascades. The surprise is supported by poor access into this peak, specifically in winter to its north slopes. Late spring and early summer, skiers can hike Trail 1345 to Peggys Pond and then climb the east side of the mountain. The route described here is attainable in winter and early spring. Although you are traveling on glaciers, there are very few open crevasses until late season.

ACCESS

The biggest challenge is getting to the starting point. You can link this tour as part of a bigger traverse or take the time and logistics (extra hiking or snowmobiling) to get to the wilderness boundary at the end of Forest Service Road 4330 north of Salmon

Mount Daniel from the east (Trevor Kostanich)

La Sac. From Roslyn drive north on State Route 903 to the Salmon la Sac winter recreation area (about 15 miles). From here, snowmobile in about 13 miles on Forest Service Road 4330 to where it ends at the trailhead at 3380 feet. It is possible to drive to the trailhead late season and climb the common route on the east side of the mountain via Trail 1345 to Peggys Pond.

TOUR

From the trailhead, skin up the Cle Elum River valley over Hyas Lake. About a half kilometer (0.3 mile) beyond the smaller, upper portion of Hyas Lake, notice a deep gully in the steep east-facing slopes. This chasm provides a more direct ascent route to the Daniel Glacier when you are certain that the snow is very stable. Continue past this gully, and drop your overnight gear at around 3600 feet (1.5 hours to here).

Climb west, avoiding the steeper south-facing slopes. Use the forested ridge on climber's left to reach a flat spot at 5200 feet, and then descend a short, steep pitch south into the base of the huge northeast cirque at 4900 feet (3.5 hours to here).

From the base of this alpine cirque, you can observe many ski options. Climb southwest up the Daniel Glacier using terrain features to set a safe and efficient track. Gain the saddle between the East and Middle Summits at 7610 feet. Continue northwest along a ridge to the Middle Summit at 7960 feet (6.5 hours to here). Look down onto the Lynch Glacier, and soak in vast acreage of treeless terrain, rare in the

Central Cascades. One of the tougher decisions of the tour comes now: will you ski the Lynch Glacier or the Daniel Glacier?

DESCENT. Return via the ascent route down the vast Daniel Glacier. Enjoy almost 3000 feet of continuous alpine skiing to the bottom of the cirque at 4900 feet. Climb north to the flat bench at 5200 feet (7.5 hours to here). Follow the ascent route down to camp at 3600 feet (9 hours to here).

Your other option is to descend to the east of a rock pillar, and drop onto the Lynch Glacier at 7600 feet. Enjoy glacial powder turns to Pea Soup Lake at 6220 feet. From Pea Soup Lake, climb east to the draw at 6250 feet (7.5 hours to here). Descend east with a steep traverse skier's left at about 5600 feet, and then ski southeast to regain your ascent route at 5200 feet. Follow your ascent route down to camp at 3600 feet (9 hours to here).

The next morning enjoy a variation in the area before returning to the trailhead and the snowmobile (or long hike) out to Salmon la Sac.

Tour Author: Trevor Kostanich

60 Mount Stuart: Cascadian Couloir

Starting elevation: 4280 feet
High point: 9415 feet
Vertical gain/loss: 8185 feet/8185 feet
Distance: 13.5 km (8.4 miles)
Time: 9–11 hours (1–2 days)
Overall difficulty: difficult
Ski skills: difficult
Fitness level: very strenuous
Technical skills: moderate
Commitment: high
Gear: the basics, plus ski mountaineering equipment
Best season: April–June
USGS map: Mount Stuart
Permits: You must display a Northwest Forest Pass or Interagency Pass to park at the trailhead. Fill out a self-issued wilderness permit at the trailhead for this tour, which is in Alpine Lakes Wilderness in the Okanogan–Wenatchee National Forest.

Mount Stuart is the crown jewel of the Wenatchee Mountains and the eastern anchor of the Alpine Lakes Wilderness. Its massive granitic bulk rises out of the U-shaped Ingalls Valley on the south and towers above the larches and steep glaciers on its north side. Stuart offers many compelling ski outings, including the Sherpa Glacier and the

Mount Stuart from the south (Scott Schell)

circumnavigation; even the Ice Cliff Glacier and the Stuart Glacier Couloir have been skied. But the long, continuous turns offered by the Cascadian Couloir make it an outing for every backcountry skier.

It is best in spring, when careful timing can yield a 5000-foot corn run. You can do this tour as a day trip, but it is worth staying overnight; you might get to hear the Teanaway wolf pack howling at night or catch a glimpse of the wolverines that have been sighted near Ingalls Pass.

ACCESS

From Cle Elum, follow State Route 970 north toward Wenatchee. After 7 miles, take a left on Teanaway Road. Follow North Fork Teanaway Road to 29 Pines Campground, where the pavement ends at a fork in the road. Take the right fork (Forest Service Road 9737), and follow it 10 miles to the Esmeralda Basin trailhead at 4280 feet (0.75

hour from Cle Elum). Expect to park somewhere short of the trailhead most years, and remember that this mileage will add to the cumulative times in the tour description.

TOUR

Follow the path of Trail 1390 up above tree line, and head for gentle Longs Pass, taking care around the cornices that hang to the north most seasons (2 hours to here). Find a break in the cornices, and descend into the head of Ingalls Creek, skiing directly toward Mount Stuart. Reach Ingalls Creek just below 5000 feet, and begin looking for a suitable crossing to the north side of the creek. Head east to the open meadows at 4800 feet and the toe of the Cascadian Couloir (2.5 hours to here). If you are spending the night, this is a great place to look for good camping.

The official Cascadian Couloir is the steep gully that runs between the "W" and the "I" in the word "Wilderness" on the USGS quad; however, in solid snowcover the larger drainages to the east also offer good possibilities. Head up the couloir, which approaches 40 degrees in a few spots, and follow it to where it emerges onto a ridge at 7600 feet (5 hours to here). Climb toward the false summit of Mount Stuart. The crux of the ascent is finding a place to cross the south spur of the false summit; the best place is near 9200 feet and should require only a short section of steep snow or third-class scrambling.

Continue on a rising traverse toward the summit, staying just below the ridge crest. Note that the gully below (Ulrichs Couloir) is long and severe, and a misstep here would have serious consequences. Third-class rock leads to the summit at 9415 feet a short way beyond for the tour's high point. Those unafraid of heights can take a peek down the wild north side of the mountain (6.75 hours to here).

DESCENT. Once you are across the head of Ulrichs and at the base of the false summit, fasten your seatbelt for a long ride. As you assess conditions, consider the drainages to the east of the Cascadian, including the gentler drainage due south of Sherpa Peak. You may be able to optimize conditions by picking your aspect. Use caution if you descend a line other than the one you ascended. Return to the meadows (and your camp) at 4800 feet (8.25 hours to here).

Skin back to Longs Pass the way you came (9 hours to here), or consider returning via Headlight Creek and Ingalls Pass to round out the tour. A quick, fun ski brings you back to the car in an even 10 hours.

Tour Author: Forest McBrian

61 Blewett Pass

Starting elevation: 3900 feet
High point: 5915 feet
Vertical gain/loss: 2000 feet/2000 feet
Distance: 8–12 km (5–7 miles)
Time: 4–7 hours
Overall difficulty: easy
Ski skills: easy
Fitness level: moderate
Technical skills: low
Commitment: very low
Gear: the basics
Best season: late December–March
USGS map: Blewett Pass
Permits: You do not need a permit to take this tour on the Okanogan–Wenatchee National Forest if you access it from near the Tronsen Campground, but you must display a Sno-Park Permit to park at Blewett Pass.

The rolling hills immediately east of Blewett Pass offer a variety of short ski tours that are accessible throughout the winter due to their proximity to a major highway. Although this region of the Cascades usually has a shallower snowpack than areas farther west do, the quality of the snow typically makes up for it. Relatedly, this area routinely has better weather than other parts of the Cascades and can offer much sunnier skiing if you need to dry out midwinter. With well-marked trails and a short approach, this area is a great venue for both new backcountry travelers and seasoned locals seeking a workout or dawn patrol spot.

ACCESS

From Leavenworth, follow US Highway 2 east just over 4 miles, and turn south on US Highway 97. Follow US 97 for about 20 miles to a small pullout along the east side of the highway at Forest Service Road 7240 for Tronsen Meadow (25 miles from Leavenworth).

From Cle Elum, follow State Route 903 east for 10 miles to join US Highway 97, and follow it north for about 15 miles. The pullout is located about 0.8 mile north of Blewett Pass at 3900 feet (25 miles from Cle Elum).

TOUR

Travel up the snow-covered Tronsen Meadow Road for 100 meters (300 feet) to the first fork. Take the right fork, ski down a short hill, and cross Tronsen Creek on a small bridge. Continue southward up the well-marked Tronsen Meadow Trail for about 100 meters (300 feet), and stay to the right at the first junction. Follow this trail up, past a meadow, to a second trail junction at 4200 feet. Again, stay right, this time on Lillaby Tie Trail, and begin a slightly steeper climb.

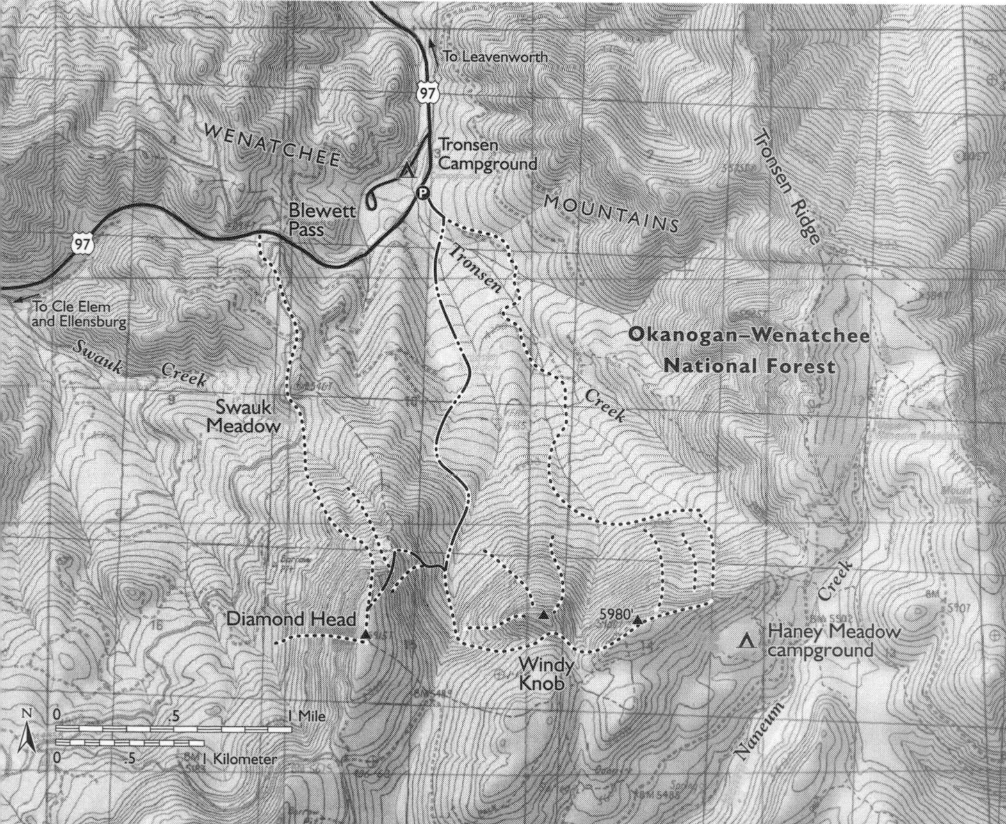

The Blewett Pass peaks from the north (Kurt Hicks)

After crossing an old road bed, the upper Tronsen Road Trail, at 4500 feet, continue a few hundred meters farther to yet another junction. Take a left onto the XC15 Haney Meadows Trail, and follow it south until you are below the northeast aspect of Diamond Head at 5000 feet (1.5 hours to here).

At the bottom of the northeast clearing on Diamond Head, tour up along its right edge to a bench at around 5500 feet on the north ridge. Continue southward, up steeper ground, to the summit at 5915 feet (2.5 hours to here).

DESCENT. The classic descent is to ski northeast off the summit down the gladed slopes you just ascended. Another option is to ski down to the north-northwest from the bench at 5500 feet. From the bottom of this run, the best exit is to skin back to the bench and then descend the northeast slope. If time and motivation allow, take another lap or two on either descent.

An interesting alternative to a second lap on Diamond Head is to continue along the Haney Meadows Trail to the top of Windy Knob, the small peak east of Diamond Head. From the summit, peel skins and enjoy the open, north-facing slopes below. Even farther east along the crest, fine descents can be found off of Point 5980.

Later in spring, it is possible to find corn skiing on the southern and western aspects of these peaks. Although snowmobilers commonly use this side of these peaks midwinter, spring sees far less traffic, especially on weekdays. It is possible to ski corn and powder here in the same day if you nail the timing! If corn skiing is your only objective, consider approaching directly from Blewett Pass (the alternate approach marked on this tour's map). But remember that you must display a Sno-Park Permit to park there.

From the base of Diamond Head, follow your ascent tracks back to your car in an easy 20-minute glide. Be cautious on the upper portion of the trail to keep from impaling yourself on the tight trees.

Tour Author: Kurt Hicks

MOUNT RAINIER

AT 14,410 FEET MOUNT RAINIER towers above its relatively gentle and forested surroundings by more than 7000 vertical feet. It is an iconic mountain in North America, the highest mountain in Washington State and the third highest mountain in the Lower 48. It is the most glaciated peak in the continental United States due to its combination of latitude, elevation, and proximity to the relentless Pacific storms.

Mount Rainier is a geologically young stratovolcano in the Cascade Volcanic Arc. Early volcanic deposits are estimated to be about 850,000 years old while the actual cone is about 500,000 years old. Many geologic signs indicate that the summit elevation may very well have exceeded 15,000 feet in the past, but the mountain is a fairly typical example of the interplay between eruption and erosion which has caused the appearance of Mount Rainier to continually change.

Its dome-shaped bulk provides a lot of terrain above the present day glacier firn line around 7000 feet and, thanks to this large glacial accumulation area, it is able to sustain an impressive amount of ice. Mount Rainier hosts 26 major glaciers and its glaciated area of 36 square miles makes up almost a quarter of all the glaciated terrain in Washington State—certainly impressive when you consider that Washington holds about 70 percent of all the glaciated terrain in the continental United States. Six important ice streams emanate from the summit dome: Winthrop, Emmons, Ingraham, Nisqually, Kautz, and Tahoma. These large glaciers are separated by an array of large and many smaller cirque glaciers and snowfields.

Mount Rainier National Park hosts a complex ecosystem in part because of its staggering vertical relief of almost 13,000 feet: the park contains forested, subalpine, alpine, and high alpine glaciated zones. As you drive into the park you will see old-growth forest of Douglas fir, red cedar, and western hemlock.

FEES, PERMITS, AND WEATHER INFORMATION

Tours in this section are located within Mount Rainer National Park. Contact information for the park, including the Henry M. Jackson Memorial Visitor Center, Longmire Museum, and Climbing Information Center are located in Resources.

Parking. An entrance fee or pass is required to enter Mount Rainier National Park. Accepted passes include a single visit pass sold at Mount Rainier National Park entrances, a Mount Rainier National Park Annual Pass, or an Interagency Pass.

Permits. A Climbing Pass is required for all trips above 10,000 feet. These can be obtained at the Wilderness Information Center, Paradise Climbing Information Center, White River Information Center, or, in the winter, the Longmire Museum.

Camping. Wilderness Camping Permits are required for all overnight stays in the Mount Rainier backcountry. Permits are limited and reservations can be made in advance. Contact the park's visitor center at Paradise to check on station hours and seasons as well as for more information about getting your permit.

Weather. In addition to the Northwest Avalanche Center and the National

Previous page: Skiing the Muir Snowfield on Mount Rainier (Erin Smart)

Weather Service websites, check the Crystal Mountain Resort and University of Washington Department of Atmospheric Sciences sites for current local weather and snowpack conditions. See Resources for web addresses.

62 Camp Muir

Starting elevation: 5420 feet
High point: 10,080 feet
Vertical gain/loss: 4660 feet/4660 feet
Distance: 13 km (8 miles)
Time: 5–7 hours
Overall difficulty: moderate
Ski skills: moderate
Fitness level: strenuous
Technical skills: low
Commitment: low
Gear: the basics
Best season: January–August
USGS maps: Mount Rainier East and Mount Rainier West
Permits: Mount Rainier National Park charges an entrance fee. You must also have a wilderness permit to camp overnight. A climbing permit is not required to visit Camp Muir.

Ski touring to Camp Muir is a great way to get a taste of skiing on Mount Rainier without the experience needed to ski from the summit. At 10,080 feet, you are often above the clouds and truly in alpine terrain. As an added bonus, if you ski all the way to the Nisqually Bridge, you can continuously ski more than 6000 vertical feet. Although there are very few crevasses on the snowfield leading up to Camp Muir, do not underestimate this tour. The weather can change rapidly, and it is very easy to get turned around if you have limited visibility.

ACCESS

From Ashford, drive east on State Route 706 until you reach the Nisqually Entrance to Mount Rainier National Park. Continue another 6 miles on the Nisqually-Longmire Road to the gate at Longmire. In winter and spring, the road is often closed here. Even when snow has not fallen recently, the gate may be closed. Call the main park headquarters before you go to check the status of the road. Tire chains are required in the winter. It is 11 miles from Longmire to the Paradise parking area and the start of the tour. See the descent description below about the Nisqually Bridge as an exit option if you have another car and want to try it.

TOUR

By late spring, there are numerous trails that depart from Paradise. Nearly all of them will get you to Camp Muir if you keep heading uphill. When in doubt, look for the cattle trail. It is not uncommon for several hundred people to go to Camp Muir on a nice summer day. In winter, there are far fewer people, and the route is a little more nuanced, especially if the avalanche hazard is elevated. From the Jackson Visitor Center in the upper parking lot, tour north, keeping to the west (climber's left) of Alta Vista.

Once you are around Alta Vista, follow low-angle terrain to the base of the steep slopes beneath Panorama Point. If the snow stability is good, the fastest line is the prominent gully on the climber's right side of the face to the ridge. If stability is questionable, the safest route is to ascend the ridge to the climber's right. The latter generally involves booting a steep stretch through small trees near the base and going through several wind rolls up higher, but it is the safest route. The two routes meet near a stone shack at 6800 feet that used to be a bathroom, but which is now locked year-round (1.5 hours to here).

From the defunct bathroom, continue up the ridge being careful of the large cornice that forms on the east side; you would not be the first person to fall off it. Depending on conditions, ski or boot crampons can be helpful on this section. At about 7000 feet, follow the ridge as it flattens and turns right toward McClure Rock. Cut in front (west) of McClure Rock, and continue working your way along the west side of the ridge. As you get higher, the ridgeline gets broader and is less defined. Stay in the rocks or on the low-angle slopes of the Muir Snowfield to the west.

At about 8800 feet, you reach the base of Moon Rocks, where the ridgeline widens and steepens slightly (4 hours to here). There are many ways through here. When you reach the top of this slope, Anvil Rock is off to your right, and Muir Peak is straight ahead. Just to the climber's left of Muir Peak sits Camp Muir at 10,080 feet (5 hours to here).

DESCENT. From Camp Muir, you have several options for descending. The easiest and safest is to retrace your ascent route. However, if conditions are appropriate, you can descend via either side of the Muir Snowfield.

The Nisqually Chute. The Nisqually Chute is a large couloir that drops from the Muir Snowfield onto the east margin of the Nisqually Glacier. Although you are technically on the Nisqually Glacier, the crevasse hazard here is pretty low. Most parties do not feel the need for a rope or other glacier gear. The entrance can be hard to find if you have never been there before, but it begins around 8500 feet. The chute itself is quite steep (up to 40 degrees in places) and drops nearly 2000 feet to the glacier below, so be sure about its stability before you drop in.

In early spring, there is often enough snow to ski all the way down to the Nisqually Bridge, which makes for a 6200-foot run from Camp Muir. If you want to do this, leave a car at the bridge, or you will have to hitchhike back to Paradise. Alternatively, you can skin back up the moraine from the bottom of the chute and ski back to Paradise. *Do not go too low because the moraine gets very steep.*

MOUNT RAINIER
0 .5 1 Mile
0 .5 1 Kilometer
Cowlitz Cleaver
Camp Muir
Ingraham Glacier
Cowlitz Glacier
Anvil Rock
Moon Rocks
Muir Snowfield
Nisqually Glacier
Kautz Glacier
Wapowety Cleaver
Van Trump Glacier
Wilson Glacier
Paradise Glacier
Cowlitz Rocks
Mount Rainier National Park
Pebble Creek
McClure Rock
Williwakas Glacier
Panorama Point
Glacier Vista
Golden Gate
Edith Creek
Van Trump Creek
Cushman Crest
Alta Vista
Sluiskin Falls
Stevens Creek
Paradise Park
Nisqually Vista
Paradise Valley
Paradise Valley Loop Rd
Mazama Ridge
Nisqually Bridge
To Longmire
Jackson Visitor Center
Paradise - Longmire Rd
Nisqually River
Nisqually - Longmire Rd
Narada Falls
Inspiration Point
Reflection Lakes
Louise Lake
To 123
Stevens Creek
River
Paradise
Stevens Canyon Rd

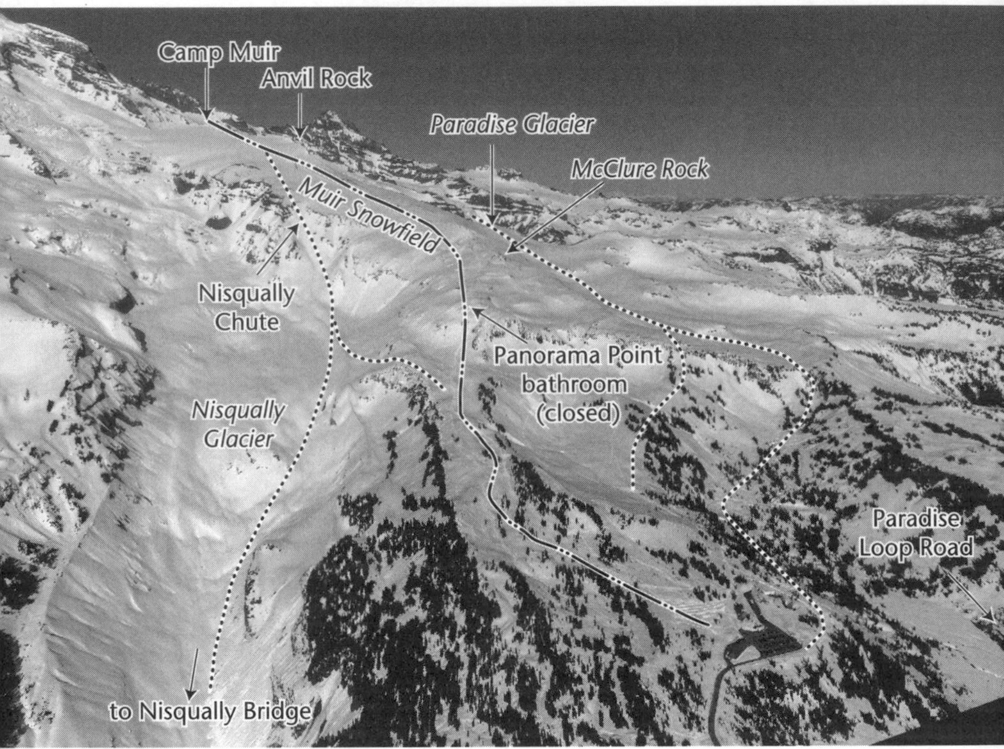

Muir Snowfield from the southwest (Scott Schell)

The Paradise Glacier. The often overlooked slopes of the Paradise Glacier can offer excellent skiing. There is certainly more crevasse hazard here than on the lower Nisqually Glacier or the Muir Snowfield, but it is still fairly benign. To access the Paradise Glacier, cut skier's left through Moon Rocks at about 9000 feet. *A couple of cracks typically form around this elevation—be careful.*

Beyond Moon Rocks, you will find good, consistent, fall-line skiing to the base of the glacier. The terrain naturally pushes you to the left. Do not fight it, or you will end up above steep cliffs to the right. Following the best skiing and drifting to the left takes you to the base of the glacier at around 7000 feet. Here, cut back to skier's right before Cowlitz Rocks, and follow the lower angled slopes to the tree line.

Depending on the time of year and amount of snow on the ground, there are a number of ways to get back to Paradise. By moving skier's right early, it is possible to access Edith Creek through Golden Gate, and return to Paradise without putting on your skins. You can also drop below Sluiskin Falls and take any number of lines down Mazama Ridge to Paradise Valley Loop Road. You will have to ascend back up to the parking lot if you choose this option.

Tour Author: Aaron Mainer

63 Fuhrer Finger

Starting elevation: 5380 feet
High point: 14,410 feet
Vertical gain/loss: 9030 feet/10,590 feet
Distance: 18.5 km (12 miles)
Time: 2–3 days
Overall difficulty: very difficult
Ski skills: difficult
Fitness level: very strenuous
Technical skills: high
Commitment: high
Gear: the basics, plus ski mountaineering and overnight equipment
Best season: April–June
USGS maps: Mount Rainier West and Mount Rainier East
Permits: Mount Rainier National Park charges an entrance fee. You must also have a wilderness permit to camp overnight. Finally, a climbing permit is also required.

The Fuhrer Finger ski descent from the summit of Mount Rainier is an exceptional line—not just for the Pacific Northwest, but anywhere in the world. Many mountain ranges have big ski lines, but a drop of 10,600 feet of continuous fall-line skiing is very hard to come by. While the steepest skiing never exceeds 40 degrees, the cumulative amount of required skills makes the Fuhrer Finger a serious endeavor and an unforgettable experience.

ACCESS

When driving up toward Paradise from Longmire, you will drive over the Nisqually Bridge. If you have two cars available, you can drop one of the cars at the parking lot just before the bridge and then shuttle up to the Paradise parking lot. Once you have checked in with the climbing rangers and have obtained your climbing permit, park the second car in the lower parking lot (below the old visitors center), and start your tour here.

If you have only one car, you can just drive up to the Paradise parking lot and then a) hitch a ride back up from the Nisqually Bridge at the end of the tour or b) simply reverse your ascent route back to Paradise.

TOUR

DAY 1. From the parking lot at 5380 feet tour up the well-traveled zone to Glacier Vista at around 6400 feet (1–1.5 hours to here). Now ski down to the lateral moraine of the Nisqually Glacier, and get onto the glacier proper at around 6250 feet. Keep

Skiing the Fuhrer Finger (Mike Hattrup)

in mind that you are venturing onto fully glaciated terrain. Tour diagonally across the glacier, and head up the steep slope on the western margin of the lower Nisqually Glacier. At about 7400 feet, you reach a bigger plateau on the lower Wilson Glacier (3 hours to here).

Now head west, avoiding the steep slopes above until you reach the gentle ridge between the western margin of the Wilson Glacier and the Van Trump Snowfields at about 7800 feet. Essentially follow this gentle ridge, and find a good camp between 9000 and 9200 feet on the eastern edge of the Van Trump Snowfields (5 hours to here). You should have good views into the lower zone of the Fuhrer Finger from your camp.

DAY 2. Timing is everything for your summit day. Essentially you are trying to get up and out of the Fuhrer Finger couloir in nicely frozen conditions, and get to the summit and back to the top of the couloir right when things are getting soft enough to ski. Please keep this in mind when you are climbing—you do not want to be in the couloir too late in the day. The rockfall hazard is real.

Leave your overnight gear at your camp, and tour north-northeast toward the high reaches of the Wilson Glacier and to the entrance of the Fuhrer Finger. At some point, it will most likely be more efficient to carry your skis, and use your crampons to reach the top of the couloir at 11,400 feet (2.5 hours to here).

You are now on the Nisqually Glacier again. Every year is a bit different, but generally the center of the upper Nisqually presents some options to tour or climb to the top. *Conditions will dictate your travel technique, but disciplined behavior in this high alpine and highly crevassed zone is obviously essential.* The summit stands at 14,410 feet (5–5.5 hours to the top).

0
.5
1 Mile
0
.5
1 Kilometer
N
Liberty Cap
Sunset Amphitheater
Mowich Glacier
MOUNT RAINIER
Winthrop Glacier
Columbia Crest
Emmons Glacier
Little Tahoma Peak
Tahoma Glacier
Disappointment Cleaver
Gibraltar Rock
Point Success
Nisqually Glacier
Nisqually Cleaver
Cowlitz Cleaver
South Tahoma Glacier
Ingraham Glacier
Success Cleaver
rockfall hazard
Camp Muir
Cowlitz Glacier
Success Glacier
Kautz Cleaver
Wapowety Cleaver
Van Trump Glacier
Wilson Glacier
Muir Snowfield
Anvil Rock
Kautz Glacier
Camp
Van Trump Snowfields
Nisqually Glacier
Mount Rainier National Park
Pebble Creek
McClure Rock
Panorama Point
Kautz Creek
Glacier Vista
Van Trump Park
Edith Creek
Cushman Crest
Sluiskin Falls
Alta Vista
Nisqually River
Paradise Park
Paradise Valley
Mazama Ridge
Paradise Valley Loop Rd
Nisqually Bridge
Paradise - Longmire Rd
Jackson Visitor Center
Nisqually - Longmire Rd
Paradise River
Reflection Lakes
Louise Lake
Stevens Canyon Rd
To 123
To Longmire

DESCENT. If all is well you should reach the summit in the middle of the morning and have plenty of time to return to the Fuhrer Finger before it gets too soft. As mentioned before, good timing is essential. Timed right, your descent down the finger should be just soft enough and very fun. From the bottom of the couloir, ski back to your camp at around 9200 feet (7 hours to here).

Do not waste too much time packing up, because you have another 5400 feet to ski down. Plus, you will experience about a 30-degree temperature swing from the summit to the Nisqually Bridge, so expect the conditions to be softer as you get lower.

From your camp, essentially reverse your ascent route until you reach the lower Nisqually Glacier. Now stay more or less in the center of the glacier until you reach its terminus zone, and then exit it on its left-hand side. Once you are off the glacier, get onto the right side of the Nisqually River. Keep skiing until you are under the bridge, and then scramble up to the parking lot just south of the bridge (9 hours to here).

Tour Author: Martin Volken

64 Van Trump Park

Starting elevation: 3610 feet
High point: 10,000 feet
Vertical gain/loss: 6750 feet/6750 feet
Distance: 13 km (8 miles)
Time: 9 hours
Overall difficulty: moderate
Ski skills: moderate
Fitness level: very strenuous
Technical skills: moderate
Commitment: low
Gear: the basics
Best season: January–May
USGS map: Mount Rainier West
Permits: Mount Rainier National Park charges an entrance fee. Since this route tops out at 10,000 feet, you do not need a climbing permit. You need a wilderness permit to camp.

Van Trump Park offers fantastic skiing on the south side of Mount Rainier. While the access and routefinding requires a bit more work than the Muir Snowfield does, the lack of crowds provides a remote experience on the south side of Washington State's largest volcano.

ACCESS

From Ashford, continue east on State Route 706 until you reach the Nisqually Entrance to Mount Rainier National Park. Continue another 6 miles on the Nisqually-Longmire

Van Trump Park from the southwest (Alasdair Turner)

Road to the gate at Longmire. In winter and spring, the road is often closed here. Call the main park headquarters before you go to check the status of the road. In winter it typically opens to the public at 9:00 AM Thursday through Monday and on holidays, but new snow can often delay it. Tire chains are required in the winter. If the road is open, from Longmire drive 4 miles toward Paradise, and park at the Comet Falls trailhead on the left side of the road.

TOUR

From the trailhead at 3610 feet, follow the trail about a half kilometer to the bridge crossing Van Trump Creek. Just before the bridge, skin northwest through large conifers eventually trending climber's right to a saddle at 4800 feet. Late spring and well into summer, you can continue on the hiking trail to access Van Trump Park. From the saddle at 4800 feet, ascend north up the west side of the ridge cresting into Van Trump Park at 5400 feet with your first good views of the mountain (2 hours to here).

Skin climber's right and traverse into the basin above Comet Falls. If you feel confident about the snow stability, follow the gully northeast, climbing the right fork at 6000 feet eventually to a flat spot at 7000 feet (3.75 hours to here). You can avoid traveling up the terrain trap of the gully by climbing steeply out to the right at any point.

From the flat spot at 7000 feet, admire the south slopes of Mount Rainier, and select your route of choice sandwiched between the Wapowety Cleaver and Wilson Glacier. Climb up to your high point near 10,000 feet (6.5 hours to here). If you have enough extra energy, top out at one of many notches that provide glorious glimpses of complex terrain east or west.

DESCENT. Follow your ascent route, and enjoy smooth, steep terrain. You will need to skin up one more time to exit the drainage above Comet Falls and regain the flat meadow area around 5500 feet. Follow your route back down through the trees, southeast over the 4800-foot saddle, and finally to the bridge and trailhead at 3610 feet (9 hours to here).

Tour Author: Trevor Kostanich

65 Lane Peak: The Zipper and The Fly

Starting elevation: 4500 feet
High point: 6012 feet
Vertical gain/loss: 1700 feet/1700 feet
Distance: 5 km (3 miles)
Time: 3–4 hours
Overall difficulty: moderate
Ski skills: difficult
Fitness level: moderately strenuous
Technical skills: low
Commitment: low
Gear: the basics
Best season: January–May
USGS maps: Mount Rainier West and Mount Rainier East
Permits: Mount Rainier National Park charges an entrance fee. You must also have a wilderness permit to camp overnight.

Lane Peak is home to two of the most iconic couloirs in Washington State: The Zipper and The Fly. Easy access, steep north-facing couloir skiing, and spectacular views of the south side of Mount Rainier mean that this peak should be on everyone's tick list. Lane Peak can also make for a great short tour if the Nisqually-Longmire Road opens late or if visibility precludes a trip higher on Rainier.

ACCESS

From Ashford, continue east on State Route 706 until you reach the Nisqually Entrance to Mount Rainier National Park. Continue another 6 miles on the Nisqually-Longmire Road to the gate at Longmire. In winter and spring, the road is often closed here. Even when snow has not fallen recently, the gate may be closed. Call the main park headquarters before you go to check the status of the road. Tire chains are required in the winter. From Longmire, it is 8 miles to the Narada Falls parking area and the start of the tour.

TOUR

From the parking lot, take the trail to the bridge across Narada Falls. From here, drop slightly and traverse skier's left at an elevation of about 4300 feet. Maintain this elevation until you hit Tatoosh Creek. Once you are across Tatoosh Creek, you should have views of Lane Peak. Ascend directly to the base at 5000 feet (1 hour to here). If you instead want to begin this tour at Reflection Lakes, park at the west end of Reflection Lakes, climb the snowbank, and drop down Tatoosh Creek until you are at the base of Lane Peak.

From the base of Lane Peak, you are looking directly up The Fly. The Zipper enters from the skier's right. Both lines are skiable, with The Fly being the easier option. Whichever one you choose, tour up the apron as high as you can until you are forced

Lane Peak from the northeast (Aaron Mainer)

to boot the rest of the way. *Of course, both of these lines are prone to avalanches—assess the snow stability carefully before you head up*. From the top of either couloir, you may choose to continue to the summit (6012 feet) via steep snow, with or without skis.

DESCENT. Ski your line of ascent, giving thought to the conditions encountered on the way up (3–4 hours total).

Tour Author: Aaron Mainer

66 The Tatoosh Traverse

Starting elevation: 4550 feet
High point: 6370 feet
Vertical gain/loss: 6080 feet/7900 feet
Distance: 22 km (13.2 miles)
Time: 2 days
Overall difficulty: difficult
Ski skills: moderate
Fitness level: strenuous
Technical skills: moderate
Commitment: low

Gear: the basics, plus overnight equipment
Best season: January–May
USGS maps: Mount Rainier East, Mount Rainier West, Tatoosh Lakes, and Wahpenayo Peak
Permits: Mount Rainier National Park charges an entrance fee. You must also have a wilderness permit to camp overnight. The park service requires bear proof food storage when staying overnight in the Tatoosh cross-country zone. This involves bear canisters if camping above tree line. Bear canisters can be borrowed at Longmire when obtaining a wilderness permit. Check with the park service for the most current food storage requirements.

The Tatoosh Range is a jagged mini-alp that runs east–west 16 miles from Boundary Peak to Eagle Peak, creating a natural southern boundary for Mount Rainier National Park. Traversing this range along the ridge top in summer is a classic route that has been profiled in climbing magazines. In winter, the same mountains are a fantastic series of bowls and couloirs, and a traverse of the range has numerous possibilities.

Good routefinding and confident avalanche hazard assessment are key. If you possess these skills and are a strong skier, this is a fantastic tour for your first backcountry overnight. With the requisite experience, you can tackle this tour in one long day, bumping up the difficulty a full grade in almost every category.

ACCESS

From Ashford, enter Mount Rainier National Park via State Route 706. Pay your fee at the Nisqually Entrance, and continue another 6 miles to Longmire. If you have more than one car in your party, you could leave one car here for when you finish your tour, or you will have to hitchhike from here back to your starting point when you exit. From Longmire, continue another 8 miles on Longmire–Paradise Road toward Paradise. Park in the designated overnight parking area near Narada Falls.

The best time for this tour straddles winter and spring, before the Stevens Canyon Road is plowed, and the park's operation changes dramatically between those two seasons. In the winter, the National Park Service requires that all vehicles have tire chains, and plowing operations may delay opening the road above Longmire (6 miles into the park). Even when snow has not fallen recently, avalanche concerns may delay the road's opening. To check road conditions and travel requirements, call the main park headquarters.

TOUR

DAY 1. At Narada Falls at 4550 feet, cross the bridge above the falls, and climb up to the Stevens Canyon Road. Follow the road for 4 kilometers (2.5 miles), where it begins its descent into the canyon at 4500 feet, and turn off onto The Bench (1.5 hours to here). Cross The Bench to Unicorn Creek, and follow the creek upstream into the basin.

Jackson Visitor Center
Paradise Valley
Longmire – Paradise Rd
River
Narada Falls
Paradise River
Reflection Lakes
Louise Lake
Stevens Canyon Rd
Nisqually
Tatoosh Creek
Possible bail-out
Creek
The Bench
Bench Lake
Mount Rainier National Park
Nisqually – Longmire Rd
Pinnacle Peak
Pinnacle Glacier
Lane Peak
Denman Peak
Camp
The Castle
RANGE
Eagle Peak
Chutla Peak
TATOOSH
Cliff Lake
Plummer Peak
Snow Lake
Unicorn
Longmire
Wahpenayo Peak
Unicorn Glacier
Unicorn Peak
Point 6800
Boundary Peak
Creek
N
0
.5
1 Mile
0
.5
1 Kilometer

The western portion of the Tatoosh Traverse from the northeast (Chris Simmons)

If you are tagging the summits of Boundary and Unicorn Peaks, take a diversion left to the saddle between Unicorn Peak and Point 6800; otherwise, head climber's right to the ridge west of Point 6800 (6150 feet and 4 hours to here). This is also a logical bivy site, but in spring, the descent from here is best when it has softened in the afternoon.

Ski almost due west as far down as you want, potentially a 2000-foot run through lightly wooded slopes and quite possibly the best descent of this tour. If you stop sooner, make sure to traverse around skier's right until you are immediately below The Castle and Pinnacle Peak. Start climbing north, aiming for the notch between them. When you reach 5800 feet in elevation, turn westward and aim instead for the saddle at 5950 feet between Pinnacle and Plummer Peaks (7.5 hours to here).

With its numerous possible variations, including a quick tour to reach the summit of Plummer Peak at 6370 feet, and bivy sites, this spot makes for a logical first or second night. The saddles between Pinnacle, Plummer, and Denman Peaks are spacious and have incredible views. They also provide logical bail-out points: skiing northwest from the Plummer-Pinnacle saddle or northeast from the Denman-Plummer saddle will take you down to 4500 feet on Tatoosh Creek, From here you have only a short 400-foot climb to the Stevens Canyon Road and back to Narada Falls.

DAY 2. The best route through this section is to cross over the Plummer via the Plummer-Pinnacle saddle, then ski the ridgeline northwest to the Denman-Plummer saddle before continuing down southwest to Cliff Lake at 5223 feet. Climb up to the Lane-Denman notch, and then ski southwest to the two small lakes on the bench at 5050 feet elevation (2 hours to here from the Plummer-Pinnacle saddle).

Climb up out of the bench, traversing across the basin to the southeast ridge of Wahpenayo Peak. Gaining this ridge is the crux of the tour and usually requires a bootpack. There are several possible routes, depending on the cornices and snow conditions, all near 5600 to 5700 feet (4 hours to here). Once you have gained the ridge, follow it up to the summit at 6231 feet (4.5 hours to here).

From the top of Wahpenayo, drop northwest into the bowl toward Chutla Peak, and stop at 5300 feet before it gets too steep. Skin back up to the notch immediately south of Chutla, and strip your skins for the last time for the last and longest descent, 2900 feet to Longmire (6.5 hours to here). If you are still tagging tops, stop at 5200 feet, and climb north to gain the notch between Eagle and Chutla Peaks. If you are doing this tour later in spring, you may find yourself hiking sooner—plan your descent to roughly follow the trail after you reach an elevation of 4300 feet. With luck, you will have a quick shuttle back to your car.

Tour Author: Chris Simmons

67 Little Tahoma: Paradise Approach

Starting elevation: 5420 feet
High point: 11,138 feet
Vertical gain/loss: 5718 feet/5718 feet
Distance: 16 km (10 miles)
Time: 9–11 hours
Overall difficulty: very difficult
Ski skills: difficult
Fitness level: very strenuous
Technical skills: very high
Commitment: moderate to high
Gear: the basics, plus ski mountaineering equipment
Best season: April–June
USGS map: Mount Rainier East
Permits: Mount Rainier National Park charges an entrance fee. You must also have a wilderness permit to camp overnight. Finally, you will also need a climbing permit.

Little Tahoma, with its summit at 11,138 feet, is the very distinct subpeak on the east flanks of Mount Rainier. Due to the approach and location, you will be treated to some of the most spectacular scenery Mount Rainier has to offer on its southern aspects, including the Nisqually ice cliffs and the imposing Cowlitz and Ingraham Glaciers. This is a fantastic ski mountaineering objective in which you travel on four glaciers and tackle a short rock scramble to the summit. When visibility is good, routefinding to Little Tahoma is straightforward, but if the weather is less than ideal, sharp navigation skills are essential.

Many people ski Little Tahoma via the Fryingpan and Whitman Glaciers, but since this is not a viable option through winter and spring, we are not describing that option. Access to that route is only available once the road to the park's White River Entrance has been plowed for the season.

ACCESS

From Ashford, drive east on State Route 706 until you reach the Nisqually Entrance to Mount Rainier National Park. Continue another 6 miles on what is now the Nisqually-Longmire Road to the gate at Longmire. In winter and spring, the road is often closed here. Even when snow has not fallen recently, there can be delays in opening the gate. Call the main park headquarters before you go to check the status of the road. All vehicles are required to carry chains in winter. From Longmire, continue another 11 miles on the Longmire–Paradise Road to the Paradise parking area and the start of the tour.

TOUR

From the north side of the parking lot, just east of the visitor center, you will generally be following the summer trail to Alta Vista, Panorama Point, and McClure Rock. Have compass bearings or GPS waypoints for these locations; they are good points of reference or benchmarks for the approach and descent. A north-northeast bearing will get you to McClure Rock (2 hours to here).

At this location, adjust to a more northerly bearing and the western edge of the Paradise Glacier. From this point forward, you will be traveling on glaciated terrain—be mindful of crevasse hazards. Maintain this course to approximately

Little Tahoma from the east (Scott Schell)

N
0 .5 1 Mile
0 .5 1 Kilometer
MOUNT RAINIER
Emmons Glacier
Fryingpan Glacier
Columbia Crest
Little Tahoma Peak
summit scramble
Whitman Glacier
Whitman Crest
Point Success
Nisqually Glacier
Ingraham Glacier
Cathedral Rocks
possible dirty boot section
Camp Muir
Cowlitz Glacier
Anvil Rock
8384'
Van Trump Glacier
Wilson Glacier
Muir Snowfield
It is critical to maintain elevation here
Paradise Glacier
Mount Rainier National Park
Cowlitz Rocks
Nisqually Glacier
Pebble Creek
McClure Rock
Williwakas Glacier
Panorama Point
Glacier Vista
summer trail
Golden Gate
Edith Creek
Sluiskin Falls
Stevens Creek
Alta Vista
Paradise Park
Nisqually River
Nisqually Vista
P
Jackson Visitor Center
To Longmire
Paradise - Longmire Rd
Paradise Valley
Paradise Valley Loop Rd
Mazama Ridge
Louise Lake
Reflection Lakes
Paradise River
Stevens Canyon Rd
To 123

8600 feet, and then adjust to a more northeast bearing at that elevation. Below this elevation, the Cowlitz Glacier is quite steep and may be heavily crevassed; stay high. Continuing to contour at about 8600 feet places you at the toe of Cathedral Rocks and the south edge of the Ingraham Glacier (4 hours to here).

To the northeast, locate a notch in the rock band that separates the Ingraham and Whitman Glaciers. This notch allows you to gain access to the Whitman and eventually to the southeast slopes on Little Tahoma. Continue to travel northeast, and contour across the Ingraham at roughly 8600 feet to reach this notch. Depending on the snowpack, this stretch may be a dirty scramble up onto the Whitman.

Using the base of the cliffs on climber's left as a handrail, continue northeast to the more open terrain of the Whitman Glacier. Once you are around the cliff band, the summit of Little Tahoma is on your left (northwest) roughly 2500 feet above (5 hours to here). The last remaining bit is a very direct ascent to just shy of the summit and an elevation of about 11,000 feet (7 hours to here). The final rock scramble is easy when dry, but exposed in places; some climbers will want a rope to help secure the ascent.

DESCENT. The descent is straightforward; follow your up track. Be diligent and avoid the temptation of descending too quickly on the traverse back across the Ingraham and Cowlitz Glaciers. If you do not maintain your uptrack elevation, you will quickly find yourself in steep and complicated terrain.

Tour Author: David Jordan

68 Liberty Ridge

Starting elevation: 4300 feet
High point: 14,410 feet
Vertical gain/loss: 11,200 feet/11,200 feet
Distance: 35 km (22 miles)
Time: 2–3 days
Overall difficulty: extremely difficult
Ski skills: extremely difficult
Fitness level: extremely strenuous
Technical skills: extremely high
Commitment: high
Gear: the basics, plus ski mountaineering and overnight equipment
Best season: March–June
USGS maps: Sunrise, Mowich Lake, and Mount Rainier West
Permits: Mount Rainier National Park charges an entrance fee. You must also have a wilderness permit to camp overnight. All parties traveling above 10,000 feet must also have a climbing permit.

Liberty Ridge from the north (Alasdair Turner)

Since the monumental first descent by Chris Landry in 1980, Liberty Ridge has become a test piece for "extreme" skiers and ski mountaineers. Remote, steep, sustained, and committing, this route is certain to get your attention. However, anything more than fantasizing about skiing this line requires a combination of excellent fitness, expert skiing ability, strong mountaineering skills, and a desire to link dozens of turns in no-fall-zone terrain. *Do not attempt this route unless you possess all of these qualities and believe that conditions will be perfect*. Like all big ski mountaineering lines, timing is everything. Because of the severity of the terrain and the consequences of a fall, we strongly recommend that you climb this line before you ski it.

ACCESS

From Enumclaw, take State Route 410 east toward Chinook Pass. After 37 miles, turn right on Sunrise Road. Follow this road 5 miles, and turn left on White River Road. Follow this to the end of the road and park at the campground. The road is closed in the winter, and usually opens sometime in May. For the latest road conditions, call the main park headquarters.

TOUR

DAY 1. From the White River Campground, walk or skin up the Glacier Basin Trail, which is usually snow covered until about the beginning of May. But even under several feet of snow, the trail should be fairly obvious. After being washed out in the floods of November 2006, it was rerouted and now ascends to Glacier Basin well above the White River.

From the bottom of the Inter Glacier, ascend to the prominent pass at 7500 feet that goes over the ridge that splits the Inter and Winthrop Glaciers. Although the col you are aiming for is just south of what is labeled as St. Elmo Pass on the USGS map, it is commonly referred to as St. Elmo's. This ascent is east-facing; get here early if solar radiation is an issue. There is often avalanche debris from wet loose slides here (5 hours to here).

From St. Elmo's, remove your skins, and drop onto the Winthrop Glacier. Choose your route carefully among the numerous crevasses, and consider roping up as conditions dictate. You have many options, but contouring around at about the 7200-foot level is the most efficient. Continue to the beginning of Curtis Ridge, being careful of the steep slopes that access the very broad ridge. Once you are safely on the ridge, there is minimal crevassing until you reach the Carbon Glacier. Eventually, you will want to make it to the western edge of Curtis Ridge at about 7200 feet where you can look out at the Carbon Glacier (6–8 hours to here).

DAY 2. From your camp on Curtis Ridge, drop onto the Carbon Glacier. Conditions will determine how you access Liberty Ridge; you usually have a couple of options, but ultimately you want to gain the climber's right side of the ridge. Although many climbing parties begin near the toe of the ridge, the slope that drops fall line from Thumb Rock to the glacier makes for a much better ski descent. There is more objective hazard from rockfall going up this way, but it is worth considering if you want to preview what you are going to ski down. Either way, you will want to end up at the base of Thumb Rock at 10,750 feet (4 hours to here).

It is possible to pass on either side of Thumb Rock; conditions will determine which way you go. Above here, you have lots of options, but you want to keep generally to the ridge crest until you reach the base of the Black Pyramid. This uppermost rock formation on Liberty Ridge will force you onto exposed snow slopes on the climber's left side of the ridge. Ascend until you reach the top of the Black Pyramid at 12,000 feet (6 hours to here).

Above this, you can cross back over the ridge onto the climber's right side and mellower terrain. Continue up until you reach the bergschrund. While you navigate this, take some time to determine how you plan on skiing through it. If you think a rappel is necessary, consider building this anchor on the way up to allow for a less complicated descent. Above the bergschrund, you encounter some of the steepest terrain on the route. Conditions will dictate exactly which way you go, but as long as you keep going up, you will reach the summit of Liberty Cap at 14,112 feet (8 hours to here).

If you want to go to the true summit, you will need to descend from Liberty Cap to

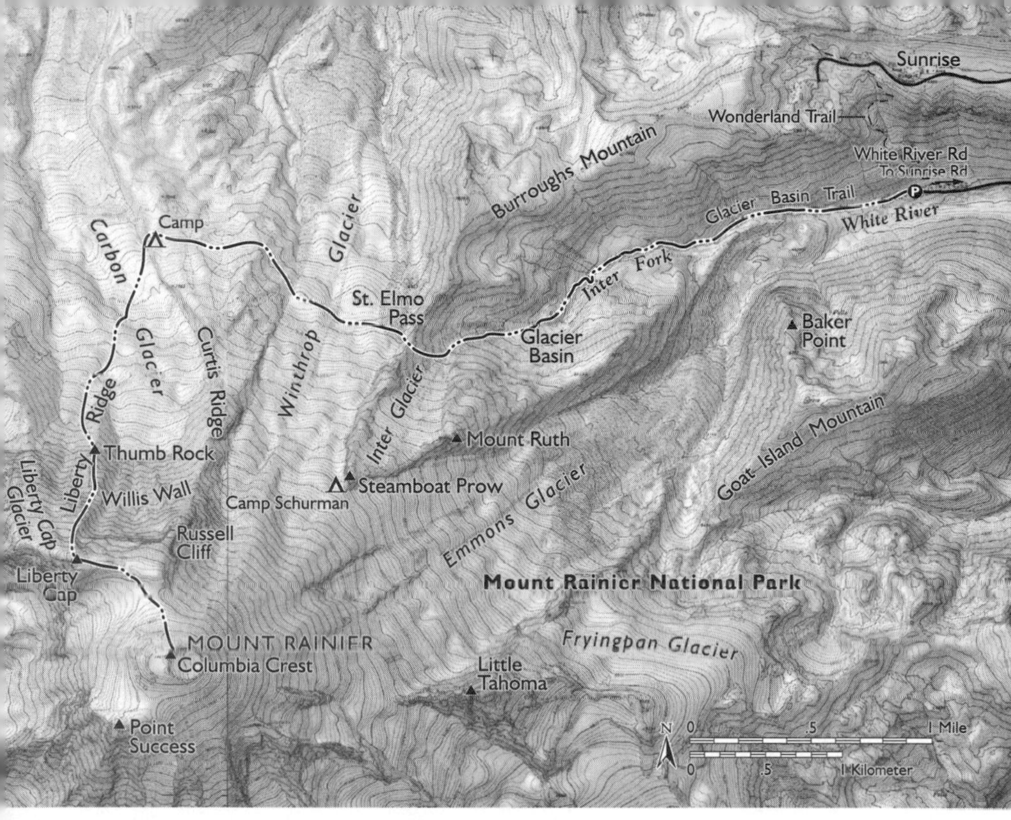

the east, and then cross the summit plateau to Columbia Crest at 14,410 feet (1 hour from Liberty Cap). This side trip can also be a good diversion while you are waiting for the snow to soften.

DESCENT. Descend the way you came up. If you do not like the conditions or are uncomfortable skiing down the ridge, consider going down the Emmons Glacier (see Tour 69, Emmons Glacier).

Tour Author: Aaron Mainer

69 Emmons Glacier

Starting elevation: 4300 feet
High point: 14,410 feet
Vertical gain/loss: 10,400 feet/10,400 feet
Distance: 25 km (16 miles)
Time: 2–3 days
Overall difficulty: very difficult
Ski skills: difficult
Fitness level: very strenuous
Technical skills: high

Commitment: high
Gear: the basics, plus ski mountaineering and overnight equipment
Best season: March–June
USGS maps: Sunrise, Mount Rainier East, and Mount Rainier West
Permits: Mount Rainier National Park charges an entrance fee. You must also have a wilderness permit to camp overnight. All parties traveling above 10,000 feet must also get a climbing permit.

There are many reasons to ski the Emmons Glacier on Mount Rainier, but the most obvious is that it is enormous. Not only is it the largest glacier on Mount Rainier, it is also the largest glacier in the contiguous United States. While its scale is impressive, the Emmons also draws skiers with its relatively easy access, facilities, and the combination of being popular without feeling overcrowded. Unlike other routes on the mountain that travel near or across rock cleavers, the Emmons Glacier has very few permanent landmarks. The route changes every year—solid glacial routefinding skills are essential.

ACCESS

From Enumclaw, take State Route 410 east toward Chinook Pass. After 37 miles, turn right on Sunrise Road. Follow this road 5 miles, and turn left on White River Road. Follow this to the end of the road and park at the campground. The road is closed in the winter, and usually opens sometime in May. For the latest road conditions, call the main park headquarters.

TOUR

DAY 1. From the White River Campground, walk or skin up Glacier Basin Trail, which is usually snow covered until about the beginning of May. But even under several feet of snow, the trail should be fairly obvious. After being washed out in the floods of November 2006, it was rerouted and now ascends to Glacier Basin well above the White River. At about 5900 feet, the trail emerges from the trees and enters a large open meadow at the base of Glacier Basin. This is a popular place to camp for those wanting to break up the ascent to Camp Schurman (3 hours to here).

From Glacier Basin, ascend west-southwest to the bottom of the Inter Glacier. The Inter Glacier has minimal crevassing, especially down low, and few parties choose to rope up here. Work your way up to an elevation of about 8600 feet, and then make your way climber's left to Camp Curtis at 8670 feet, which sits on the ridge that separates the Inter and Emmons Glaciers (7 hours to here).

From Camp Curtis, make a descending traverse south-southwest onto the Emmons Glacier. Some large crevasses form on this section of glacier; evaluate conditions and consider roping up, especially if it is getting late and the snow is soft. Either way, work your way up the glacier to the top of Steamboat Prow and Camp Schurman at 9500 feet (8 hours to here).

The Emmons Glacier from the east (Scott Schell)

DAY 2. Leave your overnight gear at Camp Schurman, and begin your trek up. Keep in mind that the Emmons Glacier is the second most popular climbing route on Mount Rainier. Unless you are climbing very early in the season, there will likely be numerous tracks going up the mountain. While you cannot trust every track, the presence of numerous guided parties means that there is typically one prominent route that goes to the summit.

The route described here works most years (at least some of the time), but glaciers are dynamic, and you should be too. For the latest route info, check the blog that the park's climbing rangers maintain (http://mountrainierconditions.blogspot.com) before you go, and check in with the climbing rangers at Camp Schurman.

From Camp Schurman, climb south-southwest (climber's left) to a flat spot on the glacier about 200 vertical feet above, known as the Emmons Flats. It is a good camping option if you cannot find a suitable place to pitch a tent at Camp Schurman or if you want a little more solitude. Continue through the Emmons Flats to a large ramp known as the "corridor" that has relatively few crevasses and is the standard route for much of the season. Work your way to the top of the corridor at approximately 11,500 feet (2.5 hours to here). Early in the season, the route may continue straight up, but more often, it cuts back to the climber's right.

Continue up to about 13,000 feet and the base of a steep headwall. At times, it is possible to ascend directly to the summit from here. If that route is not a trustworthy option for any reason, traverse right and ascend to the flat area between Liberty Cap and the summit, sometimes called Liberty Saddle at 13,600 feet (5 hours to here). From here, take the relatively mellow terrain to the summit crater and Columbia Crest at 14,410 feet (6 hours to here).

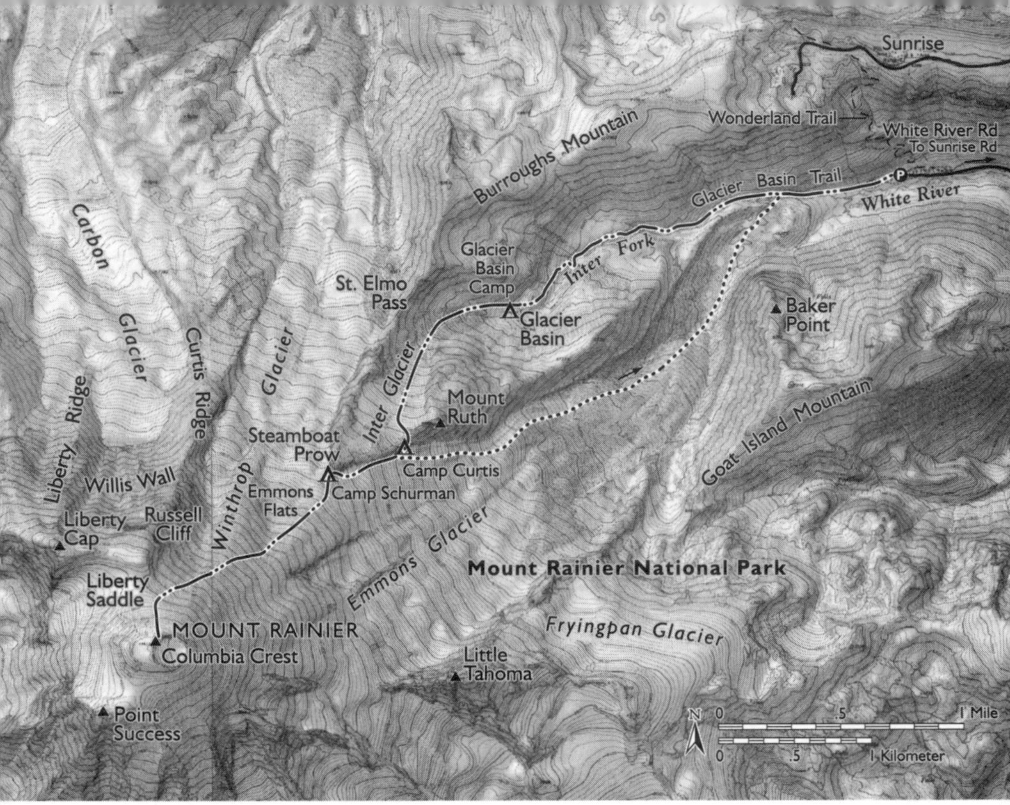

DESCENT. The descent takes you back the way you came up, which should be relatively straightforward since you were able to identify areas of concern or difficulty on your way up. If the weather is dubious, liberal use of your GPS receiver is a good idea. As previously noted, the route has very few landmarks, and it is easy to get turned around if visibility deteriorates.

Depending on what time you arrive on the summit, you may want to delay your descent by eating a sandwich or perusing the summit register. Although the Emmons is east-facing and gets early sun, the upper sections of the route can remain unpleasantly firm until late morning or early afternoon. The fact that you will be skiing more than 10,000 feet from the summit to the trailhead means that you will likely encounter bulletproof ice, perfect corn, and wet snow. Timing is everything so that you do not get too much of the former or the latter.

When you reach Camp Schurman (8 hours to here), pack up your overnight gear and get ready for the next 5000 feet of skiing. Drop onto the lower Emmons, and look for your track back up to Camp Curtis. From there, it is all downhill to the trailhead at 4300 feet (10 hours to here).

If it is early in the season and there is a lot of snow down low, you can go all the way down the lower Emmons Glacier. The skiing can be sublime. The downside is that you will probably have to put your skins back on to get across the moraine at the bottom, and getting across the Inter Fork of the White River can be a pain.

Tour Author: Aaron Mainer

70 Cowlitz Chimneys

Starting elevation: 3800 feet
High point: 7300 feet
Vertical gain/loss: 4300 feet/4900 feet
Distance: 18 km (11 miles)
Time: 8–10 hours
Overall difficulty: difficult
Ski skills: difficult
Fitness level: very strenuous
Technical skills: moderate
Commitment: high
Gear: the basics
Best season: April–May
USGS maps: White River Park, Mount Rainier East, and Chinook Pass
Permits: Mount Rainier National Park charges an entrance fee. You must also have a wilderness permit to camp overnight.

The Cowlitz Chimneys are an excellent destination if you are looking for adventurous skiing off the beaten path. Situated on the east side of Mount Rainier National Park in the vicinity of Cayuse Pass, this zone sees remarkably little traffic. We describe this tour as a point-to-point traverse, but it is possible to enter and exit from State Route 123.

ACCESS

From Enumclaw, take State Route 410 east for 37 miles. Turn right onto Sunrise Road, and drive approximately 4 miles to the Fryingpan Creek trailhead at 3800 feet. It is best to do this tour after the National Park Service opens the road to Sunrise and Cayuse Pass, which can be anywhere from mid-April to late May. For the latest road conditions, call the main park headquarters.

If you want to drop a car at the end or simply access the Chimneys from Needle Creek, continue on State Route 410 to Cayuse Pass. Bear right on State Route 123, and drive another 5 miles to the trailhead for Deer Creek Falls on your right.

TOUR

Take the short spur trail to gain the Wonderland Trail, and follow it to the basin at the head of Fryingpan Creek. If there is a lot of snow, it may be difficult to follow the trail down low. As long as you keep the creek a couple hundred meters to your left, it does not matter. At 4400 feet, the terrain steepens and the trail switchbacks right next to the creek. Follow or cut the switchback to gain flatter terrain at 4600 feet.

The trail emerges from the old-growth forest and crosses the creek via a footbridge at 5200 feet (2 hours to here). It is possible to cross here, but early in the season, it is usually easier to continue up the drainage and cross a snowbridge farther up the creek.

Continue up the bottom of the drainage until about 5500 feet where you then want to work up and left to an area known as Summer Land (3 hours to here).

The terrain opens up here and feels very big. Head southeast on a rising traverse, and pass underneath Meany Crest. There are big slopes above and below you here—make sure you feel good about their stability. Once you are past Meany Crest, aim for the col to the climber's left of Panhandle Gap (just south of Point 6945). At this col, make your first transition at 6700 feet (4 hours to here).

Make a hard traverse east-southeast to gain the broad ridgeline above and south of the Sarvant Glaciers. Once on the ridge, put your skins back on and take a rising traverse, again east-southeast, aiming for an elevation of about 7300 feet on Banshee Peak (not labeled on the USGS map). This is a beautiful ascent overlooking Ohanapecosh Park and Mount Rainier. Once you have gained your elevation, take a good look at the backside of the Cowlitz Chimneys. Aim for the 7100-foot saddle between the North (Point 7421) and Middle (Point 7605) Chimneys (5 hours to here).

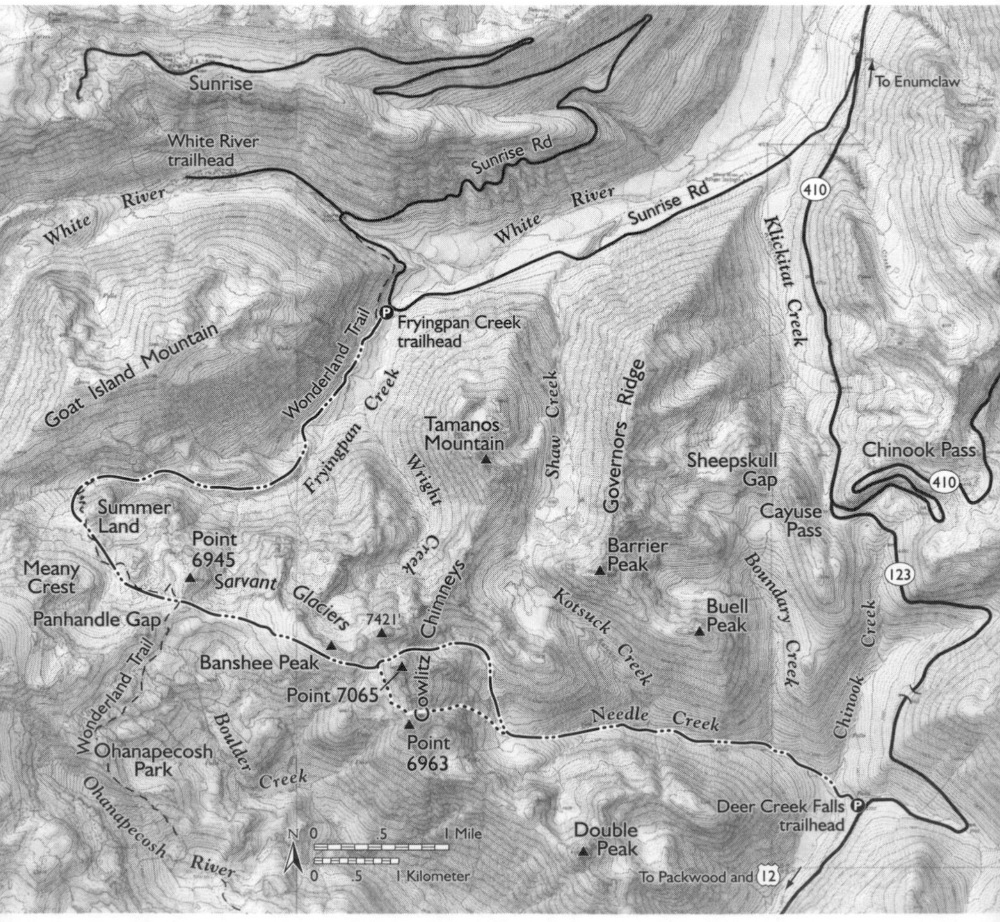

Cowlitz Chimneys from the east-southeast (Scott Schell)

Depending on the time of year and the seasonal snowpack, you may be able to ski from the summit of the North Chimney. Whether you choose to go for the summit or not, you are looking to descend the broad drainage that drops first east and then south to the meadow at the head of Needle Creek at 4500 feet (6 hours to here).

Alternate route. There is an excellent couloir that begins just north of Point 6963 on the USGS map. From the shoulder of Banshee Peak, rip your skins and traverse south-southeast on the west side of the chimneys. When you run out of elevation to work with, put your skins back on for one last climb to the notch at 6900 feet (5.5 hours to here). From here, descend east into the Needle Creek drainage. The first 600 to 800 vertical feet is fairly steep and takes you through an open couloir to a large bench.

From that bench, continue down and look for the narrow exit couloir on skier's right at 5400 feet. If the couloir has too little snow or you do not like the look of it, you can work along the benches and through small trees to skier's left down to the upper basin of Needle Creek. Both routes will take you to the meadow at the head of Needle Creek at 4500 feet (6.5 hours to here).

From the meadow, work your way down the Needle Creek drainage. When Kotsuck Creek comes in from the left, move to the north side of the creek and look for the trail that takes you all the way to State Route 123 at 3230 feet (8 hours to here).

Tour Author: Aaron Mainer

71 Fryingpan Creek Couloir

Starting elevation: 3800 feet
High point: 6790 feet
Vertical gain/loss: 3600 feet/3600 feet
Distance: 13 km (8 miles)
Time: 6–8 hours
Overall difficulty: very difficult
Ski skills: very difficult
Fitness level: strenuous
Technical skills: very high
Commitment: high
Gear: the basics, plus ski mountaineering equipment and a 50-meter rope
Best season: April–May
USGS maps: White River Park, Chinook Pass, and Mount Rainier East
Permits: Mount Rainier National Park charges an entrance fee. You must also have a wilderness permit to camp overnight.

A striking line in a spectacular setting, Fryingpan Creek Couloir has all the ingredients of a classic couloir: steep, narrow, and deep. Combine this descent with a rappel entrance, and it is guaranteed to get your heart racing.

ACCESS

From Enumclaw, take State Route 410 east 37 miles. Turn right on Sunrise Road, and drive approximately 4 miles to the Fryingpan Creek trailhead at 3800 feet. It is best to do this tour after the National Park Service has opened the road to Sunrise, which can be anywhere from mid-April to late May. For the latest road conditions, call the main park headquarters.

TOUR

To access the couloir from the top (the approach we recommend), follow the Wonderland Trail to the basin at the head of Fryingpan Creek. If there is a lot of snow, it may be difficult to follow the trail down low. As long as you keep the creek a couple hundred meters to your left, it does not matter. At 4400 feet, the terrain steepens and the trail switchbacks right next to the creek. The trail is fairly obvious here and allows you another good look at the couloir. Follow or cut the switchback to gain flatter terrain at 4600 feet. If you choose to ascend the couloir from the bottom, you will want to drop down and cross Fryingpan Creek here. To drop in from the top, continue up the climber's right side of the creek.

The trail emerges from the old-growth forest and crosses the creek via a footbridge at 5200 feet (2 hours to here). Although it is possible to cross here, it is usually easier to continue up the drainage, and cross a snowbridge farther up the creek. Continue

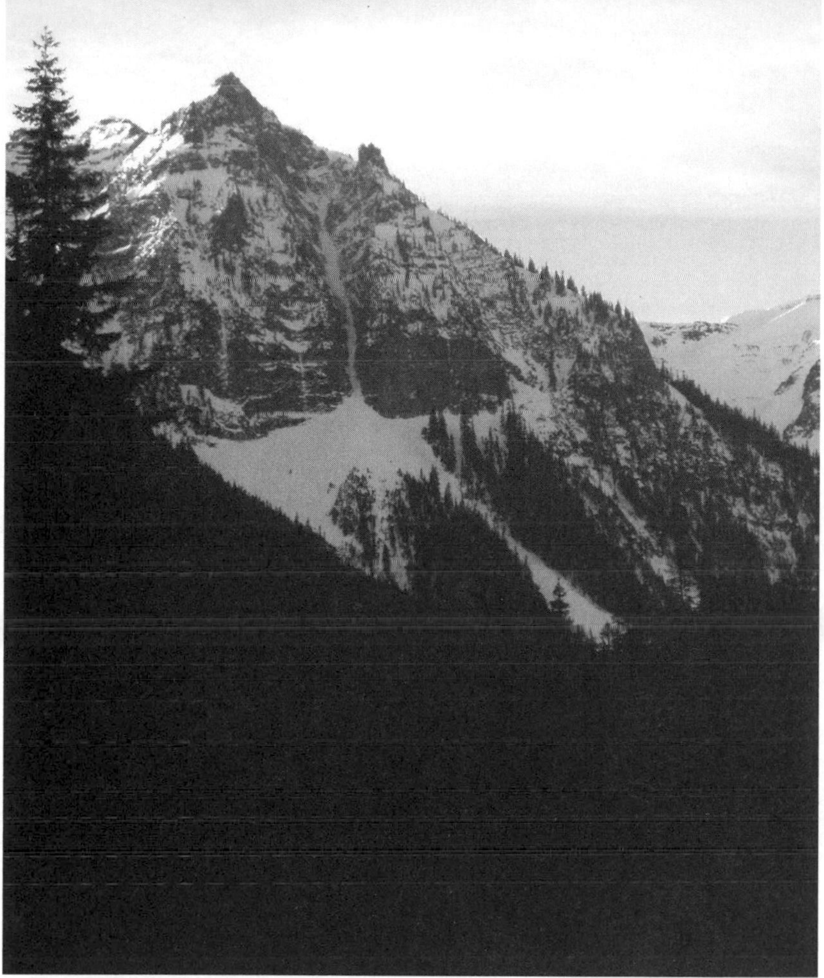

The Fryingpan Creek Couloir from the northeast (Aaron Mainer)

up the bottom of the drainage until about 5500 feet. From here, you will want to work up and left to an area known as Summerland (3 hours to here).

The terrain opens up here and feels very big. Head southeast on a rising traverse, and pass underneath Meany Crest. There are big slopes above and below you here—make sure you feel good about their stability. Once you are past Meany Crest, aim for the col to the climber's left of Panhandle Gap (just south of Point 6945 on the map). At this col, make your first transition at 6700 feet (4 hours to here).

The entrance to the couloir is on the looker's left side of the ridgeline in front of you and the quickest way there is a high traverse. Traverse to the prominent rib in the middle of the basin, being mindful of the large cornices that can form on the ridgeline above. From the rib, put your skins back on, and head for the bench above the trees on the far side. The entrance to the couloir is not obvious. It is left (north) of the last rocky point on the ridgeline and lower than you might expect at 6500 feet (5 hours to here).

You may be able to drop in from the very top of the couloir on skier's right in a very big snow year, but more than likely you will want to move down the ridgeline to a good-sized subalpine fir and rappel into the skier's left side. The rappel is anywhere between 15 and 25 meters. Be sure about the snow's stability, the conditions, and your skiing ability before you pull the rope, because it would be very difficult to climb back out.

Once you are in the couloir, there is no need for directions, but be aware of the rollover about halfway down. The couloir ends abruptly, and you exit onto a wide apron. Keep slightly left, and take this slope fall line all the way to Fryingpan Creek. Find a way across the creek, which can be the most challenging part of the tour, and ascend the bank on the other side to the trail. Take the trail back to your car at 3800 feet (6 hours to here).

Tour Author: Aaron Mainer

72 Mount Rainier Circumnavigation

Starting elevation: 4300 feet
High point: 10,080 feet
Vertical gain/loss: 16,000 feet/16,000 feet
Distance: 50–60 km (30–35 miles)
Time: 4–5 days

Overall difficulty: very difficult
Ski skills: difficult
Fitness level: very strenuous
Technical skills: extremely high
Commitment: high
Gear: the basics, plus ski mountaineering and overnight equipment
Best season: March–June
USGS maps: Sunrise, Mowich Lake, Mount Rainier West, and Mount Rainier East
Permits: Mount Rainier National Park charges an entrance fee. You must also have a wilderness permit to camp overnight. All parties traveling above 10,000 feet must get a climbing permit

Mount Rainier is the most massive volcano in Washington State, and circumnavigating it is an ambitious undertaking. The vast majority of the tour is on glaciated terrain, you must cross a number of steep slopes, and navigation errors can have grave consequences. Before you attempt this tour, you need to be sure that weather and conditions are appropriate for the scale of the objective. With that said, a successful circumnavigation of Mount Rainier takes you through consistently spectacular terrain and makes for one of the finest and most challenging ski mountaineering objectives in Washington State. Although it is possible to begin and end at any of the common access points of the park, it will be described here from the White River Campground.

ACCESS

From Enumclaw, take State Route 410 east toward Chinook Pass. After 37 miles turn right on the Sunrise Road. Take it 5 miles to the White River Road, and turn left. Follow this to the end of the road and park at the campground. This road is closed in the winter, and usually opens sometime in May. For the latest road conditions, call the main park headquarters.

TOUR

DAY 1. From the White River Campground, walk or skin up the Glacier Basin Trail, which is usually snow covered until about the beginning of May. But even under several feet of snow, the trail should be fairly obvious. It was washed out in the floods of November 2006, but it has since been rerouted and ascends to Glacier Basin well above the White River.

From the bottom of the Inter Glacier, ascend to the prominent pass at 7500 feet on the ridge that separates the Inter and Winthrop Glaciers. Although the col you are aiming for is just south of what is labeled as St. Elmo Pass on the USGS map, it is commonly referred to as St. Elmo's. Since the ascent to St. Elmo's is east facing, you want to be here early if solar radiation is an issue (5 hours to here).

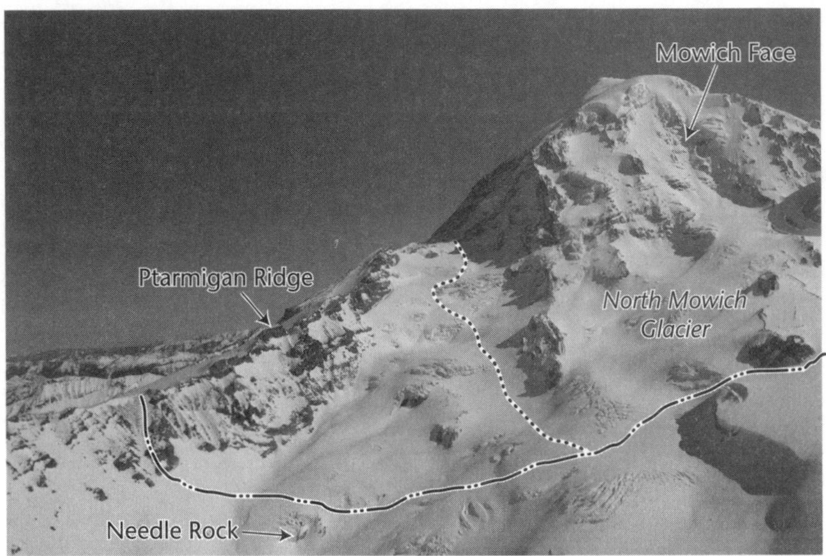

Mount Rainier from the northwest (Alasdair Turner)

From St. Elmo's, rip your skins and drop onto the Winthrop Glacier. There are numerous crevasses here, so choose your route carefully and consider roping up if conditions dictate. Contouring around at about the 7200-foot level is the most efficient option. Continue to the beginning of Curtis Ridge, being careful of the steep slopes that access the very broad ridge. Once you are safely on the ridge, you should encounter minimal crevassing until you reach the Carbon Glacier. Eventually, make it to the western edge of Curtis Ridge at about 7200 feet where you can look out at the Carbon Glacier (6–8 hours to here).

DAY 2. The second day of this tour takes you across the park's least visited glaciers and lets you view some of the more spectacular aspects of the volcano. Begin by dropping onto the Carbon Glacier from your camp on Curtis Ridge. Be aware that some large crevasses form alongside the margin of the glacier—use caution here. Cross the Carbon, aiming for the slope on the uphill side of the rock band that is exposed at approximately 7000 feet. This slope is quite steep and east facing, so it is best to get through this section early. A rising traverse brings you to the top of this slope and mellower terrain on the Russell Glacier around 7500 feet (1 hour).

From here you have a couple of options. You can either ascend to the top of the Russell Glacier and drop onto the North Mowich Glacier around 9800 feet, or you can continue with a slightly rising traverse toward Observation Rock, the prominent and craggy peak on the far side of the Russell Glacier . The Russell Glacier also offers some fantastic north-facing skiing. If you check out the high route and do not like the descent onto the Mowich, you can get great turns back down toward Observation Rock.

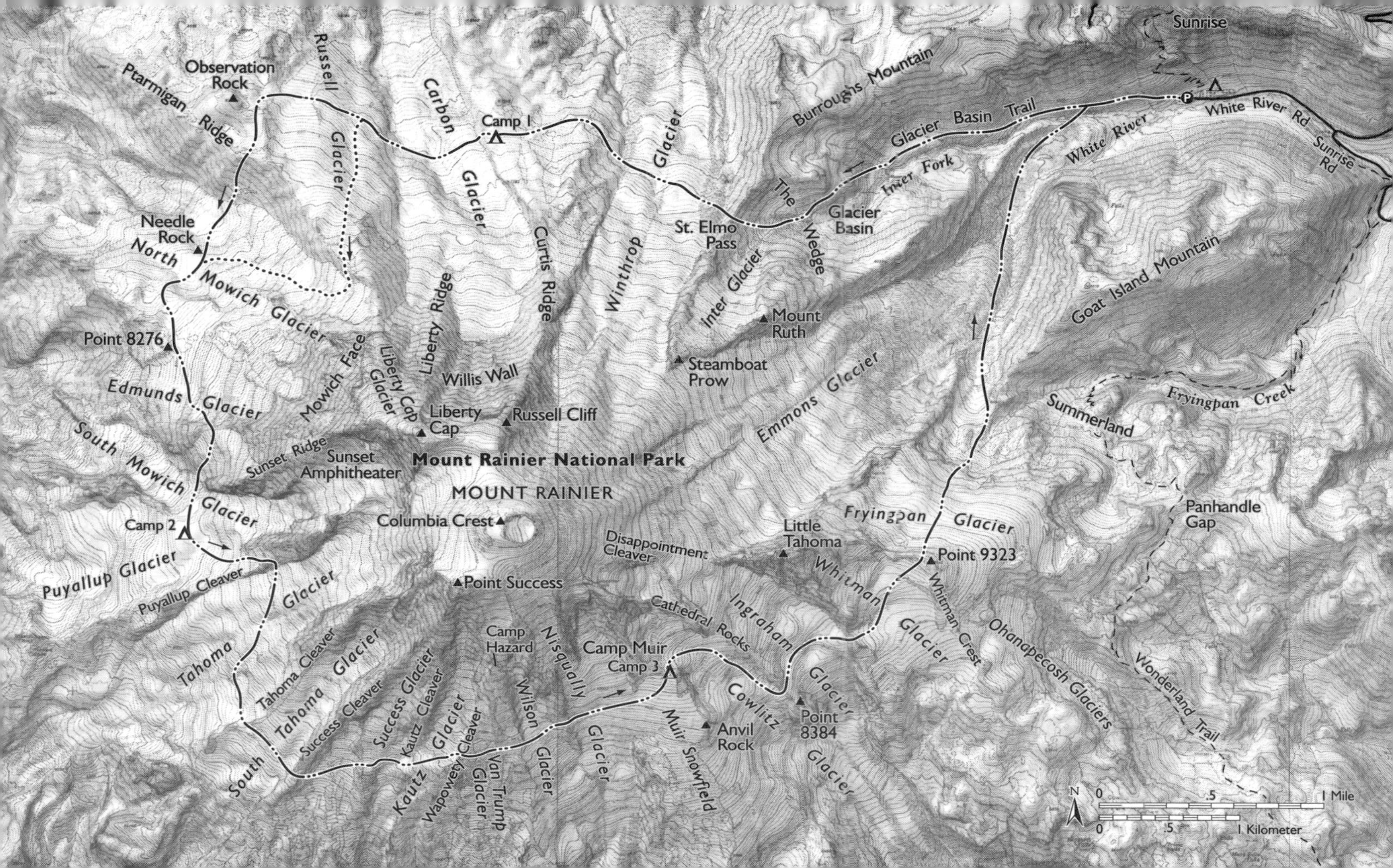

Sunrise
Burroughs Mountain
White River Rd
Sunrise Rd
Glacier Basin Trail
White River
Inter Fork
Glacier Basin
The Wedge
St. Elmo Pass
Inter Glacier
Mount Ruth
Steamboat Prow
Goat Island Mountain
Fryingpan Creek
Summerland
Panhandle Gap
Wonderland Trail
Ohanapecosh Glaciers
Observation Rock
Ptarmigan Ridge
Russell Glacier
Carbon Glacier
Camp 1
Winthrop Glacier
Curtis Ridge
Liberty Ridge
Willis Wall
Needle Rock
North Mowich Glacier
Point 8276
Mowich Face
Liberty Cap Glacier
Liberty Cap
Russell Cliff
Emmons Glacier
Edmunds Glacier
South Mowich Glacier
Sunset Ridge
Sunset Amphitheater
Mount Rainier National Park
MOUNT RAINIER
Columbia Crest
Camp 2
Puyallup Glacier
Puyallup Cleaver
Point Success
Disappointment Cleaver
Little Tahoma
Fryingpan Glacier
Point 9323
Whitman Glacier
Whitman Crest
Ingraham Glacier
Cathedral Rocks
Camp Hazard
Nisqually Glacier
Camp Muir
Camp 3
Cowlitz Glacier
Point 8384
Anvil Rock
Muir Snowfield
Tahoma Glacier
Tahoma Cleaver
Success Cleaver
Success Glacier
Kautz Cleaver
Kautz Glacier
Wapowety Cleaver
Van Trump Glacier
Wilson Glacier
South Tahoma Glacier
N
0
.5
1 Mile
1 Kilometer

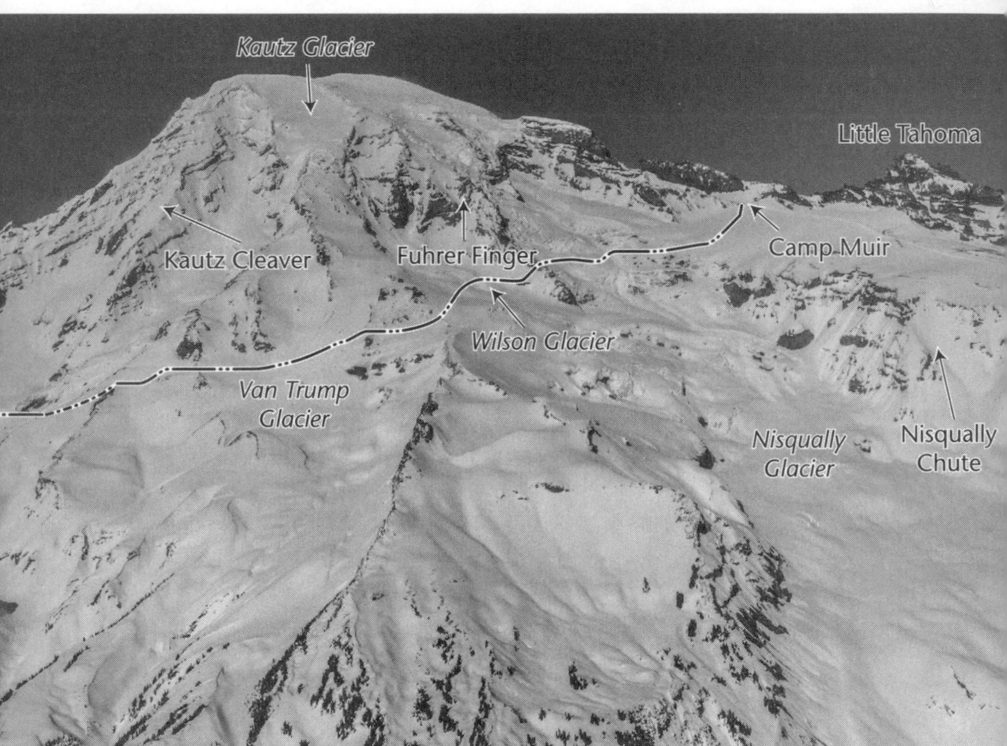

Mount Rainier from the southwest (Alasdair Turner)

If you opt for the low route, you will want to pass underneath Observation Rock and follow the small basin on its south side until you reach Ptarmigan Ridge. The terrain is fairly broken and convoluted here, but you are aiming for an elevation of 8400 feet on Ptarmigan Ridge (3–4 hours to here). There is typically a good access point onto the Mowich Glacier here, but conditions vary depending on the time of year and a number of nearby lines end in cliffs even with a very deep snowpack. Be sure that the route you choose goes through.

In the middle of the Mowich, there is a prominent nunatak that is labeled on the USGS map as Needle Rock. Cross the Mowich above this feature, and navigate the rolling terrain beyond it until you reach the edge of the Edmunds Glacier above Point 8276. From here follow a rising traverse across the Edmunds, shooting for a small saddle at 9300 feet on the next cleaver. Then descend south-southwest toward Sunset Ridge. Cross under Sunset Ridge and cruise across the South Mowich Glacier to a large flat area at 8500 feet on the Puyallup Glacier. Camp here, but be sure to probe for crevasses before you put up your tent (7–8 hours to here).

DAY 3. Day three takes you across the southern aspect of Mount Rainier. If solar radiation or warm temperatures are a concern, consider starting quite early. From your camp on the flat bench at 8500 feet, climb toward the Puyallup Cleaver. The south side of the cleaver is very steep, and you will need to cross at an elevation of 9800 feet (1 hour to here).

The slope that takes you onto the Tahoma Glacier from here is also very steep, so use good judgment. Once you are on the Tahoma Glacier, do not let your guard down as it is one of the biggest glaciers on the mountain, and it has numerous large crevasses. This can be a great ski as you make a descending traverse to 8200 feet on the far side of the glacier. Look back up the mountain to view the Sickle, the unique curving feature through the Upper Tahoma Icefall (a worthy objective in its own right for those willing to access the mountain from the Westside Road).

Once you are across the glacier, contour across the South Tahoma Glacier, and cross the Success Cleaver at the same elevation of 8200 feet (2.5 hours to here). From this point, the terrain is a bit more forgiving until you get to the Wilson Cleaver. The glaciers are not quite as broken as they are on the north and west side of the

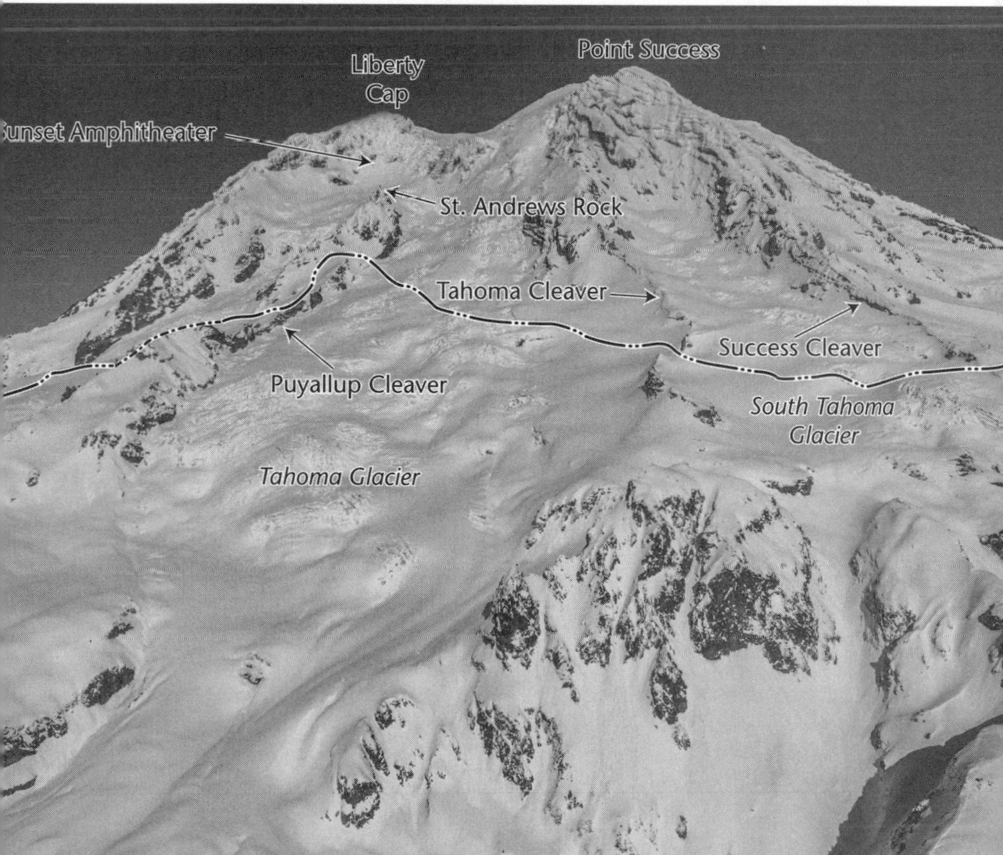

Mount Rainier from the west (Alasdair Turner)

mountain, and you can choose from among numerous options for crossing the cleavers that separate the glaciers. Do not get complacent, but ultimately you need to get to an elevation of 9500 feet on the Wilson Cleaver. If you have the time, there are numerous options for fall-line skiing in here.

Once you get to the Wilson Cleaver, be very cautious crossing the Nisqually Glacier. This is one of the most hollow glaciers on the mountain and the site of numerous crevasse falls—*strongly consider roping up across here*. Eventually the Nisqually gives way to the relatively benign Muir Snowfield, which you cross to reach Camp Muir at 10,080 feet (7 hours to here). There is a first-come, first-served public shelter at Camp Muir.

DAY 4. From Camp Muir, descend 1600 feet down the Cowlitz Glacier to Lower Cathedral Gap. Although it is not labeled as such on the map, it is the saddle 100 feet or so above Point 8384 on Cathedral Rocks. Drop onto the Ingraham Glacier, and connect mellow terrain at around 8500 feet until you reach the rock ridge that separates the Ingraham and Whitman Glaciers. Some fourth-class scrambling brings you to a prominent col here at 8800 feet (2 hours to here).

You will need to drop a couple hundred feet on the other side to get around a rocky protrusion and onto the Whitman Glacier. From here, you are shooting for the saddle to the west of Point 9323 on the Whitman Crest (3 hours to here). Rip your skins for the last time, and carefully make your way down the north side of this col and onto the Fryingpan Glacier.

At around 7600 feet, the glacier starts to get pretty steep; be sure to avoid cliffs on this stretch. There are numerous routes through here and you are heading for the broad southwest ridge of Goat Island Mountain. Once you are on the north side of this ridge, follow the basin to the lower Emmons Glacier until you reach the Glacier Basin Trail, which will take you back to the White River Campground (5 hours to here).

Tour Author: Aaron Mainer

SOUTH CASCADES

THE SOUTH CASCADES PROVIDE a unique mountain landscape where large snowy volcanoes dwarf the surrounding forested hills. This section describes tours in the Cascade Range from the Crystal Mountain Ski Area south to the Columbia River (the state border with Oregon). While Mount Rainier lies within this geographic definition, it deserves its own section based on its massive size and elevation.

With the exception of the distinct volcanoes, the mountains in the South Cascades are lower than their counterparts to the north; they typically stand about 5000 feet above sea level. The peaks of the Goat Rocks are all nearly 8000 feet but they are an anomaly of the region formed by a massive eruption of what was another stratovolcano. This large conical volcano was over 10,000 feet high over 2 milllion years ago; it left behind a series of eroded remnants named after the many mountain goats that live there. Skiers will likely see mountain goats roaming the subalpine and alpine zones on the volcanoes; at lower latitudes, the average temperatures are a little warmer than the rest of the state and the snowline correspondingly higher.

The geology in this region is primarily lava flows between higher volcanic rock. Younger than the rock found in the North Cascades where erosion has left more solid foundation, this volcanic rock is loose and unfavorable for technical climbing. Fortunately, they still hold massive amounts of snow for good alpine conditions and reliable skiing into summer. While Mount Saint Helens lost most of its glaciers during the 1980 eruption, the Goat Rocks has some remaining icefields on its northeast side, and Mount Adams boasts ten principal glaciers. Most massive is the Adams Glacier which spills 3 miles northwest from the summit of Mount Adams.

FEES, PERMITS, AND WEATHER INFORMATION

Tours in the South Cascades are located within Gifford Pinchot National Forest and Mount Baker–Snoqualmie National Forest. Contact information for these two entities, and the Mount Adams and Cowlitz Valley Ranger Stations, is located in Resources.

Parking. Many National Forest recreation sites require a parking fee. Day passes can be purchased at local vendors or your annual Northwest Forest Pass or America the Beautiful Pass will also work.

Camping. Fill out a free, self-issued wilderness permit at the trailhead. Wilderness regulations apply, and Leave No Trace practices are strongly encouraged.

Permits. A Cascade Volcano Pass is required for all climbing on Mount Adams above 7000 feet after June 1. Trips to Mount Saint Helens require a climbing permit that can be purchased at the Mount Saint Helens Institute website.

Wilderness Areas. Mount Adams Wilderness, Tatoosh Wilderness, Goat Rocks Wilderness are located within the Gifford Pinchot National Forest. The Mount Baker–Snoqualmie National Forest contains Goat Rocks Wilderness and Norse Peak Wilderness.

Weather. In addition to the Northwest Avalanche Center and the National Weather Service websites, check the Crystal Mountain Resort, White Pass, and

Previous page: The north side of Mount Adams (Scott Schell)

Mount Hood sites for current local weather and snowpack conditions. See Resources for web addresses.

73 Crystal Lakes: G-String and Shoestring

Starting elevation: 4300 feet
High point: 6595 feet
Vertical gain/loss: 6300 feet/6300 feet
Distance: 13–17 km (7.8–10.2 miles)
Time: 3–6 hours
Overall difficulty: difficult
Skiing skills: difficult
Fitness level: strenuous
Technical skills: moderate
Commitment: low
Gear: the basics
Best season: December–May
USGS maps: Norse Peak and White River Park
Permits: You do not need a permit to park or to take this tour, which starts at the Crystal Mountain Ski Area and enters Mount Rainier National Park, but it is a good idea to check in with the Crystal Mountain Ski Patrol to make sure that they are not doing avalanche control work in Silver Basin.

The G-String and the Shoestring are located in Crystal Lakes Basin inside Mount Rainier National Park. Crystal Lakes Basin is the large, triple-bow basin that lies directly south of Silver King Peak and Crystal Mountain Ski Area. Easily seen from the ski area's South Country Traverse, the twin chutes start directly on the summit of Point 6595 that defines the western terminus of the basin.

ACCESS

From Enumclaw, take State Route 410 east 33 miles to Crystal Mountain Boulevard. Turn left here, and go 6 miles to Crystal Mountain Resort.

TOUR

There are two ways to begin this tour. A ride (pass required) to the top of the High Campbell Chairlift eliminates a big chunk of the uphill skinning. Take the South Country Traverse Trail to the top of Silver Basin. Alternatively, from the base of the ski area, skin up next to the Quicksilver Chairlift being mindful of downhill traffic. From the top of the chairlift, continue up the groomed path past Hen Skin Lake until you reach Silver Basin (the basin southwest of Hen Skin Lake). Be careful through here because the skiers on this outrun for the Crystal Mountain South Country are seldom expecting uphill traffic. Gain the ridge west of Three Way Peak at the top of Silver Basin (2 hours to here).

From any point on top of the ridge, ski generally southwest to upper Crystal Lake. Cross the lake and descend to 5800 feet. At 5800 feet, contour about 0.5 kilometer (0.3 mile) to the left through a small drainage. Point 6595 is immediately to the northwest. Ascend any of the prominent east-facing gullies on the south ridge of Point 6595. These gullies are steep, often windloaded, and can be threatened by cornices from above. Be confident in your assessment of snow stability before you continue up from here. Gaining the ridge usually involves a transition to booting at the very top. Once you are on the ridge, ascend due north over much mellower, but often wind-scoured, terrain to the summit of Point 6595 (3 hours to here).

The G-String and Shoestring Couloirs from the northeast (Aaron Mainer)

The G-String and Shoestring are parallel gullies that run from the large north-facing bowl you are now standing above. The G-String to skier's right is a classic steep-walled couloir, while the Shoestring is less of a pronounced rock feature and more of a gully. Either descent option offers about 1200 feet of moderately steep, north-facing skiing before the trees become too thick for you to ski farther.

Transition back to uphill mode, and work the rolls and benches to the southeast, climbing back up to Crystal Lake. From the lake climb east-northeast toward Three Way Peak. Gain the ridge to climber's left of Three Way (Point 6706 on the map) then descend through the ski area back to your vehicle.

Tour Author: Solveig Waterfall

74 Crystal Mountain: East Peak

Starting elevation: 4400 feet
High point: 6720 feet
Vertical gain/loss: 2300 feet/2300 feet
Distance: 5.5 km (3.5 miles)
Time: 3–4 hours
Overall difficulty: easy
Ski skills: moderate
Fitness level: moderately strenuous

Technical skills: low
Commitment: low
Gear: the basics
Best season: December–April
USGS map: Norse Peak
Permits: none

East Peak is an excellent tour with easy access from Crystal Mountain and some fun skiing from the summit. It can be a good day for those new to ski touring and can also make for a good escape from the ski resort if the lines are too long or you just want to get away.

ACCESS

From Enumclaw, take State Route 410 east 33 miles to Crystal Mountain Boulevard. Turn left here and go 6 miles to the Crystal Mountain Resort.

TOUR

East Peak is not labeled on the USGS map. It is the point south of Point 6654. From the Crystal Mountain Ski Area, start up the road to Gold Hills that begins behind the chapel. Eventually this road switchbacks to the right, and a sign indicates the start of the summer trail. Ascend the bank here to an open area 30 feet above the road. The Bullion Basin Trail continues up on skier's left, but even relatively early in the season, it is possible to continue up an old run cut on skier's right, and skip a couple

East Peak from the northwest (Alasdair Turner)

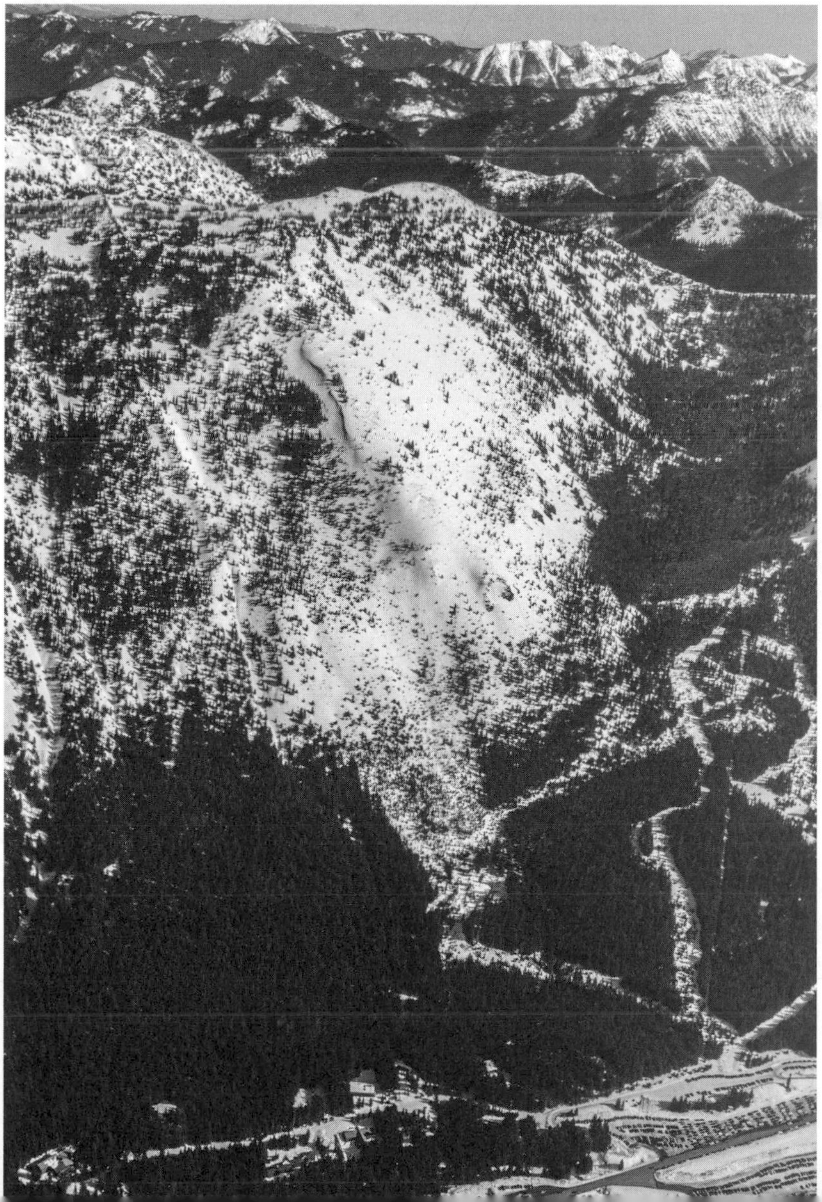

of switchbacks. Work your way through small trees until you are pushed back to the left. You are then forced up a short, steep bit before you regain the Bullion Basin Trail at 5200 feet (1 hour).

Continue up the trail to the head of Bullion Basin. The terrain above you is what you will be skiing down; while you are skinning up, you can get an idea of what looks good and where you want to ski. The trail follows a couple of small switchbacks before it emerges into an open meadow at 5800 feet (1.5 hours to here).

From here, you have a couple of options. You can work the relatively open terrain above you to the summit. This option is straightforward, but it involves ascending some fairly large and open slopes. Alternatively, it is possible to cut east-southeast across the top of the meadow, and take the ridge on the other side to the summit at 6720 feet (2.5 hours to here). The ridge requires some tricky skinning and small detours around trees and rocks, but if the open slopes above seem suspect, it can be the best way to go. When you are skiing down, keep in mind that the terrain to skier's right is generally more open.

Tour Author: Aaron Mainer

75 Sheep Lake Couloir

Starting elevation: 4400 feet
High point: 6904 feet
Vertical gain/loss: 5100 feet/5100 feet
Distance: 12 km (7.5 miles)
Time: 6–8 hours
Overall difficulty: difficult
Ski skills: difficult
Fitness level: strenuous
Technical skills: moderate
Commitment: low
Gear: the basics
Best season: December–April
USGS map: Noble Knob
Permits: You do not need a permit to park or to take this tour, which starts at the Crystal Mountain Ski Area and enters Mount Rainier National Park. But it is a good idea to check in with the Crystal Mountain Ski Patrol to make sure that they are not doing avalanche control work in Silver Basin.

The Sheep Lake Couloir is one of the finest couloirs in the immediate vicinity of Crystal Mountain. From the summit of Point 6904, the couloir boasts 1200 feet of fall-line skiing in a beautiful setting.

ACCESS

From Enumclaw, take State Route 410 east 33 miles to Crystal Mountain Boulevard. Turn left here, and go 6 miles to Crystal Mountain Ski Area.

TOUR

From the ski resort, skin up next to the Quicksilver Chairlift being mindful of downhill traffic. From the top of the chairlift, continue up the groomed path past Hen Skin Lake until you reach Silver Basin (the basin southwest of Hen Skin Lake). Be careful through here because the skiers on this outrun for the Crystal Mountain South Country are seldom expecting uphill traffic.

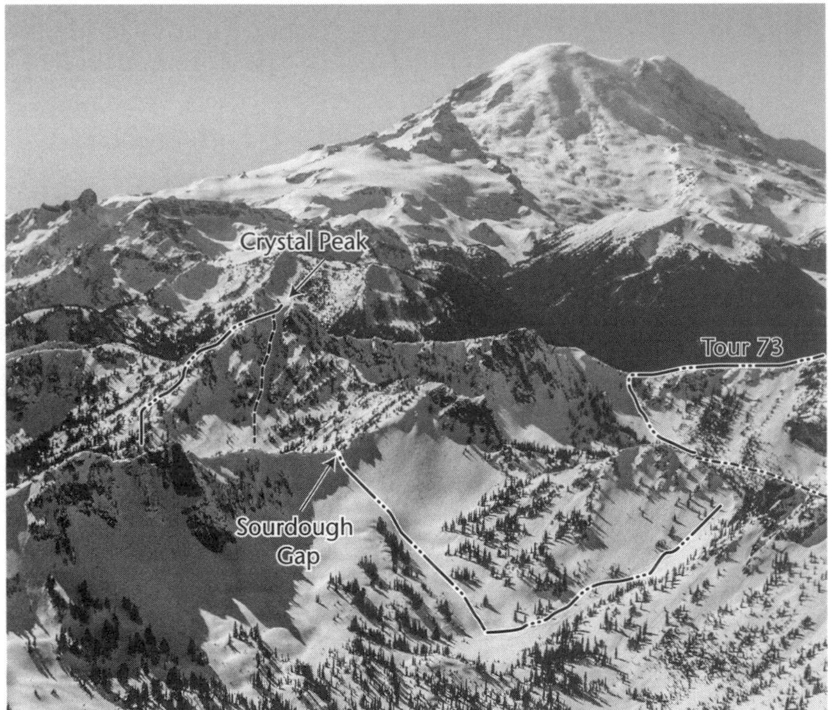

The Sheep Lake Couloir from the east (Alasdair Turner)

Once you are in Silver Basin, gain the ridgeline west of Three Way Peak. If you are here early in the morning or after a recent snowfall, be sure that there is no avalanche control work in progress. Once you are on the ridgeline at 6500 feet (2 hours to here), drop briefly into Crystal Lakes Basin, and traverse hard skier's left (south) to the obvious col that separates it from the Morse Creek Basin. Depending on how high you are able to stay on the traverse and the snow conditions up to the col, a short bootpack may be all that is required to get to the saddle. However, if the skiing looks good and you do not mind adding some length and vertical distance to your tour, you can ski down into the Crystal Lakes Basin as far as you want.

Once you are at the col, you can again make a hard descending traverse, this time to skier's right (still south), or you can drop into the Morse Creek drainage for some fall-line turns. With hard traverses and a couple of short bootpacks, you can make it all the way to Sheep Lake without putting your skins on. Of course, by doing that, you miss out on a lot of good skiing! Either way, eventually make your way to Sourdough Gap, which is at the southwest end of the Morse Creek drainage. Here, rip your skins and enjoy some turns down to Sheep Lake at 5760 feet (3.5 hours to here).

From Sheep Lake, you can look directly up the couloir. If the couloir does not look good for some reason, consider continuing on to Chinook Pass (see Tour 76, Crystal

Mountain to Chinook Pass). While it is possible to boot straight up the couloir, it is often safer and more enjoyable to access it by ascending the ridgeline to climber's left. Gain the ridge from the south end of Sheep Lake. Skinning up the ridgeline can be challenging and may require a short bootpack or two, depending on the conditions, but it will eventually lead to the summit of Point 6904 on the USGS map. *Be careful when you approach the summit—the exposure on the north side is severe.* Use caution and steer clear of any cornices that may be present (4.5 hours to here).

Before you drop into the couloir, be sure about its stability. The entrance is quite steep, and the consequences of an avalanche anywhere in it are high. It would not be an outrageous place to put someone on belay to assess conditions and test the slope stability before you drop in. Also keep in mind that since the couloir is almost directly east facing, it gets early sun exposure.

Once you are back at Sheep Lake, head back up to Sourdough Gap, and return to Crystal Mountain the way you came (7 hours to here).

Tour Author: Aaron Mainer

76 Crystal Mountain to Chinook Pass

Starting elevation: 4400 feet
High point: 6400 feet
Vertical gain/loss: 6000 feet/6000 feet
Distance: 20 km (12 miles)
Time: 8–10 hours
Overall difficulty: difficult
Ski skills: moderate
Fitness level: strenuous
Technical skills: low
Commitment: moderate
Gear: the basics
Best season: December–April
USGS maps: Norse Peak, White River Park, and Chinook Pass
Permits: You do not need a permit to park at or to take this tour, which starts at the Crystal Mountain Ski Area and enters Mount Rainier National Park. But it is a good idea to check in with the Crystal Mountain Ski Patrol to make sure that they are not doing avalanche control work in Silver Basin.

Despite its close proximity to the Crystal Mountain Ski Area, a tour to Chinook Pass feels very remote. This isolated feeling combined with fantastic views of Mount Rainier makes for a great day in the mountains.

ACCESS

From Enumclaw, take State Route 410 east 33 miles to Crystal Mountain Boulevard. Turn left here, and go 6 miles to Crystal Mountain Resort. If you plan to return via State Route 410 from Chinook Pass, you may want to drop a car at the base of Crystal Mountain Boulevard. It is usually possible to hitchhike on weekends or holidays, but this may not be an option on slow, midweek days. If Cayuse Pass is open, drop a car there for your return; it's a short way east on State Route 410 from the junction with Crystal Mountain Boulevard.

TOUR

From the Crystal Mountain Resort, skin up next to the Quicksilver Chairlift being mindful of downhill traffic. From the top of the chairlift, continue up the groomed path past Hen Skin Lake until you reach Silver Basin (the basin southwest of Hen Skin Lake). Be careful through here because skiers on this outrun for the Crystal Mountain South Country seldom expect uphill traffic.

Once you are in Silver Basin, gain the ridgeline just to the west of Three Way Peak (Point 6796). If you are here early in the morning or after a recent snowfall, be sure that there is no avalanche control work in progress. Once you are at the ridgeline at 6500 feet (2 hours to here), drop briefly into the Crystal Lakes Basin, and traverse hard skier's left (south) to the obvious col that separates it from the Morse Creek Basin.

Depending on how high you are able to stay on the traverse and the snow conditions up to the col, a short bootpack may be all that is required to get to the saddle. However, if the skiing looks good and you do not mind adding some length and vertical distance to your tour, it is possible to ski down into the Crystal Lakes Basin as far as you want.

Once you are at the col, make another hard descending traverse, this time to skier's right (still south), or drop into the Morse Creek drainage for some fall-line turns. Either way, eventually make your way to Sourdough Gap, which is at the southwest end of the Morse Creek drainage. Here, rip your skins and enjoy some turns down to Sheep Lake at 5760 feet (3.5 hours to here).

As you approach Sheep Lake, maintain some of your speed so that you end up on the far (south) side of the lake. A short bit of sidestepping with your skis on will get you over the small ridge that forms the lake's southern boundary. From here contour around to skier's right until State Route 410 and Chinook Pass, both of which are closed and snow covered in the winter, are visible. Choose your route to the road carefully as the road cut is quite steep in places. Once you are down, skin up the road a kilometer or so to the pass at 5430 feet (4 hours to here).

At Chinook Pass, you have options that depend, in part, on how much you skied on the way to it and what time it is. If you are at the pass early, you may want to check out the terrain on the west side of Naches Peak. Some excellent couloirs originate on the ridge just south of the rocky, technical summit pyramid. To get there, head south from the pass across Tipsoo Lake, and ascend directly up whichever one looks good. Of course, you will want to have a good grasp of snow and avalanche conditions before doing so.

To Enumclaw
410
To 410
Crystal Mountain Blvd
Mount Baker–Snoqualmie National Forest
Crystal Mountain Ski Area
CRYSTAL MOUNTAIN
Mount Rainier National Park
Quicksilver Chairlift
Creek
Elizabeth
Pickhandle Basin
Pickhandle Gap
Elizabeth Lake
White River
Crystal Creek
Hen Skin Lake
Bear Gap
Pickhandle Point
Silver Basin
Crystal Lakes Basin
Three-Way Peak
Morse Creek
Upper Crystal Lake
Morse Creek Basin
Placer Lake
To Sunrise
Deadwood Creek
Sourdough Gap
Crystal Peak
Klickitat Creek
Sheep Lake
To Yakima
410
410
Deadwood Basin
Deadwood Lakes
Rainier Fork American River
Mount Baker–Snoqualmie National Forest
Yakima Peak
Chinook Pass
Tipsoo Lake
Cayuse Pass
Naches Peak
123
N
0 .5 1 Mile
0 .5 1 Kilometer

Alternatively, you can ski the northwest side of Yakima Peak, which is on the opposite side of the pass. Access it by skinning north and slightly east to the broad saddle northeast of the peak. Then traverse underneath the peak until you are at the base of the obvious couloir on its northwest side. Some steep skinning or a short bootpack will bring you to the summit, which few people visit in the winter.

To get back to Crystal Mountain, you can either continue down State Route 410 where you can pole and skate your way back to the bottom of Crystal Mountain Boulevard, or you can skin back to the ski area via the Deadwood and Crystal Lakes Basins.

If you choose the latter option, follow the ridgeline that runs north from Yakima Peak until you reach the next peak to the north. It is impossible to ski from the summit of this unnamed peak, but there are two small couloirs to the west of the main summit that drop down to Deadwood Lakes at 5230 feet (5.5 hours to here). Be sure that you have enough energy and time to ascend to the ridgeline that separates these lakes from Crystal Lakes Basin afterward because you do *not* want to go down the very steep, densely vegetated Deadwood Creek.

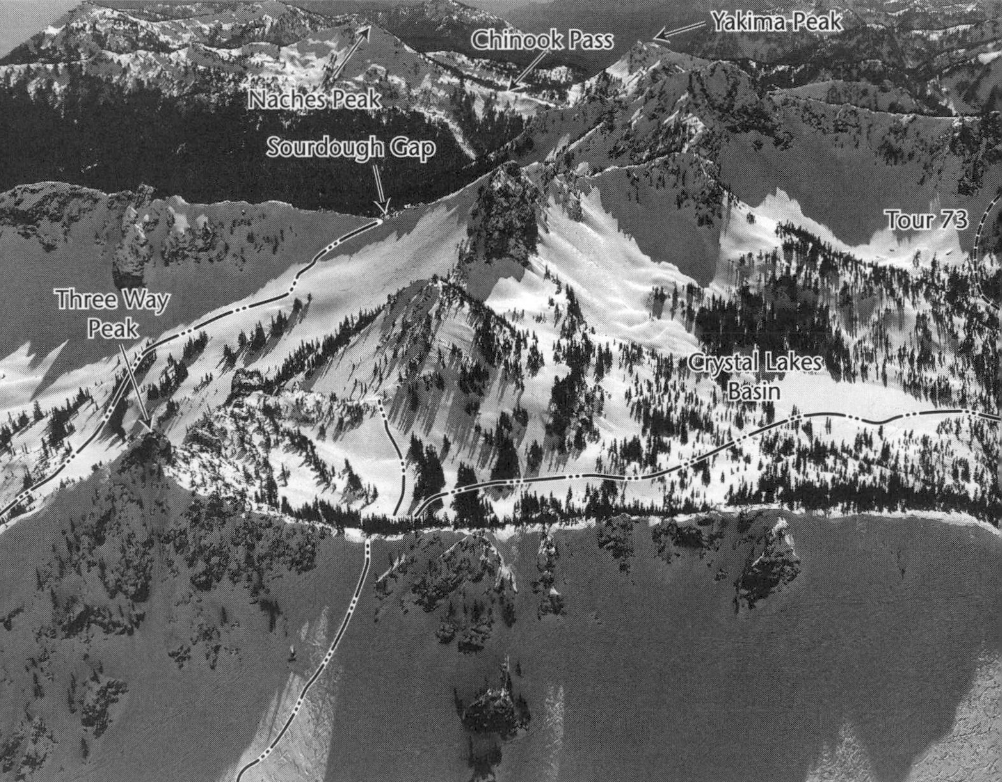

Chinook Pass and Sourdough Gap from the north (Scott Schell)

From Deadwood Lakes work the terrain to the north, heading toward Point 6706 on the USGS map. Once you have gained this ridgeline, there are several couloirs that drop into the Crystal Lakes Basin. The easiest way to descend is from the col between Points 6706 and 6595. Once you are in the Crystal Lakes Basin, work your way northeast to Upper Crystal Lake and then the ridgeline that separates Mount Rainier National Park from the Crystal Mountain Ski Area. Ski Silver Basin back to your car at 4400 feet (8 hours to here).

Tour Author: Aaron Mainer

77 Goat Rocks: Gilbert Peak

Starting elevation: 4080 feet
High point: 8201 feet
Vertical gain/loss: 4200 feet/4200 feet
Distance: 24 km (15 miles)
Time: 2 days
Overall difficulty: moderate
Ski skills: easy
Fitness level: moderately strenuous
Technical skills: moderate
Commitment: low
Gear: the basics, plus overnight gear
Best season: late April–July
USGS maps: Pinegrass Ridge, Jennies Butte, and Walupt Lake
Permits: You must display a Northwest Forest Pass or Interagency Pass to park at the trailhead. This tour takes place in the Goat Rocks Wilderness in the Gifford Pinchot and Mount Baker–Snoqualmie (administered by the Okanogan–Wenatchee) National Forests. Wilderness permits can be filled out at the start of Trail 1120.

The Goat Rocks provide a rare stretch of jagged crest in the southern part of the state's Cascades. Lying between Mount Rainier and Mount Adams, these pointy peaks are the remnants of a volcano estimated to have been more than 10,000 feet high and extinct for two million years. This area provides fantastic late season corn skiing.

ACCESS

Access is difficult at all times, and winter realistically offers only one route in via White Pass. Once the snow melts off the roads later in the spring, better access is available via the North Fork and South Fork Tieton River on the east side and Snowgrass Flats on the west side. The slopes east of the crest provide better skiing because they hold snowfields longer into the summer. The route described here comes in from Conrad

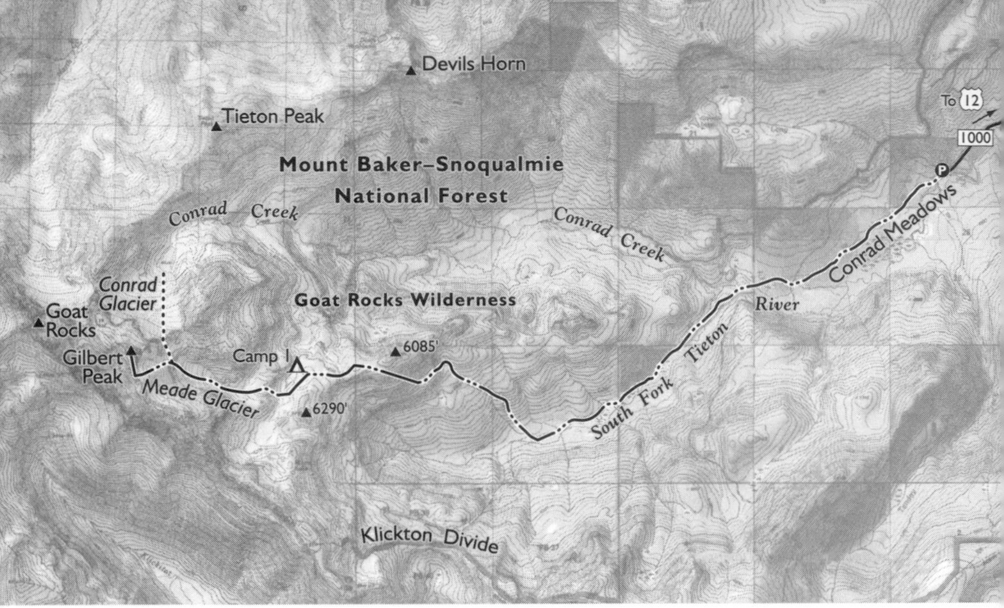

Meadows onto the Meade Glacier and Gilbert Peak (also known as Mount Curtis Gilbert), the highest point of the Goat Rocks.

Travel State Route 12 for 35 miles west of Yakima (19 miles east of White Pass). Turn left (or right, if approaching from the east) onto Forest Road 1200 (Tieton Reservoir Road). Continue for 3.6 miles until you reach Forest Road 1204 (Cold Creek); turn right onto Forest Road 1204 and follow it for 2.7 miles. Turn left onto Forest Road 750 and continue for about a mile. Turn right onto Forest Road 1000 (South Fork Tieton Road); continue 6.9 miles to the trailhead. Check with the Naches Ranger District of the Okanogan–Wenatchee National Forest for the most current access route and road conditions.

TOUR

DAY 1. Walk the road west until it curves to the right and you hit the start of Trail 1120. This trail quickly fords Long Creek before meandering through Conrad Meadows where the trail is the low point in a very wet area. Expect a soft, wet hiking surface with competing challenges of running water and cow pies. After 3 kilometers (1.9 miles), stay left, heading southwest on the trail along the South Fork Tieton River. At about 4310 feet, the trail begins climbing northwest. Soon you should be able to transition to skins, and tour to the 6000-foot saddle west of Point 6085 (4 hours to here).

Staying on the north side of the ridge, travel west to set camp in the large meadow just above 6000 feet with views west to Gilbert Peak (4.5 hours to here). If views and high points are mandatory for your camp location, continue climbing south to Point 6290.

DAY 2. Leave overnight gear at your camp, and travel west into the obvious entrance of the Meade Glacier (taking note of some fun ski options on looker's left). You can travel north to the notch onto the Conrad Glacier to further explore the Goat Rocks

Gilbert Peak towers above the Meade Glacier (Trevor Kostanich)

or continue west to the snowy bench at 7700 feet south of Gilbert Peak (1.75 hours from camp). This bench offers great views southwest to Mount Adams and is a logical high point for the skier who does not care about reaching a summit.

From this bench it is a short hike to the summit of Gilbert Peak. Caching your skis, climb northwest onto the drier side of the peak and finally scramble up the steeper rocky section to the summit at 8201 feet (2.5 hours from camp). The views northwest up the crest display the rewards of exploring Goat Rocks further.

Follow your ascent route back to the bench at 7700 feet, and then enjoy big open turns down the Meade Glacier. Collect your overnight gear, and ski down into the drainage of the South Fork Tieton River. Stay close to the trail because, sooner than you may prefer, you will begin hiking the long walk to the trailhead (5.5 hours to here).

Tour Author: Trevor Kostanich

78 Mount Saint Helens: Worm Flows and Swift Glacier

Starting elevation: 2700 feet
High point: 8365 feet
Vertical gain/loss: 5665 feet/5665 feet
Distance: 20 km (12 miles)
Time: 7–9 hours

Overall difficulty: moderate
Ski skills: difficult
Fitness level: very strenuous
Technical skills: low
Commitment: low
Gear: the basics, plus a light ice ax and crampons in firm conditions
Best season: January–May
USGS map: Mount St. Helens
Permits: To travel above 4800 feet on Mount Saint Helens, you need a permit from the Mount Saint Helens National Volcanic Monument in the Gifford Pinchot National Forest. From April 1–October 31, climbing permits are available online from the Mount Saint Helens Institute. Check www.fs.usda.gov/detail/mountsthelens for details about obtaining permits. From November 1–March 31, you can get a free winter climbing permit in person at the Lone Fir Resort in Cougar or at the Marble Mountain Snow-Park; during this period you must also display a Washington Sno-Park Permit.

Several years after the massive 1980 eruption destroyed its 9677-foot summit dome and northern aspects, Mount Saint Helens once again became a popular recreation area. Reopened to climbing and skiing travel in 1987, the southern reaches of the mountain remained intact, offering a dramatic and unique view of Cascade geology from the summit rim. Climbing or skiing into the crater itself, however, is strictly prohibited. The relatively benign remnants of the crevasse-free, post-eruption glaciers on the south aspect offer a wide variety of skiing terrain, and an easily approachable trailhead makes for an ideal day trip. Camping is allowed at the trailhead to accommodate an alpine start, or for a more relaxed schedule and scenic winter camping experience, consider setting up a base camp at tree line (around 5000 feet).

ACCESS

From Interstate 5 in Woodland, take exit 22 and turn east onto Dike Access Road. Continue straight onto Old Pacific Highway, and then bear left onto East Scott Avenue, and then bear left again onto Lewis River Road. Continue past the town of Cougar, where the road becomes Forest Service Road 90. Turn left on Forest Service Road 83, and follow it to the plowed Marble Mountain Sno-Park.

TOUR

Follow the often-traveled Swift Ski Trail (Trail 244) to reach tree line. At 3700 feet, cross to the west side of Swift Creek, just above Chocolate Falls (1.5 hours to here). From here, the terrain opens up to a series of bowls, gullies, and broad ridges. Monitor

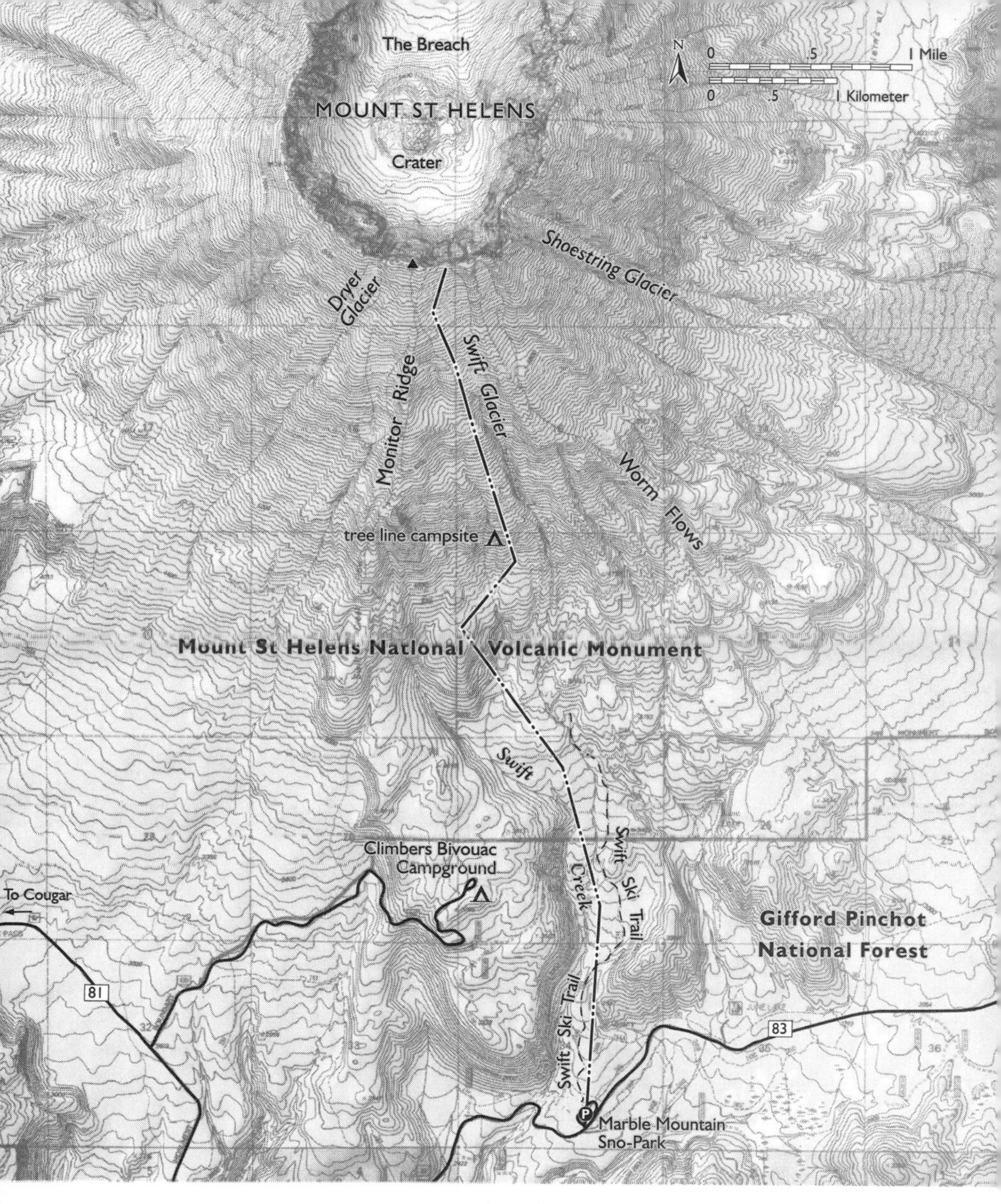

Ridge is to the west and the Worm Flows are to the east. Follow the most appealing terrain toward the small Swift Glacier above 5600 feet (4–4.5 hours to here). Near the crater rim, slope angles can tilt to around 35 degrees, but they are still easy to navigate on skis. As you approach the crater rim at 8365 feet, use extreme caution and give the corniced edge a wide berth (6.5 hours to the crater rim).

DESCENT. Once the dramatic views of active mountain building inside the crater and the grandeur of the Cascade Range begin to settle in, finish your summit snacks and transition to downhill mode. The standard ski descent retraces the ascent route back

Mount Saint Helens from the south (Alasdair Turner)

to tree line. Alternately, those seeking steeper slopes or longer days can plan a creative tour into the Worm Flow zone. Regardless of the route chosen, consider the avalanche hazard carefully, as there are many terrain traps and convexities to manage on the way down. And because this is generally a due south aspect, watch for late afternoon sluffs and wet loose avalanches on warm spring days. Much of the terrain above tree line is poorly anchored and prone to intense sun and wind effects.

Local Pacific Northwest tradition brings out many locals in May for a Mother's Day tribute climb and ski. Most do so in full costume: donning dresses, colorful wigs, excessive jewelry, and a have-fun-or-go-home attitude.

Tour Author: Solveig Waterfall

79 Mount Adams: North Face of Northwest Ridge

Starting elevation: 4600 feet
High point: 12,276 feet
Vertical gain/loss: 8970 feet/8970 feet
Distance: 23 km (14 miles)

Time: 2 days
Overall difficulty: very difficult
Ski skills: very difficult
Fitness level: very strenuous
Technical skills: high
Commitment: high
Gear: the basics, plus ski mountaineering and overnight equipment
Best season: May–July
USGS maps: Mount Adams West and Mount Adams East
Permits: This tour takes place within the Mount Adams Wilderness in the Gifford Pinchot National Forest. From June 1 through September 30, you must display a Cascade Volcano Pass when traveling above 7000 feet on Mount Adams; the pass is available from the Mount Adams Ranger Station in Trout Lake, the Cowlitz Valley Ranger Station in Randle, or by mail. During the remainder of the year, a wilderness permit is necessary; you can self-register at the Mount Adams Ranger Station or the trailhead. You must display a Cascade Volcano Pass, Northwest Forest Pass, or Interagency Pass to park at the trailhead.

Mount Adams is the second tallest peak in the state, and its southern slopes deservedly receive many ski visits. The north side of this volcano offers a more wild experience in technical terrain. While the north side offers a plethora of fun ski descents, the big open face falling off the northwest ridge begs the ski mountaineer to enjoy about 3000 feet of steep, exposed turns. Due to its north aspect and high elevation, you must wait for sunshine and high temperatures to soften the snow for a more enjoyable descent. This route describes an ascent up the north ridge on mixed rock and snow with only short sections of exposure. It offers continuous views of your desired descent down the north face of the northwest ridge.

ACCESS

The Killen Creek trailhead (Trail 113) is on Forest Service Road 2329. This area is dense with intertwined Forest Service roads that often hold snow into summer, and you must navigate several of them to get to the trailhead. Contact the Mount Adams Ranger Station for current road conditions (see Resources).

From Randle on State Route 12, turn south on State Route 131 (Forest Service Road 23). After 15 miles, veer left onto Forest Service Road 21. After 5 miles, turn right onto Forest Service Road 56. After 2.4 miles, turn right onto Forest Service Road 5603. After 4 miles, turn right onto Forest Service Road 2329. After 4.5 miles, park at Killen Creek trailhead at 4600 feet.

TOUR

DAY 1. From the trailhead, hike up the trail until there is enough snow for you to skin continuously. Cross the Pacific Crest Trail at about 6100 feet (2.25 hours to here). Continue skinning south-southeast toward a steeper slope that you can bypass by contouring around the ridge climber's right or ascend by traversing to climber's left. Set camp just above this steeper slope at 6900 feet with running water to the west (3 hours to here). This short day sets you up well for the big day to come.

DAY 2. From camp, travel south-southeast and gain the start of the north ridge at around 8100 feet (1.25 hours from camp). Follow along this north ridge, using longer snow sections on climber's left as appropriate. Around 9000 feet (2.25 hours from camp), the ridge narrows and there are a couple of short sections on steeper rock where the use of hands is helpful. Throughout the ascent, observe a desired path down the north face of the northwest ridge, specifically the mandatory traverse left at about 10,400 feet, and any crevasse crossing concerns lower on the route. Also note the descent option of the climbing route, the north ridge, in case you need an alternative.

At about 11,600 feet (4.5 hours from camp), the slope angle mellows, becoming more efficient to skin. The final few hundred feet to the true summit at 12,276 feet (5.5 hours from camp) are long but we recommend that route for multiple reasons; ascending that way allows the sun to soften the descent ridge and gives you a chance to take photos and socialize with the groups who ascended the south side.

Mount Adams from the north (Scott Schell)

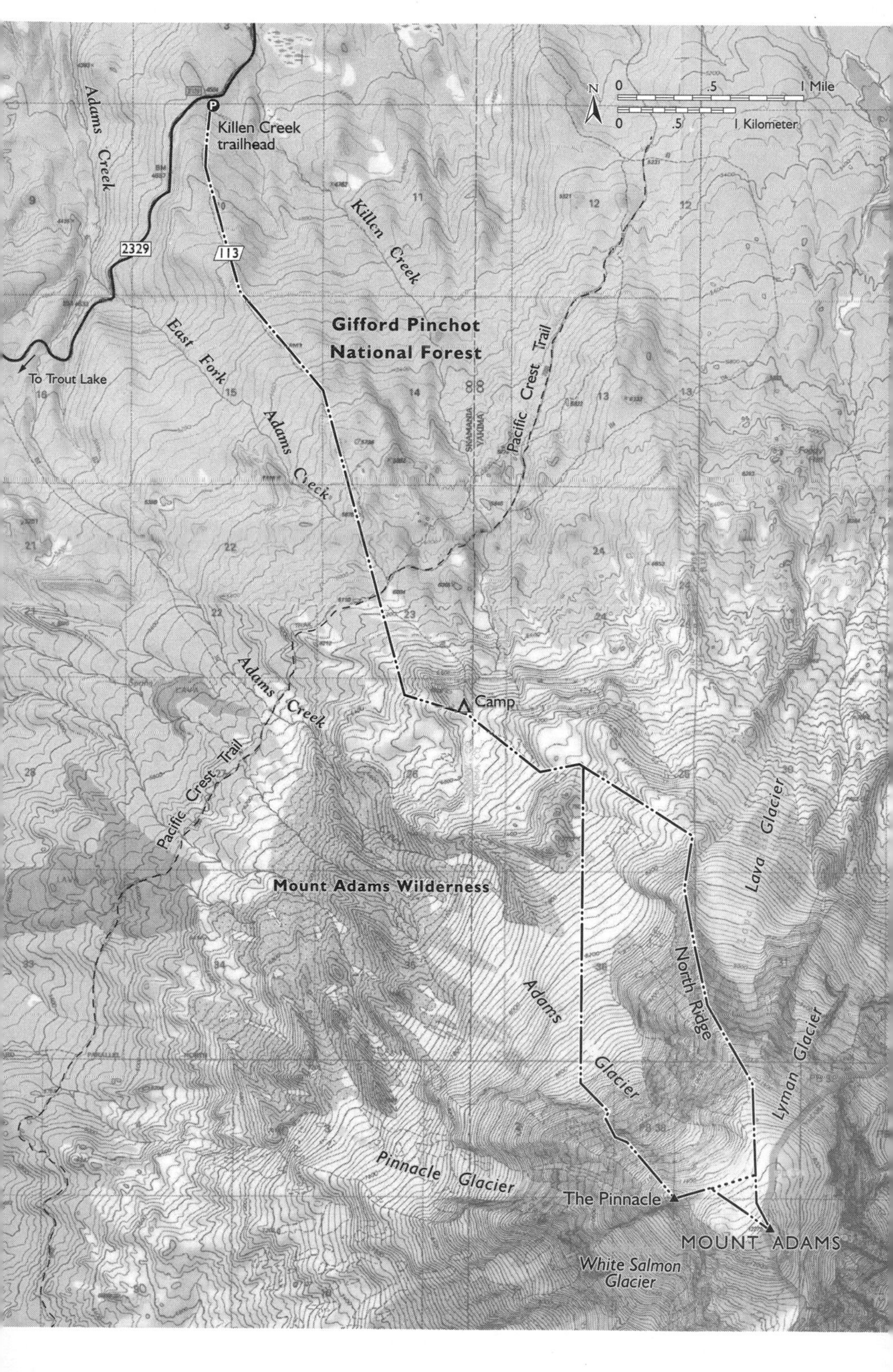

0
.5
1 Mile
0
.5
1 Kilometer
Killen Creek
trailhead
Adams Creek
Killen Creek
2329
113
Gifford Pinchot
National Forest
East Fork
Adams Creek
To Trout Lake
Pacific Crest Trail
Camp
Adams Creek
Pacific Crest Trail
Mount Adams Wilderness
Lava Glacier
North Ridge
Adams
Glacier
Lyman Glacier
Pinnacle Glacier
The Pinnacle
MOUNT ADAMS
White Salmon
Glacier

When you have had your fill of the summit, ski northwest off the summit toward the east side of The Pinnacle (the northwest summit of this vast volcano). A short climb up this gentle ridge to the summit of The Pinnacle at about 12,080 feet puts you at the top of the desired ski route (6.5 hours from camp).

If you do not care about reaching the true summit, skin southwest from 11,900 feet above the Adams Glacier to the top of The Pinnacle to shave an hour off the tour.

DESCENT. From the top of The Pinnacle, admire your surroundings and what you can see of your ski descent, which the convex slope limits. The first few hundred feet of the run are the least steep—a good place to test your comfort level with the snow's firmness. Once you are committed, enjoy the consistent pitch and vast smoothness of this big mountain face. The slope steepens about halfway down and stays steeper than 40 degrees.

At about 10,400 feet, traverse left above a small cliff band, and then descend between some rocks and possible cracks. Traverse right onto the western edge of the Adams Glacier at about 9800 feet being cautious of crevasses. Ski to the flats just below 9000 feet where you should take a well-deserved deep breath, turn around, and admire the huge face you just descended.

Traverse right below the final crevasse hazard, and enjoy a couple thousand feet of low-angle skiing back to camp at 6900 feet (8.5 hours from camp). Gather your overnight gear, and ski as low as possible before hiking the trail down to the trailhead (10.5 hours from camp).

Tour Author: Trevor Kostanich

80 Mount Adams: South Ridge and Southwest Chutes

Starting elevation: 5520 feet
High point: 12,276 feet
Vertical gain/loss: 6756 feet/6756 feet
Distance: 15 km (9.5 miles)
Time: 1–2 days
Overall difficulty: moderate
Ski skills: moderate
Fitness level: strenuous
Technical skills: low
Commitment: moderate
Gear: the basics, plus overnight gear, a light ice ax, and crampons for firm conditions
Best season: May–July
USGS maps: Mount Adams East and Mount Adams West

Permits: This tour takes place within the Mount Adams Wilderness in the Gifford Pinchot National Forest. From June 1 through September 30, you must display a Cascade Volcano Pass when traveling above 7000 feet on Mount Adams; the pass is available from the Mount Adams Ranger Station in Trout Lake, the Cowlitz Valley Ranger Station in Randle, or by mail. During the remainder of the year, a wilderness permit is necessary, and you can self-register at the Mount Adams Ranger Station or the trailhead. You must display a Cascade Volcano Pass, Northwest Forest Pass, or Interagency Pass to park at the trailhead.

For those looking for a great Cascade volcano skiing experience on relatively safe terrain, the southeast shoulder of Mount Adams is hard to beat. Standing at 12,276 feet with about 8000 feet of vertical relief, Mount Adams towers above its surroundings. Although many skiers visit the south side each year, do not underestimate its difficulty. This is a big mountain on which you may encounter conditions not unlike those of Mount Rainier. The majority of this ski tour travels through the alpine environment (above tree line); when the weather closes in, sharp navigation skills are crucial.

ACCESS

To reach the southeast shoulder, you will begin at the Cold Springs Campground on the south side of Mount Adams. From Vancouver, Washington, take State Route 14 to the town of White Salmon and then north to the town of Trout Lake. Continue north and pass a sign for Mount Adams Recreation Area Forest Service Road 8040. This road is not maintained in winter; depending on the conditions, it could be snow covered. Contact the Mount Adams Ranger Station for current road conditions. For the purpose of this description, the tour starts where Forest Service Road 8040 ends at the Cold Springs Campground at 5520 feet.

TOUR

DAY 1. This tour begins at the South Climb trailhead in Cold Springs Campground. Early in the season, this trail is not obvious, meaning that you may need to navigate cross-country, but as the season progresses, the tour begins with the typical trail approach to gain the snow line. Depending on the time of year and snowpack depth, you will need to decide which approach is suitable.

Standard approach. The well-beaten climber's trail winds through pine forest and flowery meadows indicative of a more easterly climate. Follow this abandoned road until it eventually turns into a thin, dusty trail and very slowly climbs to old lava flows at about 6800 feet. When the trail eventually ends at the snow line, continue north and skirt the west side of the Crescent Glacier at 7600 feet (3 hours to here).

Continue traveling north to what is known as the "Lunch Counter" at about 9000 feet. This popular camping area has room for several bivy sites, but it can be crowded. For a more isolated camp and better views, head east from the Lunch Counter to a plateau at 9400 feet on Suksdorf Ridge (5.5 hours to here).

Early season approach. The more direct early season approach has an appealing, secluded feel. Because it is through more open pine forest and meadows, cross-country travel is quite straightforward. From the South Climb trailhead, head generally north-northeast for about 3.5 kilometers (2.2 miles) to an elevation of about 7600 feet. You should be just west of the South Butte (2.5 hours to here).

The slope steepens slightly as you begin to gain the Suksdorf Ridge, which divides the dish-shape Crescent Glacier to your west and the Gotchen Glacier to the east. Climb roughly 1200 feet to an approximate elevation of 8800 feet. When the slope angle begins to relax, change to a due north bearing (4 hours to here). A plateau just ahead at 9400 feet makes for a great camp with outstanding views of the Mazama Glacier to the east (5 hours to here). The Lunch Counter, mentioned above, is just west of you (and also offers good camp options).

DAY 2. Even though you gain only 2800 feet on your second day, it will be strenuous—start early. You will be traveling at relatively high elevations by Cascade Range standards, and you will need to descend more than 6700 feet and almost 5 miles to your car. The first 200 feet of gain is low angle; then at about 9600 feet, the slope steepens. Travel north-northwest up the very consistent slope angle for nearly 2000 feet until you gain the bench or false summit at 11,520 feet.

If you have good visibility, this bench is obvious, but if it is obscured, be careful to maintain an accurate compass bearing. Use caution to avoid trending too far north onto the steep upper slopes of the Mazama Glacier (2 hours to here).

Once you have gained the false summit, you have an excellent view of Pikers Peak, which stands at 11,657 feet. From here you still need to gain about 700 feet of elevation to reach the summit of Mount Adams to the north. Maintaining an elevation of approximately 11,600 feet, continue north to reach the toe of the final slope. At 11,700 feet, trend north-northwest to the summit at 12,276 feet (4 hours to here).

DESCENT. Aside from the plateau at around 11,600 feet, you are now rewarded with one of the longer uninterrupted ski descents that the Washington volcanoes have to offer. Choose to retrace your tracks down the South Rib / Suksdorf Ridge, or the Southwest Chutes.

South Rib / Suksdorf Ridge. These two options are so close and similar that in many opinions they're one and the same. Follow your tracks from the summit, across the summit plateau, past the South Summit (sometimes called Pikers Peak), and continue down 2500 feet to the Lunch Counter (5.5 hours to here).

South Rib: Continue your descent skier's right, past the west side of the Crescent Glacier and toward the Cold Springs trailhead.

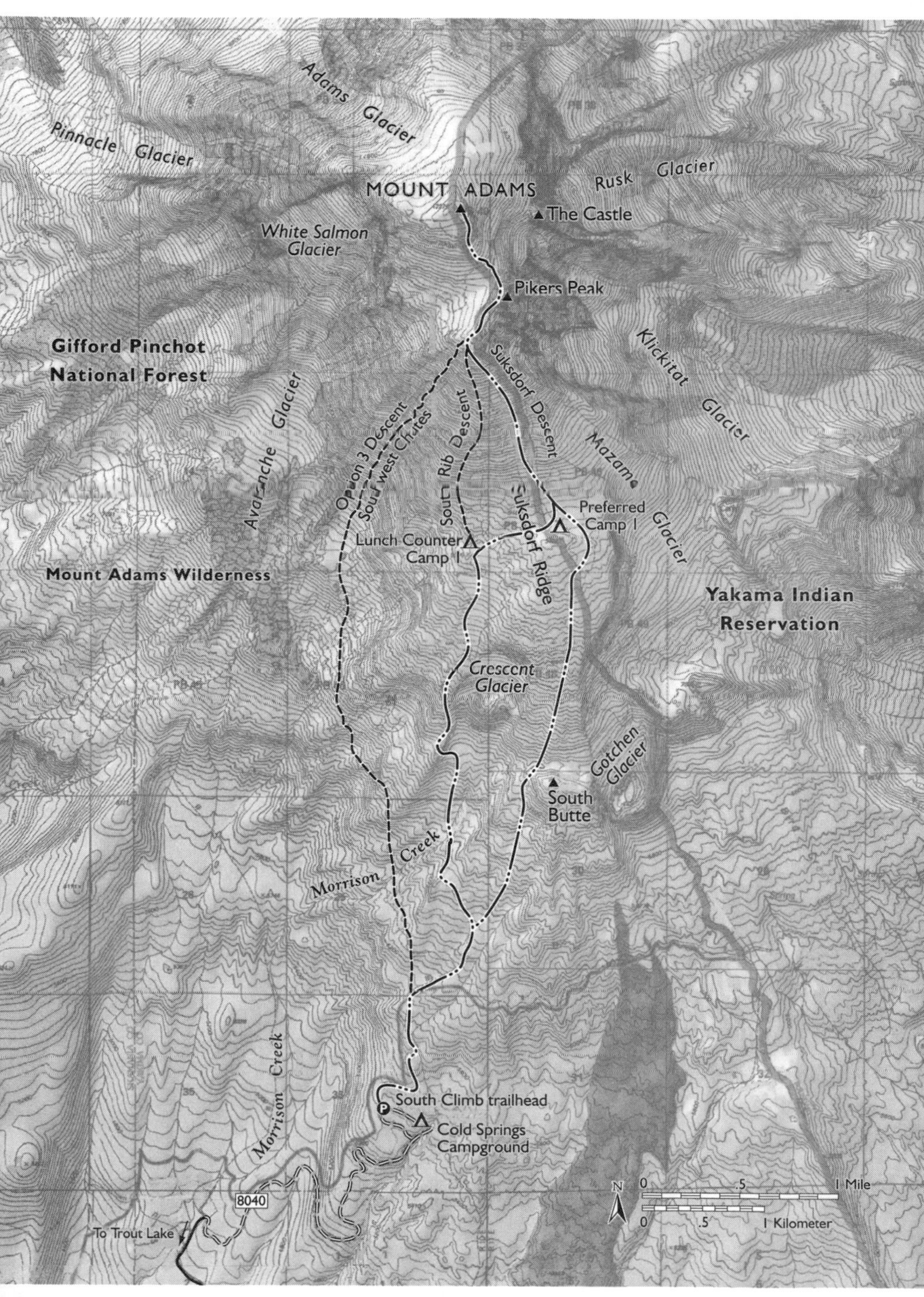

Adams Glacier
Pinnacle Glacier
MOUNT ADAMS
The Castle
Rusk Glacier
White Salmon Glacier
Pikers Peak
Gifford Pinchot National Forest
Klickitat Glacier
Suksdorf Descent
South Rib Descent
Southwest Chutes
Option 3 Descent
Avalanche Glacier
Mazama Glacier
Preferred Camp 1
Lunch Counter Camp 1
Suksdorf Ridge
Mount Adams Wilderness
Yakama Indian Reservation
Crescent Glacier
Gotchen Glacier
South Butte
Morrison Creek
South Climb trailhead
Cold Springs Campground
8040
To Trout Lake
N
0 .5 1 Mile
0 .5 1 Kilometer

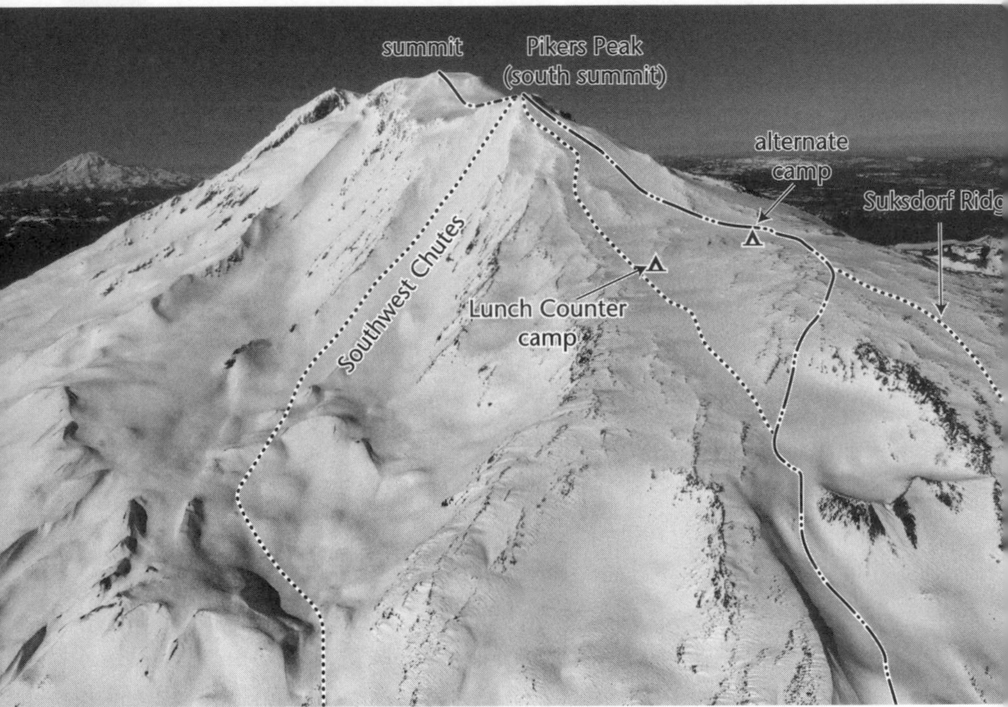

Mount Adams from the south (Scott Schell)

Suksdorf Ridge: Head skier's left along the Suksdorf Ridge toward South Butte to approximately 7600 feet, then rightwards to regain the trail to Cold Springs. The South Rib route is more direct, easier-to-navigate (therefore followed by most parties), and lasts longer into the summer; however, all those reasons make it more popular with climbers and skiers. The Suksdorf Ridge offers fewer people, and a more "alpine" descent with a series of linked-together basins on a high ridge, but melts out sooner. Both options should lead you to your car in about 7 hours.

Southwest Chutes. The Southwest Chutes are quite possibly one of the most "classic" volcano ski descents on the west coast with almost 4000 feet of completely uninterrupted 35-degree terrain. Follow your tracks from the summit, across the summit plateau, and to the South Summit. Instead of continuing to follow your up track past the South Summit and onto the upper headwall of the South Rib route, turn west until you can look over the edge. A series of parallel drainages will be visible; they are the Southwest Chutes. Begin the ski descent here. At 8000 feet, turn southeast to meet your up track. Below tree line the terrain turns into a number of gullies that flow *away* from Cold Springs Campground and the trailhead, so make doubly sure of your navigation before you commit to skiing in the trees.

Tour Authors: David Jordan and Chris Simmons

BONUS TOUR

WE OPTED TO INCLUDE THE Spearhead Traverse because we wanted to provide an example of the ski touring options to be found in the massive British Columbia Coastal Mountains. It is hard to grasp the size and quality of this high alpine playground that stretches nearly a thousand miles from the Washington border to the mountains of Southeast Alaska and the Yukon Territories.

It is safe to say that one could create hundreds of equally excellent tours in this massive mountain range. Much exploring has been done by adventurers on ski and on foot who accessed the mountains from the inland or by boat via the impressive inlets, but the remote and adventurous character of the region remains. To learn more about the ski touring terrain, purchase John Baldwin's third edition of *Exploring the Coast Mountains on Skis*.

The Spearhead Traverse offers unusually good access due to the Whistler–Blackcomb ski area. Despite the large number of people who recreate on the ski slopes of Whistler Mountain Resort, you can get away from the crowds on the Spearhead Traverse. In large part, this has to do with the absence of huts on the route; there is only the very basic Himmelsbach Hut at Russet Lake. This might change in the next few years, however, as there is a substantial effort underway to create a hut system along the Spearhead Traverse. A formal proposal was submitted to BC Parks by the Spearhead Huts Committee in the fall of 2012. Follow the progress of this project on www.spearheadhuts.org.

The Spearhead Traverse was first done on skis in 1964 by a group including Karl Ricker, a well-known Whistler resident. The route follows the Fitzsimmons Range from the Whistler Mountain/Garibaldi Provincial Park boundary at Flute Mountain around to the Spearhead Range at the edge of the Blackcomb Mountain/Garibaldi Provincial Park Boundary at the East Col. The traverse is done in both directions with Blackcomb to Whistler being most popular.

81 The Spearhead Traverse

Starting elevation: 650 meters (2132 feet) at Whistler Village
High point: 2600 meters (8530 feet) at Tremor Col
Vertical gain/loss: 6600 feet/10,725 feet
Distance: 28–30 km (about 18 miles)
Time: 3 days
Overall difficulty: moderate to difficult
Ski skills: moderate
Fitness level: strenuous
Technical skills: moderate
Commitment: moderate to high
Gear: the basics, plus ski mountaineering and overnight equipment

Previous page: Ripsaw Ridge camp, looking southeast (Martin Volken)

Best season: February–May
Maps: John Baldwin Map 1999; Whistler Backcountry
Permits: The Spearhead Traverse is located in Garibaldi Provincial Park. BC Parks charge camping fees that you can pay online or at Whistler Guest Services. Visit the park's page on the BC Parks website for up-to-date information.

The Spearhead Range is not located in Washington, but we love this classic route anyway. The access is as good as it gets, and contrary to what you might expect, you will be touring in relative solitude. This might change a bit if the proposed hut system along the tour route is built in the near future. The scenery is spectacular and alpine, but the route is moderate. It never climbs more than 1500 feet in a stretch, and the downhill portions are quite moderate.

The weather in this area is also classic for the region, and navigation on the glaciated terrain of the tour can become quite difficult. If you are a strong tourer, you might be able to blast through the described route in one day. Traveling light and fast is certainly fun, but it takes away from the area's potential. As described, the tour enables you to take advantage of the countless ski descents off the little peaks that you pass along the way. They range wildly in steepness and commitment.

We opted to describe the traverse itself, but peaks like Decker, Pattison, Tremor, or the Fissile and glaciers like the Platform or the Curtain provide possibilities for skiing and climbing entertainment for many days. These peaks and glaciers are only a few of the possible side trips that make the Spearhead Traverse what it is—a northwest super-classic.

Many skiers use the Himmelsbach Hut at Russet Lake as an overnight location during this tour. Please be aware that you cannot make a reservation to stay there. It is occupied on a first-come, first-served basis. Quite a few ski tourers approach this hut from the Whistler side and use it as a base for tours in the Fissile Peak region. Do not count on being able to stay there, and note that it is not equipped or heated.

ACCESS

Follow British Columbia Highway 99 north of Vancouver (which is about 140 miles from Seattle), to Whistler Village, and park your car in the overnight and RV parking lot of the Blackcomb Ski Area. Go to the day lodge and fill out a backcountry registration form, which enables you to get a "one ride up" lift ticket to the top of the ski area.

TOUR

DAY 1. Go to the Blackcomb Gondola at Whistler Village, and take it to the top. From the top of the gondola, go over to the Excalibur Gondola and ride this to the top. From here ski down the short distance to the Glacier Express chairlift (which is well marked), and take it up. From here take the Showcase T-Bar up to the Blackcomb Glacier entrance. Start your tour here.

Since the gondola does not start until 8:30 AM, you will probably not start this tour until around 10:00 AM. To get around this late start, you could take the last ride up in the evening and camp at the base of Decker Mountain.

From the top of the Showcase T-Bar, ascend the short hill to the entrance of the Blackcomb Glacier ski slope. Start traversing as high as possible south-southeast across the upper reaches of Blackcomb Glacier. When you reach the gentle draw that marks the entrance to Garibaldi Provincial Park at around 2200 meters (7217 feet), tour up it to the col located just northeast of Blackcomb Peak at 2350 meters (7709 feet) (1 hour to here).

From the col, ski southeast down to the Decker Glacier. In the flat spot due north of Decker Mountain at 2140 meters (7020 feet) is the previously described camp spot that is an option if you rode the chairlifts up in the late afternoon. Maintain your southeast bearing, and ascend the Decker Glacier to the ridge at 2200 meters (7217 feet) that forms that glacier's eastern border (2.5 hours to here).

You are standing on a flatter part on the ridge. From the ridge you can also see your next pass on the other side of Trorey Glacier just north of Mount Pattison. Ski down the steep but short couloir—one of the more avalanche-prone slopes of the tour—onto the Trorey Glacier.

Once you are down on the Trorey Glacier, maintain a southeast bearing, and tour across it and up to the previously mentioned pass at 2350 meters (7709 feet) (3.5 hours to here).

From here, ski the short distance down to the Tremor Glacier (do not forget to look at Mount Pattison's east slopes), and start touring up to the hidden notch behind Tremor Mountain. As you ascend, maintain a southeast bearing on one of the longest ascents of the traverse, which can seem even longer in the afternoon sun. Aim for the distinct notch at 2600 meters (8530 feet) (4.5–5 hours to here).

It is hard to imagine that anyone could tire of the view that opens up on the other side of this col. You are now standing on the northern end of the headwall of the Fitzsimmons valley, which is occupied by five glaciers of varying size: Platform, Curtain, MacBeth, Fitzsimmons, and Overlord. Tour south-southeast across the Platform Glacier, one of the smaller of those five, to the little pass between Quiver Peak and the northern edge of The Ripsaw. You are starting to tour around the head of the valley. There are good campsites at around 2600 meters (8530 feet) just below the short south face of Quiver Peak (5.5–6 hours to here).

DAY 2. This scenic portion of the tour offers more challenging navigation. In bad weather conditions, it can be quite difficult and you might be better off reaching the Himmelsbach Hut at Russet Lake via the variation described below. If the weather is fine, then follow the standard approach instead.

Variation. From camp, retrace your tracks from the previous day for about 300 to 400 meters (1000 to 1300 feet). Now start skiing a descending traverse northwest until you reach the more or less south-facing lobe of the Platform Glacier. Ski down

Alta Lake
Whistler Village
Whistler Creek
99
To Vancouver
Blackcomb
Excalibur Gondola
Excalibur Gondola
Excelerator Chairlift
Glacier Express Chairlift
Harstman Glacier
Showcase T-Bar
Blackcomb Glacier
Phalanx Glacier
Phalanx Mountain
Saucer Lake
Spearhead Glacier
The Spearhead
exit ski area
Blackcomb Peak
Whistler Village Gondola
Fitzsimmons Creek
Whistler Creek
Harmony Creek
Flute Creek
Oboe Creek
Melody Creek
SPEARHEAD
RANGE
Alternate Camp 1
Decker Glacier
Decker Mountain
Trorey Glacier
Mount Trorey
Mount Pattison
Tremor Glacier
Tremor Mountain
Shutter Glacier
Shatter Glacier
Shutter Mountain
Quiver Peak
Camp 1
Platform Glacier
Ripsaw Glacier
The Ripsaw
Curtain Glacier
Fitzsimmons Creek
bad weather variation
Mount MacBeth
Naden Glacier
Couloir Ridge
MacBeth Glacier
Fitzsimmons Glacier
Whistler Mountain
Whistler Glacier
re-enter ski area
re-enter ski area
Piccolo Summit
Flute Summit
Oboe Summit
GARIBALDI PARK
Himmelsbach Hut Camp 2
Singing Pass
FITZSIMMONS
RANGE
Russet Lake
Overlord Glacier
Overlord Mountain
Fissile Peak
Mount Iago
Iago Glacier
Diavolo Glacier
Benvolio Glacier
Refuse Pinnacle
Mount Benvolio
Mount Fitzsimmons
Detour Ridge
Whirlwind Peak
Cheakamus Mountain
Cheakamus River
Cheakamus Lake
Singing Creek
0 .5 1 Mile
0 .5 1 Kilometer
N

this lobe, and pass the little icefall on the right. This part of the ski descent is quite steep and can be dangerous when the snow is unstable. At about 2100 meters (6890 feet), you reach gentler terrain. Here the Platform and Curtain Glaciers merge. Now follow the drainage southwest all the way down to Fitzsimmons Creek at 1500 meters (4921 feet) (1 hour to here).

Follow Fitzsimmons Creek on its south side for about 1 kilometer (0.6 mile). At 1400 meters (4593 feet) of elevation, cut southwest into the forest. Maintain this bearing until you run into a major drainage, which is Russet Creek. Now tour south up this drainage until you come close at 1700 meters (5577 feet) to a very distinct moraine, the western lateral moraine of the lowest reaches of Overlord Glacier. Russet Creek flows along the west side of the moraine. Follow the creek to the northern tip of Russet Lake at 1882 meters (6174 feet) by touring generally south to about 1800 meters (5906 feet). Here you start going west until you reach the lake (3 hours to here).

If time, conditions, and mood allow it, you can do a great day tour with light packs from here. Tour up the gentle slopes on the west side of Fissile Peak southeast to the col at 2320 meters (7611 feet) between Fissile and Whirlwind Peaks (1.5–2 hours from the hut). Here you start skiing north down the Overlord Glacier with the impressive east face of Fissile Peak looming over you. Be aware that there is a crevasse zone on the west side of the glacier between 2150 and 2000 meters (7000 and 6500 feet). You can ski a bit farther to the east where the glacier is less steep. Continue this great ski descent down to the previously mentioned lateral moraine at 1700 meters (5577 feet). Here regain your ascent track from the morning back to the hut (4 hours from and back to hut).

Standard approach. Chances are that you will have great weather. In that case, continue the classic tour from your camp by Quiver Peak by traversing south on the Ripsaw Glacier. Ascend to the col at 2460 meters (8070 feet) that lets you drop onto the Naden Glacier. Here you repeat this action by traversing the Naden Glacier, still going south to a col at 2430 meters (7972 feet) and immediately northwest of Couloir Ridge (1 hour to here).

The following descent down the Macbeth Glacier marks a key spot on the tour. Ski down the MacBeth Glacier staying close to the southwest ridge of Couloir Ridge. At about 2250 meters (7382 feet), ski onto the ridge. This spot is not only a key location on the tour, but it is also an amazing piece of glaciology. Looking to your right you can see the MacBeth Glacier flowing to the west and looking to the left you see the Iago Glacier flowing to the east.

Now follow the ridge across the saddle and up to about 2250 meters (7382 feet). Here you can tour onto the Iago Glacier without having to lose any elevation. Skin south up the Iago Glacier to a broad shoulder at 2400 meters (7874 feet) (2.5–3 hours to here).

Look for a steeper entrance between rocks that connects to the south-facing slope, which in turn takes you down to the Diavolo Glacier. Ski south-southwest on this descent so that you do not lose too much elevation. Once you are on the Diavolo Glacier at about 2180 meters, start touring west up the Diavolo Glacier. Do not drift

The Overlord Glacier from the north (Martin Volken)

too far to skier's left to keep from ending up on the Benvolio Glacier, which would take longer. Rather stay close to Mount Fitzsimmons, and gain the gap at 2480 meters (8136 feet) between Mount Benvolio and Mount Fitzsimmons (4–5 hours to here).

From here, tour northwest across the upper reaches of Fitzsimmons Glacier to the northern toe of Overlord Mountain. (This section is clearly visible from the Horstman Hut at the top of the Blackcomb Ski Area.) Keep wrapping around the mountain until you come to the edge of a spectacular cirque. You are standing on a ridge at 2400 meters with rock towers to your north. Drop into the cirque, and traverse the spectacular Overlord Glacier toward the pass at 2320 meters between Fissile Peak and Whirlwind Peak (6 hours to here).

From here, ski the remaining ski descent down the gentle slopes on the west side of Fissile Peak. Maintain a northwest bearing all the way down to Russet Lake. Once you are at the lake at 1882 meters, follow it around to the north end to the hut (7 hours to here).

Variation. From the top of the Overlord Glacier, you can also ski down first north on a broad and friendly shoulder and then northwest all the way down to about 1800 meters before exiting it on the left via a steep moraine. This truly excellent descent is worth the short climb back up to the hut, but make sure you stay near the northeast face of the Fissile so that you pass a little crevasse zone on your right. Once you are off the glacier, head west up toward Russet Lake and the hut (2 hours from the top of the Overlord Glacier).

DAY 3. From the Himmelsbach Hut at Russet Lake, you are no more than two to three hours from the Whistler Ski Area. You have plenty of time to enjoy a short day tour out of the hut and then return to Whistler in the afternoon.

Optional half-day trip. You can skin up to Whirlwind Peak as a half-day trip. Another option is to ascend Fissile Peak and then choose from several different descents with varying degrees of difficulty off the summit. (You might need a rope, ice ax, and crampons for the summit traverse.)

From the Himmelsbach Hut at Russet Lake, climb the previously mentioned slopes on the west flanks of Fissile Peak up toward the pass at 2320 meters (7611 feet). At 2050 meters (6725 feet), turn east and climb up the gentler portion of the west flank to reach the summit ridge by the south summit. From here traverse the summit ridge to the summit at 2439 meters (8001 feet) (3 hours from the hut).

If conditions are favorable, you can ski the spectacular descent down the northwest couloir. But be careful because this committing descent represents a radical departure from this tour's general character. Even skiing down the steep ascent route will add an exciting finish to the traverse (4–5 hours round trip).

Out from the hut. From the hut, start touring southwest to the broad shoulder at 1970 meters (6463 feet) that lets you look down to Singing Pass. Ski down to Singing Pass, and ascend the gentle slopes of Oboe Summit on the other side. This is the easternmost of the so-called Musical Bumps (2 hours to here).

Now skirt Oboe Summit on the south, and scoot to the saddle between Oboe and Flute Summits. Ascend the slopes of Flute Summit. You are still touring northwest.

Be careful once you get to the flat summit cap. The summit drops off very steeply to the northwest and could make for an unpleasant surprise in poor visibility. Turn a bit more west here, and ski down the shoulder to the saddle at 1888 meters (6194 feet) between Flute Summit and Piccolo Summit (3–4 hours to here).

From here you can probably see the ski tracks that traverse high on the north side of Piccolo Summit and then continue to the ski slopes of the Whistler Mountain Ski Area. Ski down the remaining 1200 meters (4000 feet) of vertical to Whistler Village.

Tour Author: Martin Volken

GUIDE AND AUTHOR PROFILES

(Left to right): Aaron Mainer, Kurt Hicks, Margaret Wheeler, Erin Smart, Forest McBrian, Chris Simmons, Ben Haskell, Martin Volken, Trevor Kostanich, Dave Jordan

Martin Volken is the founder and owner of Pro Guiding Service and Pro Ski and Mountain Service. He is a Swiss IFMGA Mountain Guide and guides all facets of mountain travel. He has authored and co-authored *Backcountry Skiing Snoqualmie Pass* and co-authored *Backcountry Skiing: Skills for Ski Touring and Ski Mountaineering*. He consults for Outdoor Research and K2. He would like to thank Ben Haskell for his amazing effort in managing this group project.

Benjamin Haskell has shared his love of the Cascades with guests of Pro Guiding Service since 1999. He was certified as an AMGA ski mountaineering guide in 2001. When he isn't guiding, he is a captain with the Seattle Fire Department.

Forest McBrian grew up in western Oregon, where on a clear day he could see the Cascades. He studied English and French at Evergreen State College in Olympia and cut his teeth climbing and skiing in Chamonix. He holds IFMGA certification and guides year-round.

Trevor Kostanich is a Washington native who loves exploring snowy mountains. With decades of work and play around Snoqualmie Pass, he appreciates the continued discovery of wild terrain so close to home. He has been ski guiding in the Cascades since 2010.

Aaron Mainer began guiding after receiving a degree in international political economy from the University of Puget Sound. He has skied extensively throughout Washington, British Columbia, and Alaska, including first descents on Mount Rainier and Denali. An IFMGA-certified guide, Aaron lives in Enumclaw, Washington.

Chris Simmons learned to ski as a child in California, and moved to the Cascades in 2000 to guide. He's climbed and skied all over the world, including ski descents in the Himalaya and Antarctica. Chris is an IFMGA- and AMGA-certified mountain guide and lives in Seattle, Washington.

David Jordan began skiing and climbing at a young age. His pursuits have taken him to Europe, Africa, and throughout the US, but he calls the Cascades home. David has been a professional mountain guide since 2008.

Kurt Hicks is a native of the Pacific Northwest and began exploring the Cascades at the age of eleven. He studied public land management in college and environmental science in graduate school. He is an AMGA-certified alpine and rock guide and lives in Seattle, Washington.

Margaret Wheeler is an IFMGA- and AMGA-certified guide, leading trips throughout Europe and North America. An active member of the guiding community, she is an instructor of guide training for the AMGA and has served on its board of directors. She also works as an AIARE instructor and trainer.

Erin Smart is an AMGA-certified ski mountaineering guide and a Seattle native who grew up skiing and climbing all over the Cascades of Washington State. She has also been ski mountaineering in the French Alps since she was fifteen. She has been mountain guiding since 2010, mainly in the Cascades, her true home.

Solveig Waterfall has guided in Colorado, the Sierras, the Cascades, Alaska, Mexico, and Argentina. Personal climbing and skiing have taken her to the Indian Himalaya and British Columbia. After years of ski patrolling at Crystal Mountain, Solveig now guides full time. She is an AMGA-certified ski mountaineering guide.

Guest author **Lowell Skoog** has been skiing in the Cascades since the early 1960s. He started backcountry skiing in 1979 and has pioneered hundreds of miles of high-level ski routes in Washington. A software engineer by profession, Lowell is compiling a comprehensive history of backcountry skiing in the state.

Guest author **Jason Hummel** is a northwest native who started skiing the backcountry at age six; he has been exploring the Cascades and other mountains around the world ever since. In 2009 he left a career in personal finance to ski, hike, bike, and kayak. His photographs of these adventures can be seen in many outdoor-related publications.

RESOURCES

NATIONAL PARKS

Mount Rainier National Park
Ashford, WA 98304
360-569-2211
www.nps.gov/mora/index.htm

North Cascades National Park
Marblemount, WA 98267
360-854-7200
www.nps.gov/noca/index.htm

Olympic National Park
Port Angeles, WA 98362
General information: 360-565-3130
Road and weather information: 360-565-3131
www.nps.gov/olym/index.htm

NATIONAL FORESTS

Gifford Pinchot National Forest
Vancouver, WA 98682
360-395-3400
www.fs.usda.gov/giffordpinchot

Mount Baker–Snoqualmie National Forest
Sedro Wooley, WA 98284
360-854-7200
www.fs.usda.gov/mbs

Okanogan–Wenatchee National Forest
Wenatchee, WA 98801
509-664-9200
www.fs.usda.gov/okawen

Olympic National Forest
Forks, WA 98331
360-374-7566
www.fs.usda.gov/olympic

RANGER DISTRICTS

Cle Elum Ranger District, Cle Elum, WA; 509-852-1100
Cowlitz Valley Ranger Station, Randle, WA; 360-497-1100
Hood Canal Ranger District, Quilcene, WA; 360-765 2200
Mount Adams Ranger Station, Trout Lake, WA; 509-395-3400
Naches Ranger District, Naches, WA; 509-653-1401
Pacific Ranger District, Forks, WA; 360-374-6522
Pacific Ranger District, Quinault, WA; 360-288-2525
Skykomish Ranger District, Skykomish, WA; 360-677-2414
Snoqualmie Ranger District, North Bend, WA; 425-888-1421
Wenatchee River Ranger District, Leavenworth, WA; 509-548-2550

INFORMATION CENTERS

Climbing Information Center (Mount Rainier), Paradise, WA; 360-569-6641
Glacier Public Service Center, Glacier, WA; 360-599-2714
Henry M. Jackson Memorial Visitor Center (Mount Rainier), Paradise, WA; 360-569-6571
Longmire Museum (Mount Rainier), Longmire, WA; 360-569-6575
Marblemount Wilderness Information Center, Marblemount, WA; 360-854-7245
Mount Saint Helens Institute, mshinstitute.org/index.php/climbing/index
Sedro Woolley National Park and National Forest Information Center, Sedro Woolley, WA; 360-854-7200
Verlot Public Service Center, Granite Falls, WA; 360-691-7791

WEATHER AND SKI CONDITIONS

Blackcomb/Whistler: www.whistlerblackcomb.com/the-mountain/snow-and-weather
Crystal Mountain: www.crystalmountainresort.com
Crystal Mountain Ski Patrol: 360-663-3060
Hurricane Ridge (Olympic NP and NF): hurricaneridge.com
Mission Ridge: www.missionridge.com
Mount Baker Ski Area: www.mountbaker.us
Mount Hood Meadows, Oregon: www.skihood.com
Northwest Avalanche Center: www.nwac.us
Stevens Pass Ski Area: www.stevenspass.com
Summit at Snoqualmie: www.summitatsnoqualmie.com
Timberline Lodge, Oregon: www.timberlinelodge.com
University of Washington Department of Atmospheric Sciences: www.atmos.washington.edu/data/rainier_report.html
White Pass: www.skiwhitepass.com

INDEX

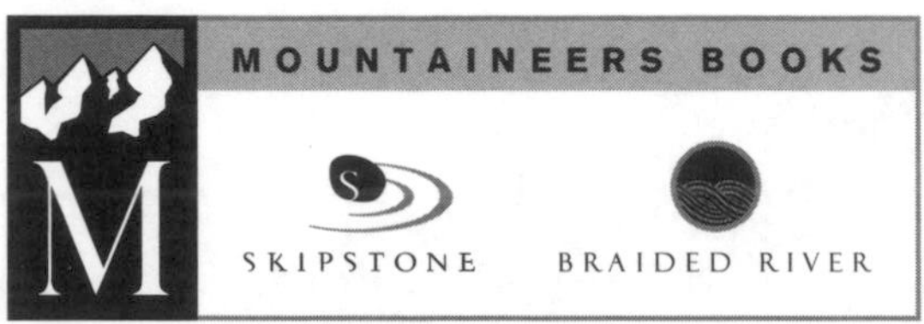

recreation • lifestyle • conservation

MOUNTAINEERS BOOKS, is a leading publisher of mountaineering literature and guides—including our flagship title, *Mountaineering: The Freedom of the Hills*—as well as adventure narratives, natural history, and general outdoor recreation. Through our two imprints, Skipstone and Braided River, we also publish titles on sustainability and conservation. We are committed to supporting the environmental and educational goals of our organization by providing expert information on human-powered adventure, sustainable practices at home and on the trail, and preservation of wilderness.

The Mountaineers, founded in 1906, is a 501(c)(3) nonprofit outdoor activity and conservation organization whose mission is "to explore, study, preserve, and enjoy the natural beauty of the outdoors." One of the largest such organizations in the United States, it sponsors classes and year-round outdoor activities throughout the Pacific Northwest, including climbing, hiking, backcountry skiing, snowshoeing, bicycling, camping, paddling, and more. The Mountaineers also supports its mission through its publishing division, Mountaineers Books, and promotes environmental education and citizen engagement. For more information, visit The Mountaineers Program Center, 7700 Sand Point Way NE, Seattle, WA 98115-3996; phone 206-521-6001; www.mountaineers.org; or email info@mountaineers.org.

Our publications are made possible through the generosity of donors and through sales of more than 500 titles on outdoor recreation, sustainable lifestyle, and conservation. To donate, purchase books, or learn more, visit us online:

MOUNTAINEERS BOOKS
1001 SW Klickitat Way, Suite 201 • Seattle, WA 98134
800-553-4453 • mbooks@mountaineersbooks.org • www.mountaineersbooks.org

Mountaineers Books is proud to be a corporate sponsor of the Leave No Trace Center for Outdoor Ethics, whose mission is to promote and inspire responsible outdoor recreation through education, research, and partnerships. • The Leave No Trace program is focused specifically on human-powered (nonmotorized) recreation. • Leave No Trace strives to educate visitors about the nature of their recreational impacts and offers techniques to prevent and minimize such impacts. • Leave No Trace is best understood as an educational and ethical program, not as a set of rules and regulations. • For more information, visit www.lnt.org or call 800-332-4100.